Canada and International Affairs

Series Editors
David Carment
NPSIA
Carleton University
Ottawa, ON, Canada

Philippe Lagassé
NPSIA
Carleton University
Ottawa, ON, Canada

Meredith Lilly
NPSIA
Carleton University
Ottawa, ON, Canada

Palgrave's *Canada and International Affairs* is a timely and rigorous series for showcasing scholarship by Canadian scholars of international affairs and foreign scholars who study Canada's place in the world. The series will be of interest to students and academics studying and teaching Canadian foreign, security, development and economic policy. By focusing on policy matters, the series will be of use to policy makers in the public and private sectors who want access to rigorous, timely, informed and independent analysis. As the anchor, Canada Among Nations is the series' most recognisable annual contribution. In addition, the series showcases work by scholars from Canadian universities featuring structured analyses of Canadian foreign policy and international affairs. The series also features work by international scholars and practitioners working in key thematic areas that provides an international context against which Canada's performance can be compared and understood.

More information about this series at
http://www.palgrave.com/gp/series/15905

Norman Hillmer
Philippe Lagassé
Editors

Justin Trudeau and Canadian Foreign Policy

Canada Among Nations 2017

palgrave
macmillan

Editors
Norman Hillmer
Carleton University
Ottawa, ON, Canada

Philippe Lagassé
Carleton University
Ottawa, ON, Canada

Canada and International Affairs
ISSN 2523-7187   ISSN 2523-7195 (electronic)
ISBN 978-3-030-08873-6   ISBN 978-3-319-73860-4 (eBook)
https://doi.org/10.1007/978-3-319-73860-4

© The Editor(s) (if applicable) and The Author(s) 2018
Softcover re-print of the Hardcover 1st edition 2018
This work is subject to copyright. All rights are solely and exclusively licensed by the Publisher, whether the whole or part of the material is concerned, specifically the rights of translation, reprinting, reuse of illustrations, recitation, broadcasting, reproduction on microfilms or in any other physical way, and transmission or information storage and retrieval, electronic adaptation, computer software, or by similar or dissimilar methodology now known or hereafter developed.
The use of general descriptive names, registered names, trademarks, service marks, etc. in this publication does not imply, even in the absence of a specific statement, that such names are exempt from the relevant protective laws and regulations and therefore free for general use.
The publisher, the authors and the editors are safe to assume that the advice and information in this book are believed to be true and accurate at the date of publication. Neither the publisher nor the authors or the editors give a warranty, express or implied, with respect to the material contained herein or for any errors or omissions that may have been made. The publisher remains neutral with regard to jurisdictional claims in published maps and institutional affiliations.

Cover image © Patsy Lynch / Alamy Stock Photo
Cover design by Henry Petrides

Printed on acid-free paper

This Palgrave Macmillan imprint is published by the registered company Springer International Publishing AG part of Springer Nature.
The registered company address is: Gewerbestrasse 11, 6330 Cham, Switzerland

For
Maureen Molot
and
the Norman Paterson School of International Affairs
on its 50th Anniversary

Preface

Canada Among Nations was first published in 1984, and it has seen the world turn many times since. Providing a scholarly description and analysis of developments and currents in Canadian foreign policy, the *Canada Among Nations* volumes have taken their place as the contemporary academic record of Canadians' approaches to the world. Our predecessors have published the research of emerging and established scholars, practitioners, and journalists, ensuring a variety of perspectives that have enriched the study of Canada's international policies. The 2017 edition, concentrating on the first two years of the Justin Trudeau government, is the first to be published with Palgrave Macmillan, as part of the newly established book series, *Canada and International Affairs*. *Canada Among Nations* will be its flagship publication.

Part of the *Canada Among Nations* tradition is a workshop, where editors and authors gather to exchange research and ideas. This year's meeting was hosted by the Bill Graham Centre for Contemporary International History at the University of Toronto. We are grateful to Mr. Graham, Trinity College, and the Centre's John English, Jack Cunningham, and Jennifer Chylinski for their generous hospitality. Out of the workshop emerged a number of themes. First, and unavoidably, Canada is not alone in facing Donald Trump as president of the United States and the uncertainty that he breeds. Second, in both Canada and the United States, a yawning gulf is apparent between rhetoric and reality, and workshoppers frequently found themselves comparing talk to action, or lack of action. Connected with that is a notable and frequent gap between political tactics and policy strategy; the former are apparent, the latter much less so, or not at all. Third, members of the workshop frequently pointed to the centrality of politics high and low, not least in the Trudeau government's (often unsuccessful) desire to differentiate itself from the previous government's international policies. Fourth, we took note of the Canadian government's emphasis on gender equality and a feminist foreign policy. Last, but importantly, the workshop concluded with the sense that chapter writers should consider the challenges that lie ahead in their issue areas.

We thank Dane Rowlands, the director of the Norman Paterson School of International Affairs when we undertook this project, and Yiagadeesen Samy, NPSIA's current director, for their steadfast support. Theresa Le Bane and Uriel Marantz carried out research and organizational work on our behalf. Joseph Le Bane prepared the manuscript as editorial coordinator, and he did a good deal more than that in rooting out errors and inconsistencies. Susan Whitney reviewed the manuscript and gave research and editorial advice to our and the authors' great benefit. David Carment, dynamic as always, was instrumental in making important arrangements with the publisher. At Palgrave, we have been assisted mightily by Senior Editor Anca Pusca, a team of peer reviewers, and Katelyn Zingg.

We dedicate this volume to Maureen Molot, esteemed friend and colleague, a former director of NPSIA, and often an author and editor in the *Canada Among Nations* series. We at the same time celebrate the 50th year of the Norman Paterson School.

Norman Hillmer
Philippe Lagassé

Contents

1 The Age of Trudeau and Trump   1
   Norman Hillmer and Philippe Lagassé

2 The Promise and Perils of Justin Trudeau's
   Foreign Policy   17
   Roland Paris

3 Promises Made, Promises Kept? A Mid-term
   Trudeau Foreign Policy Report Card   31
   Kim Richard Nossal

4 What's Not to Like? Justin Trudeau, the Global
   Disorder, and Liberal Illusions   55
   Jerome Klassen and Yves Engler

5 Canada-US Relations Under President Trump:
   Stop Reading the Tweets and Look to the Future   83
   Stephen Blank and Monica Gattinger

6 Canada's International Environmental Policy:
   Trudeau's Trifecta of Challenges   103
   Debora Van Nijnatten

7   International Trade: The Rhetoric and Reality
    of the Trudeau Government's Progressive Trade Agenda   125
    Meredith B. Lilly

8   Justin Trudeau's China Challenges   145
    Philip Calvert

9   A Promise Too Far? The Justin Trudeau Government
    and Indigenous Rights   165
    Sheryl Lightfoot

10 Canada's Feminist Foreign Policy Promises:
    An Ambitious Agenda for Gender Equality, Human
    Rights, Peace, and Security   187
    Rebecca Tiessen and Emma Swan

11 "We Will Honour Our Good Name": The Trudeau
    Government, Arms Exports, and Human Rights   207
    Jennifer Pedersen

12 The Trudeau Government, Refugee Policy,
    and Echoes of the Past   233
    Julie F. Gilmour

13 Justin Trudeau's Quest for a United Nations Security
    Council Seat   247
    Andrea Charron

14 Manning Up: Justin Trudeau and the Politics
    of the Canadian Defence Community   261
    Andrea Lane

15 Trudeau the Reluctant Warrior? Canada
    and International Military Operations   285
    Jeffrey Rice and Stéfanie von Hlatky

Index   303

Notes on Contributors

Stephen Blank is a senior fellow at the University of Ottawa's Institute for Science, Society and Policy and a former Fulbright professor at the Universities of Montreal and Ottawa.

Philip Calvert a former Canadian ambassador in Asia, is senior fellow of the China Institute at the University of Alberta and associate with the Centre for Asia-Pacific Initiatives at the University of Victoria.

Andrea Charron is an assistant professor of international relations and director of the Centre for Defence and Security Studies at the University of Manitoba's Political Studies Department.

Yves Engler is an author and activist based in Montreal specializing in Canadian foreign policy.

Monica Gattinger is an associate professor of political studies at the University of Ottawa; director of uOttawa's Institute for Science, Society and Policy; and chair of the Positive Energy project.

Julie F. Gilmour is an assistant professor at Trinity College in the University of Toronto.

Norman Hillmer is Chancellor's Professor of History and International Affairs at Carleton University.

Jerome Klassen is an associate lecturer at the University of Massachusetts, Boston, and research fellow with the Massachusetts Institute of Technology Center for International Studies.

Philippe Lagassé is the Barton Chair and associate professor of international affairs at Carleton University.

Andrea Lane is a doctoral candidate in the Department of Political Science at Dalhousie University.

Sheryl Lightfoot is the Canada Research Chair of Global Indigenous Rights and Politics and associate professor of First Nations and Indigenous Studies and Political Science at the University of British Columbia.

Meredith B. Lilly is the Simon Reisman Chair and associate professor of international affairs at Carleton University and a former foreign affairs and international trade advisor to Prime Minister Stephen Harper.

Kim Richard Nossal is a professor of political studies and a fellow at the Centre for International and Defence Policy at Queen's University.

Roland Paris is the University Research Chair in International Security and Governance at the University of Ottawa and a former senior advisor to Prime Minister Justin Trudeau.

Jennifer Pederson who received her doctorate from Aberystwyth University for her work on peace movements, researches foreign policy for the New Democratic Party of Canada.

Jeffrey Rice is a doctoral candidate in the Department of Political Science at Queen's University.

Emma Swan is a doctoral candidate in the School of International Development and Global Studies at the University of Ottawa and a Trudeau scholar.

Rebecca Tiessen is an associate professor in the School of International Development and Global Studies at the University of Ottawa.

Debora Van Nijnatten is a professor in the Department of Political Science and North American Studies Program at Wilfrid Laurier University.

Stéfanie von Hlatky is an associate professor in the Department of Political Science at Queen's University and director of the Queen's Centre for International and Defence Policy.

Acronyms

ADS	Approved Destination Status
AI	Artificial Intelligence
AIIB	Asian Infrastructure Investment Bank
APEC	Asia-Pacific Economic Cooperation
ASEAN	Association of Southeast Asian Nations
ATT	Arms Trade Treaty
BTB	Beyond the Border
CADSI	Canadian Association of Defence and Security Industries
CAF	Canadian Armed Forces
CANSOFCOM	Canadian Special Operations Forces Command
CBC	Canadian Broadcasting Corporation
CBSA	Canada Border Services Agency
CCC	Canadian Commercial Corporation
CCIC	Canadian Council for International Cooperation
CEDAW	Convention on the Elimination of All Forms of Discrimination Against Women
CERD	Committee on the Elimination of Racial Discrimination
CETA	Comprehensive Economic and Trade Agreement (Canada-European Union)
CIDA	Canadian International Development Agency
CO_2	Carbon Dioxide
COP21	Conference of the Parties, Twenty-First Session
CPC	Conservative Party of Canada
CPLC	Carbon Pricing Leadership Coalition
CPP	Carbon Pricing Panel

CSO	Civil Society Organization
DACA	Deferred Action for Childhood Arrivals
DND	Department of National Defence
DP	Displaced Person
ECCC	Environment and Climate Change Canada
ECOSOC	Economic and Social Council (UN)
EFP	Enhanced Forward Presence
EPA	Environmental Protection Agency
FPIC	Free, Prior, and Informed Consent
FTA	Free Trade Agreement
FTE	Full-Time Equivalent
G20	Group of Twenty
G7	Group of Seven
G8	Group of Eight
GAC	Global Affairs Canada
GAR	Government Assisted Refugees
GATT	General Agreement on Tariffs and Trade
GBA	Gender-Based Analysis
GCC	Gulf Cooperation Council
GDLS	General Dynamics Land Systems of Canada
GDP	Gross Domestic Product
GHG	Greenhouse Gas
HFC	Hydrofluorocarbons
IAR	International Assistance Review
IED	Improvised Explosive Device
ILO	International Labour Organization
IMF	International Monetary Fund
Industry 4.0	Fourth Industrial Revolution
IR	International Relations
IRCC	Immigration, Refugees and Citizenship Canada
IS	Islamic State
ISAF	International Security Assistance Force
ISDS	Investor-State Dispute Settlement
ISIL	Islamic State of Iraq and the Levant
ISIS	Islamic State of Iraq and Syria
LAV	Light-Armoured Vehicle
LCFS	Low Carbon Fuel Standards
LGBTQ	Lesbian, Gay, Bisexual, Trans, and Queer
LPC	Liberal Party of Canada
MP	Member of Parliament

NAFTA	North American Free Trade Agreement
NALS	North American Leaders Summit
NAP	National Action Plan
NATO	North Atlantic Treaty Organization
NDP	New Democratic Party
NFTC	NATO Flying Training in Canada
NGO	Non-governmental Organization
OECD	Organization for Economic Co-operation and Development
OPEC	Organization of Petroleum Exporting Countries
P5	Permanent Five
PMO	Prime Minister's Office
POW	Prisoner of War
PRT	Provincial Reconstruction Team
PSR	Privately Sponsored Refugee
PSRP	Privately Sponsored Refugee Program
R2P	Responsibility to Protect
RCAF	Royal Canadian Air Force
RCC	Regulatory Cooperation Council
RCMP	Royal Canadian Mounted Police
SOF	Special Operation Forces
TPP	Trans-Pacific Partnership
TRC	Truth and Reconciliation Commission
TTIP	Transatlantic Trade and Investment Partnership
UN	United Nations
UNDRIP	United Nations Declaration on the Rights of Indigenous Peoples
UNFCCC	United Nations Framework Convention on Climate Change
UNHCR	United Nations High Commissioner for Refugees
UNPFII	United Nations Permanent Forum on Indigenous Issues
UNSC	United Nations Security Council
UNSCR	United Nations Security Council Resolution
US	United States
WEOG	Western European and Other States
WPS	Women, Peace, Security
WPSN	Women, Peace and Security Network
WPSN-C	Women, Peace and Security Network-Canada
WTO	World Trade Organization

CHAPTER 1

The Age of Trudeau and Trump

Norman Hillmer and Philippe Lagassé

Two elections lie at the heart of this book. Justin Trudeau's Liberals won power in October 2015, and they entered office fully clothed in pledges to remake Canada and at the same time remake the country's place among nations. During Trudeau's first six weeks as prime minister, his widely publicized trips to meetings of the G20 in Turkey, the Asia-Pacific Economic Cooperation (APEC) Summit in Manila, the Commonwealth prime ministers' conference in Malta, and the COP21 climate talks in Paris furnished him with what one commentator called "a new, worldly, political shield" at home and a dashing image abroad.[1] Liberal internationalism was in the saddle and Trudeau its glamorous ambassador to the global community. On the eve of another election, when Donald Trump startled his way to the United States presidency in November 2016, the *Economist* magazine's cover Canadianized the Statue of Liberty, which was pictured with a smile, a maple leaf hat, and a hockey stick. The accompanying editorial purred that Trudeau's Canada was the exception to a depressing international company of "wall-builders, door-slammers and drawbridge-raisers."[2]

N. Hillmer (✉) • P. Lagassé
Carleton University, Ottawa, ON, Canada

© The Author(s) 2018
N. Hillmer, P. Lagassé (eds.), *Justin Trudeau and Canadian Foreign Policy*, Canada and International Affairs,
https://doi.org/10.1007/978-3-319-73860-4_1

Trudeau was labelled the anti-Trump by the *Washington Post* and the German newspaper *Die Welt*³ and almost universally elsewhere, but he acted with disciplined politeness when he turned his face towards the new American president. Trump too had his big promises, including a vow that American alliances and trade agreements would be scrutinized and repudiated if they did not meet his approval. Canadian interests, most prominently those tied up in the North American Free Trade Agreement (NAFTA), were directly on the line. All Ottawa governments look southwards, but the prime minister and his ministers and officials now fanned out all over the United States to make the case that Canada was too important to the United States for the ties between the two countries to be allowed to deteriorate. It was as if the fate of Canadians depended on the successful wooing of Trump's America.⁴

Justin Trudeau's election triumph brought Prime Minister Stephen Harper's near-decade-long Conservative government to an end. The Trudeau victory was not preordained, and the suspicion was that his carload of promises were a luxury that only the leader of the third party in the House of Commons could afford, since it was unlikely that he would have to form a government that would have to implement them. In the first half of an unusually (for Canada) lengthy electoral campaign, the social democratic New Democratic Party (NDP) was thought to have a much better chance of displacing Harper, and for a while there appeared the possibility that the Conservatives might cling to power after all. During the closing weeks of the campaign, however, voters opposed to the Conservatives coalesced around the Trudeau Liberals. Although future studies of the 2015 election may offer a more nuanced explanation, the Liberals had apparently succeeded in convincing voters, including many who often did not participate in the democratic process, that Trudeau was best placed to oust the Conservatives. "Real Change," the overarching Liberal message aimed directly at the unpopular Harper, propelled the Liberals to a commanding 184 seats in the House of Commons, as against 99 for the Conservatives and only 44 for the NDP.

The Trudeau electoral platform was laced with progressive policy promises and not so subtle suggestions that a Trudeau government would dismantle Harper's legacy. The Liberals talked of renewing Canadian leadership in the world, notably by confronting climate change and reengaging with the United Nations and peacekeeping operations. A new government would implement the United Nations Declaration on the Rights of Indigenous Peoples (UNDRIP), end the Canadian military's combat mission in Iraq, welcome thousands of Syrian refugees, reinvest in development assistance to the "world's poorest countries," and reexamine Canada's approach to international trade.[5] Harper had shunned the world, and Trudeau would counter his blinkered vision.

Canada Among Nations 2017 is an assessment of Trudeau's first two years of international policies. The book begins with three overview articles that revolve around the very high expectations that the prime minister fostered and with which he must now live. Roland Paris applauds Trudeau's fierce defence of economic and security interests, vocal promotion of openness and inclusion, and skilful handling of the relationship with the United States. But in his potential, Paris warns, lurks the danger that Trudeau will fail to meet his own call for global leadership. Kim Richard Nossal does a tally of promises made and promises kept in a mid-term report card that gives passing marks to the government's management of the politics and process of foreign policy. His conclusion is that the pledges of 2015 are not weighing the government down. Jerome Klassen and Yves Engler, on the other hand, deliver a scathing indictment of the prime minister's leadership, which they argue raised unrealistic hopes for "socially-progressive and liberal values, worldwide." Trudeau's cheerleading for a transcendent politics, international and otherwise, is for them an illusion or, worse, a lie. Klassen and Engler claim that, as the globe plummets into disorder, the Trudeau government stubbornly maintains Canada's allegiance to Washington, militarism, and the imperialism of corporate capitalism.

Creating distance from Stephen Harper was not as easy as it looked. Trudeau has undoubtedly shifted the rhetoric away from his predecessor's combative insistence that international amity had to be subordinated to a righteous struggle against the evils of a dangerous world.[6] In foreign policy tone is not nothing, but continuity with the recent past defines a good deal of Trudeau international policy. "What a splendid job Justin Trudeau is doing in carrying out Stephen Harper's foreign policy," contended John Ibbitson, Harper's biographer, in March 2017. Trudeau had promised his Canada would be "a caring country committed to doing its share, and he's kept his word. Canada is indeed doing it share—the same share that it contributed under the Conservatives."[7]

International trade was at the top of the Harper agenda, and it has remained there under Trudeau. The Liberal government embraced the Conservatives' Canada-European Union Comprehensive Economic and Trade Agreement (CETA) and looked towards a remodeled Trans-Pacific

Partnership (TPP), which struggled to survive without Trump, who dismissively walked away from it early in his presidency.[8] Trudeau's trade ministers have elaborated a progressive approach to trade, with an emphasis on environmental protections, worker rights, and an equitable sharing of the benefits of trade. Meredith Lilly's chapter stipulates, however, that those same progressive elements were already present in the CETA, TPP, and Canada-Korea Trade Agreement texts worked out by the previous government. Lilly also points out how difficult it is to humanize trade in negotiations with a protectionist Trump administration and a China that desires free trade without an overlay of Western values. It is hard to be a progressive without willing partners.

Indigenous voters rushed to Trudeau because he made an eloquent case that their causes were his. Speaking to the UN General Assembly in September 2017, the prime minister declared that Canada had been built on the ancestral land of Indigenous peoples, but without "the meaningful participation of those who were there first." Their experience had been "mostly one of humiliation, neglect, and abuse." Canada had campaigned and voted against the 2007 United Nations Declaration on the Rights of Indigenous Peoples, Trudeau lamented, but his government was proudly on a path of reconciliation with First Nations, Métis nation, and Inuit peoples. The Declaration was its guiding light.[9]

Trudeau's good intentions are easier to express than apply, and, as in so much, his vocabulary about Indigenous peoples gives rise to hopes that are almost impossible to fulfil. Sheryl Lightfoot's analysis recognizes the ways in which Trudeau has woven the UN Declaration on the Rights of Indigenous Peoples into his ambitions for global leadership, but at the same time makes abundantly clear the extraordinary complexities of Indigenous politics in Canada. Lightfoot is pessimistic, concluding that the government "is engaged in a difficult dance. It has promised to adopt and implement the UNDRIP, yet it is cognizant of the scope of structural changes to do so, and so it remains hesitant—even resistant—to making real change." The talk is remarkably different, but the substance "is quite consistent with the Harper government."

Jennifer Pedersen's chapter is another example of the difficulty in matching human rights aspirations with government practice. Her subject is Canada's lucrative arms export industry and, specifically, the sale of Canadian-made light-armoured vehicles (LAVs) to Saudi Arabia. The LAV deal, worth $15 billion over 15 years and generating 3,000 jobs at the General Dynamics plant in Southwestern Ontario, was concluded by the

Conservatives in 2014. It became controversial for the Trudeau government in 2016, after the Saudis carried out a mass execution of 47 dissidents. The Liberals refused to turn away from their Conservative inheritance. They tied themselves in knots with implausible assertions that the contract could not be cancelled, simultaneously declaring that their hearts bled for the victims of Saudi violence, some of whom were on the wrong end of weapons made in Canada. NDP members of Parliament were themselves in a delicate position, since one of them held the House of Commons seat where the General Dynamics plant was housed. They chose to concentrate their fire on the Liberals' lack of transparency and oversight. The government meanwhile piled poor communication skills on top of its hypocrisy.

In the Liberals' more open door to China, surely a break with the recent past was evident. Where the Harperites had been wary, Trudeau was almost giddy, to the extent that one well-placed observer accused him and his colleagues of being "smitten with the dynamic, entrepreneurial and innovative China that dominates the business pages, while remaining largely silent about the China that tramples human rights at home and intimidates rivals abroad."[10] Trudeau visited China, as his father had done as prime minister. Ottawa set about exploring a Sino-Canadian free trade agreement, eased investment rules, and allowed the sale of a Canadian technology company to a Chinese firm that the Conservatives had blocked on national security grounds. For the Trudeau government, the benefits of building stronger ties with an economic colossus and Canada's second largest trading partner outweighed the risks. Those risks included alienating a public that is suspicious of getting too close to China, or letting the Chinese security state get too close to Canadians.[11]

Philip Calvert, whose Canadian foreign service career included three periods in Beijing, is not so sure that Trudeau's China policy is all that novel, apart from the obvious transformation of "styles of engagement." The claim to a principled foreign policy and a greater emphasis on North America to the detriment of Asia in the early Harper years did lead to a cooling of relations between the two countries. But Calvert explains that the thinking soon shifted, in part because of pressures from business. He details sustained increases in trade and investment, in education links, and in the flow of Chinese tourists to Canada in the Conservative decade after 2006. What was lacking, he regrets, was a balanced and comprehensive strategy. Calvert sees none of that under Trudeau either. He offers specific recommendations about the manner in which Canadian interests can be advanced through a multifaceted and comprehensive approach based on a realistic understanding of China today and its expanding (and expansive) global presence.

When the Harper Conservatives deployed special operations forces to Iraq in August 2014 to train and assist local fighters in their battles against the Islamic State (IS), the Liberals supported the government's decision. However, when the Harper government opted to send CF-18 fighter aircraft to conduct strikes against the IS in October 2014, the Liberals resisted this overtly offensive element of the mission. Their opposition to the deployment continued throughout the following year and into the 2015 election campaign, when Trudeau was adamant that the aircraft would be withdrawn if he formed a government. While it took it several months to act on this promise, the government ultimately ended the CF-18 deployment to Iraq in 2016. At the same time, it increased the number of Canadian trainers. The Liberals continued to draw the fine distinction that the Conservatives had between a combat mission in which Canadian soldiers directly engage the adversary and a training and assistance endeavour that sees the special forces involved in firefights against the Islamic State when necessary for self-defence or in support of local allies. As Jeffrey Rice and Stéfanie von Hlatky argue in these pages, the current government puts the Iraq emphasis in a different place, yet the commitment to this undertaking and to the previous government's Latvian and Ukraine operations remains steadfast. Trudeau might appear, sometimes deliberately, the reluctant warrior and Stephen Harper the very opposite, but the similarities in military policy between their two governments are much more pronounced than the differences.

The replacement of the aged CF-18s was another area where the Liberals sought to separate themselves from the Conservatives during the 2015 election. Trudeau declared that his government would not acquire the F-35 Joint Strike Fighter and that the replacement for the CF-18s would be chosen following an open competition. Once in power, Trudeau softened his stand against the F-35, but the government has since been focused on acquiring an interim fleet of fighters to complement the legacy CF-18s in the short term, while the contest to replace Canada's fighter aircraft is only slated to begin in 2019. The Liberals have adopted the Conservatives' caution regarding this most controversial of military procurements.

The government promises to invest more in the military than the Conservatives. Benefiting from a willingness to accept prolonged and deep budget deficits, the Liberals issued a defence policy statement, *Strong,*

Secure, Engaged, which outlined significant investments in the Canadian Armed Forces (CAF).[12] The policy aims to recapitalize the military within the next decade and to enhance the CAF's capabilities in the cyber and space domains. Skeptics noted that investments in the military will only ramp up following the next federal election, leaving them vulnerable to a change of policy or government. Early on in the Harper government, the military had also been given prominence, but substantial increases in defence spending did not materialize.

Rather than merely detailing what the Trudeau government has pledged to do in its defence policy document, Andrea Lane examines the gender politics that have characterized commentaries about the military, the Liberals, and the prime minister himself. Lane notes that the questioning of Trudeau's (and Liberals') masculinity has been a routine part of defence debates. She encourages a critical consideration of the manner in which Canadians speak about military affairs and of the veil of objectivity that covers the consensus position of the defence community. Lane finds in Trudeau's reputation as an anti-militarist an opportunity to be supportive enough of the military that he can be all things to all voters—"masculine and feminine, tough and tender, killing and caring." Like his father before him, Trudeau may end up spending far more on defence equipment and in the rebuilding of the military than the Conservatives. The Liberals might accomplish in deed what the Harper government only achieved in words.

Trudeau touted a revival of peacekeeping, and explicitly linked it to his announcement in March 2016 that Canada would seek election in 2020 to a nonpermanent seat on the United Nations Security Council (UNSC).[13] This brought together two proud foreign policy practices from not-so-recent days: Canada had been a leading peacekeeping country until the early 2000s, and it had served on the UNSC in every decade from the 1940s to the 1990s. The Harper government had been indifferent to peacekeeping and to the United Nations, and it had failed in 2010 to secure a berth on the Security Council. There was no better way to prove that Canada was back in the world, the Liberals declared, than to return to a prominent role at the UN and earn the international respect thought to have been lost by the previous government.

Peacekeeping remains very popular with Canadians, three-quarters of whom (according to an Angus Reid poll) believe that Canada should focus on such missions rather than "combat preparedness."[14] The Opposition response is that modern peacekeeping often involves combat and that a risky peacekeeping expedition is being contemplated for the sake of Trudeau's global ambitions. Yet the government found it difficult to identify an appropriate UN peace operation for the Canadian military. Two years into its mandate, the government was still considering options, and it was unclear when and where the armed forces would be sent on a UN peacekeeping operation.[15] Nor will Canada easily find its way to the UNSC when the time comes. Andrea Charron's assessment of Trudeau's bid (if he is still prime minister in 2020) for the Council is that competition will be very stiff and that Canada lacks some of the appeal it once had in the international community. The election might end in defeat, a humiliation not unlike Harper's ten years before.

Some of Trudeau's promises held more promise. The welcoming of more than 40,000 Syrians to Canada was a signal achievement. The Harper reaction to the Syrian refugee crisis had been stingy. His government had admitted only 2,300 refugees from the civil war by the time of the 2015 election. Trudeau said he would perform many times better and turned the project into a personal crusade and a governmental priority—good politics plus good feelings if it worked, as Julie F. Gilmour illustrates in her chapter, but disastrous if it didn't. Gilmour demonstrates how the government tapped into a longstanding Canadian practice of private refugee sponsorship. Canadians, some of them former refugees themselves, set up collectives, raised money, made sponsorship applications to the government, put pressure on it to do more and do it more quickly, and gave "the global media a case study in engaged citizenship." In March of 2017, the *New York Times* published a front-page feature article one year after Canada had "embraced Syrian refugees like no other country." It was Month 13, when the sponsors' support of the Syrians was by agreement coming to an end. The story sensitively caught the flood of emotions on both sides as the sponsors moved away from the refugees, and the Syrians moved tentatively into Canadian society, on their own now.[16]

The prime minister did not stop with his Syrian enterprise. The day after the Trump administration imposed a 90-day ban on travellers from selected Middle Eastern and African countries, Trudeau tweeted on 28 January 2017: "To those fleeing persecution, terror & war, Canadians will welcome you, regardless of your faith." Asylum seekers poured illegally over the Canada-United States border, some 8,500 of them crossing into Quebec during the summer months of July and August. They would have to prove to the Immigration and Refugee Board, which had a backlog of more than 40,000 cases by late October, that they legitimately feared persecution and were not using the opportunity to find a better life than they had in the United States. The adjudication process was painfully slow, and at least half of the claimants would be unsuccessful, but medical care, a monthly stipend, and a work permit were available while they waited for a decision. The prime minister spoke to the media and reworded his tweet, saying that there was "no advantage to irregular migration over regular migration."[17]

The Trudeau government innovated with the adoption of a feminist international assistance policy. Pledging to empower women and girls in the developing world, the new policy is notably centred on gender equality, in contrast to the Conservatives' focus on maternal health. However, the policy did not come with an increase in development assistance spending, which languished at 0.26 per cent of gross national income (GNI), distant from the UN objective of 0.7 that was being met by Germany, the United Kingdom, and Sweden.[18] Whether the shift in emphasis will compensate for a stagnant budget is uncertain. In their contribution to this volume, Rebecca Tiessen and Emma Swan see encouraging (but not definitive) progress towards a feminist foreign policy in the aid promise and other pledges to make gender equality crucial to the government's human rights strategies. Tiessen and Swan argue that such efforts must be comprehensively pursued across all of government and underwritten by a feminist epistemological foundation. Without a deeper understanding of the power dynamics and varieties of oppression that surround gender, the goals of an avowedly feminist prime minister will fall short of achievement.

Advancing Canada as a champion in the battle against climate change was Trudeau's most visible break with Harper foreign policy. The Conservatives held that Canada's efforts against climate change had to be balanced against economic growth and the success of the country's natural resource industry. Trudeau and his forceful environment minister, Catherine McKenna, confidently assert that this argument presents a false dichotomy. Economic prosperity and efforts to better the environment can be achieved simultaneously: the latter will promote the former. One of the first major international acts of the Trudeau government was the signature of the Paris climate accord. The government subsequently brought the document before the House of Commons for a symbolic vote, reaffirming its commitment to the agreement and compelling the Opposition to vote against it, another unsurprising illustration of the fact that Trudeau and his advisors, like their counterparts from the Harper era, craft domestic victories out of their international affairs.[19]

Debora Van Nijnatten's chapter establishes that the Trudeau government from the start embedded commitments to greenhouse gas emissions, clean technology promotion, and sustainable practices into foreign and domestic policies. Multilateralist overtures reached out to the United States president, to the American states, to Mexico, and to China. The first of these environmental initiatives worked well when Barack Obama had control, at least of his own administration, but the Trump shock put an end to progress. Van Nijnatten has Trudeau and McKenna grinding on regardless, hindered by the sheer complexity of the problem, domestic political pressures, competition for scarce government resources, and the amount of oxygen being consumed in coping with Trump's America. In October 2017, the federal commissioner of the environment and sustainable development circulated reports criticizing the government's stewardship of these files.[20]

Environmentalism has been a prime target of Trump populism. As president, he quickly jettisoned the Paris accord, leading the *Guardian* newspaper to depict a deflated globe held up only by a clothespin under the headline "How US became a rogue state."[21] In the Trump grip, the United States will effectively cease to support global efforts to curb climate change. While this will not stop Canada from pursuing its own efforts on that front, an American refusal to engage with other countries will limit the effectiveness of any agreements and possibly amplify the economic impact that climate change compacts have on Canada. In light of Trump's anticipated attacks on other environmental protections and regulations, the full impact of his presidency on the Canadian environment and Canada's global environmental policies is unknown, but troubling.

Trump's first months in power were characterized by a series of astounding statements, resignations, and firings, as well as a bewildering approach to international affairs. Combining a Jacksonian worldview[22] with the temperament of a New York mobster, Trump became the pariah of the international community. He antagonized and alienated allies and threatened nuclear war, all while being remarkably gentle towards Russia. As his behaviour grew increasingly erratic, the military men that served in his White House and Cabinet did what they could to contain the president's outbursts and return American foreign policy to familiar ground. Their success has been intermittent. It is impossible to believe that they would have wanted him to speak as he did in his menacing September 2017 address to the UN, in which he threatened the destruction of North Korea and the ending of the Iran nuclear agreement.[23]

Stephen Blank and Monica Gattinger begin their chapter on Canadian-American relations with the crushing uncertainties caused by a disorganized Trump presidency: "we are pretty much left peering into a cloudy crystal ball and interpreting continuing campaign rhetoric, leaks, and, of course, tweets." They choose to look beyond Trump to broader bilateral and international trends, and in particular to the issues thrown up by profound demographic and social change, fundamental alterations in the energy and climate systems, and emerging technologies that are disrupting and transforming the domestic and global economies. In these arenas, all of which will have far more impact on the Canada-United States relationship than any president, Canada faces daunting challenges. Blank and Gattinger want much more attention paid to northern North America's long-term prospects and to problem-solving that they advise be carried out with strategic foresight and long-term planning within a collaborative continental framework.

Among America's traditional allies and partners, Canada has arguably positioned itself best to deal with the new administration. Considering the closeness between Trudeau's prime minister's office and President Barack Obama's White House, this may seem surprising. But the underlying reality of the continental relationship is that the Canadian government devotes a vast amount of time and energy to understanding and managing its southern neighbour, even more so when Washington is troublesome. Although the Trudeau government would have preferred that Hillary Clinton win the presidency, and was caught off guard by Trump's election (who was not?), the prime minister, his Cabinet, and his counsellors did what they could to retain Canadian influence in Washington and keep the mercurial president (relatively) civil towards Canada. Noting, for example, the heavy military presence in Trump's White House, the Trudeau government named former Lieutenant General Andrew Leslie as parliamentary secretary to the minister of foreign affairs, with a focus on Canada-United States relations.[24] There were also reports that Trudeau's principal secretary, Gerald Butts, had befriended Steve Bannon, who served as Trump's chief strategist until his departure from the White House in August 2017.[25] In addition, the government worked assiduously to cultivate ties with American states and cities in an effort to reinforce the importance of the Canada-United States relationship outside of Washington.

President Trump has forced the renegotiation of the United States-Canada-Mexico NAFTA. He has always mixed his messages, but left no doubt about his bias against trade pacts, which seemed to him (in the words of a *New York Times* reporter) occasions "for the United States to get mugged in a global marketplace in which countries are either pillaging or getting pillaged."[26] In mid-October 2017, Trudeau met Trump at the White House. When the two talked to the media afterwards, the prime minister kept his composure when Trump repeated his threat to terminate NAFTA. A few miles away, in the fourth round of the NAFTA talks, the United States was putting on the table demands so impossible that they seemed to stun even the American negotiators. Mexico and Canada vowed to keep calm and carry on, and the talks were extended into 2018.[27] Trudeau and his team put their faith in American business, the Congress, and US states and cities, where they had made strong allies. Ottawa had no faith in the Trump administration, called by Foreign Minister Chrystia Freeland the most protectionist US government since the 1930s.[28]

Trump warned America's NATO allies that he expected them to meet their commitment to spend two per cent of GDP on defence. When the Liberals released their defence policy in 2017, there was speculation that the spending increases announced by the government were meant to appease the United States. Although the Liberals' planned investments in the military will not meet the two per cent target, and while there are significant reasons to doubt whether the increases were intended to respond to Trump's demands, Canadian efforts to placate the president may guard against cuts to the promised defence dollars.

Though not a direct effect of any of Trump's actions or policies, brewing trade wars between Canada and the United States have complicated the Liberals' defence plans. In late 2016, Minister of National Defence Harjit Sajjan announced that Canada would consider the acquisition of 18 Boeing Super Hornet fighter aircraft. Sajjan explained that these interim fighters were needed to allow the Royal Canadian Air Force to fulfil their North American and international obligations simultaneously, without any risk management. A few months later, Boeing accused Canadian aerospace darling Bombardier of receiving unfair subsidies. Since that time, the Trudeau government has declared that it will not conduct business with Boeing, jeopardizing Canada's Super Hornet acquisition. Journalist Patrick Leblond wrote that, inspired by the president's "America First" trade policies, Boeing's moves against Bombardier reflect "Trumpism at its worst."[29]

The American president could render the Liberals' defence priorities still more complicated in the future. Contrary to his posturing during the

2016 election, Trump has increased America's international military commitments. In the summer of 2017, Trump announced an increase in the United States' efforts against the Taliban in Afghanistan. Although the details of his plan remain vague, Trump indicated that the United States would undertake more military operations in the country. To the relief of the Trudeau government, the president did not state that he expected allies to contribute forces or increase their presence in Afghanistan. No Canadian government would be keen to redeploy the military there after the CAF withdrawal in 2014. However, given the government's efforts to maintain a stable relationship with the president, Trudeau could feel compelled to answer Trump's call should it ever come.

According to media reports, the Liberals' delayed decision on a UN peacekeeping operation is partially tied to Trump's election.[30] After the American election, the reasoning goes, the Trudeau government felt that it needed to assess Trump's reaction to a Canadian peacekeeping deployment. The connection between the two is speculative, though it is possible that the Liberals did not want to risk a military mission that the United States would be unwilling to support. Trump's disdain for the United Nations could dampen Canada's campaign to obtain a seat on the Security Council as well. If the relationship with the president takes precedence over being seen as a champion of the UN, the Trudeau government could choose to play down or quietly abandon its hopes of securing a seat. There may also be no energy left in Ottawa to do anything but navigate the Trump turbulence. It is equally possible that the government will see a seat on the Council as a way of supporting the UN and the liberal international order during a disruptive Trump presidency. Truth be told, the president is unlikely to give much thought to Canada's Security Council ambitions.

Commentaries about contemporary politics are always perilous, but they become downright dangerous when the man in the White House is so unpredictable, so untethered by principle, so alienated from the system of which he is a part. As the first anniversary of Donald Trump's election to the presidency approaches, his approval ratings hover at record lows, scandal haunts his administration, Republicans in Congress war with him and themselves, and doubts accelerate about his fitness for the presidency. Yet no one can underestimate, or ignore, the Trump Effect. The Canadian government's foreign policy, for all Trudeau's sunny multilateralism, will largely succeed or fail in Washington. The Age of Trudeau is handcuffed to the Age of Trump.

Notes

1. Clark (2015, A4).
2. *The Economist* (2016, cover, 11).
3. Tharoor (2016), Geiger and Kürschner (2017).
4. Taylor-Vaisey (2017, 20–24).
5. Liberal Party of Canada (2015a).
6. Hillmer (2016, 258–268).
7. Ibbitson (2017, A5).
8. Global Affairs Canada (2017), Campion-Smith (2017, A1, A18).
9. Trudeau (2017).
10. Mulroney (2017, F7).
11. Fife and Chase (2017, A1, A4). The report also showed an uptick in support for a free trade agreement with China over the period Trudeau had been in office.
12. National Defence (2017).
13. Harris and Kent (2016).
14. Liberal Party of Canada (2015b), Angus Reid Institute (2015).
15. Berthiaume (2017, NP3).
16. Kantor and Einhorn (2017, 1, 11–13).
17. CBC News *The National* (2017), Levin (2017, A6).
18. Zilio (2017, A2).
19. Lagassé (2016).
20. Office of the Auditor General of Canada (2017).
21. Morrow (2017a, A6; b, A4).
22. Mead (2017).
23. Trump (2017).
24. Fife (2017).
25. Radwanski (2017).
26. Goodman (2017, B1, B3).
27. *The Guardian Weekly* (2017).
28. CBC Radio *The Sunday Edition* (2017).
29. Leblond (2017).
30. Blanchfield and Berthiaume (2017).

References

Angus Reid Institute. 2015. Election 2015: Canadians profess decline in international reputation in last decade by margin of 2:1. Angus Reid Institute, September 28. http://angusreid.org/election-2015-foreign-policy/. Accessed 22 Aug 2016.

Berthiaume, Lee. 2017. Officials await next mission as UN summit approaches. *Ottawa Citizen*, October 16.

Blanchfield, Mike, and Lee Berthiaume. 2017. Canada stalled on request to lead Mali mission because of Trump: Sources. *Canadian Press*, February 3.
Campion-Smith, Bruce. 2017. Away from glare of NAFTA talks, Canada eyes Pacific trade deal. *Toronto Star*, October 1.
CBC News. 2017. *The national.* September 7.
CBC Radio *The Sunday Edition.* 2017. Interview with Chrystia Freeland. October 22.
Clark, Campbell. 2015. The apprenticeship of Justin Trudeau. *Globe and Mail*, December 7.
Fife, Robert. 2017. Trudeau promotes former general Andrew Leslie to forge closer ties with U.S. *Globe and Mail*, January 17.
Fife, Robert, and Steven Chase. 2017. Poll finds most Canadians oppose sale of high-tech firms to China. *Globe and Mail*, July 3.
Geiger, Klaus, and Mareike Kürschner. 2017. Warum weder Merkel noch Trudeau der Anti-Trump ist. *Die Welt*, February 17. https://www.welt.de/politik/deutschland/article162180430/Warum-weder-Merkel-noch-Trudeau-der-Anti-Trump-ist.html. Accessed 10 Oct 2017.
Global Affairs Canada. 2017. Consultations on Canada's discussions with the remaining members of what was previously the Trans-Pacific Partnership. *Canada Gazette*, September 30. http://www.gazette.gc.ca/rp-pr/p1/2017/2017-09-30/html/notice-avis-eng.php. Accessed 1 Oct 2017.
Goodman, Peter S. 2017. Trump's unpredictable actions on global trade leave a trail of bewilderment. *New York Times*, September 29.
Harris, Kathleen, and Melissa Kent. 2016. Trudeau unveils Canada's plan to seek 2021 UN Security Council seat. *CBC News*, March 16. http://www.cbc.ca/news/politics/canada-united-nations-security-council-1.3491917. Accessed 11 Oct 2017.
Hillmer, Norman. 2016. The prime minister of the few. In *The Harper era in Canadian foreign policy: Parliament, politics, and Canada's global posture*, ed. Adam Chapnick and Christopher Kukucha, 258–268. Vancouver: University of British Columbia Press.
Ibbitson, John. 2017. Trudeau taking foreign-policy cues from Tory playbook. *Globe and Mail*, March 9.
Kantor, Jodi, and Catrin Einhorn. 2017. Embracing refugees, then letting go. *New York Times*, March 26.
Lagassé, Philippe. 2016. The constitutional politics of parliament's role in international policy. In *The Harper era in Canadian foreign policy: Parliament, politics, and Canada's global posture*, ed. Adam Chapnick and Christopher Kukucha, 56–72. Vancouver: University of British Columbia Press.
Leblond, Patrick. 2017. Boeing-Bombardier dispute is Trumpism at its worst. *Globe and Mail*, September 27.
Levin, Dan. 2017. Asylum cases are piling up, and Canada feels strain. *New York Times*, October 20.

Liberal Party of Canada. 2015a. Real change: A new plan for a strong middle class. Liberal Party of Canada. https://www.liberal.ca/wp-content/uploads/2015/10/New-plan-for-a-strong-middle-class.pdf. Accessed 10 Oct 2017.
———. 2015b. Promoting international peace and security. Liberal Party of Canada. https://www.liberal.ca/realchange/promoting-international-peace-and-security/. Accessed 14 Aug 2016.
Mead, Walter Russell. 2017. The Jacksonian Revolt: American populism and the liberal order. *Foreign Affairs*, March/April.
Morrow, Adrian. 2017a. White House lays out NAFTA agenda. *Globe and Mail*, October 16.
———. 2017b. NAFTA renegotiations turn acrimonious. *Globe and Mail*, October 18.
Mulroney, David. 2017. Trudeau's embrace of China exposes his naiveté. *Globe and Mail*, January 14.
National Defence. 2017. Strong, secure, engaged: Canada's defence policy. Government of Canada. http://dgpaapp.forces.gc.ca/en/canada-defence-policy/docs/canada-defence-policy-report.pdf. Accessed 20 Oct 2017.
Office of the Auditor General of Canada. 2017. 2017 fall reports of the commissioner of the environment and sustainable development. Government of Canada. http://www.oag-bvg.gc.ca/internet/English/parl_cesd_201710_e_42475.html. Accessed 20 Oct 2017.
Radwanski, Adam. 2017. Butts, Bannon and an unexpectedly effective courtship. *Globe and Mail*, August 16.
Taylor-Vaisey, Nick. 2017. Wooing America. *Maclean's*, September.
Tharoor, Ishaan. 2016. The many ways Canada's Trudeau is the anti-Trump. *Washington Post*, February 29. https://www.washingtonpost.com/news/worldviews/wp/2016/02/29/the-many-ways-canadas-trudeau-is-the-anti-trump/?utm_term=.5e194f06ac0c. Accessed 10 Oct 2017.
The Economist. 2016. Liberty moves North. *The Economist*, October 29–November 4.
The Guardian Weekly. 2017. Front page headline and illustration. June 9–15.
Trudeau, Justin. 2017. Prime Minister Justin Trudeau's address to the 72th session of the United Nations General Assembly. Speech, presented at United Nations General Assembly, New York, September 21.
Trump, Donald. 2017. Remarks by President Trump to the 72nd session of the United Nations General Assembly. *The White House*, September 19. https://www.whitehouse.gov/the-press-office/2017/09/19/remarks-president-trump-72nd-session-united-nations-general-assembly. Accessed 22 Sept 2017.
Zilio, Michelle. 2017. No plans to bump up foreign aid, Bibeau says. *Globe and Mail*, April 12.

CHAPTER 2

The Promise and Perils of Justin Trudeau's Foreign Policy

Roland Paris

Halfway through his first mandate, Prime Minister Justin Trudeau's foreign policy remains a work in progress, but its foundations are strong. In an era of mounting protectionism and intolerance, Trudeau has emerged as one of the world's most vocal and visible defenders of the "small-l" liberal values of openness and inclusion, earning himself—and Canada—widespread praise. He has, to date, demonstrated considerable diplomatic skill in his dealings with a mercurial president of the United States, Donald Trump, without diminishing his commitment to policies—from combating climate change to welcoming refugees—that are at odds with the US administration. He has renewed Canada's partnership with its closest allies, deploying Canadian forces to lead a North Atlantic Treaty Organization (NATO) battle group in Eastern Europe, and has made gender equality the focus of Canada's development policy. He has also pursued a vigorous trade-expansion strategy, finalizing a major trade agreement with the European Union and promoting a model of "progressive" trade that emphasizes sharing the benefits of trade more equitably.

R. Paris (✉)
University of Ottawa, Ottawa, ON, Canada

© The Author(s) 2018
N. Hillmer, P. Lagassé (eds.), *Justin Trudeau and Canadian Foreign Policy*, Canada and International Affairs,
https://doi.org/10.1007/978-3-319-73860-4_2

Trudeau's brand of internationalism, which blends liberal idealism and interest-based realism, has worked well for Canada in the past and stands to do so in the future. With global challenges proliferating and international leadership in short supply, Trudeau is well-positioned to advance Canada's interests while rallying international action to address some of these challenges. He also has the potential to achieve a breakthrough in Canada's trade relations with large emerging countries in Asia, which are increasingly at the centre of global economic growth and whose importance in global affairs will grow. Further, his foreign minister, Chrystia Freeland, is better equipped than most of her predecessors to advance Trudeau's international agenda; and the Canadian public continues to support an activist foreign policy, rather than succumbing to isolationist tendencies that have gained prominence elsewhere. In short, this is a moment of unusual promise for Canadian foreign policy.

Yet it is also one of perils. Two loom, in particular. The first is the danger of a rupture in relations with the United States, Canada's most important economic partner and ally, whose unpredictable president has denounced some of America's closest partners and questioned the value of existing trade accords, including the North American Free Trade Agreement (NAFTA). A serious disruption could result in significant economic costs for Canada, as well as potential political costs for Trudeau and his party at the polls. The second peril is less visible, but related to the first: the urgent and complex demands of managing Canada-US relations could end up overshadowing other important international priorities, which also require the attention of the prime minister and his cabinet. Neglecting these priorities would represent more than a missed opportunity to capitalize on Canada's current advantages and to realize Trudeau's post-election promise of Canada assuming a global leadership role. In a world of rising powers, mounting competitive pressures, and other international challenges that bear on the security and well-being of Canadians, protecting Canada's interests necessitates a strategic, globally engaged foreign policy.

In June 2017, the federal government issued three international policy statements—on foreign policy, defence, and international development assistance—the full implications of which will not be known for some time. This chapter therefore offers a snapshot of an evolving situation, along with some reflections on the future. I begin by describing the development of

Trudeau's foreign policy to date, focusing on three periods: (1) the months prior to the October 2015 federal election, (2) the first year in office from the 2015 election until Trump's victory in November 2016, and (3) the ensuing period until the fall of 2017. Then I consider the international risks and opportunities facing the Trudeau government in the coming months and years.

The reader should know I approach this subject with a particular set of experiences and views. I served as an advisor to Trudeau immediately before and after the 2015 election, taking a leave from my university position until the summer of 2016. Although this was my fourth job in government, it was my first political appointment. I am not a partisan person by inclination, but I was happy to advise Trudeau for two reasons. First, I had long been concerned about the directions of Canadian foreign policy (under preceding Conservative and Liberal governments) and I welcomed the opportunity to offer recommendations on how to improve it. Second, I liked the way that Trudeau thought about international affairs. We shared a vision of a Canada assertively pursuing its national interests while working constructively with other countries to address global problems. At a time of unusual promise and peril, he has the potential to become one of Canada's great foreign-policy prime ministers. Whether he ultimately realizes this potential, however, remains to be seen.

Preparation: The Lead-Up to the 2015 Election

An enterprising scholar or journalist will eventually piece together the development of Trudeau's foreign-policy views before he became prime minister. I know only a small part of this story, the part I witnessed. In September 2014, I was invited to meet with Trudeau, who was then the leader of the third party in Parliament, and to brief him on the situation in the Middle East. Also present were several of his senior staff and members of his International Affairs Council of Advisors, a group that convened periodically to discuss foreign-policy issues. In the ensuing weeks, working with Trudeau's aides, I provided feedback on the policy elements of draft speeches and statements he was scheduled to deliver. Later that fall, I was asked to draft a foreign-policy plan for a future Liberal government.

Much of the raw material for this exercise had already been assembled by Trudeau's staff (drawing on his previous policy pronouncements and Liberal Party positions) and by the two co-chairs of the International Affairs Council: Marc Garneau, a Member of Parliament who was then the

Liberal foreign affairs critic, and Andrew Leslie, a former army general who would be elected to Parliament the following year. They had commissioned a number of short briefing notes from a variety of people on foreign-policy issues. I spent the next two months collecting and reflecting on such documents, doing additional research, and reaching out to experts and stakeholders in various fields. The result was a 31-page draft that Trudeau read and we discussed in January 2015. The document went through several subsequent revisions and ultimately provided grist for speeches and policy statements prior to the election, parts of the Liberal campaign platform and mandate letters that the prime minister wrote to his international ministers after the election.[1]

In broad summary, the document set out a number of goals, including:

pursuing a North American strategy on climate change and energy;
concluding the Paris climate negotiations and establishing a domestic framework to meet Canada's greenhouse gas commitments;
expanding Canada's trade relationships, most notably with China and other fast-growing markets in Asia, which had been neglected for too long;
reaffirming Canada's commitment to counterterrorism and the coalition against the Islamic State of Iraq and the Levant (ISIL);
contributing further to NATO's "reassurance measures" in Eastern Europe;
revitalizing Canada's multilateral diplomacy at the United Nations (UN) and in other forums in order to advance Canadian goals and to strengthen the machinery of international cooperation;
championing human rights and pluralism—most notably the rights of women, children, minorities, and refugees—in an increasingly divided and sectarian world;
reorganizing and expanding Canada's approach to helping fragile states, such as by contributing badly needed specialized capabilities to the new generation of UN peace operations;
resuming diplomatic contacts with "troublesome" countries, such as Russia and Iran, while continuing to oppose their aggressive actions;
adopting more innovative forms of development programming, including earmarking a portion of the international assistance budget for new aid-delivery pilots and taking promising pilots to scale;

expanding international education for young Canadians in order to prepare the next generation of private- and public-sector leaders to succeed in an increasingly complex world;
reinvesting in the instruments of Canada's international policy—military, development assistance, and foreign service—all of which had been underfunded for years; and
capitalizing on Canada's standing in the world by mobilizing broad coalitions of like-minded states and international non-state actors to support these foreign-policy goals.

Some of these recommendations were accepted. Others were overtaken by events or were not pursued at all. Still others required further consideration and development. Because majority governments enter office with a reasonable expectation of four years in power, Trudeau's cabinet had the time to consider its strategic options, launching reviews of defence and development policy, for example. But the new government also had to make immediate decisions and to begin laying the groundwork for policy changes. By an accident of timing, Trudeau was to attend four major summits, including the Group of Twenty (G20) meeting in Turkey, the Asia-Pacific Economic Cooperation (APEC) summit in Manila, the Commonwealth conference in Malta, and the UN climate change conference in Paris, as well as two bilateral visits to France and Britain, all within six weeks of taking office. Because my informal advisory role had gone from casual to intensive in the preceding months, I was invited to join the "transition team" after the election and then to come into the Prime Minister's Office (PMO) to continue advising the prime minister.

Salad Days: From the 2015 Election to Trump

Many had assumed that foreign policy was not Trudeau's strong suit. During the election campaign, at a leaders' debate on international affairs in Toronto, the audience had snickered when New Democratic Party leader Thomas Mulcair had questioned how Trudeau would perform in a face-to-face meeting with Russian leader Vladimir Putin. Now Trudeau was plunging into intensive diplomacy, just days after becoming prime minister.

This initial flurry of travel turned out to be a blessing. International meetings serve a "forcing function" in government—they compel officials and political leaders to focus on issues and define objectives relevant to those meetings. In his summit sessions and bilateral encounters, the prime minister had the opportunity to explain his policy priorities to fellow leaders, arguing, for example, for the importance both of maintaining open international trade and of sharing the benefits of growth more equitably. By the end of this intensive period of travel, Trudeau had met the leaders of many of the world's major countries and Canada's principal partners (including the United States, the United Kingdom, France, Germany, Italy, Japan, and China) and had begun building personal relationships with each.

The single less-than-positive encounter was by design: Trudeau's first conversation with Vladimir Putin on the margins of the Group of Twenty (G20) summit in Turkey. Trudeau was clear-eyed about Putin, who was no friend of the West or Canada. Prior to their meeting, I was thinking about former US President John F. Kennedy's first encounter with then-Soviet leader Nikita Khrushchev in 1961, when Khrushchev thought he could exploit Kennedy's relative inexperience and youth. It was important for Trudeau to begin his relationship with Putin from a position of resolve and strength. Once this position was clearly established, Ottawa could then gradually expand normal diplomatic contacts with Russia, which the Conservative government under Stephen Harper had restricted. One minor challenge, however, was to find an opportunity for Trudeau to speak with Putin; they did not have a formal meeting scheduled at the summit. Although the two leaders crossed paths and shook hands at one point between sessions, a simple handshake was not the message Trudeau wanted to convey, either to Putin or to Canadians. After some manoeuvring, he approached Putin in the meeting room at the end of the summit and delivered a pointed message: Canada would continue to oppose Russia's interference in Ukraine and to support the people of Ukraine, and he expected Russia to fully implement the Minsk II peace accords.

Canadian journalists accompanying the prime minister on these early trips were particularly interested in the reactions of Canadian allies to Trudeau's planned withdrawal of Canada's six CF-18s from combat operations over Iraq and Syria. Trudeau had adopted this position a year before the election, after reflecting on how Canada could best contribute to the coalition campaign against ISIL. He had concluded that the most effective and sustainable strategy was to enable local forces to carry out the anti-ISIL campaign, rather than doing the fighting for them. For Trudeau, this enabling role included training, advising, and assisting local forces, and other types of support to the international coalition. It did not include conducting airstrikes or sending Canadian troops into front-line combat against ISIL fighters. I might have drawn the line somewhat differently, but I respected Trudeau's decision. I also came to understand that he would not shy away from using armed force, there or elsewhere, if it were in Canada's interests to do so. In any event, one of the striking things about his initial round of meetings with foreign leaders was that this issue rarely came up, and when it did, Trudeau was not pressured. German Chancellor Angela Merkel, for instance, asked Trudeau to explain his position on the CF-18s but did not challenge it, and US President Barack Obama seemed unperturbed when they met for the first time in Manila. The fact that Trudeau simultaneously recommitted Canada to the anti-ISIL coalition and pledged to boost Canada's training role likely helped to defuse any concerns.

Rumours of a "bromance" between Obama and Trudeau were not exaggerated. The president and his senior advisors regarded Trudeau as a kindred spirit who reminded them of a younger Obama. Whether this impression was accurate or not, it served Trudeau's aim of resetting Canada's relationship with the US administration. Relations with Mexico also improved when Trudeau reaffirmed his intention to remove visa restrictions on Mexican travellers to Canada, which had caused considerable tension in the relationship. Conditions were therefore ripe to make progress on a number of bilateral and trilateral issues, including a continental agreement on reducing methane emissions, a major source of greenhouse gases. Everyone was aware, however, that Obama had only a few months left in office and that any long-term US commitments had a potential expiry date. On some issues, moreover, the warm feelings between Obama and Trudeau were not enough to overcome deeper resistance. Canada was particularly concerned about the looming threat of new US tariffs on Canadian softwood lumber, but Obama showed no inclination to face down the US lumber lobby.

Meanwhile, the Trudeau government was laying the groundwork for the rest of its foreign policy. Just minutes after he was sworn in, the prime minister called upon Canadian ambassadors and heads of mission to communicate with "other diplomats, host government officials, civil society, and the media—in all manner of ways—through direct contact, the media, and social media," relaxing the previous government's restrictions. The new government also:

launched the defence and international assistance reviews;
revised Canada's military mission in Iraq and expanded the number of trainers;

announced that Canadian forces would lead the NATO battle group in Latvia;

initiated negotiations with the provinces on a pan-Canadian plan to implement the Paris climate agreement;

pledged $2.65 million over five years to support developing countries deal with the adverse effects of global warming;

helped raise nearly $13 billion from other countries and private sources to expand the global fight against HIV-AIDS, malaria, and tuberculosis;

welcomed tens of thousands of Syrian refugees to Canada and increased support for refugees in Jordan and Lebanon;

transformed the foreign ministry's Office of Religious Freedom into a larger human rights bureau;

concluded the Canada-EU economic and trade agreement;

initiated exploratory discussions for possible free trade negotiations with China; and

announced Canada's bid for a UN Security Council seat in 2021–22.

However, the government was arguably less effective at explaining its foreign policy to Canadians. The prime minister opted not to present a comprehensive statement of the government's international priorities in the form of a speech or document, leaving this task largely to his foreign minister, Stéphane Dion. A serious, smart, dedicated man who readily immersed himself into the details of policy, Dion nevertheless had difficulty conveying the government's goals and dealing with a handful of controversial issues, including the sale of armed troop-transport vehicles to Saudi Arabia.

Donald Trump's unexpected election in November 2016 was the first real foreign-policy crisis to hit the Trudeau government, prompting a reorganization of the ministry—including Dion's removal and Chrystia Freeland's appointment as foreign minister. While a relatively permissive international environment during Trudeau's first year in office had allowed for the gradual rollout of international initiatives, red lights were now flashing in Ottawa and across the country.

ALL HANDS ON DECK: AFTER TRUMP'S ELECTION

Although Ottawa had done some planning for the possibility of a Trump victory, the US election was a shock. The prime minister had earlier made the decision not to weigh into the US presidential campaign—for good reason: publicly supporting Hillary Clinton's bid would not have improved her electoral prospects, and it could have backfired badly on Canada.

Trump's election in November prompted the prime minister's principal secretary and chief of staff, Gerald Butts and Katie Telford, to quickly make contact with the president-elect's closest advisors, including Jared Kushner (Trump's son-in-law) and Steve Bannon, the erstwhile head of *Breitbart News*, who had joined the Trump campaign in its latter stages. They also reached out to intermediaries who had relationships with Trump and people rumoured to be candidates for senior posts in the Trump Administration, and they sought advice from a range of Canadians with experience in Canada-US relations, regardless of partisan affiliations. Chrystia Freeland, who was then still minister of international trade, and David MacNaughton, Canada's ambassador to the United States, were also instrumental in these outreach efforts.

In January 2017, the government reorganized in advance of Trump's inauguration. In addition to moving Freeland into the foreign minister's job and appointing François-Philippe Champagne as the new Minister of International Trade, Freeland's former chief of staff was brought into the PMO to coordinate a whole-of-government approach to US relations. Meanwhile, Trudeau was communicating with provincial premiers and Canada's big-city mayors, and over the coming weeks a coordinated advocacy campaign took shape, mobilizing Canadian political and business leaders across the country as well as allies throughout the United States. Its overarching message was simple: the Canada-US economic relationship is beneficial to both countries, including to the millions of Americans whose jobs depend on it. Trilateral negotiations aimed at "modernizing" NAFTA, along with the delicate task of managing relations with Trump, himself, quickly became Ottawa's top foreign-policy priority.

These circumstances informed Freeland's major speech to Parliament in June 2017, which set out the broad directions and purposes of the government's approach to international affairs.[2] Without naming the president, she took aim at Trump's "America First" renunciation of America's postwar commitment to uphold the liberal international order, his characterization of international trade as harmful to American workers, and his appeals to nativism and anti-immigrant (and anti-Muslim) sentiments. She presented the case for Canada continuing to pursue an activist international policy on a global scale, arguing that upholding the framework of international institutions and rules served Canadians' interests and reflected their values. She also highlighted two other priorities: reinvesting in the military and promoting "progressive trade that works for working people." Details were scarce, but as a policy-framing exercise, Freeland's address was reminiscent of a speech given by another foreign minister—Louis St. Laurent's "Gray Lecture" of 1947—in which he also made the case for a global, activist Canadian foreign policy at a time of uncertainty and change in the world.

One day after her address, the government announced that it would increase defence spending by a substantial amount, although the bulk of the increases were scheduled for future years. A new development policy statement followed a few days later. Its centrepiece was a plan to increase the proportion of Canadian development spending dedicated to women's health and empowerment, from two to 15 per cent. However, the government committed no new funds to this goal, instead reallocating existing budgetary resources at a time when Canada's development spending was trending towards its lowest level in 50 years (as a percentage of gross domestic product). Nor did Freeland pledge additional funding for Canada's foreign service, which had also been depleted over the preceding years. This was awkward for a government that had emphasized the necessity for Canada to play a leadership role in the world; implementing Freeland's vision would seem to require reinvesting in all the tools of international policy, not just the military.

Looking Ahead: Promise and Perils

The absence of a plan to reinvest in the diplomatic and development instruments of Canadian foreign policy pointed to a broader question facing the government: how serious was Trudeau's commitment to pursuing the ambitious foreign policy that he had repeatedly promised? This remains an open question. The prime minister himself is an internationalist—he believes that Canada should play an energetic, constructive role in the world. As he said in 2016 when he first addressed the United Nations General Assembly, "We're Canada and we're here to help." He has spoken many times about the need for global action on a range of issues, including climate change, inclusion and diversity, gender equality, the rights and well-being of refugees, and maintaining the rules-based international order. Yet, halfway through his first mandate as prime minister, it is unclear how he intends to translate these aspirations into a programme of action that would meet his own call for global leadership.

Those hoping for clarification of Trudeau's intentions in his second speech to the UN General Assembly in September 2017 would have been disappointed. He used the occasion to highlight Canada's efforts to redress its historical injustices committed against Indigenous peoples—an important national objective, to be sure, and one that was consistent with broader international efforts to recognize the rights of Indigenous people around the world—but the speech shed little light on Trudeau's foreign-policy plans. Although responsible behaviour at home can earn Canada plaudits and might serve as a model to others, addressing global problems ultimately requires countries that are willing to lead international campaigns to tackle these problems.

Canada has often provided this type of international leadership in the past. Louis St. Laurent played an important role in the creation of NATO after the Second World War. Lester Pearson was instrumental in developing the institution of peacekeeping. Pierre Elliott Trudeau tried to build a new dialogue between the developed and developing worlds and to achieve a global agreement on arms control, efforts that were not ultimately successful, but he did bring about a historic opening in Canada's relations with China. Brian Mulroney negotiated the Canada-US and North American free trade agreements, concluded an acid rain accord, and was instrumental in the campaign against South African apartheid. Jean Chrétien and his foreign minister, Lloyd Axworthy, achieved an international treaty banning anti-personnel landmines and played an important role in creating the International Criminal Court. Even Stephen Harper, who questioned Canada's liberal internationalist traditions, launched a global initiative on maternal, newborn, and child health that achieved significant results and continues to this day. In all of these cases, Canadian leaders left their marks in international affairs by investing their own political and diplomatic influence in special initiatives to address specific international challenges.

Justin Trudeau is now in a strong position to do the same. He benefits from an international profile and positive global reputation that may exceed that of any previous Canadian prime minister. He could use these assets to mobilize a broad coalition of like-minded countries, private foundations, advocacy groups, international agencies, and individual citizens in an organized campaign to address one or more of the global issues that matter to him. For example, the world is facing an unprecedented refugee crisis, with tens of millions of people stuck in the limbo of protracted displacement with little prospect of returning home or being resettled elsewhere. These situations risk becoming time bombs of hopelessness for millions of young refugees who are not receiving education or learning employable skills. Canada could mount an international campaign aimed at providing 100 per cent of refugee youth with quality primary education and older youths with skills training, thus creating hope for their future, lowering the risk of radicalization and future instability, reducing incentives for refugees to risk dangerous onward journeys, and empowering girls and young women—another one of the prime minister's goals.

Canada needs an activist foreign policy not just to help others, but also to help ourselves. Today's historic shift in global economic and political power towards emerging countries has far-reaching implications for both the security and economic well-being of Canadians. How can Ottawa contribute to the process of integrating these countries into the existing international order, which for decades has underpinned an unprecedented period of prosperity and relative peace for Canada? How can we best help to adapt that order so that it better reflects new power realities while simultaneously upholding the interlocking network of institutions and rules that have provided a modicum of stability in international affairs? With protectionist sentiments on the rise in the United States, how can Canada diversify its trade relationships and adjust to the centre of global economic activity shifting towards Asia? Canada lags far behind our competitors in accessing the Chinese market, for example, and our trade remains overwhelmingly with slow-growth countries, which limits Canada's own economic prospects, but closer engagement with China also involves risks. Beijing does not play by the same rules as Canada's traditional trading partners, and some of its domestic policies are odious, including the repression of political dissidents. Balancing these conflicting pressures is just one example of the challenges facing Canada's leaders in a more complex and increasingly multipolar world. Some may be tempted to turn away from these challenges, but that would leave Canada both sidelined and disadvantaged in international affairs.

Yet there is a real risk that the Trudeau government will be so consumed by its relations with the United States that it will fail to make real breakthroughs in other areas of its foreign policy.

Managing Canada-US relations is a vital interest, but it should not come at the expense of pursuing a strategic and energetic foreign policy beyond North America. This will require sustained attention from the prime minister and his cabinet, along a commitment to achieve substantive rather than merely symbolic results. Trudeau, in short, still needs to convert his ambitious foreign-policy language into concrete initiatives and achievements, translating aspiration into action. Political leaders' time and attention are the most precious commodities in Ottawa. Will there be enough to spare for a foreign policy that secures Canada's interests in a rapidly changing world while also providing Canadian leadership to address specific global problems?

Conclusion

Halfway through its first mandate, the Trudeau government has laid a solid foundation for its foreign policy, but it is still only a foundation, and dangers loom. Trudeau's success or failure to protect Canada's interests with the Trump Administration will almost certainly be a defining element of his foreign-policy record as prime minister. On the other hand, focusing too narrowly on relations with the United States would also be risky. Canada's interests extend well beyond North America, and current conditions are unusually promising for Trudeau to pursue an ambitious and effective foreign policy. Failing to capitalize on this moment—due to a lack of attention, strategic clarity, or ambition—would also figure in Trudeau's eventual foreign-policy legacy: as a missed opportunity of historic significance.

Notes

1. I also used this document as a basis for writing (Paris 2015), "Time to make ourselves useful: An open letter to the 2015 federal election winner."
2. Global Affairs Canada (2017).

References

Global Affairs Canada. 2017. Address by Minister Freeland on Canada's foreign policy priorities. Government of Canada, June 6. https://www.canada.ca/en/global-affairs/news/2017/06/address_by_ministerfreelandoncanadasforeignpolicypriorities.html. Accessed 8 Aug 2017.

Paris, Roland. 2015. Time to make ourselves useful: An open letter to the 2015 federal election winner. Literary Review of Canada, March 2015. http://reviewcanada.ca/magazine/2015/03/time-to-make-ourselves-useful/. Accessed 15 Sept 2017.

CHAPTER 3

Promises Made, Promises Kept? A Mid-term Trudeau Foreign Policy Report Card

Kim Richard Nossal

Election promises in Western democracies are notorious for their evanescence. Parties and candidates seeking office invariably try to attract votes by making promises that they believe will resonate with the electorate. Frequently, however, those promises are embraced without a careful consideration of what would happen if the candidate making the promises actually won the election and took power. For that reason, election campaigns cast a long shadow, often shaping (and sometimes mis-shaping) policy once the party that had made the promises comes to power.

The Liberal government of Justin Trudeau came to power in 2015 having spent the election campaign making not only a number of specific foreign policy promises, but also a generalized promise to pursue a very different kind of foreign policy than the Conservative government under Stephen Harper had pursued between 2006 and 2015. Two years on, and halfway through its term, has that promise of change been met? The purpose of this chapter is to provide a mid-term assessment of the Trudeau government's international policy based on the promises that the Liberals made while in opposition or during the election campaign.

K. R. Nossal (✉)
Queen's University, Kingston, ON, Canada

© The Author(s) 2018
N. Hillmer, P. Lagassé (eds.), *Justin Trudeau and Canadian Foreign Policy*, Canada and International Affairs,
https://doi.org/10.1007/978-3-319-73860-4_3

At mid-term, it can be argued that in its first two years in office the Trudeau government was indeed able to forge a different path in global affairs than the Conservatives, but it is a difference primarily of tone. In many areas of policy, inertial forces imposed themselves—not at all surprisingly, given the broader economic and geostrategic structural determinants of Canada's location in global affairs. Taken as a whole, the specific international policy promises made by the Liberals during the 2015 campaign did not cast a negative shadow. And one election promise that will come back to haunt a future government, Trudeau's insistence that a Liberal government would not acquire the Lockheed Martin F-35 Lightning II as a possible replacement for Canada's fleet of CF-18 Hornet jet fighters, was likely put off sufficiently into the future that it will not be an issue in the 2019 election.

Ironically, it is clear that at the Trudeau government's mid-term that the foreign policy promises that it made during the 2015 election have been almost entirely eclipsed by a phenomenon that was only dimly taking shape in the fall of 2015: the rise of Donald J. Trump as president of the United States. It can also be argued that at mid-term, the defining feature of the Trudeau government's foreign policy has been its management of the challenges posed by Trump.

The Electoral Context

The foreign policy promises made by the Liberals during the 2015 election campaign cannot be understood unless they are placed in the context of the party's standing at the outset of the campaign. At dissolution, the Liberals held just 36 of the 308 seats in the 41st Parliament. On 2 August, when the writs were issued for the election on 19 October, the Liberals were in third place in the polls, and well behind not only the official opposition, the New Democratic Party (NDP) under Tom Mulcair, which spent the first half of the campaign in first place, but also the Conservatives under Stephen Harper.

Moreover, Trudeau's foreign affairs record in the two years that he had been leader of the Liberal Party did not look promising. In particular, two thoughtless off-the-cuff comments about international affairs dogged him. Six months into his leadership, at what was described as a "ladies night" fundraiser,[1] Trudeau was asked which nation he admired most besides Canada. He responded: "There's a level of admiration I actually have for China. Their basic dictatorship is actually allowing them to turn their economy around on a dime."² The comment was widely derided. The NDP likened him to Sarah Palin, the Republican vice-presidential candidate in 2008 who had a well-established reputation for foolish gaffes. For their part, the Conservatives claimed that the comment showed that Trudeau was "in over his head."³

The second gaffe came in October 2014. In a "fireside chat" with journalist Don Newman at a Canada 2020 conference, Trudeau was asked about his party's policy on Islamic State in Iraq and the Levant (ISIL, also known as Islamic State in Iraq and al-Shām, or Daesh, its Arabic acronym). Trudeau responded by noting that the Liberals supported the provision of humanitarian aid, but opposed military involvement. But he went on to wonder why the Harper Conservatives refused to focus on humanitarian assistance "rather than … trying to whip out our CF-18s and show them how big they are."⁴ Again, he was widely criticized, with Conservative and NDP critics deriding his "childish" and "juvenile" locker-room humour.⁵

Not surprisingly, the Conservatives used the lack of experience revealed by these gaffes as a central theme of their campaign in 2015. The series of attack ads that began airing three months before the writs were issued stressed Trudeau's inexperience. They featured a group of interviewers assessing Trudeau's resume, and wondering if he had the experience to become prime minister. The general conclusion, written in red on his resume by one of the interviewers, was that he was "just not ready" to be prime minister, with another interviewer adding, mockingly, "Nice hair, though."⁶ While the longer-term impact of these ads on the electors continues to be debated,⁷ the "just not ready" theme appeared to resonate with voters in the first part of the campaign.⁸

However, the 2015 campaign was a long one, at 78 days the longest since 1872, and far longer than the average length of the previous ten campaigns—45.8 days. By most accounts,⁹ Harper called the election six weeks early in a cynical bid to give the Conservative Party a major advantage over the NDP and the Liberals, since newly revised electoral spending rules favoured the Conservatives, who had raised much more money than the other parties. Indeed, Conservative officials admitted that the long campaign was explicitly designed to "exhaust the other parties' finances."¹⁰

But it is clear in retrospect that the longevity of the campaign worked against the Conservatives. Had the election been held 45 days after the writs were issued—in other words, in the middle of September—polls suggest that there would have been a minority parliament, since Conservatives,

Liberals, and the NDP were all polling around 30 per cent each at that point. But in the additional 30 days, there was a major reversal of fortune. By voting day, the Liberals had surged to 39.5 per cent, the NDP had plunged to 19.7 per cent, while the Conservatives had remained at 31.9 per cent.[11] The Liberals ended up winning 184 of the 338 seats in the expanded House of Commons, giving the party a commanding majority in the 42nd Parliament.

Promises, Promises

The various foreign policy promises of the Liberal Party during the 2015 campaign can best be gleaned from the formal Liberal platform as well as the statements made at events like the Munk Debate on Foreign Policy, which organized a leaders' foreign policy debate on 28 September.[12] The published platform devoted just ten pages of their 88-page platform to international policy. While there were promises on immigration, development assistance, trade promotion, and national defence, there was no foreign policy section per se. The closest was a short statement on Canada's role in global politics. At just 149 words, the Liberal statement on foreign policy was even shorter than the brief 171 words on foreign policy that the Conservative Party had written for the 2005–2006 campaign.[13] It can thus readily be cited in full:

> Canada has a proud tradition of international leadership, from helping to create the United Nations after the Second World War, to the campaign against South African apartheid, to the international treaty to ban landmines.
>
> Unfortunately, under Stephen Harper, our influence and presence on the world stage has steadily diminished. Instead of working with other countries constructively at the United Nations, the Harper Conservatives have turned their backs on the UN and other multilateral institutions, while also weakening Canada's military, our diplomatic service, and our development programs.
>
> Whether confronting climate change, terrorism and radicalization, or international conflicts, the need for effective Canadian diplomacy has never been greater than it is today.
>
> Our plan will restore Canada as a leader in the world. Not only to provide greater security and economic growth for Canadians, but because Canada can make a real and valuable contribution to a more peaceful and prosperous world.[14]

This general promise to restore Canadian leadership in the world was accompanied by a range of other promises. On peace and security, the platform committed a Liberal government to renew Canada's commitment to peacekeeping operations and to allocate resources to the United Nations (UN), particularly on civilian police training and peace operations. On defence, the Liberals committed to maintain current spending levels and to launch a review of defence policy. The platform did, however, embrace three very specific promises. One focused on the replacement for the fleet of CF-18 Hornet jet fighters: "We will not buy the F-35 stealth fighter-bomber." Instead, a Liberal government would "immediately launch an open and transparent competition" to replace the existing CF-18 fleet but would not allow Lockheed Martin to compete (How it was possible to run an "open" competition while refusing to allow one of the primary competitors to compete was not addressed). The second specific promise related to the Canadian operations in Iraq and Syria against ISIL: a Liberal government would end the combat mission, "refocus Canada's military contribution in the region on the training of local forces, while providing more humanitarian support," and admit 25,000 Syrian refugees immediately. Third, the platform promised to remain "fully committed" to the existing military contributions to the North Atlantic Treaty Organization (NATO) assurance measures in Central and Eastern Europe.

To a consideration of these peace and security promises, and how they fared under the new Liberal government at mid-term, we now turn.

"Canada Is Back"

"To this country's friends all around the world," Justin Trudeau told a Liberal victory rally the day after the election, "many of you have worried that Canada has lost its compassionate and constructive voice in the world over the past ten years. Well, I have a simple message for you: on behalf of 35 million Canadians: We're back."[15] The "Canada is back" meme quickly became the hallmark of the new government's approach to global politics.

The declaration that Canada was "back" in global affairs was a pithy, but loaded, phrase. While only a few remembered that Stephen Harper and the Conservatives had used precisely the same catchphrase when they came to power in 2006,[16] it was designed to signal that the Trudeau government was promising to change course in a number of key foreign policy areas. It signalled an end to Canada's antipathy towards the UN, so much in evidence between 2006 and 2015; there would be no more disparaging it as a "gabfest for dictators."[17] No longer would the government in Ottawa conduct foreign policy by insult: no longer would it "lecture and leave," in former foreign minister Joe Clark's memorable phrase.[18] It signalled an end to what Jeffrey Simpson of the *Globe and Mail* so accurately called "bullhorn diplomacy."[19] Finally, the phrase was intended to signal an end to the relentless cynicism in foreign policy that was so much a mark of the Harper Conservatives, reflected in the efforts to politicize almost every foreign policy issue in an undisguised and unapologetic attempt to maximize their electoral support—and to maximize the skewering of the opposition parties.[20]

After the election, there was indeed a marked change in tone. Trudeau's approach to participation in the UN climate change Twenty-First Conference of the Parties (COP21) in Paris in November 2015 was indicative. During the Harper years, the opposition parties would be routinely excluded from Canadian delegations to global climate change conferences; but then, just to rub it in, the Conservative front bench would take particular delight in criticizing the opposition for not attending these conferences. As prime minister, however, Trudeau chose not to play tit-for-tat with the Conservative opposition. Instead, he invited the opposition parties to join him as part of the delegation to Paris, and even tweeted a picture of himself surrounded by premiers and three opposition MPs: Ed Fast, the Conservative environment critic; Tom Mulcair, the NDP leader; and Elizabeth May, the leader of the Green Party. The message accompanying the picture would have been unthinkable before 19 October 2015: "To fight climate change, we're all in this together."[21] The same non-partisanship was evident some days later at Toronto airport, when the prime minister welcomed the first planeload of Syrian refugees to Canada. Once again, he invited the opposition to join him, for this was intended to be a *Canadian* welcome, not a partisan affair from which the opposition would be excluded so that the governing party could capture maximum political credit.[22]

But the change in tone was accompanied by some changes in policy as the new government moved to implement its election promises.

Canada as Internationalist Peacekeeper

The Liberals had a clear purpose in putting the recommitment to peacekeeping operations at the forefront of its election campaign. They were playing to the strong public support for the idea that Canada is a peacekeeping country, an idea that the Harper Conservative government had supposedly abandoned.²³ Indeed, in 2014, Roland Paris, a professor of international relations at the University of Ottawa, published a widely cited article that showed conclusively that, despite the efforts of the Harper Conservatives to alter the "Canada as peacekeeper" narrative, "there remains an important reservoir of public support for liberal internationalism."²⁴ (After the election, Trudeau appointed Paris to serve as his foreign policy adviser for six months).

To underscore the return to internationalism, Trudeau focused on one of the key markers of Canadian international engagement—a non-permanent UN Security Council seat. Canada had been elected to the Security Council once a decade between the late 1940s and the late 1990s, and had only lost an election twice: in the election for the very first Security Council in January 1946, and in October 2010. The 2010 defeat was in part the result of mismanagement: the Harper government had at first decided not to run, and then changed its mind part way through the long campaign. It was also in part a consequence of the sneering attitude of the Conservatives towards the UN.²⁵ Trudeau wasted little time in seeking a symbolic reset of Canadian policy towards the UN: in March 2016, he announced that Canada would be a candidate for the 2021–2022 session of the Security Council.²⁶

Moreover, once in power, the Trudeau government moved to make good its promise to restore Canada as a peacekeeping nation. In August 2016, Harjit Sajjan, the minister of national defence, travelled to five African countries to find an appropriate UN peacekeeping mission to join. The intention was to be able to announce the Canadian decision in September, when a UN Summit on Peacekeeping was taking place in London.²⁷ Mali was the favoured location for the new deployment. But the new deployment never materialized, partly because of the rise of Donald Trump, discussed below, and partly because of another promise that the Liberals had made during the election campaign: a promise to maintain Canada's commitment to reassurance missions in Eastern Europe.

Central and Eastern Europe

The Liberal platform had promised that "We will remain fully committed to Canada's existing military contributions in Central and Eastern Europe."²⁸ Little had been made of this promise during the campaign itself. Canada's contribution to NATO's reassurance and deterrence efforts in Central and Eastern Europe had been agreed to by the

Conservative government in early 2014 as relations between the Russian Federation and NATO countries deteriorated following the Euromaidan protest movement in Ukraine in late 2013. When the Russian Federation seized Crimea from Ukraine in February 2014 and subsequently incorporated it into the Russian Federation and then launched a military intervention in the Donbass region of eastern Ukraine, relations deteriorated even further. The nadir came in July 2014, when a Russian SA-11 Buk surface-to-air missile fired from rebel-held territory in the Donbass destroyed a Malaysian Airlines Boeing 777, killing all 298 passengers and crew.

The reaction of Western countries to the events in Ukraine in 2014 included both sanctions, including expelling Russia from the Group of Eight (G8), and military measures. A number of Western states, including Canada, sought to contribute to Ukrainian efforts at self-defence. Under Operation UNIFIER, the Canadian Armed Forces (CAF) shipped non-lethal military equipment to Ukraine, and in December 2014 signed an agreement for joint military training with the Ukrainian armed forces; the training mission started in September 2015.

Ukraine is not a NATO ally, but the deterioration in relations with Russia spilled into other parts of Central and Eastern Europe, which did affect NATO allies. In April 2014, NATO embraced a series of measures designed to provide reassurance to those members of the alliance, to deter Russia from destabilizing NATO allies in Central and Eastern Europe, and to de-escalate the mounting tensions with Moscow. Over the course of 2014 and 2015, Canada contributed air, naval, and land forces to this reassurance mission. Operation REASSURANCE involved an air task force deployed to the Baltics and Romania; a maritime task force deployed to the Mediterranean Sea, the Black Sea, and the eastern Atlantic Ocean; and a land task force that deployed in exercises across Central and Eastern Europe.

When the Trudeau government took office in November 2015, the Conservative policy was continued. In March 2017, the government extended its military training commitment to Ukraine for a further two years. In Central and Eastern Europe, the Trudeau government decided to ramp up its commitment to the reassurance mission, announcing in July 2016 that Canada would lead a multinational battle group in Latvia.[29] In June 2017, Enhanced Forward Presence battle group Latvia was stood up, with 450 Canadian forces joined by forces from Albania, Italy, Poland, Slovenia, and Spain.

The Counter-ISIL Promise

When ISIL emerged in Syria and western Iraq in 2013 and launched an offensive in 2014 that resulted in the declaration of a caliphate, the Conservative government joined the US-led multinational Global Coalition against ISIL. In October 2014, the CAF launched Operation IMPACT, which deployed two CF-18s, a CP-140 Aurora, and a CC-150T Polaris air refueller to Kuwait for integration into the Global Coalition's air strikes against ISIL targets. In March 2015, the Harper government not only extended the Canadian mission for a year, but expanded combat operations into Syria. As leader of the Liberal Party, Trudeau had opposed a combat role for Canada in the Counter-ISIL Coalition, arguing that Canada should limit itself to humanitarian contributions only. Although his position attracted considerable opposition within his own party, Trudeau began promising that, if a Liberal government were elected in the October 2015 elections, it would end the CF-18 bombing strikes against ISIL, and would focus on training for what he argued was a "civil war" in Iraq. During the election campaign, he repeated his promise, prompting a pithy response from Harper: "If your policy is humanitarian assistance without military support, all you're doing is dropping aid on dead people."[30]

Once in power, however, the Trudeau government was faced with considerable pressure to reverse its campaign pledge, particularly after the jihadist attacks in Paris on 13 November 2015 that killed 130 people. Although ministers tried to assure Canadians that Canada's friends and allies were comfortable with the decision to pull the CF-18s, it was clear that not everyone was happy. Two days after the election, the Kurdish *peshmerga* claimed publicly that the promise was "bad news for us."[31] And Canada was pointedly excluded from a meeting of allied defence ministers held in Paris on 20 January to discuss the campaign against ISIL.[32] There was also considerable domestic opposition, with numerous voices criticizing the government for refusing to back down.[33] Even the normally sympathetic *Toronto Star* pressed Trudeau to be clearer about his anti-ISIL policies, arguing in an editorial on 20 December that "It's time to dispel the fog."

Following the jihadist attacks in Ouagadougou and Jakarta in January 2016 that killed seven Canadians, relatives of two of the victims, Maude Carrier and Yves Carrier, openly criticized Trudeau for his policies on ISIL. Camille Carrier, the mother of Maude and ex-wife of Yves, told media that she was "revolted," "ashamed," and "outraged" that Trudeau was abandoning the fight against ISIL by withdrawing the CF-18s. "Cet homme-là se promène avec une belle petite coupe de cheveux et a toujours des formules vides et convenues," she told TVA, "Il condamne les choses, mais il n'est même pas capable d'aller se battre avec les autres qui appuient les Français" ("He walks around with his nice little haircut and always has empty pat phrases. He condemns things, but he isn't even capable of going to fight with others who are supporting the French").[34] And when Trudeau phoned Yves Richard, Maude's husband, to offer condolences, Richard reported to the media that "je lui ai demandé d'arrêter son bla-bla politique" ("I asked him to stop his political blah-blah-blah"), and then rudely hung up on Trudeau for offering him nothing more than canned platitudes ("une formule tout à fait cassette").[35]

Despite the criticism, Trudeau remained unmoved. On 8 February 2016, he held a press conference to announce the withdrawal of the CF-18s. However, the other aircraft were left in place as part of the counter-ISIL Coalition's military operations. The number of personnel deployed to the training mission in Iraq was tripled and, in addition, the government committed to participation in a NATO-led training mission in Jordan.[36] It should be noted that neither the prime minister nor any other member of his government offered a coherent rationale for withdrawing the CF-18s, either before or after taking office. On the contrary: Trudeau simply avoided the question. For example, Terry Milewski of the CBC's *Power and Politics* asked Trudeau in June 2015 under what circumstances he would support airstrikes: "If you don't want to bomb a group as ghastly as ISIS, when would you ever support real military action?" Trudeau quickly dismissed him with the retort: "Terry, that's a nonsensical question; you know that very well."[37] After the election, in an interview at the World Economic Forum at Davos in January 2016, Fareed Zakaria bluntly asked him on CNN about the CF-18 withdrawal: "Why? What's the logic behind this?" Trudeau chose not to address the question at all; instead he talked at length about Canada's putative "comparative advantage" in military training.[38] (As David Akin, the parliamentary bureau chief for Sun Media, tweeted after the interview, "Trudeau gives Zakaria same logic-free answer on CF-18s he's given journos and Parliament for weeks."[39]) Not even when the withdrawal was formally announced on 8 February was this "logic-free" approach abandoned: the new policy was just announced, with Trudeau making no effort to explain why it was necessary to withdraw the CF-18s.

However, despite the range of opposition, the promise to withdraw from the counter-ISIL combat mission was implemented without any longer-term political damage to the government. By the mid-term, the issue was no longer on the agenda.

Syrian Refugees

The promise to admit 25,000 refugees was central to the Liberal campaign, and the promise appeared in two separate locations in the 2015 platform, as part of the promises on immigration and refugees and as part of the Liberal policy on countering ISIL.

The refugee crisis had emerged from the uprisings of early 2011 that had blossomed into civil war by early 2012 and had intensified with the rise of ISIL in 2014. By the summer of 2015, the civil war had produced over four million registered refugees,[40] and the Canadian response under the Conservative government had been limited. In July 2013, the minister of immigration, Jason Kenney, had promised to admit 1300 Syrian refugees by the end of 2014. In January 2015, Kenney's successor, Chris Alexander, promised that Canada would accept 10,000 Syrian refugees by the end of 2017. By the summer of 2015, however, only 2300 refugees had been settled.[41]

The Syrian refugee crisis of 2015 was initially not an issue in the Canadian election campaign. On 2 September, however, news outlets around the world published a photograph of the lifeless body of Alan Kurdi, a three-year old Syrian boy, drowned on a Turkish beach. The Kurdi family had been trying to flee to Greece from the Syrian civil war when their overloaded inflatable boat capsized. Alan, his mother, and his brother drowned. While that powerful image of Alan Kurdi had a transformative impact on the refugee crisis globally, it had particular resonance in Canada when it was discovered that the Kurdis were eventually trying to join Alan's aunt in Coquitlam, British Columbia.

While the fate of the Kurdi family's refugee application to Canada became a brief issue, the image of Alan Kurdi had a lasting impact on the campaign. In response to the publication of the photograph, the question of how many Syrian refugees Canada would admit assumed greater salience. Tom Mulcair promised that an NDP government would admit 10,000 refugees. For his part, Harper promised that his government "had plans to do more" for Syrian refugees, though he cautioned that "we can't lose sight of the fact that refugee resettlement alone cannot in any part of the world, solve this problem." He claimed that military action against ISIL, who were causing the refugee crisis, was necessary.[42]

The Liberals were able to mark themselves off from the other parties on this issue. Since at least 2013, Trudeau had been on the record as supporting a much more open and generous policy towards Syrian refugees,[43] and the Liberals had incorporated a promise to admit 25,000 Syrian refugees into their election platform.[44] The sudden emergence of this issue allowed the Trudeau campaign to underscore the Liberal commitment to a generous Canadian approach to refugees—and to call out the Conservatives for trying to tweak their Syrian refugee policy in the wake of Alan Kurdi's death. As Trudeau put it, "you don't get to suddenly discover compassion in the middle of an election campaign."[45] It can be argued that Trudeau's Syrian refugee promise played an important part in transforming the trajectory of opinion in the last 30 days of the election campaign.

The campaign had shifted in the middle of September, when a court ruled that women had the right to wear a niqab while taking the oath of citizenship. This prompted the Conservatives to double down on their antipathy to the niqab, which was accompanied by a promise to introduce a "barbaric cultural practices" snitch line.[46] Trudeau and NDP Leader Mulcair spoke out against the Conservative tactics. Trudeau criticized Harper for "playing very reckless and dangerous games, pitting Canadians against one another for a narrow political goal."[47] Mulcair, for his part, called for tolerance.[48] It was after this that NDP support drifted downward, particularly in Quebec, where Mulcair's position on the niqab was highly unpopular, while Liberal support rose, not only in Quebec, but in Ontario as well. The Syrian promise cemented the Liberals as the tolerant alternative to the Conservatives.

The promise to resettle 25,000 Syrian refugees was fulfilled, even if the process of moving so many people to Canada took longer than the Liberals had originally promised and even if the number was well below what European countries were accepting. For all of the difficulties in meeting the target, this promise was widely considered to be a success.

The F-35 Promise

On 20 September 2015, in the middle of the campaign, Trudeau promised that a Liberal government would not buy the Lockheed Martin F-35 joint strike fighter as a replacement for Canada's existing fleet of CF-18 Hornets, even though Canada is one of the nine nations involved in the multinational Joint Strike Fighter program. Instead, Trudeau promised to run an "open" competition, although Lockheed Martin would not be allowed to compete in this competition. Canada would buy from "one of the many, lower-priced options that better match Canada's defence needs," as the Liberal platform put it.[49] Moreover, the substantial savings putatively generated by not buying the F-35 would be reallocated to the Royal Canadian Navy.

This promise was embraced for purely electoral reasons; there was no strategic or military rationale. The claim that it would save huge amounts of money was, in a word, false. But the F-35 was deeply connected to the Conservative government, which had badly mismanaged the procurement and politicized the F-35 selection. And partly encouraged by the politicization of the F-35 by the Conservatives, the Liberals had been playing political games with the F-35 procurement well before Trudeau took over the leadership of the party in 2013.[50]

Because Liberal gamesmanship with the F-35 had been so successful in attacking the Conservatives between 2010 and 2012, it was not surprising that Trudeau decided to continue what his predecessors had started. Indeed, he decided to take a leaf directly from the playbook of an earlier Liberal leader. In the middle of the 1993 election campaign, Jean Chrétien, then the leader of the opposition, had promised that a Liberal government would cancel a contract that the Progressive Conservative government of Brian Mulroney had signed for a fleet of EH101 maritime and search and rescue helicopters to replace the Sea Kings and Labrador helicopters that had entered service in the early 1960s.

Chrétien was as good as his word: the new Liberal government cancelled the EH101 contract, in a stroke throwing away $478 million in cancellation fees and paid-for work. The Chrétien government then spent the next decade grappling with the awkward consequences of what had been a casual promise designed to attract votes, spending considerably more on new helicopters than if the original contract had been allowed to stand.[51] However, as a political ploy, it was successful: Chrétien and the Liberals never suffered any political consequences as a result.

When Trudeau was elected in 2015, he moved to make good his F-35 promise. One key part of that promise—not allowing the F-35 to compete in any competition—had to be abandoned after the new cabinet was told that barring the F-35 not only broke a number of Canadian laws, but would expose the government to massive lawsuits. But the other part of the promise—not buying the F-35—remained in play. So Trudeau tried to do to the F-35 what the Chrétien government had done to the EH101 after 1993: it found numerous ways to torque the selection process to ensure that some other jet fighter—any other jet fighter—would be selected. The prime minister openly disparaged the F-35, telling Parliament that the F-35 "does not work and is a long way from ever working."[52]

Over the course of 2016, Minister of National Defence Sajjan, who had been directed by the prime minister to find a way to ensure that the F-35 was not acquired, found just what was needed. In a clever bit of legerdemain, Sajjan determined that the existing fleet of 76 CF-18 Hornets left Canada with what he called a "capability gap." In other words, there would be too few fighters in the event that Canada were for some reason called on to undertake a range of missions at the same time. Although this "gap" was news to the Royal Canadian Air Force, which was long on the record as requiring only 65 aircraft to fulfil all of Canada's air missions, the Trudeau government announced in November 2016 that it was going to procure 18 Boeing Super Hornets on a sole-source basis to fly alongside the "legacy" CF-18 Hornets and postpone the replacement decision for the CF-18 fleet for five years.[53] However, this plan quickly fell apart when Boeing Co., the manufacturer of the Super Hornet, launched a trade complaint against Bombardier Inc., claiming that Bombardier had dumped its C-series airliner in the US market. In September 2017, Trudeau walked back the Super Hornet plan, promising that Canada "won't do business with a company that's busy trying to sue us and put our aerospace workers out of business."[54]

The mess that Trudeau created with his rash promise in September 2015 will have long-term costs. Just as the Chrétien decision in 1993 increased costs and reduced capability, the Trudeau decision in 2015 will have huge costs for Canadians into the 2020s. If Canada does not acquire the F-35, all those Canadian firms anticipating participation in Lockheed Martin's global supply chains will be excluded. Finally, Canadian interoperability with the United States and numerous other allies that have chosen the F-35 will be affected.

Trudeau and the Rise of Trump

Any mid-term assessment of Trudeau's foreign policy must recognize that the long shadow of the 2015 election campaign was in essence eclipsed by the rise of a phenomenon that was only dimly anticipated in Canada in the fall of 2015: the rise of Donald J. Trump. When Trudeau and the Liberals took office in November 2015, Trump had been a formal candidate for four months, and his campaign was already marked by the kind of radical rhetoric and equally radical policy ideas that would in 2016 sweep away 16 other candidates for the Republican presidential nomination and then secure him the presidency of the United States.

There is little doubt that Trump's election presented the Trudeau government with a major dilemma. For the new US president came to office openly opposing two of the core elements of Canadian foreign policy, the North American Free Trade Agreement and the North Atlantic Treaty Organization, and virtually all of his known positions on a wide range of policy issues promised to negatively affect Canadian interests. Moreover, Trump's highly idiosyncratic and unpredictable personality posed an unprecedented challenge for all leaders of other states who had to deal with him.

In the event, the third-place leader in 2015 who was widely mocked as being "just not ready" proved more than ready to deal with the challenges of a Trump presidency. For Trudeau moved expeditiously to ensure that Canadian interests were as protected as possible given the unpredictable nature of the new administration in Washington.

First, eschewing the off-the-cuff tendencies that had marked his time in opposition, Trudeau was highly disciplined in his statements about Trump. Even before it was clear that Trump would emerge victorious, Trudeau was cautious. When he was asked in March 2016 about a possible Trump victory, the prime minister responded: "The reality is we will work alongside our neighbors and allies regardless of the political choices that they make. We have too much of our economy that is wrapped up in the United States, too much that we depend on each other for."[55] By the time Trump was in the White House, Trudeau had developed a mantra from which he never deviated. Whenever he was asked to criticize Trump, his response was a variant of his response to a question posed to him at a news conference in Calgary in January 2017 about whether he thought that Trump was a misogynist. After a brief pause, Trudeau responded: "It is not the job of a Canadian prime minister to opine on the American electoral process. It is the job of the Canadian prime minister to have a constructive working relationship with the president of the United States and that is exactly what I intend to do."[56] He also imposed the same tight discipline on his caucus, ensuring that he did not have to deal with the kind of anti-American sentiments that so marked the Liberal caucuses of Jean Chrétien and Paul Martin.[57]

Second, just before the inauguration in Washington, Trudeau shuffled his cabinet. Stéphane Dion, who had been given the foreign affairs portfolio in November 2015, was moved out of the portfolio, and offered an ambassadorship in Europe. In his place, Trudeau appointed the minister of international trade, Chrystia Freeland. There were a number of reasons for the shuffle. Dion, described as an "unlikely diplomat," was seen by some as not having the "people skills" necessary to deal with the new administration, particularly given Trump's tendency to take offence.[58] Freeland, by contrast, not only had a good grasp of the trade portfolio that promised to be front and centre in Canadian-American relations under Trump but had a considerable network of contacts in the United States from her time as a journalist and editor at Reuters and the *Financial Times* in New York City.

Third, Trudeau adopted a broadly strategic approach to the Canada-United States relationship. He brought policy-makers with knowledge and experience, such as former Prime Minister Mulroney, into the process. His government deployed Canada's diplomatic and political assets widely across the American political system, embracing not only Congress but state and municipal governments in what one observer called the "doughnut strategy"—in other words, working around the "hole" that was the Trump White House.[59] Trudeau even reached out to Ivanka Trump, the president's daughter, in what was described as "daughter diplomacy" (prompting John Higginbotham, who was the minister in the Canadian embassy in Washington from 1994 to 2000, to observe, "It is just so *Game of Thrones*").[60]

Finally, the Trudeau government moved to recalibrate its foreign and defence policies: within months of Trump's inauguration, the government had put out new policy statements. In early June, Freeland delivered a major address that reaffirmed Canada's commitment to the liberal international order, and committing Canada to working to uphold that order despite the obvious reluctance of some in the United States to maintain it.[61] Two days later Defence Minister Sajjan released a new defence policy that featured promises of a significant increase in Canadian defence spending.[62] Sajjan had launched a defence policy review in April 2016, with a new policy statement anticipated by the end of the year. However, the emergence of Trump prompted a major reset in defence policy. Not only was Canada's search for a new African peacekeeping mission slowed to a complete crawl (and then a standstill), but the new defence review was rewritten to take account of Trump's highly critical attitudes towards America's allies.

Conclusion

The purpose of this chapter has been to look at how the Trudeau government managed the key peace and security promises made during the election campaign of 2015. Coming to power with a different tone and approach, the Trudeau government established an important distance from the Harper Conservatives, even if in some cases, such as the assurance missions in Central and Eastern Europe, it just continued the Conservative government's policies. At least one of its election promises was a major success: the Syrian refugee initiative was popular in Canada and redounded to Canada's credit internationally. One of its promises that looked problematic at the time, the promise to withdraw from the combat role in Iraq, proved to be quite unproblematic politically and simply dropped from the agenda. And in the one case where a promise will have negative implications in the future—the F-35 promise—the Trudeau government can count itself fortunate that it kicked the CF-18 replacement can sufficiently far down the road that it will not face any significant blowback in the 2019 election. Whatever financial or operational difficulties created by Trudeau's promise in 2015 will instead haunt whichever party forms government in the early 2020s.

Mid-term assessments are intended to provide a guide for the remainder of the term. But in the case of Trudeau's foreign policy, any assessment will necessarily be eclipsed by what happens in the remaining two years of the Liberal mandate. Although the government has put in place both the mechanisms and the strategic elements for dealing with an unusual presidency, the Trudeau Liberals will likely be judged on how they actually manage the Trump era rather than on how they managed their first two years in power. As journalist John Ibbitson noted in his own mid-term report card, success or failure on the Canadian-American relationship could well define the Trudeau government.[63]

Notes

1. Humphreys (2013).
2. Akin (2013).
3. Gerson (2013).
4. CBC News (2014).
5. Hume (2014).
6. Conservative Party of Canada (2015).
7. Blais (2015).

8. CBC News (2015b).
9. For example, Dornan (2015, 12), CBC News (2015a), Clark (2015).
10. Clark (2015).
11. Elections Canada (2015).
12. Munk debate on foreign policy (2015).
13. Conservative Party of Canada (2006, 44–45).
14. Liberal Party of Canada, (2015, 68).
15. Quoted in Simpson (2015a).
16. Chin (2015).
17. Nossal (2016a).
18. The phrase does not appear in his book on Canadian diplomacy (J. Clark 2013); he used it in an interview with Campbell Clark of the *Globe and Mail* (C. Clark 2013).
19. Simpson (2014).
20. Nossal (2014).
21. Trudeau (2015).
22. Joseph (2015).
23. Nossal (2013).
24. Paris (2014, 306).
25. Nossal (2016a).
26. Harris and Kent (2016).
27. Chase (2016).
28. Liberal Party of Canada (2015, 71).
29. Berthiaume (2016).
30. Canadian Press (2015).
31. Chase (2015).
32. Fife (2016).
33. For example, Castonguay (2015), Den Tandt (2015), Gurney (2015), Simpson (2015b), Gagnon (2016).
34. TVA Nouvelles (2016), Hopper (2016).
35. Bellavance (2016).
36. Zilio (2016).
37. Milewski (2015).
38. Zakaria (2016).
39. Akin (2016).
40. UNHCR (2017).
41. Petrou (2015).
42. Taber and Thanh Ha (2015).
43. MacDonald (2013).
44. Liberal Party of Canada (2015, 64).
45. Taber and Thanh Ha (2015).
46. Andrew-Gee (2015).

47. Kennedy (2015).
48. Hamilton (2015).
49. Liberal Party of Canada (2015, 70).
50. For details, see Nossal (2016b, 71–88).
51. Plamondon (2010), Nossal (2016b, 60–71).
52. Trudeau spoke in French, claiming that the Conservatives "se sont accrochés à un avion qui ne fonctionne pas et qui est loin de pouvoir fonctionner," which Hansard translated as "The Conservatives threw in their lot with a plane that does not work and is a long way from ever working" (House of Commons 2016).
53. Brewster (2016).
54. Sheetz (2017).
55. Collins (2016).
56. Bickis and Canadian Press (2017), Austin (2017).
57. Nossal (2008).
58. Chase (2017).
59. Fisher (2017).
60. Dale (2017).
61. House of Commons (2017).
62. National Defence (2017).
63. Ibbitson (2017).

References

Akin, David. 2013. Trudeau admires China's 'basic dictatorship.' *Toronto Sun*, November 8.

Akin, David (@davidakin). 2016. Trudeau gives Zakaria same logic-free answer on CF-18s he's given journos and Parliament for weeks. @WEF. *Twitter*, January 20, 9:48 a.m. https://twitter.com/davidakin/status/689821761710338048. Accessed 24 Aug 2017.

Andrew-Gee, Eric. 2015. Conservatives vow to establish 'barbaric cultural practices' tip line. *Globe and Mail*, October 2.

Austin, Ian. 2017. Justin Trudeau, facing pressure to oppose Donald Trump, opts to get along. *New York Times*, February 3.

Bellavance, Joël-Denis. 2016. Ouagadougou: le conjoint de Maude Carrier raccroche au nez de Justin Trudeau. *La Presse*, Janvier 21.

Berthiaume, Lee. 2016. Canada to send 450 troops to Latvia as NATO faces off against Russia. *Globe and Mail*, July 8.

Bickis, Ian, and Canadian Press. 2017. Trudeau navigates perils of energy, climate, Trump as liberals wrap defeat. *National Newswatch*, January 24. https://www.nationalnewswatch.com/2017/01/24/canada-can-forge-ties-with-trump-while-sticking-up-for-values-hajdu-says-2/#.WenhI2hSyUk. Accessed 25 Aug 2017.

Blais, Eric. 2015. Conservatives' Trudeau attack ads worked, but maybe not 'forever.' *CBC News*, October 16. http://www.cbc.ca/news/politics/canada-election-2015-attack-ads-trudeau-conservatives-1.3270164/. Accessed 25 Aug 2017.

Brewster, Murray. 2016. Liberals to buy 18 Boeing Super Hornet fighter jets to fill 'capability gap.' *CBC News*, November 22. http://www.cbc.ca/news/politics/fighter-jet-purchase-announcement-1.3862210. Accessed 25 Aug 2017.

Canadian Press. 2015. Liberal, NDP anti-terror strategy 'just dropping aid on dead people': Harper. *Globe and Mail*, August 11.

Castonguay, Alec. 2015. Premier test pour Trudeau: le monde. *l'Actualité*, Novembre 10.

CBC News. 2014. RAW Trudeau: Don't just 'whip out CF-18s.' *CBC News*, October 2. http://www.cbc.ca/player/News/Politics/ID/2539526631/. Accessed 24 Aug 2017.

———. 2015a. Canada federal election 2015: Stephen Harper confirms start of 11-week federal campaign. *CBC News*, August 2.

———. 2015b. 'Just not ready' Trudeau ad may be getting to voters, poll suggests. *CBC News*, September 5. http://www.cbc.ca/news/politics/conservative-attack-ads-not-ready-justin-trudeau-1.3217203. Accessed 25 Aug 2017.

Chase, Steven. 2015. Kurdish fighters call Trudeau plan to withdraw CF-18 fighter jets 'bad news.' *Globe and Mail*, October 21.

———. 2016. Defence Minister to tour Africa on mission to learn about peacekeeping. *Globe and Mail*, August 4.

———. 2017. Dion, an unlikely diplomat, dropped as Liberals retool for Trump era. *Globe and Mail*, January 10.

Chin, Jessica. 2015, Justin Trudeau's not the first prime minister to say 'Canada Is Back,' *Huffington Post Canada*, December 1. http://www.huffingtonpost.ca/2015/12/01/canada-is-back-trudeau-harper_n_8688282.html. Accessed 25 Aug 2017.

Clark, Campbell. 2013. Joe Clark's new book: Canada is the country that 'lectures and leaves.' *Globe and Mail*, November 1.

Clark, Joe. 2013. *How we lead: Canada in a century of change*. Toronto: Random House Canada.

Clark, Campbell. 2015. Harper's early election call a clever ploy to gain edge on campaign spending. *Globe and Mail*, August 2.

Collins, Eliza. 2016. Trudeau: I'll work with Trump if I have to. *Politico*, March 7. http://www.politico.com/blogs/2016-gop-primary-live-updates-and-results/2016/03/justin-trudeau-donald-trump-220380. Accessed 26 Aug 2017.

Conservative Party of Canada. 2006. *Stand up for Canada: Federal election platform*. Ottawa.

———. 2015. The interview. Cpcpcc video, 0:01:03, May 25. https://www.youtube.com/watch?v=c86-9HitWg0. Accessed 24 Aug 2017.

Dale, Daniel. 2017. Daughter diplomacy: Trudeau's unorthodox play for Donald Trump's approval. *Toronto Star*, March 16.

Den Tandt, Michael. 2015. Why Trudeau should keep CF-18s in the fight against ISIL. *National Post*, December 22.

Dornan, Christopher. 2015. The long goodbye: The contours of the election. In *The Canadian federal election of 2015*, ed. Christopher Dornan and Jon H. Pammett, 7–21. Toronto: Dundurn Press.

Elections Canada. 2015. Forty-second general election 2015: Official voting results. http://www.elections.ca/res/rep/off/ovr2015app/41/table9E.html. Accessed 24 Aug 2017.

Fife, Robert. 2016. Canada shut out of IS coalition meeting. *Globe and Mail*, January 18.

Fisher, Max. 2017. Canada's Trump strategy: Go around him. *New York Times*, June 22.

Gagnon, Lysiane. 2016. Where is the PM when Quebec needs him? *Globe and Mail*, January 20.

Gerson, Jen. 2013. At Toronto fundraiser, Justin Trudeau seemingly admires China's 'basic dictatorship.' *National Post*, November 8.

Gurney, Matt. 2015. Canada should stay in the fight against ISIL. *National Post*, December 17.

Hamilton, Graeme. 2015. Tom Mulcair appeals for tolerance as NDP's niqab policy at odds with Party's Quebec base. *National Post*, September 23.

Harris, Kathleen, and Melissa Kent. 2016. Trudeau unveils Canada's plan to seek 2021 UN Security Council Seat. *CBC News*, March 16. http://www.cbc.ca/news/politics/canada-united-nations-security-council-1.3491917. Accessed 25 Aug 2017.

Hopper, Tristan. 2016. Condemn Burkina Faso terror attack 'with planes,' not just words, victim's mother tells Trudeau. *National Post*, January 18.

House of Commons. 2016. *Debates*, 42nd Parl., 1st Sess., June 7, 14h20.

———. 2017. *Debates*, 42nd Parl. 1st Sess., June 6, 10h25.

Hume, Jessica. 2014. It's 'not about whipping out our CF-18s to show how big they are': Trudeau. *Toronto Sun*, October 2. http://www.torontosun.com/2014/10/02/its-not-about-whipping-out-our-cf-18s-to-show-how-big-they-are-trudeau. Accessed 24 Aug 2017.

Humphreys, Adrian. 2013. Justin Trudeau hosts 'ladies night' fundraiser despite 'firestorm' of controversy over 'patronizing' ad. *National Post*, November 7.

Ibbitson, John. 2017. Trudeau's Liberals: A midterm report card. *Globe and Mail*, April 18.

Joseph, Rebecca. 2015. 1st planeload of Syrian refugees land on Canadian soil. *Global News*, 10 December.

Kennedy, Mark. 2015. Trudeau channels his father on minority rights. *Ottawa Citizen*, October 7.

Liberal Party of Canada. 2015. *Real change: A new plan for a strong middle class.* Ottawa, October 5.

MacDonald, Michael. 2013. Trudeau says Canada should accept more Syrian refugees. *CTV News*, August, 30.

Milewski, Terry. 2015. CBC, power and politics. *CBC News video*, 0:04:35, June 23. http://www.cbc.ca/player/play/2670343050. Accessed 24 Aug 2017.

Munk Debate on Foreign Policy. 2015. The Munk Debate on Canada's foreign policy. *Cpac video*, 1:48:46, September 29. https://www.youtube.com/watch?v=osbXcR8L2Po. Accessed 24 Aug 2017.

National Defence. 2017. *Strong, secure, engaged: Canada's defence policy.* Ottawa.

Nossal, Kim Richard. 2008. A thermostatic dynamic? Electoral outcomes and anti-Americanism in Canada. In *The political consequences of anti-Americanism*, ed. Richard A. Higgott and Ivona Malbašić, 129–141. London: Routledge.

———. 2013. The liberal past in the conservative present: Internationalism in the Harper era. In *Canada in the world: Internationalism in Canadian foreign policy*, ed. Heather A. Smith and Claire Turenne Sjolander, 21–35. Toronto: Oxford University Press.

———. 2014. *Primat der Wahlurne*: Explaining Stephen Harper's foreign policy. International Studies Association, March 29. http://post.queensu.ca/~nossalk/papers/Nossal_2014_Harper.pdf. Accessed 24 Aug 2017.

———. 2016a. Canada and the General Assembly: A global bully pulpit. In *Canada and the UN: Legacies, limits and the Harper shift*, ed. Robert Teigrob and Colin McCullough, 161–182. Montreal/Kingston: McGill-Queen's University Press.

———. 2016b. *Charlie foxtrot: Fixing defence procurement in Canada.* Toronto: Dundurn Press.

Paris, Roland. 2014. Are Canadians still liberal internationalists? Foreign policy and public opinion in the Harper era. *International Journal* 69 (3): 274–307.

Petrou, Michael. 2015. How has Canada fared on resettling Syrian refugees? *Maclean's*, July 15.

Plamondon, Aaron. 2010. *The politics of procurement: Military acquisition in Canada and the Sea King helicopter.* Vancouver: University of British Columbia Press.

Sheetz, Michael. 2017. Justin Trudeau says Canada will not buy from Boeing while it is 'busy trying to sue us.' *CNBC.com*, September 18. https://www.cnbc.com/2017/09/18/justin-trudeau-says-canada-will-not-buy-from-boeing-while-it-is-busy-trying-to-sue-us.html. Accessed 2 Oct 2017.

Simpson, Jeffrey. 2014. The trouble with bullhorn diplomacy. *Globe and Mail*, May 2.

———. 2015a. Want to be a world player, Canada? Get ready to spend. *Globe and Mail*, October 30.

———. 2015b. As allies gear up, Trudeau ramps down. *Globe and Mail*, November 17.

Taber, Jane, and Tu Thanh Ha. 2015. Immigration Minister Chris Alexander suspends re-election campaign. *Globe and Mail*, September 3.

Trudeau, Justin (@JustinTrudeau). 2015. To fight climate change we're all in this together. Canada is back. #COP21. *Twitter*, November 30, 2:02 p.m. https://twitter.com/justintrudeau/status/671403931025698816. Accessed 24 Aug 2017.

TVA Nouvelles. 2016. Ouagadougou: la mère d'une victim en colère contre Trudeau. *TVA Nouvelles*, Janvier 18.

UNHCR. 2017. Syria emergency. UNHCR. http://www.unhcr.org/en-us/syria-emergency.html. Accessed 24 Aug 2017.

Zakaria, Fareed. 2016. Justin Trudeau reaffirms Canada's position on the fight against ISIS in Davos. *CBC News video*, 0:01:42, January 20. https://www.youtube.com/watch?v=efWSz7c3NaY. Accessed 24 Aug 2017.

Zilio, Michelle. 2016. Canada to pull fighter jets, triple training mission against Islamic State. *Globe and Mail*, February 8.

CHAPTER 4

What's Not to Like? Justin Trudeau, the Global Disorder, and Liberal Illusions

Jerome Klassen and Yves Engler

When the Liberal Party of Canada won a majority government in the parliamentary elections of 19 October 2015, the world took notice. The Liberal Party had not simply ousted the incumbent Conservatives, but had done so under the charismatic leadership of Justin Trudeau, whose platform of "Real Change" was, in several respects, the most progressive on offer. In the context of economic, political, and military turbulence globally, including signs of far-right resurgence, Trudeau's victory was a catalyst of hope for socially progressive and liberal values, worldwide. These values were integral to the Liberal Party platform, particularly to its pledges on global affairs. During the election campaign, Trudeau promised to restore a positive Canadian engagement with the United Nations (UN); to redirect Canadian foreign assistance towards the poorest members of global society, particularly towards women and girls; and to foster more diverse

---

J. Klassen (✉)
MIT Center for International Studies, Cambridge, MA, USA

Y. Engler
Independent Scholar, Montreal, QC, Canada

© The Author(s) 2018
N. Hillmer, P. Lagassé (eds.), *Justin Trudeau and Canadian Foreign Policy*, Canada and International Affairs,
https://doi.org/10.1007/978-3-319-73860-4_4

global relations, especially with India and China. Most prominently, Trudeau announced that a Liberal government would immediately sponsor the settlement of 25,000 Syrian refugees.

In government, Trudeau moved quickly to realize these promises. In November 2015, the government created Global Affairs Canada as the public designation of the Department of Foreign Affairs, Trade and Development. In doing so, it signalled a new conceptualization of Canada's linkages to the world as something more meaningful, even transformational, than the official department title suggests. In the same month, Trudeau also announced at the UN climate summit in Paris that "Canada is back, and here to help." Trudeau made several financial commitments, including $2.65 billion to a climate adaptation and mitigation fund, $300 million annually to a green technology fund, and $30 million to immediately assist the world's poorest countries in combating climate change.[1] In January 2017, the Liberal government announced that it had welcomed more than 40,000 Syrian refugees through public and private sponsorship programs.[2] In June 2017, the government also announced a *Feminist International Assistance Policy* to support "gender equality and the empowerment of women" as "the best way to build a more peaceful, inclusive and prosperous world."[3]

Such initiatives have won Trudeau effusive praise from liberal commentators in other countries, particularly in the United States. For the *New York Times*, "with the rise of Justin Trudeau, Canada is suddenly…Hip."[4] More seriously, as the *New York Times Magazine* observed, "Trudeau's most radical argument is that Canada is becoming a new kind of state, defined not by its European history but by the multiplicity of its identities from all over the world. His embrace of a pan-cultural heritage makes him an avatar" of what Trudeau himself advocates: "openness, respect, compassion, willingness to work hard, to be there for each other, to search for equality and justice."[5] In March 2016, US President Barack Obama concurred: "He [Trudeau] campaigned on a message of hope and of change. His positive and optimistic vision is inspiring young people. At home, he's governing with a commitment to inclusivity and equality. On the world stage, his country is leading on climate change and he cares deeply about development. So, from my perspective, what's not to like?"[6]

For many liberals, then, Trudeau seems to embody the values of a fair, inclusive, and democratic society. From their standpoint, Trudeau is a transcendent leader, whose support for progressive causes, including gender equality and immigrant rights, might suppress or supersede emergent trends of xenophobia, authoritarianism, and bellicose nationalism worldwide.

A liberal theory of international politics underpins such views. In this perspective, international relations are determined primarily by the domestic political character of states as well as by the ideas and volitions of individual leaders. In Michael Doyle's synthesis of this perspective, the world order is divided into two types of states—liberal, market-friendly democracies, and illiberal, state-centric regimes.[7] The democratic states hold a common culture of rules-based and participatory governance and share the gains of international trade and investment. For these reasons, democracies are constrained in their external relations and generally form a peaceful bloc of states with shared interests in multilateral governance. Democratic states, however, are threatened by illiberal regimes. These regimes are not constrained by popular representation and thus frequently commit human rights abuses domestically and act belligerently towards other states. In this context, liberal states are rightly compelled—in the interests of human rights, peace, and economic development—to contain and, if necessary, intervene in and remove illiberal regimes. The fundamental point of liberal theory, though, is that international politics are driven ultimately by the internal culture of states and the policy agenda of individual leaders. For these reasons, it is entirely feasible for liberals such as Trudeau to make progressive impacts globally.

Realist theories of international relations contest such optimism.[8] For realists, the liberal theory amounts to a voluntarist account of global politics, one that is based on the political will of individuals and on other contingent factors. By contrast, realists advocate a scientific approach, which begins, materially, with the international state system and its structural imperatives. More specifically, realism proceeds from the institutional reality of the nation-state system and its logic of anarchy. Lacking an overarching sovereign, the nation-state system induces a regulating principle of "self-help": a systemic pressure for states to secure their own prosperity without regard for the needs and interests of others. In this context, the "security dilemma" emerges as the hinge of world politics. That is, as one state seeks to increase its security and prosperity, it compels other states to balance against it in a zero-sum competition. The history of international politics is the history of the balance of power, which any state actor must engage with as the core concern of the national interest. With this in mind, realists believe that liberal advocates of a democratic peace through multilateral governance are peddling false promises.[9] At the end of the day, political leaders, whatever their values, should make decisions based on the national interest of the state. It follows that leaders—such as Trudeau—should forego their ideals in favour of institutionalized, national security concerns.

If realism denies the importance of political agency, and if liberalism overstates it in an idealistic manner, Marxism, as the third major theory of international relations, seeks a dialectical balance. The starting point of this analysis, as Marx observed, is that "[human beings] make their own history, but they do not make it as they please; they do not make it under self-selected circumstances, but under circumstances existing already, given and transmitted from the past. The tradition of all dead generations weighs like a nightmare on the brains of the living."[10] For Marxists, the social relations of capitalism are the "circumstances" of the extant world order. Indeed, capitalist production depends upon and works through a social relation between the working class, which sells its labour power in exchange for a wage, and the capitalist class, which expropriates the surplus value added in production as profit.[11] The accumulation of capital is therefore coterminous with social inequality and, consequently, with class struggle. At the same time, the whip of competition creates a systemic drive for productivity increases through technological innovations, which, over time, reduce the capacity of capital to extract surplus labour as the sole source of profit. A specific contradiction emerges: the very dynamic of revolutionary growth under capitalism also undermines the accumulation process by reducing the rate of profit and thus precipitating crisis.[12]

For Marxists, the state is inextricable from the class relations and accumulation dynamics of capitalism. The capitalist state is formally autonomous from the social relations of production, but it functions to mediate the class struggle politically and to manage the accumulation process on capital's terms. Marxists contend that the uneven rate of capital accumulation between states creates an unequal world economy, in which the leading units of capital, based primarily in core economies, compete systematically in the world market, by exacting "super profits" in the periphery. The result is an imperialist structure of world order—a competitive global hierarchy of economic and political power.[13] More precisely, the world politics of capitalism are shaped by three intersecting relations: (1) the "vertical" relations of class conflict between capital and labour, both within states and across their borders; (2) the "horizontal" relations of market competition between capitals based in many states and the resulting inter-imperialist rivalries; and (3) the "lateral" relations of economic interdependence between core states, which cooperate in the domination and exploitation of peripheral ones.[14]

In this context, the grand strategies of states are driven primarily by the political interests of the hegemonic faction of capital within them. National security strategies are permeated by capitalist class interests. For example, by establishing rules for international trade and investment, securing resources for industrial production, and disciplining any states or social movements that threaten such imperatives, capitalism creates a world not of peace and security, but of competition and conflict. It follows that liberal dreams of the sort Trudeau proffers are little but illusions. More than this, they obfuscate the class character of the state and the imperialist nature of capitalist foreign policy.

To further this argument, this chapter analyses Canadian foreign policy in light of current dynamics in the global political economy. It argues that the neoliberal period of economic and political governance under US hegemony has reached an impasse; that new tendencies in the world economy and state system are upending US primacy and engendering new patterns of multi-polarity and geopolitical conflict; that Canadian foreign policy during the neoliberal period has supported the primacy strategy of Washington and the economic interests of Canadian capital; and that, despite new patterns of global disorder, the same logic of Canadian foreign policy will likely persist under Justin Trudeau. For case studies, the chapter focuses on two flashpoint regions in which Canadian foreign policy is currently engaged—the Middle East and Eastern Europe.

Liberal Hegemony: US Grand Strategy Since the Second World War

To contextualize the argument, it helps to return to the period of the Second World War, when US elites devised a grand strategy of "liberal hegemony."[15] The liberal element of the strategy was to expand capitalism on a global scale, particularly into the postcolonial world. The hegemonic element was to achieve what the American State Department termed a "preponderance of power" for the United States itself.[16]

With respect to the world market, the US-led Bretton Woods Agreement (1944) established a new international monetary system of fixed exchange rates, in which the US dollar was pegged to gold and served as world money. Fearing the rise of leftist forces in Western Europe, the United

States also funded the Marshall Plan (1947) as a means of backing European reconstruction and the expansion of US capital on the continent. The General Agreement on Tariffs and Trade (1947) also begat successive rounds of tariff reductions. US hegemony was also evident in the reconstruction of inter-state relations. At the Dumbarton Oaks Conference (1944), the United States led negotiations on the future structure of the United Nations, which was founded at the San Francisco Conference (1945) under heavy US direction and surveillance.[17] Previously, through negotiations on the Atlantic Charter, Lend Lease, and Bretton Woods, the United States also forced the British Empire to commit to scaling back imperial trade preferences.[18] Alongside this, US military power was deployed globally through a network of bases, air transit rights, and strategic zones of influence.[19]

With Harry S. Truman's presidency, the United States largely initiated the Cold War as a plank of America's overarching strategy.[20] For example, the founding of the North Atlantic Treaty Organization (NATO 1949) embodied the logic of hegemonic liberalism. It was designed, specifically, to preempt "neutralism" in Western Europe, to guard European capitalism from "internal subversion" by leftist forces, and to "keep the Americans in, the Russians out, and the Germans down," as NATO's first secretary general explained.[21] Towards the Third World, US efforts were similar; though promising a liberal vision of decolonization, US doctrine identified "economic nationalism" as a critical threat to "assured access to vital bases and raw materials."[22] For these reasons, the United States backed several recolonization efforts by the British and French and sponsored coups and military dictatorships from Iran to Guatemala.[23]

In the mid-1960s, however, American strategy reached an impasse. Economically, new competition from exporters in Western Europe and Japan created balance of payments deficits, which caused speculation on the dollar-gold exchange and culminated in US President Richard Nixon's 1971 abrogation of the Bretton Woods Agreement. Likewise, US political strategy was thoroughly discredited by the wars in Indochina, as well as by support for authoritarian regimes across the Third World.[24] In this context, US elites looked for new methods of reasserting primacy.

The political economy of neoliberalism can be traced to these efforts. Neoliberalism is the US-led model of economic and political governance, which aimed to restore the class power of capital in the United States and around the world.[25] Its core features include trade and investment liberalization, financial deregulation, tax cuts for corporations and wealthy individuals, and austerity for social programs. As a regime of capital accumulation, neoliberalism was successful, as demonstrated by rising rates of corporate profit across the 1980s and 1990s.[26] At the international level, neoliberal strictures were imposed on dozens of Third World countries during the 1980s debt crisis.[27] Predictably, the neoliberal program had deleterious impacts on Third World development. In contrast to the 1960s and 1970s, average growth rates for developing countries in the 1980s and 1990s were cut in half, and the globalization agenda produced a negative net transfer of financial resources from the poorest to richest states.[28] Summarizing these trends, the UN observed that, during the neoliberal period, the world economy had experienced "no convergence in income."[29]

Neoliberalism, as an imperial project of US power, was also imposed by force. In 1973, the military coup in Chile was supported by US covert action, and the resulting dictatorship imposed a radical, free-market program. Over the 1980s, the United States supported violent proxy wars in Central America, Southern Africa, and Afghanistan.[30] With the collapse of communism, US militarism was unfettered. The *Defense Planning Guidance* of the Bush I presidency (1989–1993) called for a strategy to "preclude the emergence of any potential global competitor."[31] In line with this, the Bill Clinton administration called for the US military to "sustain American global leadership" and to "secure uninhibited access to key markets, energy supplies and strategic resources."[32] Similarly, the Bush II government (2001–2009) declared a plan to "dissuade potential adversaries from pursuing a military build-up in hopes of surpassing, or equaling, the power of the United States."[33] The *National Security Strategy* of Obama's first presidency called on the US military to "underwrite global security."[34] Through such military efforts, the American state advanced the project of liberal hegemony.

Global Disorder: Crisis, Multi-polarity, and Resistance

Plans for a second American century, however, were a conceit of empire. The period of neoliberal economic expansion came to an end in the late 1990s, when the rate of profit for US capital reached a peak and began the slow descent into the 2008 financial crisis. The decline in the rate of profit forced capital into the financial sector, which in turn sought higher returns through debt markets in housing, consumer credit, and student loans.[35]

The bursting of the credit bubble exposed the class nature of the neoliberal project, particularly in how the state bailed out financial titans but not homeowners and workers. The crisis also spread quickly to Europe, where financial institutions had invested heavily in fictitious US financial assets and where the neoliberal strictures of the eurozone amplified its internal imbalances, especially those between surplus and deficit states. The austerity agenda in Europe and the United States further exposed the predatory interests of North Atlantic capitalist classes, which tried to resolve the crisis through savage attacks on social programs, pensions, and unions. A new dynamic of social resistance emerged—for example, from Occupy Wall Street in the United States to riots and general strikes across Europe. The underlying causes of these new class struggles are stagnant economic conditions and the growing inequality of wealth and income in advanced capitalist economies.[36]

The systemic crisis of neoliberalism, though, has allowed space for new development strategies in the periphery. According to the UN, the "Rise of the South"—the rapid industrialization of key developing countries—has been driven by "a proactive developmental state, tapping of global markets and determined social policy and innovation."[37] In this context, developing countries have increased their share of world merchandise trade, strengthened trading linkages amongst themselves, and become a growing source of capital exports. As a result, the UN notes that "[b]y 2020…the combined economic output of three leading developing countries alone—Brazil, China and India—will surpass the aggregate production of Canada, France, Germany, Italy, the United Kingdom and the United States."[38] The post-neoliberal period of development, then, is producing a realignment of world economic power.

The shift towards multi-polarity has also occurred in the realm of global politics. After the attacks of 11 September 2001, the US military campaign for primacy was asserted, first, in Afghanistan. The Taliban government was replaced by force and the United States and NATO helped establish a new government of sectarian warlords under Hamid Karzai's centralized presidency. A neoliberal development program was imposed on Afghanistan, further undermining the state's ability to meet long-term development objectives.[39] The Taliban reemerged as a powerful insurgency, which the United States and NATO failed to contain.[40]

The US-led "global war on terror" was used as a pretext for the 2003 war on Iraq. The war and occupation were not policy blunders of the neoconservative faction in Washington, but a rational, high-stakes gamble of the US ruling class and state apparatus to impose American hegemony in the region. Specifically, the war gamble was designed to remove an independent and nationalistic government; to liberalize Iraqi oil production and trade; and to bolster the power of US strategic allies in the Middle East.[41] The US military occupation dismantled Iraq's state and security services, engendered sectarian forms of politics, deployed extensive violence against Iraqi society, and created a context for al-Qaeda and later, the Islamic State (IS), to take root.[42] The failed occupation further undermined US abilities to dictate outcomes in critical conflict zones.

The war and occupation also destabilized the region in unintended ways. First, Iran emerged as the regional victor of the war. Specifically, Iran benefitted from the destruction of Saddam Hussein's hostile regime; from the rise of Shia parties in Iraqi government; and from the ignominious withdrawal of US military forces. In this context, "Iran has become…the most critical country in the world's most critical region," and the United States "is on the verge of losing its strategic position in the Middle East."[43] Second, Saudi Arabia entered a multi-faceted crisis zone. It faced, for the first time since the death of Egyptian President Gamal Abdel Nasser, a new regional competitor: Iran. Saudi Arabia also stood against Arab public opinion on the war in Iraq and on the unaddressed conflict in Palestine. Saudi Arabia faced a crisis of legitimacy domestically in that American counter-terrorism policies threatened core Wahhabi principles of the state.[44] The failure of US interventions in the Middle East, however, has reinforced the Saudi position in the US alliance system. Indeed, despite the fact that "donors in Saudi Arabia constitute the most significant source of funding to Sunni terrorist groups worldwide,"[45] the United States has doubled down on its strategic relationship with the kingdom, trading arms for petrodollars and facilitating Saudi military efforts and covert operations in Yemen, Bahrain, Syria, and elsewhere.[46]

The United States has also lost immense credibility in the Israel-Palestine conflict. The roots of this conflict lie in the Zionist colonization of Palestine, with British imperial support. Despite increasing levels of Jewish flight to Palestine, in 1947 Palestinian Arabs still constituted more than two-thirds of the population and owned 90 per cent of privately controlled land. Yet, the 1947 UN partition resolution created, without support of the indigenous population, a Jewish state on 55 per cent of Palestine. Before and during the war that followed Israel's declaration of independence, a systematic expulsion of Palestinians took place. More than 400 Palestinian villages were destroyed, 750,000 Palestinian refugees were forced into exile, and 78 per cent of the former British Mandate of Palestine was seized by the new Israeli state.[47] In 1967, Israel grabbed the West Bank, the Gaza Strip, and East Jerusalem on spurious grounds,[48] and soon after launched a settlement project in the Occupied Territories.

Today, the Palestinian nation endures what UN-commissioned international law experts describe as apartheid: deliberate and systemic acts of racial oppression and domination.[49] For strategic reasons, including projecting and maintaining hegemony in the energy-rich Middle East, the United States, from the start, forged a deep relationship with Israel.[50] As part of this, it has consistently backed Israeli wars on regional states and the Palestinian people and played a "rejectionist" role in peace negotiations,[51] favouring instead "conflict management" of the extant apartheid system. According to Aaron David Miller, who advised six US secretaries of state on Arab-Israeli negotiations, the United States has served as "Israel's lawyer." Indeed, "[f]ar too often, particularly when it came to Israeli-Palestinian diplomacy, our departure point was not what was needed to reach an agreement acceptable to both sides but what would pass with only one—Israel."[52] US imperial power has failed to support a peace process, allowing Israel to pursue expansionist policies.

Although the Syrian conflict has domestic roots in authoritarian governance and neoliberal class formation, and regional roots in the "Arab Spring,"[53] the United States and its allies played a major role in compounding the conflict. Before the Syrian uprising began, the United States was running covert operations in Syria, with the goal of destabilizing the regime.[54] Although US officials were divided from 2003 onward between "reform" and "regime change" in Syria, the latter approach won out as the conflict unfolded. In the wake of Iraq, Obama refused any direct military invasion, but allowed, in stages, the Pentagon and the Central Intelligence Agency to arm and train an insurgency, with the support of Saudi Arabia, Turkey, and Qatar.[55] From early on, the White House was aware that extremist groups, including al-Qaeda, dominated the Syrian insurgency.[56] Yet, US-vetted rebels frequently fought alongside and shared weapons with those same extremist forces.[57] At the same time, the United States failed effectively to rein in Turkish, Gulf Arab, and Israeli support for extremist groups.[58] The key point is that the hegemonic strategy of a declining US empire pulled its policies in contradictory directions, such as working with the Gulf Arab monarchies to promote democracy in Syria and waging a counter-terrorism war against IS while instrumentalizing other extremist factions in the same theatre. After the 2015 al-Qaeda-led summer offensive in Aleppo and Idlib provinces, Russia entered the war, reversed the tide of the conflict, and blocked any regime change effort.[59] On the Syrian battleground multi-polarity has been revealed by force of arms.

Beyond the Middle East, common dynamics of multi-polarity and social resistance are apparent. To address one further example, consider the Ukraine crisis and the resulting "New Cold War" between NATO and Russia. In liberal discourse, Russia is the real culprit of the Ukraine crisis, primarily because of "Russian internal political dynamics," including "protests" against "fraudulent...elections," which President Vladimir Putin suppressed through "unconstrained, erratic adventurism."[60] However, despite Russian intervention in Ukraine, including support for armed rebels in Donbass and the annexation of Crimea,[61] the "taproot of the trouble is NATO enlargement, the central element of a larger strategy to move Ukraine out of Russia's orbit and integrate it into the West."[62]

In fact, in February 1990, as part of preliminary talks with Russian officials on German reunification, US Secretary of State James Baker made "iron-clad guarantees" that NATO would not move "one inch eastward." The quid pro quo was that Russia would agree to German membership in NATO and that the United States would curb NATO enlargement. However, within weeks, the US National Security Council was debating whether and when to "signal to the new democracies of Eastern Europe NATO's readiness to contemplate their future membership."[63] In 1999 and 2004, two rounds of NATO expansion occurred, and in 2008 Georgia and Ukraine were promised membership, despite repeated Russian warnings that NATO would thereby constitute a direct threat to Russian national security. As Richard Sakwa observes, it was "[t]he failure to establish a genuinely inclusive and equal European security system" that "imbued European international politics with powerful stress points," including the "international earthquake we call the Ukraine crisis."[64]

These regional stress points intersected with Ukraine's internal political divisions. In his judicious study,[65] Sakwa locates the "Ukrainian crisis" in different understandings of Ukrainian statehood. On one side is the "Orange" tendency, which "thinks in terms of a Ukraine that can finally fulfill its destiny as a nation state, officially monolingual, culturally autonomous from other Slavic nations and aligned with 'Europe' and the Atlantic security community." On the other side is the "Blue" tendency, which symbolizes "a rather more plural understanding of the challenges facing Ukraine, recognizing that the country's various regions have different historical and cultural experiences, and that the modern Ukrainian state needs to acknowledge this diversity in a more capacious constitutional settlement."

As the Ukrainian crisis unfolded, US and European backing for the Orange camp, including the unconstitutional transfer of power on 21 February 2012, helped precipitate the civil war and Russian intervention. In fact, as Sakwa elaborates, "[for the Kremlin], 21 February was the turning point, with the EU unwilling or unable to honour its own agreements[66] and condoning the illegal seizure of power. The "Ukrainian crisis" at this point became internationalized and turned into the "Ukraine" crisis, with the Kremlin enraged by the coming to power of Russophobic nationalists. The seizure of power by monist nationalists allied with unsavoury right-wing elements alienated pluralists and raised fears that the exclusive form of nationalism…would now be given free reign. In Crimea, Odessa, and above all in the Donbass, the scene was set for confrontation, loss of territory, and civil war."[67]

In sum, the fading fortunes of US hegemony have sparked common dynamics of geopolitical and social conflict in flashpoint zones of the global political economy, resulting in the current state of global disorder.

TRUDEAU AND THE GLOBAL DISORDER: CANADA IN THE MIDDLE EAST AND EASTERN EUROPE

During the neoliberal period, three dynamics have transformed the political economy of Canadian foreign policy. First, from the mid-1980s to the present, the Canadian state has pursued a project of continental neoliberalism.[68] Under the direction of corporate policy groups and think tanks, the goal of this strategy has been to integrate the US and Canadian economies in free-market ways.

Second, the Canadian state worked to globalize production and investment on a broader scale.[69] In fact, the regional strategy of continental neoliberalism was designed as a stepping-stone for Canadian corporate expansion in the world economy, particularly through foreign direct investments. By 1996, Canada had become a net exporter of direct investment capital, and Canadian corporations became leaders in several global sectors, including energy, mining, finance, aerospace, and information-and-computer-technologies. Directorship interlocks between the top-tier firms of Corporate Canada and the top firms globally also increased, with Canadian corporate elites expanding their position in the "North Atlantic ruling class."[70]

Third, Liberal and Conservative governments began to rethink Canadian foreign policy in light of the globalization agenda and Washington's primacy strategy. With support of the corporate community and defence lobby, Canadian governments have articulated a new grand strategy of armoured neoliberalism: a fusion of militarism and class warfare in Canadian state policies and practices.[71] The aims have been threefold: globalize Corporate Canada's reach; elevate Canada's position in the US-led geopolitical hierarchy, particularly through new forms of cooperative specialization; and discipline any opposition forces—both state and non-state—in the world order. From Afghanistan to Haiti and Honduras, Canadian foreign policy worked precisely to such ends.[72]

Given this context, how has Trudeau engaged with the current global disorder, particularly in the Middle East and Eastern Europe? To begin, in the Middle East, the Trudeau government has largely maintained the prior government's pro-Saudi and pro-Israel policies. The Liberals also retained the previous government's posture towards other crises in the region. The Trudeau government largely ignored Saudi Arabia's bombing of Yemen, which left over 10,000 civilians dead and millions hungry and sparked a cholera epidemic.[73] Rather than oppose this humanitarian calamity, Ottawa armed the Saudis and openly aligned itself with Riyadh. For example, the government signed off on a $15 billion Canadian Commercial Corporation Light Armoured Vehicle (LAV) contract with the kingdom. Over a decade and a half, General Dynamics Land Systems Canada is to provide upwards of a thousand vehicles equipped with machine guns and medium- or high-calibre weapons to Saudi Arabia. The largest arms export contract in Canadian history, it includes maintaining the vehicles and training Saudi forces to use the LAVs.[74]

Video emerged of Canadian-made LAVs targeting civilians in Yemen.[75] Other weaponry procured in Canada was also used in Yemen.[76] Some of the Saudi pilots bombing Yemen were likely trained in Alberta and Saskatchewan. Since 2011 Saudi pilots have trained with NATO's Flying Training in Canada (NFTC), which is run by the Canadian Forces and CAE Inc. (formerly Canadian Aviation Electronics).[77] The Montreal-based flight simulator company trained Royal Saudi Air Force pilots in the Middle East, as well as the United Arab Emirates Air Force, which joined the Saudi-led bombing of Yemen.[78] With the LAV sale under a court challenge, in late 2016 federal government lawyers described Saudi Arabia as "a key military ally who backs efforts of the international community to fight the Islamic State in Iraq and Syria and the instability in Yemen. The acquisition of these next-generation vehicles will help in those efforts, which are compatible with Canadian defence interests."[79] In a further sign of Ottawa aligning with Riyadh's foreign policy, the Canadian Embassy in Saudi Arabia noted in 2017 that "the Saudi government plays an important role in promoting regional peace and stability."[80]

Within six weeks of taking up his new post, Foreign Minister Stéphane Dion met his Saudi counterpart in Ottawa.[81] According to briefing notes for the meeting, Dion was advised to tell the Saudi minister, "I am impressed by the size of our trade relationship, and that it covers so many sectors...You are our most important trading partner in the Middle East and North Africa (MENA) region."[82] The Trudeau government also sought to deepen ties to the Saudi-led Gulf Cooperation Council (GCC), whose members almost all intervened in Yemen.[83] Announced in 2013, the Canada–GCC Strategic Dialogue has been a forum to discuss economic ties and the conflicts in Syria, Iraq, and Yemen. Dion attended the May 2016 meeting with GCC foreign ministers in Saudi Arabia, and another gathering was set for late 2017.[84]

According to figures compiled by defence industry publisher IHS Jane's, Canada was the second biggest arms exporter to the Middle East in 2015.[85] Canadian diplomats, the Canadian Commercial Corporation (CCC), and the Canadian Association of Defence and Security Industries (CADSI) promoted arm sales to the GCC monarchies.[86] With support from Global Affairs Canada and the CCC, a slew of Canadian companies flogged their wares at the Abu Dhabi-based International Defence Exhibition and Conference (IDEX) in 2016 and 2017, the largest arms fair in the Middle East and North Africa.[87] Furthermore, Canadian companies and officials sold weapons to monarchies that armed anti-government forces in Syria. In an effort to oust the Bashar al-Assad regime, GCC countries supported extremist Sunni groups, which have had ties to IS.[88]

In early 2016, the Trudeau government withdrew Canadian bombers from the US-led Iraq/Syria mission that began in October 2014. The government, however, maintained two reconnaissance aircraft and an in-air refuelling tanker to support a mission that bombed Syria without Damascus' permission, a contravention of international law.[89] The Trudeau government continued with the previous government's low-level support for regime change in Syria.[90] It provided aid to groups opposed to Assad and supported US cruise missile strikes on a Syrian military base in April 2017 after the chemical incident in Khan Sheikhoun.[91]

The Trudeau government also tripled the number of Canadian special forces on the ground in the region. More than 200 highly skilled soldiers provided training, weaponry, and combat support to Kurdish forces often accused of ethnically cleansing areas of Iraq that they have captured.[92] Despite being framed as a "training" mission, the Canadians repeatedly engaged in battle.[93] Canadian soldiers provided indirect support to Shia government forces, some of which massacred Sunnis in areas of Iraq captured from IS.[94] A tactical helicopter detachment, intelligence officers, and a combat hospital in Iraq, as well as 200 Canadian forces members at a base in Kuwait, supported the Canadian special forces.[95] There is also a Canadian frigate in the region, and two dozen Canadian forces members were part of US-led operations in Bahrain and Qatar.[96]

The Trudeau government continued to isolate Canada from world opinion on Palestinian rights. Canada voted against numerous UN resolutions, supported by almost the entire world, upholding Palestinian rights. In November 2016, for instance, Ottawa joined Israel, the United States, Marshall Islands, Micronesia, and Palau in opposing a motion titled "Israeli settlements in the Occupied Palestinian Territory, including East Jerusalem and the occupied Syrian Golan."[97] In all, 156 countries voted in favour of the motion, while six abstained.[98] In spring 2016, Dion criticized the UN Educational, Scientific and Cultural Organization (UNESCO) for defending Palestinian rights and the UN Human Rights Council for appointing University of Western Ontario law professor Michael Lynk as "Special Rapporteur on Palestine."[99] In May 2017, Trudeau linked the fighting of anti-Semitism to those opposed to political Zionism, Israel's state ideology.[100]

With Israel, Saudi Arabia, and the United States generally antagonistic to Iran, there has been only a minor shift away from the Harper government's hostile position towards that country. The Trudeau government dialled down the previous government's most bombastic rhetoric against Tehran but has not restarted diplomatic relations or removed that country from Canada's state sponsor of terrorism list.[101] One aim of the Canada-GCC Strategic Dialogue is to isolate Iran. A communiqué after the May 2016 Canada-GCC ministerial meeting expressed "serious concerns over Iran's support for terrorism and its destabilizing activities in the region."[102] The Trudeau government continued to criticize Iran for their human rights abuses while regularly ignoring more flagrant rights violations by the rulers of Saudi Arabia. In the fall of 2016, Canada again led the effort to have the United Nations General Assembly single Iran out for human rights violations.[103]

Turning to Eastern Europe, the Trudeau government increased Canada's military presence on Russia's doorstep (Ukraine, Poland, and Latvia). Eight hundred Canadian military personnel, a naval frigate, and a half dozen CF-18 fighter jets were dispatched to the region.[104] Alongside the United Kingdom, Germany, and the United States, Canada led a NATO battle group to supposedly defend Eastern Europe from Moscow. About 450 Canadian troops were in Latvia, while the three other NATO countries led missions in Poland, Lithuania, and Estonia. Canada also has 200 troops working out of a NATO command centre in Poland and a naval frigate patrolling the Black Sea and Mediterranean.[105] In March 2017, Canada's military training mission in Ukraine was renewed for two more years and simultaneously had its mandate expanded. Two hundred Canadians troops effectively emboldened far-right militarists responsible for hundreds of deaths in Eastern Ukraine.[106]

Canada's military build-up in Eastern Europe was the outgrowth of the coup in Kiev. While much is made about Russia's influence in Ukraine, there is little attention given to Canada's role in stoking tensions there. In July 2015, the Canadian Press reported that opposition protesters were camped in the Canadian Embassy for a week during the February 2014 rebellion against the president. "Canada's embassy in Kyiv was used as a haven for several days by anti-government protesters during the uprising that toppled the regime of former president Viktor Yanukovych," the story noted.[107]

Since at least the mid-2000s, Ottawa has actively supported opponents of Russia in Ukraine. Federal government documents from 2007 explain that Ottawa was trying to be "a visible and effective partner of the United States in Russia, Ukraine and zones of instability in Eastern Europe."[108] At the time, the government announced $16 million in aid to support "democratic reform" in Ukraine.[109] The previous Liberal government also intervened in Ukraine's 2004–2005 elections, supporting the so-called Orange Revolution.[110] In April 2017, the two countries signed the Canada-Ukraine Defence Cooperation Agreement.[111] The bilateral accord is designed to increase cooperation in various areas of military policy. Nine months before the Defence Cooperation Agreement was inked, Prime Minister Trudeau travelled to Kiev to sign a Canada-Ukraine Free Trade Agreement.[112] For Washington and Ottawa, Ukraine is a proxy to weaken Russia.

Conclusion

The progressive credentials of Justin Trudeau are greatly overstated with respect to core issues of international security. Structural dynamics at the global level, and in the political economy of Canada, create systemic pressures around which Trudeau has assimilated Canadian foreign policy. At the global level, the world order is defined by the crisis of neoliberalism, the decline of US hegemony, the emergence of multi-polarity, and new patterns of social resistance. As case studies from the Middle East and Eastern Europe demonstrate, Trudeau's foreign policy has continued the structural logic of Canadian foreign policy in the neoliberal period. Specifically, it has aligned with the primacy strategy of Washington, around which it has offered "cooperative specialization" of disciplinary militarism. Simultaneously, Trudeau has supported the further internationalization of Canadian capital, especially in the arms industry. Trudeau's public relations efforts to rebrand Canadian foreign policy should be viewed with caution. Whether they are deliberate obfuscations or liberal illusions, they fail to address, let alone supersede, the contradictions of global disorder. To begin to do that, a politics of anti-imperialism and social transformation is needed.

Notes

1. TheStar.com and Canadian Press (2015).
2. For a more in-depth analysis, see Government of Canada (2017a).
3. Government of Canada (2017b).
4. Haldeman (2016).
5. Lawson (2015).
6. Obama (2015).
7. Doyle (1986).
8. Mearsheimer (2001), Waltz (1979).
9. Ibid. (1994).
10. Marx (1937).
11. Ibid. (1976).
12. Shaikh (2016). Also, for a more introductory explanation of Marxist crisis theory, see Roberts (2016).
13. Callinicos (2009).
14. For more on these concepts, see various publications by Alexander Anievas especially, Anievas (2014).
15. Hearden (2002), Ikenberry (2006), Klassen (2014).

16. Leffler (1992).
17. Gowan (2003), Schlesinger (2004).
18. Early Cold War concerns later encouraged more flexibility in US demands towards dismantling the British Empire's preferential trading system (Zeiler 1997).
19. Leffler (1984, 349–51).
20. Layne (2006), Leffler (1984, 1992), Lundestad (1986).
21. Klassen (2014, 69–70).
22. Central Intelligence Agency (1948).
23. Kolko (1988).
24. Chomsky and Herman (1979), Chomsky (1996).
25. Harvey (2005).
26. Duménil and Lévy (2013).
27. Amsden (2007).
28. Chang (2008, 27), United Nations (2005, 75).
29. United Nations Development Programme (2010, 4, 72).
30. Tirman (2011, 182–192).
31. United States (1992).
32. Ibid. (1997).
33. Ibid. (2002).
34. Ibid. (2010).
35. Duménil and Lévy (2013).
36. Krugman (2012); Milanovic (2016).
37. United Nations Development Programme (2013, 65).
38. Ibid. (2013, iv).
39. Klassen (2013).
40. Chandrasekaran (2013).
41. Stokes (2009).
42. Rosen (2010).
43. Leverett and Leverett (2013, 6–7).
44. Abukhalil (2004, 31–32).
45. United States (2009).
46. Mazzetti and Schmitt (2016), Mazzetti and Apuzzo (2016), Bayoumy (2016).
47. Finkelstein (2003), Pappe (2006).
48. Finkelstein (2003).
49. United Nations Economic and Social Commission for Western Asia (2017).
50. Gendzier (2015).
51. Finkelstein (2003).
52. Miller (2005).
53. For a general overview, see Gelvin (2015). On neoliberal class formation in Syria, see Haddad (2011).

54. WikiLeaks (2016).
55. Chivers and Schmitt (2013).
56. Allam (2015).
57. Lister (2015).
58. See, for example, JPost.com Staff (2015), Chulov (2015).
59. Entous (2015).
60. McFaul et al (2014).
61. Ploeg (2017, 199–205).
62. Mearsheimer (2014).
63. Shifrinson (2016a, b).
64. Sakwa (2016, x).
65. Ibid. (ix).
66. On the night of February 20–21, Ukrainian leaders from all sides signed an agreement to resolve the crisis through the formation of a national unity government, witnessed by Russian and European Union officials (Sakwa, 2016, 88).
67. Sakwa (2016, 99).
68. Klassen (2014, 87–114).
69. Ibid. (117–119).
70. Carroll and Klassen (2010), Klassen and Carroll (2011).
71. Klassen (2014, 183).
72. Ibid. (220–248); Shipley (2017).
73. Ghobari (2016), Masters (2016), McKernan (2017).
74. Chase (2016c); Ling (2016).
75. Chase and Fife (2016).
76. Ayed et al. (2016).
77. Pugliese (2014).
78. Lake (2015), CAE (2017).
79. Ling (2016).
80. Government of Canada (2017c).
81. Global Affairs Canada (2015).
82. Kapelos (2016).
83. Chase (2016b).
84. Global Affairs Canada (2016).
85. Chase (2016a).
86. Canadian Association of Defence and Security Industries (2015).
87. Ibid. (2017).
88. Norton (2016).
89. Brewster (2017).
90. CTV News (2015).
91. Zimonjic and Tasker (2017).
92. Postmedia News (2016).

93. Canadian Press (2017).
94. Campion-Smith (2017).
95. Brewster (2017).
96. Cossette (2017).
97. United Nations (2016).
98. Ibid. (2016).
99. Engler (2016).
100. Trudeau (2017).
101. Berthiaume (2016a).
102. Chase (2016b).
103. Akin (2016).
104. Berthiaume (2016b).
105. *Defence 24*, 2016; Chase (2015).
106. Losh (2017), de Ploeg (2017, 137–145).
107. Brewster (2015).
108. Department of Foreign Affairs and International Trade (2006).
109. Blanchfield (2007).
110. MacKinnon (2007).
111. National Defence (2017).
112. Berthiaume (2016c).

References

Abukhalil, As'ad. 2004. *The battle for Saudi Arabia: Royalty, fundamentalism, and global power*. New York: Seven Stories Press.

Akin, David. 2016. Canada will use UN to knock Iran on human rights. *Toronto Sun*, July 12. http://www.torontosun.com/2016/07/12/canada-will-use-un-to-knock-iran-on-human-rights. Accessed 2 July 2017.

Allam, Hannah. 2015. Warnings of jihadists among Syria rebels came early, were ignored. *McClatchy*, August 13. http://www.mcclatchydc.com/news/nation-world/national/national-security/article31018362.html. Accessed 2 July 2017.

Amsden, Alice. 2007. *Escape from empire: The developing world's journey through heaven and hell*. Cambridge: MIT Press.

Anievas, Alexander. 2014. *Capital, the state, and war: Class conflict and geopolitics in the thirty years' crisis, 1914–1945*. Ann Arbor: University of Michigan Press.

Ayed, Nahlah, Joanne Levassuer, Jacques Marcoux, and Tracy Seeley. 2016. Canadian rifles may have fallen into Yemen rebel hands, likely via Saudi Arabia. *CBC News*, February 22. http://www.cbc.ca/news/canada/manitoba/canadian-rifles-may-have-fallen-into-yemen-rebel-hands-likely-via-saudi-arabia-1.3455889. Accessed 2 July 2017.

Bayoumy, Yara. 2016. Obama administration arms sales offers to Saudi top $115 billion: Report. *Reuters*, September 7. http://www.reuters.com/article/us-usa-saudi-security-idUSKCN11D2JQ. Accessed 2 July 2017.

Berthiaume, Lee. 2016a. No plan to stop calling Iran a state sponsor of terror, Foreign Affairs Minister Stéphane Dion says. *Ottawa Citizen*, May 2. http://nationalpost.com/news/politics/no-plan-to-stop-calling-iran-a-state-sponsor-of-terror-foreign-affairs-minister-stephane-dion-says/wcm/aeaa8023-07f0-4ce5-b055-54aca78e6969. Accessed 2 July 2017.

———. 2016b. Canada to send 450 soldiers, up to 6 fighter jets to Eastern Europe. *Canadian Press*, July 8. https://www.thestar.com/news/canada/2016/07/08/trudeau-says-canada-will-send-troops-fighter-jets-to-eastern-europe.html. Accessed 2 July 2017.

———. 2016c. Trudeau to sign free-trade deal with Ukraine. *Canadian Press*, July 10. https://www.theglobeandmail.com/news/world/trudeau-to-sign-free-trade-deal-with-ukraine/article30848223/. Accessed 2 July 2017.

Blanchfield, Mike. 2007. A 'counterbalance' – Canada's democracy can counter Russian negativity: MacKay. *Canada.com*, July 19. http://freerepublic.com/focus/f-news/1868328/posts. Accessed 2 July 2017.

Brewster, Murray. 2015. Canadian embassy used as safe haven during Ukraine uprising, investigation finds. *Canadian Press*, July 12. http://www.cbc.ca/news/politics/canadian-embassy-used-as-safe-haven-during-ukraine-uprising-investigation-finds-1.3148719. Accessed 2 July 2017.

———. 2017. Canada brings home 1 of 2 Aurora surveillance planes from anti-ISIS mission. *CBC News*, May 24. http://www.cbc.ca/news/politics/sajjan-iraq-isis-cp-140-1.4129219. Accessed 2 July 2017.

CAE. 2017. CAE awarded contract to provide comprehensive RPA training solution to UAE Air Force & air defence. *CAE*, May 8. http://www.cae.com/CAE-awarded-contract-to-provide-comprehensive-RPA-training-solution-to-UAE-Air-Force-Air-Defence/?contextualBUID=103. Accessed 2 July 2017.

Callinicos, Alex. 2009. *Imperialism and global political economy*. Cambridge: Polity Press.

Campion-Smith, Bruce. 2017. Canada's top general 'horrified' by images of Iraqi abuse. *Toronto Star*, June 12. https://www.thestar.com/news/canada/2017/06/12/canadas-top-general-horrified-by-images-of-iraqi-abuse.html. Accessed 2 July 2017.

Canadian Association of Defence and Security Industries (CADSI). 2015. CADSI receives funding to promote Western Canadian companies at international security and defence events. *CADSI*, July 24. https://www.defenceandsecurity.ca/media/article&id=277&t=c. Accessed 2 July 2017.

———. 2017. Participate in the Canadian pavilion at the IDEX 2017. *CADSI*. https://www.defenceandsecurity.ca/events/details&evtID=295. Accessed 2 July 2017.

Canadian Press. 2017. Canadian special forces taking more active role in Iraq as Liberals extend ISIS mission. *Canadian Press*, March 31. http://globalnews.ca/news/3348510/canadian-armed-forces-iraq-isis-mission/. Accessed 2 July 2017.

Carroll, William K., and Jerome Klassen. 2010. Corporate Canada hollowing out? Changes in the corporate network since the 1990s. *Canadian Journal of Sociology* 35 (1): 1–30.

Central Intelligence Agency. 1948. The break-up of the colonial empires and its implications for U.S. security. *Central Intelligence Agency*, September 3. https://www.cia.gov/library/readingroom/docs/DOC_0001166383.pdf. Accessed 2 July 2017.

Chandrasekaran, Rajiv. 2013. *Little America: The war within the war for Afghanistan*. New York: Vintage.

Chang, H-Joon. 2008. *Bad Samaritans: The myth of free trade and the secret history of capitalism*. New York: Bloomsbury Press.

Chase, Steven. 2015. Canada to station troops at NATO command centre in Poland. *Globe and Mail*, June 9. https://www.theglobeandmail.com/news/politics/harper-begins-next-leg-of-european-visit-with-stop-in-poland/article24870280/. Accessed 2 July 2017.

———. 2016a. Canada now the second biggest arms exporter to Middle East, data show. *Globe and Mail*, June 14. https://www.theglobeandmail.com/news/politics/canada-now-the-second-biggest-arms-exporter-to-middle-east-data-show/article30459788/. Accessed 2 July 2017.

———. 2016b. Ottawa keeps under wraps plan to foster ties with Arab Gulf states. *Globe and Mail*, June 21. https://www.theglobeandmail.com/news/politics/ottawa-keeps-under-wraps-plan-to-foster-ties-with-arab-gulf-states/article30551168/. Accessed 2 July 2017.

———. 2016c. The big deal. *Globe and Mail*, February 5. https://www.theglobeandmail.com/news/politics/the-saudi-arms-deal-why-its-a-bigdeal/article28568660/. Accessed 2 July 2017.

Chase, Steven, and Robert Fife. 2016. Saudis appear to be using Canadian-made combat vehicles against Yemeni rebels. *Globe and Mail*, February 22. https://www.theglobeandmail.com/news/politics/saudi-arms-used-against-yemeni-rebels-seem-to-match-canadian-lavs/article28846678/. Accessed 2 July 2017.

Chivers, C.J., and Eric Schmitt. 2013. Arms airlift to Syria rebels expands, with aid from C.I.A. *New York Times*, March 24. http://www.nytimes.com/2013/03/25/world/middleeast/arms-airlift-to-syrian-rebels-expands-with-cia-aid.html. Accessed 2 July 2017.

Chomsky, Noam. 1996. *World orders, old and new*. New York: Columbia University Press.

Chomsky, Noam, and Edward S. Herman. 1979. *The Washington connection and third world fascism: The political economy of human rights*. Boston: South End Press.

Chulov, Martin. 2015. Turkey sends in jets as Syria's agony spills over every border. *The Guardian (Observer)*, July 25. https://www.theguardian.com/world/2015/jul/26/isis-syria-turkey-us?CMP=share_btn_tw. Accessed 2 July 2017.

Cossette, 2017. Canada extends maritime security mission in Middle East to 2021. *CBC News*, May 29. http://www.cbc.ca/news/politics/canada-extends-operation-artemis-2021-1.4135904. Accessed 2 July 2017.

CTV News. 2015. Defence Minister Sajjan on Syria: Assad must go. *CTV News*, November 22. http://www.ctvnews.ca/politics/defence-minister-sajjan-on-syria-assad-must-go-1.2669381. Accessed 2 July 2017.

de Ploeg, Chris Kaspar. 2017. *Ukraine in the crossfire*. Atlanta: Clarity Press.

Defence 24. 2016. Canadian soldiers arrive in Poland. *Defence 24*, August 26. http://www.defence24.com/435947,canadian-soldiers-arrive-in-poland. Accessed 2 July 2017.

Department of Economic and Social Affairs. 2005. World economic and social survey 2005. *United Nations*, 2005. http://www.un.org/en/development/desa/policy/wess/wess_archive/2005wess_eng.pdf. Accessed 2 July 2017.

Department of Foreign Affairs and International Trade. 2006. Archived – RPP 2006–2007: 3.1 Summary of plans and priorities for 2006–2009. *Treasury Board of Canada Secretariat*, August 26. https://www.tbs-sct.gc.ca/rpp/2006-2007/fait-aeci/fait-aeci03-eng.asp. Accessed 2 July 2017.

Doyle, Michael W. 1986. Liberalism and world politics. *American Political Science Review* 80 (4): 1151–1169.

Duménil, Gerard, and Dominique Lévy. 2013. *The crisis of neoliberalism*. Cambridge: Harvard University Press.

Engler, Yves. 2016. Canada isolating itself from world opinion on Palestinian rights. *Huffington Post* (Canada), November 23. http://www.huffingtonpost.ca/yves-engler/justin-trudeau-palestine_b_13147828.html. Accessed 2 July 2017.

Entous, Adam. 2015. U.S. sees Russian drive against CIA-backed rebels in Syria. *Wall Street Journal*, October 5. https://www.wsj.com/articles/u-s-concludes-russia-targeting-cia-backed-rebels-in-syria-1444088319. Accessed 2 July 2017.

Finkelstein, Norman. 2003. *Image and reality of the Israel-Palestine conflict*. London: Verso.

Gelvin, James L. 2015. *The Arab uprisings: What everyone needs to know*. 2nd ed. Oxford: Oxford University Press.

Gendzier, Irene L. 2015. *Dying to forget: Oil, power, Palestine, and the foundations of U.S. policy in the Middle East*. New York: Columbia University Press.

Ghobari, Mohammed. 2016. U.N. says 10,000 killed in Yemen war, far more than other estimates. *Reuters*, August 30. http://www.reuters.com/article/us-yemen-security-toll-idUSKCN11516W. Accessed 2 July 2017.

Global Affairs Canada. 2015. Minister Dion welcomes Saudi counterpart. *Government of Canada*, December 16. https://www.canada.ca/en/global-affairs/news/2015/12/minister-dion-welcomes-saudi-arabian-counterpart.html?=undefined&wbdisable=true. Accessed 2 July 2017.

———. 2016. Joint communique: Second joint ministerial meeting on strategic dialogue between the Gulf Cooperation Council and Canada. *Global Affairs Canada*, May 23. http://www.international.gc.ca/name-anmo/gcc-canada-ccg.aspx?lang=eng. Accessed 2 July 2017.

Government of Canada. 2017a. #WelcomeRefugees: Canada resettled Syrian refugees. *Government of Canada*. http://www.cic.gc.ca/english/refugees/welcome/index.asp. Accessed 2 July 2017.

———. 2017b. Canada's feminist international assistance policy. *Government of Canada*. http://international.gc.ca/world-monde/issues_development-enjeux_developpement/priorities-priorites/policy-politique.aspx?lang=eng. Accessed 5 August 2017.

———. 2017c. Embassy of Canada to Saudi Arabia. *Government of Canada*, July 27. http://www.canadainternational.gc.ca/saudi_arabia-arabie_saoudite/index.aspx?lang=eng. Accessed 2 July 2017.

Gowan, Peter. 2003. US: UN. *New Left Review* 24, November/December. https://newleftreview.org/II/24/peter-gowan-us-un. Accessed 2 July 2017.

Haddad, Bassam. 2011. *Business networks in Syria: The political economy of authoritarian resilience*. Redwood City: Stanford University Press.

Haldeman, Peter. 2016. With the rise of Justin Trudeau, Canada is suddenly … hip? *New York Times*, January 16. https://www.nytimes.com/interactive/2016/01/15/style/canada-justin-trudeau-cool.html. Accessed 2 July 2017.

Harvey, David. 2005. *A brief history of neoliberalism*. Oxford: Oxford University Press.

Hearden, Patrick J. 2002. *Architects of globalism: Building a new world order during World War II*. Fayetteville: University of Arkansas Press.

Ikenberry, G. John. 2006. *Liberal order & imperial ambition*. Cambridge, UK: Polity Press.

JPost.com Staff. 2015. Report: Israel treating al-Qaida fighters wounded in Syria civil war. *Jerusalem Post*, March 13. http://www.jpost.com/Middle-East/Report-Israel-treating-al-Qaida-fighters-wounded-in-Syria-civil-war-393862. Accessed 2 July 2017.

Kapelos, Vassy. 2016. Saudi Arabia Canada's 'most important' trading partner in the Middle East: Government documents. *Global News*, March 30. http://globalnews.ca/news/2608640/saudi-arabia-canadas-most-important-trading-partner-in-the-middle-east-government-documents/. Accessed 2 July 2017.

Klassen, Jerome. 2013. Methods of empire: State building, development, and war in Afghanistan. In *Empire's ally: Canada and the war in Afghanistan*, ed. Jerome Klassen and Greg Albo, 139–180. Toronto: University of Toronto Press.

———. 2014. *Joining empire: The political economy of the new Canadian foreign policy.* Toronto: University of Toronto Press.

Klassen, Jerome, and William K. Carroll. 2011. Transnational class formation? Globalization and the Canadian corporate network. *Journal of World-Systems Research* 17 (2): 379–402.

Kolko, Gabriel. 1988. *Confronting the third world: United States foreign policy.* Boston: Beacon Press.

Krugman, Paul. 2012. *End this depression now!* New York: W.W. Norton.

Lake, Jon. 2015. Simulators for the Gulf [IDX15D3]. *Janes.com*, February 25. http://www.janes.com/article/49390/simulators-for-the-gulf-idx15d3. Accessed 2 July 2017.

Lawson, Guy. 2015. Trudeau's Canada, again. *New York Times Magazine*, December 8. https://www.nytimes.com/2015/12/13/magazine/trudeaus-canada-again.html. Accessed 2 July 2017.

Layne, Christopher. 2006. *The Peace of Illusions: American Grand Strategy from 1940 to the Present.* Ithaca: Cornell University Press.

Leffler, Melvyn P. 1984. The American conception of national security and the beginnings of the Cold War, 1945–48. *The American Historical Review* 89 (2): 346–381.

———. 1992. *A preponderance of power: National security, the Truman administration, and the Cold War.* Redwood City: Stanford University Press.

Leverett, Flynt, and Hillary Mann Leverett. 2013. *Going to Tehran: Why the United States must come to terms with the Islamic Republic of Iran.* New York: Metropolitan Books.

Ling, Justin. 2016. Canada isn't being totally honest about its plan to sell weapons to Saudi Arabia. *Vice News*, July 12. https://news.vice.com/article/exclusive-canada-isnt-being-totally-honest-about-its-plan-to-sell-weapons-to-saudi-arabia. Accessed 2 July 2017.

Lister, Charles. 2015. Why Assad is losing. *Foreign Policy*, May 5. https://foreignpolicy.com/2015/05/05/why-assad-is-losing-syria-islamists-saudi/. Accessed 2 July 2017.

Losh, Jack. 2017. Ukraine turns a blind eye to ultrarightist militia. *Washington Post*, February 13. https://www.washingtonpost.com/world/europe/ukraine-turns-a-blind-eye-to-ultrarightist-militia/2017/02/12/dbf9ea3c-ecab-11e6-b4ff-ac2cf509efe5_story.html?utm_term=.3eee214d87e8. Accessed 2 July 2017.

Lundestad, Geir. 1986. Empire by invitation? The United States and Western Europe, 1945–1953. *Journal of Peace Research* 23 (3): 263–277.

MacKinnon, Mark. 2007. Agent orange: Our secret role in Ukraine. *Globe and Mail*, April 14.

Marx, Karl. 1937. *Eighteenth Brumaire of Louis Bonaparte.* Moscow: Progress Publishers.

———. 1976. *Capital: A critique of political economy.* London: Penguin.

Masters, James. 2016. Yemen food crisis leaves millions at risk of starving. *CNN*, October 28. http://www.cnn.com/2016/10/27/middleeast/yemen-world-food-program/. Accessed 2 July 2017.

Mazzetti, Mark, and Matt Apuzzo. 2016. U.S. relies heavily on Saudi money to support Syrian rebels. *New York Times*, January 23. https://www.nytimes.com/2016/01/24/world/middleeast/us-relies-heavily-on-saudi-money-to-support-syrian-rebels.html. Accessed 2 July 2017.

Mazzetti, Mark, and Eric Scmitt. 2016. Quiet support for Saudis entangles U.S. in Yemen. *New York Times*, March 13. https://www.nytimes.com/2016/03/14/world/middleeast/yemen-saudi-us.html. Accessed 2 July 2017.

McFaul, Michael, Stephen Sestanovich, and John J. Mearsheimer. 2014. Faulty powers: Who started the Ukraine crisis? *Foreign Affairs*, November/December. https://www.foreignaffairs.com/articles/eastern-europe-caucasus/2014-10-17/faulty-powers. Accessed 2 July 2017.

McKernan, Bethan. 2017. Yemen: Almost one death per hour as cholera epidemic spreads like wildfire. *The Independent (UK)*, June 9. http://www.independent.co.uk/news/world/middle-east/yemen-war-deaths-cholera-epidemic-dying-every-hour-a7782341.html. Accessed 2 July 2017.

Mearsheimer, John J. 1994. The false promise of international institutions. *International Security* 19 (3): 5–49.

———. 2001. *The tragedy of great power politics*. New York: W.W. Norton.

———. 2014. Why the Ukraine crisis is the West's fault. *Foreign Affairs*, September/October. https://www.foreignaffairs.com/articles/russia-fsu/2014-08-18/why-ukraine-crisis-west-s-fault. Accessed 2 July 2017.

Milanovic, Branko. 2016. *Global inequality: A new approach for an age of globalization*. Cambridge: Harvard University Press.

Miller, Aaron David. 2005. Israel's lawyer. *Washington Post*, May 23. http://www.washingtonpost.com/wp-dyn/content/article/2005/05/22/AR2005052200883.html. Accessed 5 August 2017.

National Defence. 2017. Government of Canada signs defence cooperation arrangement with Ukraine. *Government of Canada*, April 3. https://www.canada.ca/en/department-national-defence/news/2017/04/government_of_canadasignsdefencecooperationarrangementwithukrain.html. Accessed 2 July 2017.

Norton, Ben. 2016. Leaked Hillary Clinton emails show U.S. allies Saudi Arabia and Qatar supported ISIS. *Salon.com*, October 11. http://www.salon.com/2016/10/11/leaked-hillary-clinton-emails-show-u-s-allies-saudi-arabia-and-qatar-supported-isis/. Accessed 2 July 2017.

Obama, Barrack. 2015. Remarks by President Obama and Prime Minister Trudeau of Canada in joint press conference. *Office of the Press Secretary*, March 10. https://obamawhitehouse.archives.gov/the-press-office/2016/03/10/remarks-president-obama-and-prime-minister-trudeau-canada-joint-press. Accessed 2 July 2017.

Pappé, Ilan. 2006. *The ethnic cleansing of Palestine*. Oxford: Oneworld.
Postmedia News. 2016. The 'ripple effect': Canada's training of Kurds could also empower them to separate from Iraq. *National Post*, February 6. http://news.nationalpost.com/news/canada/the-ripple-effect-canadas-training-of-kurds-could-also-empower-them-to-separate-from-iraq. Accessed 2 July 2017.
Pugliese, David. 2014. Canadian fighter pilots were sent to U.S. due to problems with training program. *Ottawa Citizen*, July 29. http://ottawacitizen.com/news/national/canadian-fighter-pilots-were-sent-to-u-s-due-to-problems-with-training-program. Accessed 2 July 2017.
Roberts, Michael. 2016. *The long depression: Marxism and the global crisis of capitalism*. Chicago: Haymarket Books.
Rosen, Nir. 2010. *Aftermath: Following the bloodshed of America's wars in the Muslim world*. New York: Nation Books.
Sakwa, Richard. 2016. *Frontline Ukraine: Crisis in the borderlands*. London: I.B. Tauris.
Schlesinger, Stephen C. 2004. *Act of creation: The founding of the United Nations*. New York: Basic Books.
Shaikh, Anwar. 2016. *Capitalism: Competition, crisis, conflict*. Oxford: Oxford University Press.
Shifrinson, Joshua R. Itskowitz. 2016a. Deal or no deal? The end of the Cold War the U.S. offer to limit NATO expansion. *International Security* 40 (4): 7–44.
———. 2016b. Russia's got a point: The U.S. broke a NATO promise. *Los Angeles Times*, May 30. http://www.latimes.com/opinion/op-ed/la-oe-shifrinson-russia-us-nato-deal--20160530-snap-story.html. Accessed 5 August 2017.
Shipley, Tyler. 2017. *Ottawa and Empire: Canada and the Military Coup in Honduras*. Toronto: Between the Lines Books.
Stokes, Doug. 2009. The war gamble: Understanding US interests in Iraq. *Globalizations* 6 (1): 107–112.
TheStar.com, and Canadian Press. 2015. 'Canada is back,' says Trudeau in Paris. 'We're here to help.' *TheStar.com* and *Canadian Press*, November 30. https://www.thestar.com/news/canada/2015/11/30/busy-day-for-trudeau-at-paris-climate-change-talks.html. Accessed 5 August 2017.
Tirman, John. 2011. *The deaths of others: The fate of civilians in America's wars*. Oxford: Oxford University Press.
Trudeau, Justin. 2017. Statement by the Prime Minister of Canada on Israel Independence Day. *Prime Minister's Office*, May 2. http://pm.gc.ca/eng/news/2017/05/02/statement-prime-minister-canada-israel-independence-day. Accessed 2 July 2017.
United Nations. 2005. *World Economic and Social Survey 2005*. New York: United Nations, Department of Economic and Social Affairs.
United Nations. 2016. Draft resolutions on Palestine refugees, Israeli practices in occupied Arab lands among 12 approved as Fourth Committee concludes its

work. *United Nations*, November 8. http://www.un.org/press/en/2016/gaspd628.doc.htm. Accessed 2 July 2017.

United Nations Development Programme. 2010. *Human development report 2010*. New York: United Nations.

———. 2013. *Human Development Report 2013*. New York: United Nations.

United Nations Economic and Social Commission for Western Asia. 2017. *Israel practices towards the Palestinian people and the question of apartheid*. Beirut: United Nations.

United States. 1992. Department of Defense. *Draft FY 94–99 Defense Planning Guidance*. Washington, DC.

———. 1997. *The report of the quadrennial defense review*. Washington, DC: Department of Defense.

———. 2002. *The national security strategy of the United States of America*. Washington, DC: White House.

———. 2009. Secretary of State. Cable. Terrorist finance: Action request for senior level engagement on terrorism finance. *WikiLeaks*, December 30. https://wikileaks.org/plusd/cables/09STATE131801_a.html. Accessed 2 July 2017.

———. 2010. *The national security strategy of the United States of America*. Washington, DC: White House.

Waltz, Kenneth. 1979. *Theory of international politics*. Long Grove: Waveland Press.

WikiLeaks. 2016. *The WikiLeaks files: The world according to US empire*. London: Verso.

Zeiler, Thomas W. 1997. GATT fifty years ago: U.S. trade policy and imperial tariff preferences. *Business and Economic History* 26 (2): 709–717.

Zimonjic, Peter, and John Paul Tasker. 2017. Canada was briefed on and 'fully supports' U.S. missile strikes against Syria: PM. *CBC News*, April 7. http://www.cbc.ca/news/politics/trudeau-canada-airstrikes-syria-1.4060061. Accessed 2 July 2017.

CHAPTER 5

Canada-US Relations Under President Trump: Stop Reading the Tweets and Look to the Future

Stephen Blank and Monica Gattinger

Shortly after Donald Trump's inauguration as president of the United States, Prime Minister Justin Trudeau came to New York City and was a great hit. His graceful and intelligent welcome to some 600 Canadians and friends of Canada invited to attend the made-in-Canada Broadway show (Trudeau told us this included 125 United Nations ambassadors), *Come from Away*, was much appreciated and—to many in the audience—a glowing contrast to President Donald Trump. The good people of New York City loved the good Canadian. Americans like Canada. Some 75 percent view Canada favorably and more than 40 percent of Americans would prefer to have Trudeau rather than Trump in the White House.[1] But this is not money in anyone's bank, although *Come from Away* made out handily.

Trump worsens Canadians' uncertainties about their future. A world turning upside down, rising ethnic conflict, collapsing international institutions, and climate change—all echo inside "sunny" Canada. Trump has

---

S. Blank (✉) • M. Gattinger
University of Ottawa, Ottawa, ON, Canada

jammed his (small) thumb in every sore. Relations with the United States did not really change under Obama, but Canadians were crazy about him and that smoothed the edges of dealing with the United States. Now, Donald Trump's arrival in the White House and the uncertainty and volatility it has brought puts government officials, industry, and Canada-US watchers on edge, with much hand-wringing, concern, and speculation about what the Trump presidency means for Canada-US relations. Will the country get swept up or side-swiped by the president's decisions or pronouncements? Did any of the president's overnight tweets mention Canada?

We encourage decision-makers to take the long view when it comes to Canada-US relations. Certainly, there are immediate issues to address in the relationship (we sketch a number of these out below), but, in our view, the most important issues in Canada-US relations are those that are now emerging over the horizon. Bilateral relations will become more complex over the next decades. Fundamental demographic and social changes, transformations in energy and climate systems, and technological revolutions in both economies will reshape Canada, the United States, and bilateral relations.

This is not to say that the two countries no longer need each other: they do and will. Critical issues confront, and will confront, both nations, and developing the best solutions will require close collaboration. However, Canada and the United States have tended to take their relationship for granted, thinking about it only when forced to by necessity. Future collaboration will depend on strategic foresight and more comprehensive forward-looking planning. Canada and the United States must learn to view themselves as two similar but different nations, sharing a single geographic space, facing many of the same powerful challenges, but often responding in different ways based on their domestic and international realities. The core task will be constructing mechanisms that foster collaboration and coordination to maximize both countries' capacities to respond effectively to current and emerging challenges.

Our aim in this chapter, although we will touch on existing arrangements, dynamics, and issues, is to look forward and identify emerging situations and issues that will reshape the relationship. In addition, we propose three key strategies to manage the Canada-US relationship: the importance of long-term foresight (not short-term "near sight"), the need to challenge conventional wisdom and assumptions about the drivers and underpinnings of Canada-US relations, and the necessity to develop "deep collaboration" that moves well beyond the capitals of both countries.

We begin this chapter with some context on Canada-US relations under Prime Minister Trudeau and President Trump and then move to the broader international and global pictures, highlighting three core issues that we believe will transform Canada-US relations: large-scale demographic and social change, fundamental transformations in the energy and climate systems, and the fourth industrial revolution (emerging technologies disrupting and transforming the domestic and global economies). We point to the potential impacts of these changes on essential areas of the bilateral relationship and underscore the importance of strategic foresight, deep collaboration, and challenging conventional wisdom when it comes to managing Canada-US relations.

1. What's Up Under Trudeau and Trump?

In June 2016, before the Republican and Democratic conventions and the presidential election, the North American Leaders Summit (NALS) produced an impressive list of "deliverables," touching on a raft of important topics.[2] For Canada and the United States, this reflected the continuing work of the Beyond the Border (BTB) and Regulatory Cooperation Council (RCC) projects (mirror bilateral initiatives were undertaken between the United States and Mexico). After years of false starts, from the post-North American Free Trade Agreement (NAFTA) Working Groups (that didn't) to the Security and Prosperity Partnership (that collapsed when the anti-NAFTA tribe blew on it), the BTB and RCC initiatives were making substantial progress in removing barriers to trade and investment. While neither initiative was intended to transform Canada-US relations—they were chiefly about removing long-standing irritants at the operational level—the 2016 NALS meeting may well have been the highwater mark of continental collaboration by the three national leaders.

And now? Well, for now, everything is suspended in the uncertainty of the Trump presidency. Trump's grim view of NAFTA ("history's worst trade deal") has not been expressed clearly in policies. Indeed, the *New York Times* line that Trump was "talking loudly and brandishing a small stick"[3] has pretty much continued. An early draft letter from the Acting US Trade Representative directed to the "US House of Representatives/Senate" was leaked (the Trump administration's communication system relies heavily on tweets and leaks). The letter said that President Trump intended to "initiate negotiations on NAFTA and its architecture." What followed was a substantial list of topics for consideration. Most trade specialists would find the topics reasonable—not to "tear up" NAFTA, but to reform it and bring it up to date. Negotiations are now underway and while Trump continues to brandish that stick ("I don't think we can make a deal because we've been so badly taken advantage of"), uncertainty reigns. Trump has railed about areas of concern to Canada—dispute settlement, auto content requirements, and supply management come to mind—but the Trudeau government has stated that the renegotiations are an opportunity and has pursued the country's interests with the usual Canadian trope of highlighting the importance of trade with Canada to the US economy. What has been different, this time around, is the greater level of collaboration and involvement of provincial premiers and state governors in the process and the increased focus on ministers visiting US destinations outside the Washington beltway. A smart approach, but it is not yet clear whether it will pay off.

At the bureaucratic level, while none of the three partner governments created an agency with specific responsibilities for North American affairs, in the United States at least, work on the BTB and the RCC has been deeply embedded in various sections of the government. This is good news and means that there is an informed constituency in Washington's bureaucracy for many US-Canada trade/border issues. But, as of the early fall 2017, many upper-level appointments across the government have still not been made and that expertise and interest will erode if not used. Until people are in place, we are pretty much left peering into a cloudy crystal ball and interpreting continuing campaign rhetoric, leaks, and, of course, tweets.

This said, we can be pretty certain that between wrestling with health care, the budget, Russian inquiries, North Korea, rebellious Republicans, neo-Nazis, travel bans, and more, Trump and his top advisors—those who remain—cannot be worrying too much about Canada. At the moment, any and all bandwidth for Canada is likely dedicated to the NAFTA negotiation process. Given this highly uncertain and volatile context, instead of focusing our attention on tea leaves and tweets, we believe that Canada should identify, analyze, and proactively respond to factors and trends that will shape its relations with the United States in the decades to come. We sketch these out below and then discuss their prospective and collective impact on Canada-US relations.

2. Canada and the United States in a Changing World: Demographic and Social Change

Demographics are not conclusive, but projections from the UN 2015 report, *World Population Prospects*,[4] suggest dramatic changes in the world Canada and the United States will inhabit over the coming decades. Most importantly for Canada, UN data shows that the postwar world in which the country flourished as a "middle power," punching far above its weight, is long gone.

In 2050, India and China will still be the world's population giants, but the fastest growing populations will be in sub-Saharan Africa. Of the 2.4 billion people projected to be added to the global population between 2015 and 2050, 1.3 billion will be Africans. Europe's population will be older and declining, and its share of the world population is projected to fall from 11 to 7 percent. Canada will do fairly well, by today's developed nation standards, with modest population growth. But in the world pool, Canada will be a very small fish. (The United States is the outrider here, expected to reach 400 million people in 2050—another development which may increase the distance between Canada and the United States.)

Canada will have to adapt to a world of new players which will demand greater roles in global governance—Nigeria or Ethiopia pushing to the front row in the United Nations or International Monetary Fund (IMF). Older, postwar, Euro-North American-centric institutions will be pressured to adapt to these players, to new demands and issues. The Group of Twenty (G20) was a good step, but far more will need to be done. A global question of enormous scale will be whether African nations can overcome weak institutions and deep political cleavages to become new growth centers with growing middle classes (like Taiwan, South Korea, and Malaysia) or whether they will collapse, creating vast waves of human distress and flight.

Closer to home, aging populations create new challenges in both countries. Canada will be much older: the share of Canadians 60 years old and over will reach nearly a third of the population in 2050 (for Indigenous people, the picture's very different: almost half, 46 percent, of Indigenous Canadians are under the age of 20, compared to 30 percent for non-Indigenous people).[5] The United States, because of its larger young immigrant population, will be less so: the share of Americans over 60 years old will only reach 27.5 percent in 2050. The countries' total population profile differs. In the United States, the 15–64 age group is expected to grow substantially, by more than 40 percent. In contrast, Canada's working age population is expected to decline. Both countries must deal with larger, older, populations, but the United States will enjoy a brief but useful "demographic dividend" of a larger working age population. For Canada, demographic change will drive heightened dependency rates, changes in labor force composition, and possible declining productivity, a real concern for a country that already has a productivity gap.

The United States will also look different; it will certainly be less white. In 1980, nearly half of US counties had populations that were 98 percent or more white. In 2010, that metric described fewer than 5 percent. How to read this is not clear. In the 50 years after the 1952 Immigration and Nationality Act rewrote US immigration policy, nearly 59 million immigrants have arrived in the United States. These immigrants and their descendants account for just over half the nation's population growth, and have reshaped its racial and ethnic composition.[6] Rising levels of interracial marriage and changing definitions of self-identity will probably make racial boundaries less rigid. Still, racial tensions are on the rise in the United States and were manifest in the 2016 election—particularly for groups, often less educated and less skilled, who felt their "white identity" was threatened.[7]

Canada is changing too; the percentage of visible minorities in 2011 was 19.1 percent and is expected to grow to 30.6 percent by 2031. Vancouver and Toronto are expected to become "majority-minority" cities, with three out of five people belonging to a visible minority group by then.[8] In comparison to the United States, racial relations have been harmonious in Canada. However, as the country (notably cities) becomes more and more multicultural, the potential for "white-first" movements to emerge could grow. To date, some of the most visible tensions have been seen in Quebec, with substantial debate—even a government commission—on "reasonable accommodation" for "cultural communities."

The United States and Canada will look less alike in the future. How will this affect our interests? President Trump's current Mexico policy notwithstanding, might an increasingly large and influential Hispanic US community look increasingly to the south? Ronald Reagan said of Canada, "We're more than friends and neighbors and allies; we are kin, who together have built the most productive relationship between any two countries in the world today." We will not be such close kin in the emerging decades. We have never developed a "North American" identity and the "Anglosphere" vision that tied US and Canadian (mostly Anglophone) elites for decades will fray.

In addition to demographic change, both Canada and the United States are or will be affected by broader political and social trends. A shift toward populism and economic nationalism is occurring in many parts of the world, notably in parts of Europe and the United States. Is Canada immune from this? Perhaps, perhaps not.[9] Will these sorts of trends drive the United States and Canada apart, as attentions turn evermore inward? Or, might it be possible that shared perceptions of beleaguered white identity could lead to new forms of cross-border ties? It remains to be seen.

Canada is not immune from other social and political trends affecting Western industrialized democracies. Extensive, widespread, and permanent social and value change has taken place since the 1950s. Levels of public trust in government, industry, and experts have declined across Western industrialized democracies in the post-1945 period.[10] Successive results of the Edelman Trust Barometer document this change, with the 2017 annual study noting that "trust is in crisis around the world," including trust in government, industry, non-governmental organizations (NGOs), and the media.[11] Citizens' deference to authority of various kinds (elite, government, industry, medical, etc.) has also declined over the decades.[12] Social values have become more individualistic than group-/community-oriented over the years, with individual or small group interests able to trump community/national interests. When citizens' preoccupations are centred more on individual/local interests than on national/group interests, appeals to the "national interest" or broader regional/group interests, including the importance of bilateral economic relations, for example, may get less traction or fall on deaf ears. Closer to home, some would say that emerging populism and economic nationalism, along with disarray in the Republican Party and economic dislocation in many parts of the United States, created the wave that Donald Trump rode to the White House.

How will Canada respond to these forces that threaten to overthrow the world that it has performed well in over the past 70 years? How might these changes affect Canada-US relations? We return to this below. For now, we turn to a second fundamental set of changes affecting both countries and Canada-US relations in the short and long terms.

3. Fundamental Transformations in the Energy and Climate Systems

Global energy systems are set for fundamental transformations in the coming decades. Chief among these will be efforts to reduce the carbon intensity of energy production and consumption. President Trump has repudiated the Paris Climate accord, in which countries agreed to contain the rise in the global average temperature to well below 2 degrees Celsius above pre-industrial levels and aimed to limit the increase to 1.5 degrees. The Canadian government committed to ambitious targets for reducing national greenhouse gas (GHG) emissions as part of this process: reducing emissions by 30 percent of 2005 levels by 2030 (this equates to a decrease from roughly 750 megatons carbon dioxide equivalent down to about 525 megatons in 2030). This is a steep ask, and one that most serious analysts agree is physically, if not politically, socially, fiscally, and economically, impossible given the country's current energy system. US commitments were similar to Canada's. President Barack Obama committed to reducing US emissions by 26–28 percent below 2005 levels by 2025, although the absolute emissions volumes in question are almost ten times those in Canada, given the relative size of the two economies. While Canadian emissions have declined somewhat from their 2005 levels, they are a long way from the abrupt downward trajectory to which the government is committed. In the United States, meanwhile, emissions have declined relatively more than in Canada in percentage terms, but most of this is due to fuel switching in the electricity sector, where abundant natural gas supplies are replacing coal-fired generation. Canada's electricity system is already extremely clean—between large-scale hydro and nuclear, it is 80 percent non-emitting—leaving less "low-hanging fruit" to go after.

From a policy perspective, climate change is a juggernaut. Energy systems have long-lived capital-intensive infrastructure, making stranded assets a substantial concern for industry and capital markets, and consumer behavior and expectations for cheap, reliable, and abundant energy can make it politically difficult to enact policy that will raise energy prices. Moreover, the stepwise technological changes required to move to lower carbon energy systems can be capital intensive and economically risky. All of this generates requirements for multiple forms of government intervention. While economists agree that a carbon tax is the most efficient and effective means of effecting emissions reductions, in Canada there is increasing recognition that the tax would need to be very high in order to achieve the reductions required and that other government tools like subsidies and regulations will be needed.[13] This is a tall ask for political leaders: public outrage over high taxes could be devastating at the polls (even if the tax is designed to be revenue neutral) and most governments do not have spare change lying around at the moment. And given the climate policy differences between the Trudeau and Trump camps, Canadian business, whether in energy or the broader economy, is understandably concerned about the impacts on competitiveness, investment, and trade.

At the same time, as the two countries are moving in opposite directions on climate policy, the twin technological developments of hydraulic fracturing and horizontal drilling have enabled shale gas and tight oil resources to be profitability produced. The so-called shale revolution has transformed the United States from a hydrocarbon-scarce to an oil- and gas-rich country, with oil and gas production at levels not seen for close to 50 years. The rapid expansion of oil and gas production in the United States has transformed the country's energy picture, displacing imports from the Middle East and other suppliers belonging to the Organization of the Petroleum Exporting Countries (OPEC), and displacing gas imports from Canada. It has also substantially driven down global oil prices (OPEC has mostly resisted cutting production) and led to floor prices in natural gas. As a result, the United States has experienced a manufacturing renaissance in some industries and is now an exporter of natural gas (US liquid natural gas has just arrived in Latvia, competing with Russian exports), and in a previously unimaginable move, Congress removed the country's ban on crude oil exports. For Canada, the shale revolution in the United States has generated considerable uncertainty about the future prospects for the country's oil and gas exports. Its largest (only) consumer is becoming a competitor, and for the first time in its energy history, it needs to get its oil and gas resources to international markets beyond North America. This is anything but a slam dunk, as inter-regional, environmental and Indigenous opposition to oil and gas pipelines, increased tanker traffic, and liquefied natural gas facilities have stymied getting the country's resources to market to date.[14]

Where all of this will go and what it will ultimately mean for Canada-US energy and climate relations (more on this further on in the chapter) is highly uncertain. A recent report from Norway's Statoil lays out a provocative analysis of the future. Depending on the evolution of drivers like economic growth, geopolitics, technological change, and energy and climate policies, the company projects that the future could be characterized by three very different scenarios: market forces coexisting with climate policy in a way that does not come close to meeting the ambitions of the Paris agreement (reform), substantial progress toward energy sustainability and limiting global warming to 2 degrees Celsius (renewal), or a multipolar world of self-interested populism, nationalism, and climate skepticism (rivalry).

In the midst of much energy uncertainty, it is clear that climate change is real. There is no doubt that it is having and will have substantial global, regional, and domestic impacts. Climate scientists generally agree that most of Canada will experience warming over the next decades—almost surely most of it in the Arctic and perhaps at least in some of the Atlantic region. But within this general perspective, significant regional disparities are charted. In the Prairies, temperatures are slated to go up, but precipitation won't increase in kind, meaning a much warmer drier prairie climate. This will put stress on agriculture, longer growing seasons notwithstanding.[15] And melting glaciers could much reduce water flows, even if precipitation did increase. The picture for the United States seems worse: "… mega-droughts are projected to hit the main agricultural regions in the United States—both the California and the Midwest 'breadbaskets.' The chronic water shortages that are anticipated in these regions under the business-as-usual scenario would make farming, as well as ranching in the American southwest, nearly impossible."[16]

Coastal regions of both countries will face rising sea levels, and more frequent and powerful storm surges. We cannot be unaware of the impact of climate change on US coastal regions. Some studies warn that Canada will be affected as well: "changing climate is increasingly affecting the rate and nature of change along Canada's highly dynamic coasts, with widespread impacts on natural and human systems."[17]

Changes in the Arctic are likely to be one of Canada's most critical issues and of serious concern for the United States as well. Canada's Arctic coast is the frontline of new northern transportation, mining, and fishing ventures, and Canada will be forced to make hard decisions about how it will bear this responsibility: how many resources it is prepared to devote to its northern regions and how it will seek to organize collaboration with other countries, including the United States, with major interests there. Changes in the Arctic also raise security concerns, as well as heightened potential for conflict over underwater oil and gas resources.

Globally, climate change will alter global patterns of production and transportation and is already creating "climate refugees." Many of the world's most important ports will face climate-driven threats in the next decades, stressing the global trade system. Greater variability in temperature and precipitation could cause more rapid deterioration in road and rail infrastructure.

The impacts on Canada-US relations will be profound and unprecedented. We chart some of these out below. Before that, we explore the third major transformation facing both countries: the fourth industrial revolution (Industry 4.0).

4. The Fourth Industrial Revolution: Disruptive Technologies, Competitiveness, Innovation, and Trade

In the last years of the 1990s, the parameters of industrial competitiveness were reset by advances in communications and transportation technologies. The Fordist model of the highly integrated localized factory system ("rubber and iron ore in, autos out") had given over to new systems of extended supply chains that crossed oceans and borders on just-in-time schedules. We wrote that "much of North America's economy could be visualized as a deeply integrated continental system of supply chains structured by networks linking production centers and distribution hubs across the continent."[18]

Today, technology is again changing the rules of the game. The fourth industrial revolution, the "fusion of technologies that is blurring the lines between the physical, digital, and biological spheres. ... [and is distinct in its] velocity, scope, and systems impact,"[19] is transforming the nature of production, supply, and distribution and may well alter the criteria for competitive advantage. It is intensifying social transformation and, most importantly, creating a widening gap between "winners" in the new environment and "losers"—with, in the United States at least, stunning political impact.

From the earliest colonial times, the economies of what would become Canada and the United States were closely linked. In the early twentieth century, the two countries' growing industrial cores—automobiles, energy, telephony, and chemicals—transcended the border. In the 1980s, responding to intensifying international competition, firms integrated Canadian branch plants into single North American divisions creating the "bottom-up" pressures that helped lead to the Canada-US free trade agreement.[20] In the new industrial era, the future of these cross-border networks is not guaranteed. In automobiles, the classic example of a "North American" industry, many new players in different industries are involved in the movement toward autonomous vehicles. New supply chains are emerging, linking firms with little history of cross-border ties. The United States rust belt states, widely viewed as playing leading roles in artificial intelligence (AI) and robotics, could look south or southwest rather than north, across the border.

How is Canada faring in this new industrial world? So far, the news hasn't been good. In an opinion piece in the *Globe and Mail* Kevin Lynch, the former clerk of the Privy Council and now vice-chair at BMO Financial Group, notes that Canadian rankings in productivity and innovation from the World Economic Forum, the Organization for Economic Co-operation and Development (OECD) and the IMF "all point in the same distressingly downward direction."[21] And a recent report by the Canadian Manufacturers and Exporters association and The Canadian Manufacturing Coalition complains that "Canada's manufacturing sector is being overlooked at the very time that the world of manufacturing is transforming—a transformation that brings with it tremendous opportunities as well as risks."[22]

In the potentially huge autonomous vehicle industry, Canada is "late to the party." Barrie Kirk of the Canadian Automated Vehicles Centre of Excellence observes: "When I look at the G7 and the ways in which the G7 countries are getting ready for autonomous vehicles, Canada is dead last."[23] Still, there are positive signs: Ontario's Advanced Manufacturing Consortium among McMaster University, Western University, and the University of Waterloo is a $35 million, five-year commitment; the McMaster Automotive Resource Centre ("where a high-performance lab meets a garage"); and the announcement from both General Motors and Ford that they will set up research and development centers in Ontario, a breakout from Canada's traditional role of assembler and parts producer. The government has committed some $125 million investment in AI over the coming years to position the country on the leading edge of the technology. Given how late Canada is to the party, however, these are very high hopes.[24]

5. So What Might All of This Mean for Canada, the United States, and Bilateral Relations?

The impact of these transformations on Canada, the United States, and their bilateral relations will be far-reaching and long-lasting. While the ultimate shape of things to come remains highly uncertain—and indeed this informs our recommendation that governments substantially beef up their capacities for foresight and scenarios work—we point here to a number of key potential impacts facing both countries in the years to come. We frame many of them as central questions that leaders would do well to address. We also identify promising strategies for managing bilateral relations in this emerging, uncertain, and transformative context.

On demographic change, Canada will surely have to rethink its global options. How will it recast its historic Atlantic-Euro-focused identity and commitments in an increasingly Asian-African-centered world? What role is the country prepared to play and capable of playing in this new environment? What resources exist or will need to be found to enable it to do so?[25] The direction that the United States takes will be a critical element in determining how this will play out. Can—should—Canada rely on US leadership in a tumultuous world? Under a Trump administration, this would be ill-advised (to put it mildly), but going forward, will (should) the United States and Canada collaborate on approaches and policies for this new world? Both of these questions merit careful consideration and can also be posed when it comes to energy and climate system transformations and Industry 4.0 (more on this below).

Domestically, both countries are likely to continue to see population shifts toward urban—better, urban-regional—areas. A more useful map of North America in the next few decades might highlight emerging megaregions. The other side of this coin is the depopulation of significant segments of the two countries. These patterns will affect cross border relations. While long segments of the border regions, Canada's prairies, and the US north central regions in particular, will be emptier, emerging cross-border megacities will be denser and probably more interconnected. This will pose significant challenges for Canada, including how to deal with the increasing power of some city governments and the weakening of some provincial governments, and whether to encourage or discourage deeper integration of major cross-border megacities.

For Canada, east-west distances in economic and cultural terms may increase, while north-south distances diminish. Emerging cross-border "mega-regions" in Greater Vancouver-Greater Portland-Seattle or Southern Ontario-US Rust Belt could be on the horizon. Indeed, as we note further below, economic success and competitiveness for major Canadian communities in the new technological-industrial world may depend on deepening north-south ties. Canadian communities outside these new growth regions may suffer considerably.[26] Combined with climate impacts, some areas could face the perfect storm of depopulation, economic dislocation, and environmental devastation. In a context of individualism, low trust in government and preoccupation with risk, the potential for populist backlash looms large. How will political leaders respond? Crucial will be the building of new vehicles for cross-border collaboration in emerging mega-regions.

On energy and climate, both countries will need to determine how they will reconcile the need to lower GHG emissions with their status as major oil and gas producers. The global list of top energy producers and reserve holders includes a very small number of Western industrialized democracies. Canada and the United States are among them, along with Norway and Australia. Will Canada and the United States work together to show the world that they can develop their oil and gas resources responsibly for domestic and global consumption while driving down their GHG emissions and transitioning to lower carbon energy systems in the long term? Will they collaborate on developing the energy technologies, policy frameworks, and game-changing innovations needed to do so?

On climate adaptation, both governments will have to decide whether to pump huge sums of money into defending existing infrastructure or to abandon threatened structures and build a new—or some combination of the two. While some Canadians are concerned that the United States will press for new deals to take Canadian water, in the end, much of that water may be sold south of the border in the form of Canadian grain, vegetables, and fruits, replacing the bounty of dried up farm land in the United States. Of course, adding to the list of emerging bilateral issues, to do this would require vast innovation in north-south cross-border freight transport. As for the North, there is disagreement about the extent of the security threat.[27] Regardless, the Canadian and US governments will have to work out new arrangements for cooperating and remaining resilient in the face of these new conditions.

In the new industrial era, the future of cross-border networks is not guaranteed. Canada and the United States must work to maintain their vitality. To maintain vigorous cross-border links, Canada must be at the cutting edge of Industry 4.0, but the pace, scale, and scope of change make this a challenging proposition. And cross-border integration is a challenging file to begin with. The interminable machinations getting to the second Windsor-Detroit bridge (construction of which had not yet begun at time of writing) symbolize the challenge. Although North America's twentieth-century auto industry continued to improve in a highly competitive global environment, even without the new bridge and with the thickened borders that came in the wake of 11 September 2001, success in the twenty-first century industry of autonomous vehicles, smart infrastructure, complex hardware, and software producer networks will demand far more collaboration across more industrial sectors and among governments at all levels in our federal systems.

And there is another, darker, side to these technological transformations. While new and exciting avenues for jobs and careers are emerging, many people are and will be left behind, particularly those who are older, less educated, lower skilled, and less mobile. For them, "innovation" and "Industry 4.0" may become four-letter words, if they are not already. And this is not just a matter of individuals, many of whom will require government support to transition (or to not transition) to the new world of work. The more serious threat is that entire geographic or socioeconomic communities are left derelict, raising the specter of populist and economic nationalist movements growing and gaining strength. In the United Kingdom ("Brexit") and the United States (Trump), studies reveal how these changes widen economic, social, and political cleavages. These developments are already affecting Canada-US relations, viz., anti-NAFTA sentiment and rhetoric in the United States (the fact that automation drove down jobs and not trade is beside the point). Is Canada immune from these tendencies inside its borders? We think not. But are leaders seriously considering the prospects of this and how to proactively address it? Unfortunately, we also think not.

To effectively respond to both the challenges and opportunities of these transformations as they unfold, we propose governments pursue three key strategies:

- Foresight not near sight. The unpredictability and volatility of the Trump White House militates toward focusing on the short term, but those engaged in and managing bilateral relations should position their short-term tactics within a much longer-term view. Given the scale and pace of change in the offing, both countries will need

to develop their domestic and bilateral capacities for horizon scanning, foresight, and scenarios work, along with policy and program flexibility, adaptability, and resilience, to adjust to rapid and wide-scale change.
- Challenge usual assumptions. The relatively stable postwar environment of trade liberalization, economic growth, and predictable geopolitical fault lines is being replaced by an increasingly complex, fast-moving, and unpredictable environment. The futures of trade liberalization, multilateralism, and elite-driven politics are very much open questions. In this context, decision-makers must consistently challenge their usual assumptions about "how the world works"—not only for Canada-US relations but globally—now and into the future.
- All hands on (a coordinated) deck. Those managing Canada-US relations will need to expand their toolkit and approach substantially. The challenges of an increasingly complex world will require "deep collaboration": much more decentralized and extensive relations moving well out of Ottawa and Washington into the provinces, states, and municipalities, and building, leveraging, and mobilizing multiple ongoing constituencies of political, industrial, and civil society leaders at the national, regional, and local levels.

This will not be easy, but it is essential if Canada and the United States are to effectively navigate their domestic and cross-border environments.

6. Conclusion: The Shape of Things to Come

Might the Canada-US Council for Advancement of Women Entrepreneurs and Business Leaders be a precedent? The Council was launched at a roundtable discussion with female business leaders held during Prime Minister Trudeau's February 2017 visit to the White House. Since its creation, the Council indicates it has been "hard at work" on vital topics like women in science, entrepreneurship, and private sector leadership, along with access to capital, and that it will release recommendations in the coming months.[28] While one can be skeptical about how committed anybody is to the Council idea, interestingly, all members of the Council lead organizations that are in the thick of the demographic, energy, climate and industrial transformations that are underway: General Electric, General Motors, Catalyst, TransAlta, Linamar, T&T Supermarkets,

Investissement Québec, Schnitzer Steel, Accenture, and NRStor. A formidable group, and one that we would welcome expanding its activities, partners, and ambit to "go rogue" and look at the future of Canada-US relations in the long term.

Well-structured scenarios and foresight work are in desperate need by those charting the future of bilateral relations and those managing them in the present. A process along these lines would also be a compelling illustration of the ways in which players on both sides of the border—business, government, and civil society—could begin constructing the much-needed underpinnings of "deep collaboration" in the years to come. Further, it would challenge the usual assumptions of how Canada-US relations are managed and who exercises thought leadership in the process. A process spearheaded by mayors would be an equally novel approach.

While there is much uncertainty about the future, the relationship will undoubtedly be shaped by powerful and disruptive trends. The countries may move in quite different directions over the next decades, as both undergo significant structural transformations to their economies, energy and environment systems, and populations. They will confront important and complex issues that require deep collaboration and strong relationships, challenging usual assumptions and looking far into the future to inform actions in the here and now. This will require new approaches, strong relationships, and thought leadership on both sides of the border. A tall order to be sure, but an essential one to fill if Canada and the United States are to thrive in the coming decades.

Notes

1. Ferreras (2017).
2. We particularly liked the creation of the North American Center for Collaborative Development to pursue joint research and foster exchanges between academics and others on climate change, energy, manufacturing, economic integration, and Indigenous peoples.
3. Appelbaum (2016).
4. United Nations (2015).
5. Statistics Canada (2015).
6. Pew Research Center (2015, 8).
7. Vavreck (2017).
8. Quan (2014).
9. Preston Manning, former leader of the populist Reform Party, thinks not. In the absence of mechanisms for grassroots concerns to be expressed and

addressed in the political system, there is always the potential of populist backlash in Canada. See Manning (2017).
10. See Giddens (1990).
11. See Edelman (2017).
12. See Nevitte (1996, 2011).
13. See Coad et al. (2017).
14. For a full discussion of Canada's energy relations with the United States in this context, see Gattinger and Aguirre (2016).
15. Pilger (2015).
16. Nuccitelli (2015).
17. Lemmen et al. (2016, 3).
18. See Blank (2015, 208).
19. Schwab (2016).
20. See Stanley (2010).
21. Lynch (2015).
22. Canadian Manufacturers and Exporters (2016, 4).
23. Owram (2017).
24. See Bernstein et al. (2017).
25. A recent examination of Canada in Africa observes: "Caught between these competing pressures to 'do something,' but also to limit exposure and entanglements, the result has been a pattern of un-sustained and incoherent engagements, shallow relationships, and limited understanding. But because the *results* of these initiatives are of little concern or consequence to most Canadians, there is typically little political price to be paid for their inadequacies" (Black 2016, 2).
26. See the work of Brian Crowley on "Atlantica," a North American region by-passed by globalization (Crowley n.d.).
27. See Plouffe et al. (2016).
28. See Business Council of Canada (2017).

REFERENCES

Appelbaum, Binyamin. 2016. President's growing trade gap: A gulf between talk and action. *New York Times*, April 1, 2017.

Bernstein, Alan, Pierre Boivin, and David McKay. 2017. It's time for Canada to invest in developing artificial intelligence. *Globe and Mail*, March 26.

Black, David. 2016. Canada in Africa: Finding our footing? Canadian Global Affairs Institute, December, 2016. https://d3n8a8pro7vhmx.cloudfront.net/cdfai/pages/1365/attachments/original/1480623737/Canada_in_Africa_Finding_our_Footing.pdf?1480623737. Accessed 10 Sept 2017.

Blank, Stephen. 2015. How do we get to North America? In *Regional governance in post-NAFTA North America*, ed. Brian Bow and Greg Anderson, 207–229. Abingdon: Routledge.

Business Council of Canada. 2017. Canada-United States council for advancement of women entrepreneurs and business leaders. Business Council of Canada, July 8. http://thebusinesscouncil.ca/initiatives/women-entrepreneurs-and-business-leaders/. Accessed 5 Sept 2017.

Canadian Manufacturers and Exporters and the Canadian Manufacturing Coalition. 2016. *Industrie 2030, manufacturing growth, innovation and prosperity for Canada*. Toronto: Canadian Manufacturers and Exporters.

Coad, Len, Robyn Gibbard, Alicia Macdonald, and Matthew Stewart. 2017. *The cost of a cleaner future: Examining the economic impacts of reducing GHG emissions*. Ottawa: Conference Board of Canada.

Crowley, Brian. n.d. Atlantica powerpoint presentation. Atlantic Institute for Market Studies. http://aims.wpengine.com/site/media/aims/Atlantica AugustaSlides.pdf. Accessed 5 Sept 2017.

Edelman. 2017. 2017 Edelman trust barometer. *Edelman*, January 17. http://www.edelman.com/global-results/. Accessed 5 Sept 2017.

Ferreras, Jesse, 2017. Trudeau over Trump: More Americans prefer PM as their president: Ipsos poll. *Global News*, February 7. http://globalnews.ca/news/3231630/trudeau-over-trump-more-americans-prefer-pm-as-their-president-ipsos-poll/. Accessed 5 Sept 2017.

Gattinger, Monica, and Rafael Aguirre. 2016. The shale revolution and Canada-US energy relations: Game changer or déjà-vu all over again? In *Canada in the international political economy*, ed. Greg Anderson and Chris Kukucha, 409–435. Toronto: Oxford University Press.

Giddens, Anthony. 1990. *Consequences of modernity*. Cambridge: Polity Press.

Lemmen, Donald S., Fiona J. Warren, Thomas S. James, and C.S.L. Mercer Clarke, eds. 2016. *Canada's marine coasts in a changing climate*. Ottawa: Government of Canada.

Lynch, Kevin. 2015. Global rankings tell worrisome tale about state of Canadian innovation. *Globe and Mail*, September 15.

Manning, Preston. 2017. Canada's elites could use a crash course in populism. *Globe and Mail*, March 15.

Nevitte, Neil. 1996. *The decline of deference: Canadian value change in comparative perspective 1981–1990*. Toronto: Broadview Press.

———. 2011. The decline of deference revisited: Evidence after 25 years. Paper presented at mapping and tracking global value change: A Festschrift conference for Ronald Inglehart. Irvine California, University of California, March 11.

Nuccitelli, Dana. 2015. Nasa climate study warns of unprecedented North American drought. *The Guardian*, February 16.

Owram, Kristine. 2017. Car wars: Why 'Canada is dead last' in the potentially huge self-driving industry. *Financial Post*, February 2.

Pew Research Center. 2015. Modern immigration wave brings 59 Million to U.S., driving population growth and change through 2065. Pew Research Center, September 28. http://www.pewhispanic.org/2015/09/28/modern-immigration-wave-brings-59-million-to-u-s-driving-population-growth-and-change-through-2065/. Accessed 5 Sept 2017.

Pilger, Gerald. 2015. Canada meets climate change. *Country Guide*, April 8. https://www.country-guide.ca/2015/04/08/canada-meets-climate-change/46410/. Accessed 5 Sept 2017.

Plouffe, Joël, Stéphane Roussel, and Jusin Massie. 2016, September. *Renewing the Arctic dimension to Canada's national defence policy*. Toronto: Canadian Global Affairs Institute.

Quan, Douglas. 2014. Have Canada's changing demographics made it time to retire the concept of 'visible minority'? *National Post*, June 27.

Schwab, Klaus. 2016. The fourth industrial revolution: What it means, how to respond. *World Economic Forum*, January 14. https://www.weforum.org/agenda/2016/01/the-fourth-industrial-revolution-what-it-means-and-how-to-respond/. Accessed 5 Sept 2017.

Stanley, Guy. 2010. Borders and bridges: Free trade, supply chains, and the creation of a joint trading platform: Canada-US industrial development since 1980. In *Borders and bridges: Canada's policy relations in North America*, ed. Monica Gattinger and Geoffrey Hale, 306–323. Toronto: Oxford University Press.

Statistics Canada. 2015. Aboriginal peoples: Fact sheet for Canada. *Statistics Canada*, November 30. http://www.statcan.gc.ca/pub/89-656-x/89-656-x2015001-eng.htm#a3. Accessed 5 Sept 2017.

United Nations, Department of Economic and Social Affairs, Population Division. 2015. *World population prospects: The 2015 revision, key findings and advance tables*. Working paper no. ESA/P/WP.241. New York: United Nations.

Vavreck, Lynn. 2017. The political payoff of making whites feel like a minority. *New York Times*, August 8.

CHAPTER 6

Canada's International Environmental Policy: Trudeau's Trifecta of Challenges

Debora Van Nijnatten

In its attempt to push forward with an activist international environmental agenda, the Trudeau government confronts a complex bundle of challenges, some of which are enduring issues for Canada's foreign environmental policy and some of which are unique to the present day. The most obvious is ascertaining whether—and in what ways—Canada can pursue its environmental agenda internationally in the face of vociferous US opposition to just about everything it wants to do, particularly on climate change. While this question implicates Canada's continuing struggle to balance bilateralism versus multilateralism in its foreign environmental policy, the severity of the current situation is unique—put simply, how can one deal with the unpredictable and potentially punitive Trump Effect?

The current policy environment also throws into sharp relief Canada's long-standing internal debate about the appropriate balance between economic pragmatism and environmental ideals in its foreign policy. This challenge is interwoven with the Trump Effect, since the new US administration is threatening to upend current trade and economic relationships,

D. Van Nijnatten (✉)
Wilfrid Laurier University, Waterloo, ON, Canada

© The Author(s) 2018
N. Hillmer, P. Lagassé (eds.), *Justin Trudeau and Canadian Foreign Policy*, Canada and International Affairs,
https://doi.org/10.1007/978-3-319-73860-4_6

and Canadian officials may face trade-offs between the pursuit of climate and clean energy initiatives and more traditional sectoral concerns. Furthermore, the context is one that appears to muddy rather than clarify where Canada should be directing its multilateral environmental efforts as it looks to find alternative strategic partners. While a series of overtures have been made to China, particularly in terms of fostering alternative energy markets, Latin America—via Mexico—offers opportunities as well.

This chapter explores each of these dynamics and shows the ways in which they are interlinked, thereby deepening Canada's international environmental policy difficulties. Yet the Trudeau government has shown considerable commitment to its policy objectives, at the same time that it has responded nimbly to changing conditions on this file. In particular, the Trudeau government has been able to work through the various national channels of influence in the United States while also operating across government levels to build support with like-minded states, to maintain a calm but firm diplomatic demeanour in the face of often threatening US rhetoric, and to look elsewhere for strategic partners on environmental initiatives internationally, even as the United States pulls back from such relationships.

Trudeau's International Environmental Agenda

In a CBC News article, boldly entitled "Trudeau team looks to put new face on Canada's climate policy," Canada's former ambassador to the United Nations (UN), Paul Heinbecker, was quoted as saying that Trudeau's team would have to show up at the UN climate talks in Paris in December 2015 "with a different team and a different tone,"[1] if it wanted to demonstrate that it intended to fully depart from the Harper government's approach. And, indeed, both the tone and the team departed from that of the previous administration, as the new Trudeau Liberal government seemed set to pursue an ambitious set of environmental goals based on an internationalist and activist framework.

In its campaign materials in 2015, the Liberals had sought to paint themselves as a forward-thinking and globalist alternative to a cynical and reactionary Harper Conservative government. Trudeau committed the Liberals, if elected, to re-establishing Canada's multilateralist credentials and re-engaging in the UN and other international processes. After noting that the Harper Conservatives had "turned their backs on the UN and other multilateral institutions," the Liberal plan was to "restore Canada as a leader in the world."[2] In concrete policy terms, this would mean, according to Liberal campaign documents and speeches, working with the United States and Mexico to develop an ambitious North American clean energy and environment agreement; aligning Canada's international negotiation positions with a new goal to be an efficient and responsible energy producer; and following through on G20 commitments to phase out fossil fuel subsidies.[3] On other environmental files, the party promised to re-commit and achieve the goals of the 2010 International Convention on Biodiversity and the Aichi Biodiversity Targets for protecting freshwater, marine, and coastal habitats.[4] Plans were also made finally to join the UN Convention on Desertification.

The backgrounds and policy leanings of the architects of the new framework certainly lent credence to claims that there would be a significant break from Harper era policy. The head of the transition team as the Liberals took office, Peter Harder, was a former deputy minister in several departments, including Foreign Affairs and International Trade, and had participated in negotiations on the Kyoto Protocol.[5] Other advisors in the new administration's inner circle included the principal author of former Liberal leader Stéphane Dion's "Green Shift" platform, Mike McNair, and a former CEO of World Wildlife Fund-Canada, who had also helped fashion Ontario's green energy plan, Gerald Butts. Butts, in particular, had a very close, long-term relationship with the prime minister[6] and was seen as a key force across policy planks, from energy to climate to national unity. Foreign policy expert Roland Paris was also brought onto Trudeau's advisory team, to help insert "liberal internationalist" principles into Canada's approach to the United States and the UN and in bilateral relationships.[7] A firm critic of the isolationist and instrumentalist Harper foreign policy and a proponent of multilateralism, Paris' appointment sent clear signals as to the more global vision preferred in the Prime Minister's Office (PMO).

Moreover, it is worth noting that the environment, and particularly climate change, was incorporated into the mandate letters of ministers with both domestic and also international portfolios, including Environment and Climate Change Canada (ECCC), Natural Resources Canada, Indigenous and Northern Affairs Canada, and, significantly, for our purposes here, Foreign Affairs and Trade. For the minister of environment and climate change, Catherine McKenna, her "overarching goal" was to "take the lead in implementing the government's plan for a clean environment and a sustainable economy," and she was expected to "help restore

Canada's reputation for environmental stewardship."[8] She was also to "[w]ork in partnership with the United States and Mexico and the Minister of Natural Resources and Foreign Affairs to develop an ambitious North American clean energy and environment agreement."[9] For the minister of foreign affairs (Chrystia Freeland was shifted into the portfolio in early 2017), the task was to seek "leadership opportunities for Canada and Canadians in multilateral institutions" and "in collaboration with the Minister of Environment and Climate Change, make Canada a leader of international efforts to combat climate change."[10] The minister of international trade was to "[s]upport the Ministers of Environment and Climate Change, Innovation, Science and Economic Development and Natural Resources to make strategic investments in clean technology and our resource sectors. We want Canadian firms to be world leaders in the use and development of clean and sustainable technology and processes that can be exported globally." In this way, then, climate change was imbedded into the leadership, policy advisory, and departmental infrastructure supporting the new government's domestic and foreign policy.

The Trudeau team was to be broader and extend outside of government inner circles, as the Trudeau Liberals repeatedly promised to work more closely with the provinces and the private sector. Provinces were to be extensively consulted on international environmental matters and included at international conferences. The first concrete manifestation of this commitment was to invite all provincial premiers to travel with the Canadian delegation to the UN climate talks in Paris in December 2015. The Liberal government has also placed a premium on bringing large business onto the climate policy scene; Environment and Climate Change Minister Catherine McKenna has worked closely with large corporations in Canada who have chosen to sign on to the Carbon Pricing Leadership Coalition (CPLC), discussed below.[11]

The aspirations emerging from this new climate policy infrastructure are indeed ambitious. The initial, strong signal came during the 21 session of the Conference of Parties (COP21) in Paris at the 2015 United Nations Framework Convention on Climate Change (UNFCCC), where Canada firmly committed to reducing greenhouse gas (GHG) emissions by 30 per cent from 2005 levels by 2030. Along with this target came historically generous support for clean growth strategies in developing countries,[12] as well as enthusiasm for a much more aggressive move into the global business of renewable energy development and application, seen as a "tremendous opportunity for Canada."[13] Also, at the signing ceremony for the

Paris COP21 agreement in New York in April 2016, Trudeau, as a member of the newly created Carbon Pricing Panel (CPP), convened by World Bank Group President Jim Yong Kim and International Monetary Fund Managing Director Christine Lagarde, agreed to a global target to expand carbon pricing to cover 25 per cent of global emissions by 2020, double the current level, and to achieve 50 per cent coverage within the next decade.[14] These new aspirations were layered atop a continuing commitment to supporting sector-by-sector emission reductions (especially in the transportation sector) as well as short-lived (high-impact) climate pollutants such as methane and hydrofluorocarbons (HFCs), both of which had already been initiated by the previous Harper government. As discussed below, the Trudeau government has shown considerable commitment to these policies, even as it faces pressure from its neighbour and critics at home to turn its attention elsewhere or even back away from its environmental aspirations.

The Bilateral Blockage in Multilateral Aspirations

As Laura Macdonald argued in a 2010 article on Canada's foreign policy, "bilateralism and multilateralism in the North American setting are not two distinct and contradictory trends, but have been closely linked together in a delicate balancing act since the Second World War."[15] Canada has long sought to achieve its foreign policy goals by building or joining coalitions of like-minded countries within diverse international organizations and processes, and multilateralism also offers Canada a potentially useful counterweight to the influence of its neighbour and largest trading partner, the United States. However, given the long and deep economic and political shadow cast by the United States over North America, Canada must constantly be engaged in fostering and nurturing its most significant bilateral relationship. Allan Gottlieb sees these as twin impulses that embody different visions of Canada's raison d'être—one "to improve the relationship with the colossus to the south and make Canada more secure," the other "to support countervailing forces against the colossus and try to create new norms, or rules, to constrain its power"—and yet co-exist in the Canadian foreign policy psyche.[16]

The United States is never far from Canada's mind when it pursues policy objectives multilaterally, particularly when these objectives might place it out of step with its southern neighbour. This has certainly been the case with climate politics and policy. Several studies have contrasted

Canada's visionary climate rhetoric in multilateral UNFCCC forums with its disappointing follow-through on commitments made in these forums, due in part to Canada's desire to maintain parity in position with the United States.[17] With the advent of the Harper Conservatives in 2006, the climate policy rhetoric was aligned consciously and firmly with the implementation realities in Canada and the position of the Americans on such matters; as Harper declared repeatedly, it made no sense for Canada to bind itself to any international climate pact that failed to include the United States, as this would hurt Canada's competitiveness. As Harper faced a new and more environmentally activist Obama administration, the rhetoric softened somewhat to indicate an openness to act when and how the United States did.[18]

When the Trudeau Liberals found themselves with a majority government in late 2015 and the opportunity to turn their climate policy aspirations into reality, the US administration appeared to be a staunch (if congressionally constrained) ally. The newly minted Prime Minister and US President Barack Obama had their first meeting at the Paris COP21 talks in December 2015, which produced much praise for Trudeau's ambitious climate policy commitments. Key to the renewed bilateral relationship on climate and environment, however, was Trudeau's highly successful state visit to Washington in March 2016, where the two governments agreed to reduce methane and HFCs, to continue driving forward on emission standards for vehicles, to adopt a carbon offset measure for the aviation sector and, interestingly, to align the ways the two countries assess the impact of GHG emissions caused by major projects as well as coordinate measures to reduce those emissions.[19] Scott Vaughan, president of the International Institute for Sustainable Development, said the common ground staked out by Trudeau and Obama was "the first time in 15, 16 years that you've got two political leaders in Canada and the U.S. that are of the same mind to be able to talk about climate."[20]

As a very visible follow-up to the March White House visit by Trudeau, a high-level meeting between the Canadian minister of environment and climate change, Catherine McKenna, and US Environmental Protection Agency (EPA) Administrator, Gina McCarthy, took place in Ottawa in April 2016. The two participated in several substantive discussions with Canadian stakeholders, including energy sector stakeholders, clean energy advocates, and government officials. They released a joint statement at the conclusion of their visit, reiterating that they "shared a common vision...

[o]ne that offers new jobs and new opportunities stemming from advancements in clean technologies and more sustainable use of our natural resources."[21]

Later in 2016, Trudeau hosted the North American Leaders Summit, where climate and energy policy integration was at the top of the agenda. The policy background for the summit had already been set out in the *Memorandum of Understanding on Climate Change and Energy Collaboration*, signed in February of that year between the United States, Canada, and Mexico. In both the document and at the summit, the three leaders made several commitments in terms of transitioning to a low-carbon economy: (1) a regional goal of 50 per cent of clean energy power generation by 2025; (2) ramping down short-lived climate pollutants such as methane, HFCs (a goal which Canada and the United States had advanced in previous meetings), and black carbon; and (3) promoting clean and efficient transportation.[22]

These North American commitments aligned nicely with international climate and environment dynamics and Canada's multilateral aspirations regarding clean growth and technologies (especially in the transportation sector), renewable energy expansion, and action on climate change-inducing pollutants. The prime minister also announced an historic level of support—$2.65 billion over 2015–2020—to help developing countries tackle climate change,[23] in line with UNFCCC commitments. On carbon pricing, Canada's policy was directly aligned with that of Mexico and other European partners in the CPP. The United States was not active in this forum, although the Obama administration had long made known its support for carbon pricing and concrete efforts at the state and regional level have continued to move the United States forward.[24] Further, Canada, Mexico, and the United States were working together in the Climate & Clean Air Coalition, a global initiative involving governments, civil society, and the private sector, and aimed at reducing short-lived climate pollutants across sectors.[25]

Then came the November US presidential election, with its surprising outcome. Although many held out hope that the rhetoric on the campaign trail would remain just that, the new president has followed through on environmental and climate policies that challenge the very basis of the Trudeau government's environment policy platform and place continental environmental and international relationships in direct opposition. Indeed, actions taken by the White House since Donald Trump was sworn in have fulfilled the worst fears of environmental interests around the globe, not to mention Trudeau officials. Perhaps most significantly, Trump had announced during the 2016 election campaign that he would "cancel" the Paris climate agreement; certainly, while the new US administration cannot unilaterally dismantle the 2015 UNFCCC agreement, it can defect from it. On 13 April 2017, the new EPA administrator, Scott Pruitt, a staunch supporter of the fossil fuel industry, stated his opinion that the Paris agreement is "a bad deal" that "we need to exit,"[26] although other forces in the administration were apparently in favour of staying in the agreement but adopting a lower GHG reduction target. Weeks of speculative news coverage followed, indicating a fierce battle was being raged between Paris agreement opponents and defenders both inside and outside the US administration's inner circles.[27]

On 1 June 2017, President Trump announced that the United States would no longer be party to the Agreement. In a press release entitled "America Puts Jobs First," the president laid out the arguments supporting the pullout: the United States had already achieved significant carbon dioxide (CO_2) cuts; additional cuts would be harmful to the economy and cost jobs; the United States was carrying a disproportionate burden of CO_2 reductions relative to other countries; and the Paris Agreement was, in any case, too weak to produce significant reductions globally.[28] The Trudeau government did not mask its disappointment, though it responded diplomatically. The PMO immediately issued a statement in response to the United States' decision to withdraw from the Paris Agreement, noting: "We are deeply disappointed that the United States federal government has decided to withdraw from the Paris Agreement. Canada is unwavering in our commitment to fight climate change and support clean economic growth."[29]

On other climate policy measures, the Trump administration response has been swift and brutal. An Executive Order signed on 28 March 2017 ordered all departments to "review existing regulations that potentially burden the development or use of domestically produced energy resources and appropriately suspend, revise, or rescind those that unduly burden the development of domestic energy resources," with a report on proposed actions to be taken across government in line with this new approach due within months.[30] Obama administration executive orders and reports were also rescinded by President Trump's Climate Action Plan, including provisions on power sector carbon pollution standards and methane emissions, and directives were issued to rework the legal and policy documentation underlying Obama's Clean Power Plan and related regulations. Along with these commitments has come a directive for the director of the Office of Management and Budget to "propose a plan to reorganize governmental functions and eliminate unnecessary agencies ... components of agencies, and agency programs."[31] This has widely been seen as a not-so-veiled attempt to radically reduce the size and power of the EPA.

In the current moment the policy actions taken by the Trump administration greatly complicate Canada's internationalist vision of climate action and its more concrete GHG reduction aspirations. First, given the US decision not to remain under the Paris umbrella, Canada is now in the rather delicate position of underscoring publicly its support for the Agreement and the measures taken under the Agreement, while refraining from open criticism of the Trump administration on its climate policy stances. Here, then, we see the tension between bilateralism and multilateralism. Second, in terms of policy on-the-ground, the Trump administration's orientations on environment, not to mention its very real intent to change the terms of trade in North America through a renegotiation of the North American Free Trade Agreement, have empowered domestic critics of Trudeau's carbon pricing strategy under the Pan-Canadian Framework on Clean Growth and Climate Change, released in 2016. As Saskatchewan Premier Brad Wall announced shortly after Trump's election, "it makes no sense for our federal government to push ahead with imposing a national carbon tax, when our biggest trading partner—and our biggest competitor for investment and jobs—is not going to have one."[32] And he is not alone, as interests in different regions of the country oppose the Framework actions.

Trudeau has said he plans to work with Donald Trump on shared interests, but missing from that list of interests was mention of climate change. The Joint Statement which emerged out of Trudeau's first visit with Trump in February 2017 included a muted reference to more conventional avenues of environmental cooperation: "We also look forward to building on our many areas of environmental cooperation, particularly along our border and at the Great Lakes, and we will continue to work together to enhance the quality of our air and water."[33] One might have expected support for green economic innovation and commercialization to be a politically palatable emphasis for US-Canada relations, given the size of the alternative energy industry in the United States and statements by Trump on green technologies.[34] This could have opened channels for international discussion between the United States and Paris-friendly countries, thereby making Canada's international environmental situation easier. Thus far, however, this approach has had little traction with the Trump administration, focused as it is on fostering fossil fuels.

Yet, even given the hurdles now facing North American and international efforts to address climate pollutants and to support developing countries, it is worth noting that the Trudeau government has not shown any signs of changing its policy commitments, though it might be delaying some initiatives by spreading funding out over a longer time period.[35] And a change in tactics may be underway. While the Canadian government has at many points in the US-Canadian relationship sought to recruit the support of, and coordinate policy with, like-minded US states, this approach appears to be accelerating. Very recently, the Canadian federal government has moved to put in place a national Low Carbon Fuel Standards (LCFS) under the Pan-Canadian Framework on Clean Growth and Climate Change.[36] In following through on its commitment in the Pan-Canadian Framework to "develop a clean fuel standard to reduce emissions from fuels used in transportation, building and industry," Environment and Climate Change Canada has initiated stakeholder involvement via workshops and discussions over late 2016 and 2017. The ECCC has reached out to key decision-makers on California's Air Quality Resources Board (CARB), in order to gain information on the California experience but also with a view to ensuring the inter-operability of a proposed Canadian LCFS with the existing California LCFS.[37] Indeed, a March 2017 Stakeholders Workshop on the Clean Fuel Standard began with a presentation from the Chief of the Transportation Fuel Branch of the California Air Resources Board.[38]

In this case, an increased emphasis on "diagonality" in Canada-US state relations may come to characterize bilateral relations in the coming years. This does not, however, make the bilateral-multilateral balancing act any less delicate as the Trudeau government navigates the new terrain of US-Canada relations; in fact, it may add further diplomatic complications.

THE PULL OF PRAGMATISM: CLIMATE VERSUS ECONOMY?

Those who have closely studied the foundations of the Harper government's environmental diplomacy have argued that its international activities were underlain not so much by a simple retreat from the normative framework associated with the international environmental system, but rather by a conscious "narrowing" of this framework to emphasize

Canada's interests.[39] As Craik and Prior suggest, Canada under Harper moved from a broad acceptance of the principles which underlay climate and other environmental agreements to a weighing of the costs and benefits of particular commitments, that is, "accepting those rules that favour Canada's self-interest and rejecting those that do not."[40] For Harper, self-interest was assessed on the basis of how Canada's economic competitiveness might be impacted by particular international commitments, especially with respect to climate change. This orientation was completely in keeping with the broader policy aims of the Conservative government, namely, an emphasis on getting and keeping Canada's finances in order (particularly after the global economic jolts of 2008–2009) and on growing the economy through aggressive expansion of the oil and gas sector under the umbrella of "Responsible Resource Development."[41]

However, it is important to note that, while the Harper Conservative approach was perhaps more explicit in the way that it portrayed trade-offs between economic well-being and environmental protection, this is a longer-running theme in Canadian environmental policy. Criticisms of the Jean Chrétien/Paul Martin years from 1993 to 2006 also abound; while the pro-climate and pro-global rhetoric was consistent, strong Liberal commitments to trade liberalism, resource promotion, and deficit-fighting overshadowed climate policy. As the federal Commissioner of Environment and Sustainable Development declared in a special report in 2002, "[d]uring this first decade after Rio, our findings have highlighted the serious and recurrent shortcomings in the federal government's efforts to protect the environment and promote sustainable development."[42] Successive federal administrations have been criticized for their inability to integrate climate policy aims into domestic and foreign policy in a horizontal and thorough-going fashion.

The Trudeau Liberals set out to change this pattern. One of the key planks of the Liberal campaign platform was that the economy and environment go hand-in-hand. With a rallying cry of "you can't have a strong economy without a healthy environment," Trudeau has repeatedly argued that Canada had

> allowed other countries to take the lead in the race to create new, high-tech, clean jobs. This [Harper] government has failed to deliver a sensible, credible approach to the environment and the economy … pretending that we have to choose between the two is as harmful as it is wrong. … The Liberal plan will ensure that Canada can tap into the economic opportunities of our environment and create the clean jobs of tomorrow.[43]

Upon assuming power, the Trudeau government has sought to follow through on this vision, weaving commitments to GHG reduction, clean technology promotion, and sustainable practices through international portfolios and policies. The insertion of climate policy obligations into various ministerial mandate letters, as discussed above, is one example. But this marrying of climate/environment and economy also appears in the government's stances on infrastructure funding, pipeline development, and trade promotion.

Trade promotion, and the renewed focus on relations with China, is a good example of the way in which climate and economy are linked in federal policy. The minister of environment and climate change, Catherine McKenna, led a clean technology mission of Canadian businesses to China in December 2016 in order to "deepen clean-energy ties and to help Canadian business capitalize on new opportunities."[44] As international executive vice-chair of the China Council for International Cooperation on Environment and Development, an organization that Canada helped create in 1992, McKenna co-chaired the Council's annual general meeting with China and undertook high-level bilateral meetings aimed at enhancing the range of cooperative clean technology partnerships between the two countries.[45]

However, several developments will likely test the commitment of the Liberals to climate-economy integration. The first leads us, of course, back to Trump. As the US administration considers the imposition of trade and other policy measures, border adjustment taxes on US imports, punitive measures against dairy supply management in Canada, country-of-origin labelling, and nationalist procurement policies—to name just a few—the Liberal government has mobilized the full machinery of the federal government (ministers and senior staff across departments, parliamentarians, business and interest groups, and former politicians and diplomats, not to mention the prime minister himself, who travelled frequently to the United States in 2017) to fan out across Washington and at all levels of government and send a clear message to US policymakers and legislators: the US benefits from access to Canada markets and cross-border trade.[46] And, as the Canadian federal government mobilizes to push back on punitive trade and potentially security measures, climate change appears to have quietly slipped down on the list of priority issues, though it is certainly not off the agenda.

There are two additional conditions that complicate the Trudeau government's ability to marry its climate and economic policies. While it is in any case difficult to argue for the "sustainable development" of pipelines aimed at bringing higher quantities of fossil fuels to foreign markets, the government has argued, beginning on the campaign trail in 2015 and on to the present day, for a "balanced" approach that recognizes the dependence of various regions of the country on oil and gas development at the same time that it signals and follows through on its intent to price carbon and change incentive structures in the industry. Firstly, many climate policy advocates have been quite critical of this stance, seeing pipeline development as incommensurate with effective climate policy. Secondly, it seems clear that financial constraints on the Liberals will pose a challenge for their ability to balance commitments to fostering a green economy and providing funding for green infrastructure, a big-ticket political promise. This will perhaps be further complicated by turbulent economic times ahead, depending on the fallout from US trade and economic actions. Nevertheless, Trudeau's attempts to bring about economic and environmental linkages, such that each benefits, continue to grind through the wheels of government programming, both domestically and in its foreign policy motivations.

Regional Connections and Trade-Offs

In the international climate change game, it is natural for Canada to seek out strategic regional partners as it pursues its aims. Does Canada's recent engagement in Asia mean that its international environmental focus has shifted/should shift to China? Given the enhanced focus on China as a trade partner, natural resource investor, and clean technology ally, wouldn't this be a natural fit? As Catherine McKenna noted before her visit to China:

> Canada has made it a top priority to establish a stronger and long-term relationship with China. As a major player on the world stage, China plays a lead role in accelerating the shift to a clean-growth economy. This clean-energy revolution provides great opportunities for Canada and for Canadian businesses who can offer clean-technology solutions to the world. By working together with key international partners such as China, we can address climate change in a practical way that creates economic growth, good jobs, and a better world for future generations.[47]

The short answer is certainly, but not solely. The Americas, for example, offer several other avenues for cooperative endeavours, most of which lead through Mexico.

Canada and Mexico, particularly since the election of the Trudeau Liberals in 2015, have established a stronger cooperative policy infrastructure in several climate-related areas. The two countries work together on energy efficiency programming through the Canada-Mexico Partnership, the International Partnership for Energy Efficiency Cooperation (IPEEC), and the Canada-Mexico "Fleet Smart" and "Transporter Limpio" programmes. As noted above, the two countries are founding members of the Clean Air Climate Coalition, which focuses on short-lived climate pollutant reductions, oil and gas methane partnerships, and diesel vehicles. Further, Canada and Mexico are also participants in the US-Caribbean-Central American Energy Summit, which works to advance regional energy cooperation and support clean energy integration. The role of the United States in supporting this organization is clearly in question at the present time, though the group could continue regardless. Critically, Mexico is a key partner for Canada in terms of carbon pricing: Mexico has already put in place a carbon tax on fuels, has established a Voluntary Carbon Exchange as a precursor to a mandatory carbon pricing regime, has a full legislative framework for trading in place, and there have been serious discussions about Mexico providing a source of offsets for other carbon markets, including Canada.

Interestingly, subnational cooperation between Canadian provinces and Mexican states may also provide strategic support for Canadian climate policy to reach to southward. At the Climate Summit of the Americas in August 2016, Ontario, Quebec, and Mexico signed a Joint Declaration on Climate Change, intended to support their common commitment to carbon pricing through the sharing of information and expertise and potential cooperation on clean energy innovations.[48] Canadian and Mexican subnational governments are also linked in forums such as the Compact of States and Regions, which engages states and regional governments in fostering climate change mitigation through the development of GHG inventories, target-setting, and programme development.

Looking Forward

As the discussion above highlights, the triad of international environmental policy challenges facing the Trudeau government is interlinked in rather interesting ways. An unpredictable Trump Effect seems likely to spin through, and muddle even further, both Canada's continuing attempts to balance bilateralism and multilateralism as well as the country's more determined attempts to meld environmental sustainability with economic initiatives. Obviously, strategies for working around these challenges must be interlinked.

Of increasing importance will be the ways that the Trudeau government can "work around" the Trump administration to make things happen, without raising animosity as it does so. If we look deeper into the transboundary environmental policy infrastructure that networks the two countries together at multiple levels, the tentacles of the relationship are many and overlapping, which offers possibilities for managing the current, more complex, situation.[49] Robert Pastor, a close observer of North American relations, noted in 2011 that "[b]oth Canada and Mexico have organized their entire governments to deal with the United States. They have little choice given the weight of their neighbour on their economy and society...."[50] On climate policy, these tentacles, including those connecting national and subnational governments, are perhaps less well developed than in other policy areas. It is not clear whether such infrastructure will serve to keep the lines of bilateral communication open as Canada pursues its multilateral climate obligations, or whether these lines will serve to block Canada's more globalist inclinations in this policy area. To this point, however, the Trudeau government has sought to use all avenues and instruments that are available to it, including tapping into bases of knowledge and influence that may not generally be prioritized by Liberal governments.

It seems likely that the Trudeau government will make more progress on some climate and environmental files than others; perhaps not surprisingly, those files that appear most promising for the short and medium term seem linked to cooperative relations both above and below the Trump administration. Certainly, the North American initiatives on clean energy and climate pollutant reductions, which relied on bilateral goodwill, are dead. However, the Liberals have shown no inclination to back away from their domestic initiatives under the Pan-Canadian Framework on Clean Growth and Climate Change, including the carbon pricing programme, clean energy initiatives such as LCFS, and a ratcheting up of emission and efficiency requirements on the transportation sector. As it moves forward with these programmes, the Trudeau government continues to seek strategic partners among US states—and there appears to be goodwill from various subnational neighbours to the south, especially California. Further, carbon pricing is being given some high-level "lift" from the multilateral CPLC. The Trudeau government has also followed through on its commitments for clean energy technology funding; the April 2017 federal budget was heralded as a "watershed moment for the clean-technology industry in Canada," with $2.2 billion in new spending not only on research and development but also on "boosting the demonstration, adoption and export of Canadian energy and environmental technologies."[51] This, in turn, fits well with Canada multilateral and regional strategies, particularly cooperation with China and Mexico.

There are certainly parts of the Trudeau climate platform that may be more suspect. For example, it is not entirely clear what concrete steps the federal government will take towards implementation of its promise to phase out coal-burning power plants by 2030. Moreover, its pipeline aspirations are also likely to continue to prove vexing in terms of the awkward fit with climate politics but also Canada's relations with the United States. Finally, domestic budgetary pressures may work their way through some multilateral commitments, such as funding for developing countries, in less "climate-friendly" ways. This picture will become clearer over the course of successive budgets and policy pronouncements. Without a doubt, this government will need to be highly creative as it moves forward on its climate policy aspirations—and in a context quite different than it likely expected.

NOTES

1. MacDiarmid (2015).
2. Liberal Party of Canada (2015b).
3. Ibid., (2015c).
4. Ibid., (2015a).
5. MacDiarmid (2015).
6. Berthiaume (2014).
7. Ibid. (2015).
8. Office of the Prime Minister of Canada (2015a).

9. Ibid.
10. Office of the Prime Minister of Canada (2017c).
11. For information on the Carbon Pricing Leadership Coalition, please see https://www.carbonpricingleadership.org/
12. Office of the Prime Minister of Canada (2015b).
13. Mas and Cullen (2016).
14. The World Bank (2016).
15. Macdonald (2010, 111–124).
16. Gottlieb (2005).
17. See, for example, Macdonald and Smith (2000, 107–124), Smith (2002, 286–298).
18. Van Nijnatten (2014).
19. Office of the Prime Minister of Canada (2016a).
20. Blanchfield (2016).
21. United States Environmental Protection Agency (2016).
22. Office of the Prime Minister of Canada (2016b).
23. Ibid., (2015).
24. Van Nijnatten and Lopez-Vallej (forthcoming).
25. For information on the Climate & Clean Air Coalition, please see http://www.ccacoalition.org/en/partners
26. Mooney and Dennis (2017).
27. Holland and Volcovici (2017), Milman (2017).
28. The White House (2017c).
29. Office of the Prime Minister of Canada (2017b).
30. The White House (2017b).
31. Ibid., (2017a).
32. CBC News (2016).
33. Office of the Prime Minister of Canada (2017a).
34. For example, Trump sought to reassure European leaders in early June 2017 that America "remains committed to … robust efforts to protect the environment," noting "America's strong record in reducing emissions and leading the development of clean energy technology" (The White House 2017d).
35. Demerse (2017).
36. For information on the Framework, please see https://www.canada.ca/en/services/environment/weather/climatechange/pan-canadian-framework.html
37. Environment and Climate Change Canada (2017a).
38. Ibid., (2017b).
39. Craik and Prior (2016, 197–216).
40. Ibid., 211.
41. Van Nijnatten (2016, XII–XIII).

42. Commissioner of Environment and Sustainable Development (2002).
43. Liberal Party of Canada (2015a).
44. Environment and Climate Change Canada (2016).
45. Office of the Minister of Environment and Climate Change Canada (2016).
46. Wherry (2017).
47. Office of the Minister of Environment and Climate Change Canada (2016).
48. Office of the Premier of Ontario (2016).
49. Craik and Van Nijnatten (2016, 1–40).
50. Pastor (2011).
51. Rand and Hamilton (2017).

References

Berthiaume, Lee. 2014. The man behind the curtain: Why Gerald Butts is Trudeau's most trusted advisor. *Ottawa Citizen*, October 21. http://ottawacitizen.com/news/politics/the-man-behind-the-curtain-why-gerald-butts-is-trudeaus-most-trusted-adviser. Accessed 27 Mar 2017.

———. 2015. A return to multilateralism: Meet Roland Paris, the man behind Justin Trudeau's foreign policy. *National Post*, December 29. http://news.nationalpost.com/news/canada/canadian-politics/a-return-to-multilateralism-meet-roland-paris-the-man-behind-justin-trudeaus-foreign-policy. Accessed 27 Mar 2017.

Blanchfield, Michael. 2016. Justin Trudeau seeks to build momentum as Obama hands him the climate torch. *Huffington Post*, March 11. http://www.huffingtonpost.ca/2016/03/11/obama-hands-trudeau-the-climate-torch-as-prime-minister-seeks-to-build-momentum_n_9436032.html. Accessed 27 Mar 2017.

Carbon Pricing Leadership Coalition. 2017. Why is everyone talking about carbon pricing? Carbon Pricing Leadership Coalition. https://www.carbonpricingleadership.org/. Accessed 4 Oct 2017.

CBC News. 2016. Wall: Trump win shows Canada shouldn't enact carbon tax. *CBC News*, November 9. http://www.cbc.ca/news/canada/saskatchewan/premier-brad-wall-trump-elected-1.3843350. Accessed 30 May 2017.

Commissioner of Environment and Sustainable Development. 2002. The commissioner's perspective – 2002 – the decade after Rio, 2002 report. Office of the Auditor General of Canada. http://www.oag-bvg.gc.ca/internet/English/parl_cesd_200210_00_e_12406.html. Accessed 27 Mar 2017.

Craik, Neil, and Tahnee Prior. 2016. Retreat from principle: Canada and the system of international environmental law. In *Canadian environmental policy and politics: The challenges of austerity and ambivalence*, ed. Debora L. Van Nijnatten, 197–216. Don Mills: Oxford University Press.

Craik, Neil, and Debora Van Nijnatten. 2016. Bundled' transgovernmental networks, agency autonomy and regulatory cooperation in North America. *North Carolina Journal of International Law* XLI: 1–40.

Demerse, Clare. 2017. Despite Trump, Canada's budget stays the course on climate change. Clean Energy Canada, March 22. http://cleanenergycanada.org/despite-trump-canadas-budget-stays-course-climate-change/. Accessed 22 June 2017.

Environment and Climate Change Canada. 2016. Remarks from the Honorable Catherine McKenna, Minister of Environment and Climate Change at the Toronto region board of trade. Environment and Climate Change Canada, November 25. https://www.bot.com/Portals/0/NewsDocuments/1125201 6Canada%E2%80%99s%20Strategy%20for%20a%20Clean%20Growth%20 Century.pdf. Accessed 1 Apr 2017.

———. 2017a. Clean fuel standard: Discussion paper. Environment and Climate Change Canada, February. http://www.ec.gc.ca/lcpe-cepa/D7C913BB-13D0-42AF-9BC7-FBC1580C2F4B/CFS_discussion_paper_2017-02-24-eng.pdf. Accessed 15 May 2017.

———. 2017b. Environment and Climate Change Canada. Clean Fuel Standard Workshop, March 6. https://drive.google.com/drive/folders/0B0uMvHfE8 C2uTEYzZnhOZEhMaFU. Accessed 10 Aug 2017.

Gottlieb, Allan. 2005. Romanticism and realism in Canada's foreign policy. Policy Options, February 1. http://policyoptions.irpp.org/magazines/canada-in-the-world/romanticism-and-realism-in-canadas-foreign-policy/. Accessed 4 Apr 2017.

Liberal Party of Canada. 2015a. Real change: A new plan for Canada's environment and economy. Liberal Party of Canada. https://www.liberal.ca/wp-content/uploads/2015/08/A-new-plan-for-Canadas-environment-and-economy.pdf. Accessed 28 Mar 2017.

———. 2015b. Real change: Canada's leadership in the world. Liberal Party of Canada. https://www.liberal.ca/realchange/canadas-leadership-in-the-world/. Accessed 28 Mar 2017.

———. 2015c. Real change: Climate change. Liberal Party of Canada. https://www.liberal.ca/realchange/climate-change/. Accessed 28 Mar 2017.

MacDiarmid, Margaret. 2015. Trudeau team looks to put new face on Canada's climate policy. *CBC News*, October 23. Available at: http://www.cbc.ca/news/politics/trudeau-government-environment-paris-climate-conference-1.3286345. Accessed 27 Mar 2017.

Macdonald, Laura. 2010. A fine balance: Multilateralism and bilateralism in Canadian policy in the North American region. *Canadian Foreign Policy* 16 (2): 111–124.

Macdonald, Douglas, and Heather Smith. 2000. Promises made, promises broken: Questioning Canada's commitments to climate change. *International Journal* 55 (1): 107–124.

Mas, Susana, and Catherine Cullen. 2016. Justin Trudeau signs Paris climate treaty at UN, vows to harness renewable energy. *CBC News*, April 22. http://www.cbc.ca/news/politics/paris-agreement-trudeau-sign-1.3547822. Accessed 12 Apr 2017.

Milman, Oliver. 2017. Trump aides postpone meeting as clashes over Paris climate deal continue. *The Guardian*, May 9. https://www.theguardian.com/us-news/2017/may/09/paris-climate-deal-trump-advisers. Accessed 20 July 2017.

Mooney, Chris, and Brady Dennis. 2017. Scott Pruitt calls for an 'exit' from the Paris accord, sharpening the Trump administration climate rift. *Washington Post*, April 14. https://www.washingtonpost.com/news/energy-environment/wp/2017/04/14/trumps-epa-chief-scott-pruitt-calls-for-an-exit-to-the-paris-climate-agreement/?utm_term=.a4e10330c0b3. Accessed 15 Apr 2017.

Office of the Minister of Environment and Climate Change Canada. 2016. Canada's Minister of Environment and Climate Change leads clean-technology business delegation to China and meets with the China Council for International Cooperation on Environment and Development. Office of the Minister of Environment and Climate Change Canada, December 3. http://news.gc.ca/web/article-en.do?nid=1164579. Accessed 6 Apr 2017.

Office of the Premier of Ontario. 2016. Ontario working with Québec and Mexico to advance carbon markets: Province signs joint declaration on climate change in Guadalajara. Office of the Premier of Ontario, August 31. https://news.ontario.ca/opo/en/2016/08/ontario-working-with-quebec-and-mexico-to-advance-carbon-markets.html. Accessed 25 Mar 2017.

Office of the Prime Minister of Canada. 2015a. Minister of Environment and Climate Change mandate letter. Prime Minister's Office. http://pm.gc.ca/eng/minister-environment-and-climate-change-mandate-letter. Accessed 28 Mar 2017.

———. 2015b. Prime Minister announced investment in global climate change action. Prime Minister's Office, November 27. http://www.pm.gc.ca/eng/news/2015/11/27/prime-minister-announces-investment-global-climate-change-action. Accessed 10 Apr 2017.

———. 2016a. US-Canada Joint Statement on Climate, Energy and Arctic Leadership. Prime Minister's Office, March 10. http://pm.gc.ca/eng/news/2016/03/10/us-canada-joint-statement-climate-energy-and-arctic-leadership. Accessed 11 Apr 2017.

———. 2016b. Leaders statement on a North American Climate, Clean Energy and Environment Partnership. Prime Minister's Office, June 29. http://pm.gc.ca/eng/news/2016/06/29/leaders-statement-north-american-climate-clean-energy-and-environment-partnership. Accessed 13 Apr 2017.

———. 2017a. Joint statement from President Donald J. Trump and Prime Minister Justin Trudeau. Prime Minister's Office, February 13. http://pm.gc.ca/eng/news/2017/02/13/joint-statement-president-donald-j-trump-and-prime-minister-justin-trudeau. Accessed 5 May 2017.

———. 2017b. Statement by the Prime Minister of Canada in response to the United States' decision to withdraw from the Paris Agreement. Prime Minister's Office, June 1. http://pm.gc.ca/eng/news/2017/06/01/statement-prime-minister-canada-response-united-states-decision-withdraw-paris. Accessed 1 Apr 2017.

———. 2017c. Minister of Foreign Affairs mandate letter. Prime Minister's Office. http://pm.gc.ca/eng/minister-foreign-affairs-mandate-letter. Accessed 28 Mar 2017.

Pastor, Robert A. 2011. *The North American idea: A vision of a continental future*. New York: Oxford University Press.

Rand, Tom, and Tyler Hamilton. 2017. Federal budget sets new standard for Canadian clean tech. *Globe and Mail*, April 3. https://www.theglobeandmail.com/report-on-business/rob-commentary/federal-budget-sets-new-standard-for-canadian-clean-tech/article34566088/. Accessed 25 July 2017.

Smith, Heather. 2002. Dollar discourse: The devaluation of Canada's natural capital in Canadian climate change policy. In *Canadian environmental policy: Context and cases*, ed. Debora L. Van Nijnatten and Robert Boardman, 2nd ed., 286–298. Don Mills: Oxford University Press.

Steve, Holland, and Valerie Volcovici. 2017. Trump advisers to debate Paris climate agreement. *Reuters*, May. https://www.scientificamerican.com/article/trump-advisers-to-debate-paris-climate-agreement/. Accessed 20 Aug 2017.

The White House, Office of the Press Secretary. 2017a. Presidential executive order on a comprehensive plan for reorganizing the executive branch. The White House, Office of the Press Secretary, March 13. https://www.whitehouse.gov/the-press-office/2017/03/13/presidential-executive-order-comprehensive-plan-reorganizing-executive. Accessed 11 Apr 2017.

———. 2017b. Presidential executive order on promoting energy independence and economic growth. The White House, Office of the Press Secretary, March 28. https://www.whitehouse.gov/the-press-office/2017/03/28/presidential-executive-order-promoting-energy-independence-and-economi-1. Accessed 1 Apr 2017.

———. 2017c. America puts jobs first. The White House, Office of the Press Secretary, June 1. https://www.whitehouse.gov/the-press-office/2017/06/01/president-trump-puts-american-jobs-first. Accessed 15 July 2017.

———. 2017d. Readout of President Donald J. Trump's telephone calls with Chancellor Angela Merkel of Germany, President Emmanuel Macron of France, Prime Minister Justin Trudeau of Canada, and Prime Minister Theresa May of the United Kingdom. The White House, Office of the Press Secretary, June 1. https://www.whitehouse.gov/the-press-office/2017/06/01/readout-president-donald-j-trumps-telephone-calls-chancellor-angela. Accessed 15 July 2017.

The World Bank. 2016. Leaders set landmark global goals for carbon pricing pollution. *World Bank News Release*, April 21. http://www.worldbank.org/en/news/press-release/2016/04/21/leaders-set-landmark-global-goals-for-pricing-carbon-pollution. Accessed 12 Apr 2017.

United States Environmental Protection Agency. 2016. Statement from ECCC Minister Catherine McKenna and EPA Administrator Gina McCarthy. Office of the Administrator, April 7. https://www.epa.gov/newsreleases/statement-eccc-minister-catherine-mckenna-and-epa-administrator-gina-mccarthy. Accessed 10 Apr 2017.

Van Nijnatten, Debora. 2014. Environmental policy in Canada and the United States: Climate change and continuing distinctiveness. In *Differences that count*, ed. David Biette and David Thomas, 4th ed., 340–360. Toronto: University of Toronto Press.

———. 2016. Introduction. In *Canadian environmental policy and politics: The challenges of austerity and ambivalence*, ed. Debora L. Van Nijnatten, XII–XIII. Don Mills: Oxford University Press.

Van Nijnatten, Debora, and Marcela Lopez-Vallejo. forthcoming. Canada-United States relations and a low-carbon economy for North America? In *Transboundary environmental governance across the world's longest border*, ed. Stephen Brooks and Andrea Olive. East Lansing: Co-publication of the Michigan State University Press and the University of Manitoba Press.

Wherry, Aaron. 2017. Trudeau sends more ministers to U.S. amid NAFTA and border tax worries. *CBC News*, April 18. http://www.cbc.ca/news/politics/liberals-ministers-united-states-nafta-1.4073017. Accessed 18 Apr 2017.

CHAPTER 7

International Trade: The Rhetoric and Reality of the Trudeau Government's Progressive Trade Agenda

Meredith B. Lilly

Justin Trudeau's Liberals swept to power in October 2015 on the promise of being radically different from the previous Conservative government under Stephen Harper. The Conservative government had been a strong proponent of international trade, concluding nine new trade agreements with nearly 40 countries between 2006 and 2015. Notably, the Conservatives concluded agreements with the 28 nations of the European Union (EU), and with South Korea, as well as a handful of smaller trade deals.[1]

So resolute was Stephen Harper's belief in, and defence of, international trade that he took the extraordinary step of finalizing Trans-Pacific Partnership (TPP) negotiations during the writ period of the 2015 federal election campaign, just two weeks before election day.[2] Unlike Canada's free-trade election of 1988, in which Conservative Prime Minister Brian Mulroney staked his political future on implementing Canada's first

M. B. Lilly (✉)
Carleton University, Ottawa, ON, Canada

© The Author(s) 2018
N. Hillmer, P. Lagassé (eds.), *Justin Trudeau and Canadian Foreign Policy*, Canada and International Affairs,
https://doi.org/10.1007/978-3-319-73860-4_7

free-trade agreement with the United States,[3] the 2015 election was not a proxy referendum on the benefits of free trade. Public support for free trade among Canadians had grown and was generally non-controversial.[4] Despite the Conservatives' election defeat, the result was not attributed to opposition to trade or Harper's management of the trade portfolio.

Justin Trudeau's 2015 campaign platform contained few specific trade commitments to either guide or constrain the Liberals' governance on international trade following the election. The platform loosely committed to building trade relations with emerging economies, such as India and China, and to developing stronger export capacity in green technologies. The Liberals declined to take a position on Harper's move to finalize the TPP, opting instead to consult Canadians if elected.[5] While in opposition, the Liberals supported the Canada-EU Comprehensive Economic and Trade Agreement (CETA),[6] compelling them to continue the ratification process once elected.

This chapter outlines the Liberals' trade policies during their first 18 months in power from November 2015 to April 2017. It outlines the Liberal government's efforts to shift away from merely implementing the previous Conservative government's initiatives to gradually developing its own "progressive" trade agenda. I argue that the unexpected election of Donald Trump to the US presidency in 2016 severely disrupted the Liberals' momentum toward realizing this progressive agenda, requiring Trudeau to prioritize the North American trade relationship above other interests. Finally, I discuss the importance of Canada's approach to free trade with China as a test of the Liberals' depth of commitment to this new progressive agenda moving forward.

Transitioning from the Conservative Government's Achievements

Unlike many policy areas, the international trade portfolio experienced little disruption during the Liberals' first months in office. Indeed, Prime Minister Trudeau's November 2015 mandate letter to the newly appointed trade minister, Chrystia Freeland, did not include any unique or new initiatives for the trade portfolio. Freeland was tasked with continuing all of the Harper government's initiatives: ratify CETA, implement newly completed agreements with Israel, Chile, and Ukraine, and consult Canadians on the TPP. The letter further tasked the minister with encouraging exports and foreign investment and supporting other ministers to do the same in their areas of responsibility (innovation, culture, green technologies, and development financing). Following this mandate, Minister Freeland focused her first six months in office on two files: TPP consultations and CETA's ratification.

The Liberals launched TPP consultations immediately upon assuming office in November 2015. When Chrystia Freeland signed TPP on behalf of Canada during the consultation phase in February 2016, she issued a statement pointedly noting that "signing does not equal ratifying" and merely represented a technical step in the process.[7] Similarly, when Canadian trade officials issued an economic evaluation in September of 2016 indicating that TPP would be beneficial to the Canadian economy,[8] the Liberal government had yet to officially endorse the deal, nor had they released the results of the public consultations.

Justin Trudeau indicated positive signals on TPP,[9] and it was widely believed his government would ratify the agreement following its approval in the US Congress, which never happened. The Obama administration's failure to push TPP through Congress in 2016 meant the deal's future hung in the balance of the US presidential election that fall. Immediately upon assuming office in January 2017, President Donald Trump withdrew the United States from TPP, effectively killing the deal. Despite efforts by remaining TPP partners to continue the pursuit of a deal without the United States, Canada remained largely on the sidelines of this endeavour.

With respect to CETA's ratification, Canada's new trade minister took a greater activist approach, engaging the Europeans early and effectively. Before the Liberals were even elected in 2015, the European Commission began to face opposition from its own member states—notably Germany— over the agreement's investor-state dispute settlement (ISDS) provisions. The debate was largely internal to Europe, rather than a dispute between Canada and Europe. For example, much of the debate surrounding ISDS stemmed from fears about Europe's trade negotiations with the United States via the Transatlantic Trade and Investment Partnership (TTIP) and the perception that major US companies would use CETA-like ISDS provisions in TTIP to undermine the health and safety of Europeans.[10] As anti-globalization sentiment gained momentum in Europe, CETA's ISDS chapter became a proxy target for such concerns. In 2015, EU Trade Commissioner Cecilia Malmström famously quipped that ISDS had become the "most toxic acronym in Europe."[11]

Freeland and Canada's long-standing chief negotiator for CETA, Steve Verheul, worked diligently with EU counterparts to address Europe's concerns. Negotiations were kept quiet and labelled part of the "legal scrub" to avoid reopening other parts of the agreement, with Canada ultimately accepting Europe's revised proposal.[12] The revised ISDS mechanism created a standing panel of independently appointed members to arbitrate cases as well as a separate appeal process.[13] These amendments were part of a broader effort, led by Malmström, to embed similar ISDS provisions in all of Europe's trade agreements moving forward, especially with the United States. As the first G7 country to accept the EU's proposal, Canada's agreement represented a major achievement for the EU and its goal of setting the standards for ISDS provisions globally. Over time, Malmström intends to supplant CETA's own ISDS mechanism with a permanent multilateral investment court.[14]

Although the amendments made to CETA's ISDS provisions under Trudeau's Liberal government are both important and substantive, they represent a tiny fraction of the overall agreement. Furthermore, the degree to which these amendments represent genuine solutions to the broader debates surrounding ISDS continues to be debated.[15] Claims that Freeland's team also modified CETA to better protect the rights of states to regulate in the public interest[16] are not supported by the evidence. Previous draft versions of the CETA text, as well as analysis produced by the EU prior to 2015, verify that the agreement negotiated under Canada's previous Conservative government already fully protected the rights of states to regulate in the public interest.[17] Rather, Freeland's 2016 emphasis on this issue was primarily a communication tactic to assuage a European audience that has grown leery of CETA as a precursor to Europe's trade agreement with the United States.

Despite the Liberals' minor policy contribution to finalizing the text of the agreement, their successful efforts to gain support among Europeans represented a major achievement for the government. For example, in her 2016 tour to promote CETA to European leaders, Freeland outlined the ways in which the Canadian society and the CETA agreement reflected elements of EU Trade Commissioner Malmström's 2014 "Trade for All" strategy.[18] Freeland touted CETA's progressive approach to labour protections, environmental standards, ISDS, and the rights of states to regulate in the public interest.[19] In December 2016, Freeland told an audience of Toronto business leaders that the communication of Canada's progressive values in her view played an important part in CETA's successful ratification: "We were able to make the case, based on who we are, that Canada is a progressive country with progressive values which would make a good partner for the EU. By the way, our diversity was an essential element there."[20]

Despite several tense weeks in the fall of 2016 resulting from opposition to CETA by Wallonia, a subnational region of Belgium, Freeland's efforts were ultimately successful: CETA was signed in October 2016 and ratified by the EU Parliament in February 2017. Although much attention has been paid to a Joint Interpretive Declaration[21] signed between the EU and Canada at that time, it was largely a political gesture for both sides and was not associated with changes to the agreement's text. Despite this, the events in Wallonia did result in CETA's investment chapter being placed on its own delayed implementation schedule, requiring first an opinion from the European Court of Justice on whether the ISDS provisions fall under the EU's exclusive jurisdiction. This latter issue has been overshadowed, but is arguably more important since it will leave CETA without any legal ISDS mechanism until resolved.[22]

Notwithstanding the clear and heavy influence of CETA's ratification on Canada's progressive trade rhetoric, the Liberals have repeatedly claimed that progressive trade is central to their broader trade agenda. If that is the case, what does progressive trade mean and imply for Canadian trade policy moving forward?

Progressive Trade: Policy or Politics?

Influenced by her previous journalism career in which she wrote a book[23] focused on the relationship between globalization and income inequality, Freeland was instrumental in applying Malmström's progressive trade ideas to the Canadian context. In 2016, Freeland began to advance a deliberate trade strategy that links Canadian progressive social policies with increasingly liberalized trade. In her address to the Conference of Montreal in June 2016, Freeland outlined her vision for progressive trade as a counterweight to populist-oriented protectionism and the "attack on open society" she believed was occurring in the United States and Europe.[24] She explicitly viewed populist hostility toward globalization, technological advancement, and immigration as components of a single phenomenon that could be counteracted by Canadians through commitments to immigration, open society, and progressive trade.

In that speech and elsewhere, Freeland explicitly linked the wellbeing of the "middle class" to this progressive trade agenda, advocating for the expansion of domestic social programmes such as child benefits and pension benefits to ensure that free trade could benefit "everyone," rather than a narrow class of "elites."[25] This alignment of progressive trade to the expansionist and redistributive role of government tied Freeland's policy direction more closely with the broader Liberal government's campaign commitments targeting the middle-class and its overall vision for governance.[26] As foreign affairs minister, Freeland has synthesized these sentiments into her broader vision for Canadian foreign policy priorities.[27]

Although Freeland was the architect of Canada's new progressive trade agenda, Prime Minister Trudeau fully supported the vision she outlined. In his 2017 address to the EU Parliament upon CETA's ratification, Trudeau reiterated Freeland's approach:

> Now, we live in a time when some people are worried that the current system only benefits society's narrow elite. And their concern is valid. This anxiety towards the economy and trade – the worry that our kids won't have access to the same jobs and opportunities that we have – can be addressed only if we ensure that trade is inclusive, and that everyone benefits. And this agreement – the Comprehensive Economic and Trade Agreement – is a terrific example of just that. Because, at its heart, CETA is a framework for trade that works for everyone.[28]

Later in the speech, Trudeau again referenced the elements of CETA that reflect Canada's "truly progressive trade agenda": the rights of states to regulate in the public interest, labour protections, "responsible" investment provisions, and environmental standards.

It remains to be seen what this progressive trade agenda will mean—if anything—for Canada's approach to international trade negotiations moving forward. From a policy perspective, the difficulty facing the Trudeau government's choice to highlight CETA as the "gold-standard" of progressive trade is that—notwithstanding a handful of revised pages in the 1600-page document—*all* of the elements the Liberals reference as being "progressive" were reflected in the CETA text negotiated by the previous Conservative government. In addition, many of those elements are reflected in other Canadian trade treaties, including the Canada-Korea Free Trade Agreement as well as the defunct Trans-Pacific Partnership. In fact, Canada's shift to comprehensive trade agreements has occurred incrementally over decades, influenced as much by the capacity and ambition of Canada's trading partners as our own domestic factors. In this way, it can be convincingly argued that *if* CETA is the embodiment of Canada's progressive trade policy, then Canadians should expect very little of policy substance to change under the Liberal government compared to the previous Conservative one.

If, however, as Freeland has suggested, CETA was intended to be a launching point for the Liberals to pursue an increasingly more progressive trade agenda over time,[29] the plan was severely disrupted by the election of President Trump in November 2016. To better understand the influence that Trump's election has had on Canada's broader trade agenda, we turn now to Canada's trade relations with the United States.

DONALD TRUMP'S DISRUPTION OF CANADA-US RELATIONS

Despite the overwhelmingly positive tone of bilateral relations between the newly elected Trudeau government and the US administration led by President Barack Obama, little if any meaningful progress was made on key bilateral trade issues during Trudeau's first year in office. For example, during their bilateral meetings in March and June of 2016, Trudeau and Obama were unable to reach a solution on the soon-to-expire softwood lumber agreement,[30] nor did Trudeau seek to revisit Obama's rejection of the Keystone XL pipeline. For Canada's part, Trudeau's government refused to take an official position on TPP, despite strong urging by Obama.[31]

One year into Trudeau's mandate, Donald Trump was unexpectedly elected president of the United States, shocking many and disrupting the Trudeau government's preparations for a Hillary Clinton victory. Trump had vowed to withdraw from TPP, renegotiate the North American Free Trade Agreement (NAFTA), and pursue "America first" protectionism. In defiance of the trends in technological automation that contributed to manufacturing job losses in the United States, Trump planned to restore American jobs through reshoring and addressing barriers to US exports. Although Mexico was Trump's primary North American target, Canada would certainly be impacted. In addition, Trump's broader border policies risked badly sideswiping Canadian trade interests.[32] In effect, Trump's unexpected electoral victory posed the largest challenge to Canada-US trade relations in more than two decades. The only bright spot for Canada-US relations was Trump's approval of the Keystone XL pipeline,[33] a mixed blessing for Trudeau that could only complicate his government's delicately crafted domestic roll-out of other pipeline approvals balanced with environmental protection initiatives.

Given that nearly 75 per cent of Canadian exports were to the United States,[34] Trudeau's government was forced to immediately prioritize the Canada-US trade relationship above other interests. In January 2017, Chrystia Freeland was appointed minister of foreign affairs, but would also retain the NAFTA portfolio to ensure a streamlined approach to bilateral relations with the United States.[35] The thrust of Trudeau's bilateral efforts in the early days of the Trump administration was to underscore the importance of Canada to American economic interests and the balanced trading relationship. The strategy appeared to be successful at first and, during Trudeau's visit to Washington in February 2017, Trump underscored the important and positive bilateral relationship.[36]

However, in the months that followed Trudeau's visit, relations deteriorated. In April 2017, Trump publicly attacked NAFTA, singling out unfair trading practices by Canadian dairy and softwood lumber sectors. The following week, US Commerce Secretary Wilbur Ross introduced punitive tariffs averaging 20 per cent on Canadian softwood lumber imports to the United States over long-standing US complaints regarding Canadian subsidies.[37] Days later, Trump mused publicly about withdrawing from NAFTA entirely, only to reverse course the following day.[38] A few weeks after that, US Trade Representative Robert Lighthizer formally notified Congress of his intention to renegotiate NAFTA beginning in August 2017.[39] This rapid succession of negative statements and actions toward Canada very quickly erased any remaining optimism that the Trump administration would not target Canada in NAFTA negotiations.

Uncertainty remains high among Canadian policymakers and business leaders about what aspects of NAFTA will be reopened when negotiations begin. Lighthizer's May 2017 letter to Congress[40] referenced the inclusion of several chapters that were not covered in NAFTA, including digital trade, labour, and environment provisions: these are items on which Canada and the United States could likely agree through the adoption of previously negotiated chapters from TPP.[41] However, it is difficult to predict how some of the other items listed by Lighthizer will be scoped in any negotiating mandate. For Canada's part, the fact that TPP was negotiated by a previous Conservative government gives Trudeau some leverage when negotiating the same issues for NAFTA. Never having adopted an official position on the United States-led TPP, Trudeau's team can embrace elements of the deal that further Canadian interests while distancing itself from others.

Setting aside the substance of negotiations, it is clear that NAFTA's unexpected re-emergence in the policymaking sphere placed the Trudeau government on its heels. No longer in control of its own trade agenda, the Trudeau government will be focused on NAFTA and trade relations with the United States for the remainder of its mandate. Ultimately, Mexico's electoral calendar will have a major influence on the direction and level of ambition for negotiations. If negotiations extend into 2018—a virtual certainty—little progress is likely to be made before Mexico's presidential election and the United States's own mid-term elections sidetrack talks. By extension, Canada's 2019 election could become a referendum on Trudeau's success at managing NAFTA negotiations with Trump and the Canada-US relationship overall.

This reality has a series of downstream effects on Canada's other trade relationships, including bilateral negotiations with China. It also reduces the likelihood of initiating or resuming negotiations with other trade partners, notably stalled talks with India. For example, Canada's newly appointed trade minister, François-Philippe Champagne, was issued a restricted mandate focused primarily on implementing existing initiatives and starting exploratory discussions with China.[42]

The Trudeau government's progressive trade agenda has been deeply influenced by Trump's election. In his February 2017 visit to the White House, Trudeau predictably abandoned the language of "inclusion" and "progressive trade" in favour of defending "middle-class" workers on both sides of the border.[43] Nevertheless, despite the clear shift in orientation toward the United States, Minister Champagne has continued actively to promote the progressive trade agenda,[44] especially with other internationalist governments. The degree to which this rhetoric addresses a political goal versus a genuine policy objective remains to be seen. In this respect, Canada's trade negotiations with China will become an important test of the Trudeau government's commitment to deepening and expanding the progressive trade agenda beyond CETA. We turn now to the only area of the Trudeau government's trade agenda that represents a major departure from the previous Conservative government's trade agenda: Trudeau's approach to China.

Will Trudeau Pursue Progressive Trade with China?

The Conservatives, led by Stephen Harper, made incremental progress on trade relations with China: they concluded and implemented a Foreign Investment Protection and Promotion Agreement[45]; established a renminbi trading hub in Toronto, the first in the Americas[46]; and oversaw a more than $40 billion expansion in bilateral trade and investment between 2009 and 2014.[47] Nevertheless, overall progress by Harper on trade with China was constrained by a perceived inconsistent foreign policy toward the Chinese more broadly.[48] For example, the Harper government severely restricted the ability of state-owned enterprises to acquire Canadian oil sands following the 2012 takeover of Nexen by a Chinese state-owned firm, a move seen as singling out China.[49]

In 2015, Canada was among a handful of developed economies *not* to join China's $100 billion Asian Infrastructure Investment Bank (AIIB) as a founding member. While some regarded this as another snub by the Conservatives toward China,[50] others have suggested that Canada was merely being prudent. For example, President Barack Obama was deeply opposed to the bank and no other countries in the Americas joined at that time.[51] Furthermore, since no infrastructure projects based outside of Asia were eligible for loans through the bank, Canada had better options for infrastructure investment that could benefit Canadians directly.[52]

Justin Trudeau's government resolved to approach China differently and to build broad bilateral and trade relations, like previous Liberal governments led by Jean Chrétien and Paul Martin.[53] During his September 2016 visit to China, Prime Minister Trudeau announced that Canada would apply to join the AIIB; the bank subsequently granted Canada provisional membership in March 2017.[54] This was done to advance bilateral relations rather than to offer any real economic benefit to Canadians, since the bank's rules already allowed Canadian companies to compete for contracts and projects financed through the bank regardless of Canada's membership status.[55] Furthermore, Canada's capital contribution of $256 million[56] provides negligible influence over the bank's investment decisions.[57]

The most significant development occurred a few weeks after Trudeau's visit to Beijing when Chinese Premier Li visited Canada and the two countries agreed to launch exploratory free-trade talks.[58] It is noteworthy that this announcement was made during the 2016 US presidential campaign, when Hillary Clinton was expected to win. Not surprisingly, since Trump assumed office, the Trudeau government has dramatically scaled back its public promotion of trade talks with China. For example, contrary to expectations, Chrystia Freeland's May 2017 speech outlining Canada's foreign policy priorities made no mention of free trade with China.[59] Some believe Trump's anti-NAFTA rhetoric highlights an urgent need for Canada to diversify its trade relationship with China.[60] Others argue that any move to launch formal bilateral negotiations with China while NAFTA is under threat only strengthens China's negotiating power while simultaneously undermining Canada-US relations.[61]

Negative public opinion among Canadians about trade with China is another challenge facing the Trudeau government.[62] Canadians' concerns about free trade with China stem primarily from non-economic factors such as China's undemocratic nature and lack of respect for human rights.[63] In March 2017, the Liberal government quietly launched a 90-day public consultation period on a potential free-trade agreement with China. Included was the following reference to the concerns of Canadians:

> Canadians may have concerns about China, including issues relating to the environment, labour, gender equality, rule of law and human rights. Canada's comprehensive dialogue with China is central to a healthy relationship and allows Canada to relay the concerns of Canadians and to engage with a country that hosts one sixth of the world's population. A free trade agreement with China would not deter Canada from urging and working with China to meet its international obligations in these areas. As Canada pursues future trade agreements, it will ensure policy flexibility is reserved to protect the health, safety and environment of Canadians.[64]

This acknowledgement of public unease by the government is uncharacteristic of such notices.

Should formal bilateral negotiations proceed, the scope and direction of the negotiating mandate will provide an important indication of the Liberal government's commitment to a broader progressive trade agenda. In March 2017, Canada's ambassador to China, John McCallum (a former Trudeau Cabinet minister), was quoted in the press as indicating that any trade agreement with China would include chapters on human rights and labour protections. This was in response to statements from Beijing suggesting that China would seek to exclude these issues from negotiations, as well as preventing limits on Chinese investments in Canada.[65] If

Trudeau pursues a strategy for China that downgrades Canada's comprehensive approach to trade that is reflected in the CETA, TPP, and Korea trade agreements, the Liberals' commitment to progressive trade will be fundamentally questioned.

Canada's approach to trade with China will have broader consequences for the Trudeau government's strategy for other Asian countries as well, especially Japan, which aims to press forward on TPP without the United States. While Canada and Mexico would be challenged to ratify TPP in its current state without the United States (due to competing provisions in NAFTA), there is strategic value for Canada in remaining at the TPP table. Asia will continue to be the world's most dynamic and fast-growing economic region for decades to come, and Canada's efforts to diversify trade relationships with several Asian partners can act as a counterweight to overreliance on any single large market, be it the United States or China. In this respect, it will be interesting to observe whether Champagne and his team seek to make greater inroads with the Association of Southeast Asian Nations (ASEAN) or bilaterally with Japan.

Conclusion

This chapter has outlined the Trudeau government's approach to international trade during its first year and a half in power. It has outlined steps the Liberal government has taken gradually to transition from implementing the previous Conservative government's plan to pursuing its own progressive trade agenda. The unexpected election of Donald Trump to the US presidency undermined the Liberals' strategy, requiring Trudeau's government to prioritize the Canada-US trade relationship above all other interests.

Should the Liberal government succeed in pursuing new and truly "progressive" trade initiatives, they will be small in scope and focused primarily on developing economies via the international development portfolio. For example, Chrystia Freeland and the international development minister, Marie-Claude Bibeau, have unveiled Canada's new feminist international assistance policy, which references support for progressive trade, "inclusive growth that works for everyone," and promotes women's entrepreneurship and small business development in Africa.[66]

If circumstances allow, there may be room for Canada to establish a more progressive trade agenda among like-minded developed economies over the long term. Should the EU gain traction for its initiative to establish a multilateral investment court to arbitrate ISDS claims, Canadian participation would represent support for continuing globalization and multilateralism. However, new approaches to trade require willing partners and the current global context is less open to further liberalization than to retrenchment and protectionism. For Canada's largest and most important trading partner to the south, maintaining status quo trade arrangements will be difficult enough. The years ahead will determine whether the Liberal government's progressive trade agenda is a long-term policy approach that was temporarily blown off course or whether it is merely a symbolic effort that has already peaked.

Notes

1. Harper government bilateral agreements were also completed with Ukraine, Honduras, Colombia, Peru, Jordan, and Panama, as well as the four-country pact with non-EU countries in Europe (Iceland, Liechtenstein, Norway, and Switzerland).
2. Conservative Party of Canada (2015).
3. Then Liberal leader John Turner and NDP leader Ed Broadbent both opposed the free-trade agreement with the United States during the "free-trade election" of 1988.
4. Gravelle (2014, 453–474).
5. Liberal Party of Canada (2015b).
6. Ibid. (2013).
7. Global Affairs Canada (2016e).
8. Ibid. (2016d).
9. Prime Minister of Canada (2016a).
10. Bierbrauer (2014), European Commission (2014b).
11. Ames (2015).
12. Von Der Burchard (2016), Reinisch and Stifter (2016), Lévesque (2016).
13. VanDuzer (2016), Lévesque (2016).
14. European Commission (2015, 2016).
15. Schneiderman (2016), VanDuzer (2016).
16. Global Affairs Canada (2016a, b).
17. Bierbrauer (2014), European Commission (2014a, b).
18. European Commission (2014b).
19. Global Affairs Canada (2016a).
20. Ibid. (2016c).
21. Council of the European Union (2016).
22. Biel and Wheeler (2016).
23. Freeland (2012).

24. Global Affairs Canada (2016a).
25. Ibid. (2016b, c).
26. Liberal Party of Canada (2015a).
27. Global Affairs Canada (2017c).
28. Prime Minister of Canada (2017a).
29. Global Affairs Canada (2016a).
30. Prime Minister of Canada (2016b).
31. Ibid. (2016a).
32. Lilly (2017).
33. White House Office of the Press Secretary (2017).
34. Simoes and Hildago (2017).
35. Prime Minister of Canada (2017c).
36. Ibid. (2017b).
37. Graham (2017).
38. Schlesinger and Nicholas (2017).
39. United States Trade Representative (2017).
40. Ibid.
41. Lilly (2017).
42. Prime Minister of Canada (2017d).
43. Ibid. (2017b).
44. Global Affairs Canada (2017a, b).
45. Ibid. (2017d).
46. Finance Canada (2015).
47. McCormick (2017, 474–495).
48. Burton (2015, 45–63), McCormick (2017, 474–495).
49. Dobson and Evans (2016).
50. Paltiel (2016, 40–53).
51. Brazil applied to join as a founding member of the Asian Infrastructure Investment Bank, but did not ratify its membership, possibly due to the required capital contribution.
52. Lilly (2016).
53. Burton (2015, 45–63).
54. Asian Infrastructure Investment Bank (2017a).
55. Ibid. (2015).
56. Finance Canada (2017).
57. Asian Infrastructure Investment Bank (2017b).
58. Prime Minister of Canada (2016c).
59. Global Affairs Canada (2017c).
60. Massot (2016).
61. Panetta (2017).
62. Dobson and Evans (2016), Massot (2016).
63. Allen (2015, 286–308).

64. Government of Canada (2017b).
65. Blanchfield (2017).
66. Government of Canada (2017a).

References

Allen, Nathan. 2015. Keeping rising Asia at a distance: Canadian attitudes toward trade agreements with Asian countries. *International Journal* 70 (2): 286–308.

Ames, Paul. 2015. ISDS: The most toxic acronym in Europe. *Politico*, September 17. http://www.politico.eu/article/isds-the-most-toxic-acronym-in-europe/. Accessed 17 Sept 2015.

Asian Infrastructure Investment Bank (AIIB). 2015. AIIB articles of agreement. AIIB. https://www.aiib.org/en/about-aiib/basic-documents/_download/articles-of-agreement/basic_document_english-bank_articles_of_agreement.pdf. Accessed 5 Sept 2017.

———. 2017a. AIIB welcomes new prospective members. AIIB. https://www.aiib.org/en/news-events/news/2017/20170323_001.html. Accessed 5 Apr 2017.

———. 2017b. Members and prospective members of the bank. AIIB. https://www.aiib.org/en/about-aiib/governance/members-of-bank/index.html. Accessed 20 June 2017.

Biel, Erin, and Mattie Wheeler. 2016. The uncertain future of the European investment court system. *Yale Journal of International Law*, October 30. http://campuspress.yale.edu/yjil/the-uncertain-future-of-the-european-investment-court-system/. Accessed 1 June 2017.

Bierbrauer, Elfriede. 2014. Negotiations on the EU-Canada Comprehensive Economic and Trade Agreement (CETA) concluded. Directorate-General for External Policies Policy Department, October, 2014. http://www.europarl.europa.eu/RegData/etudes/IDAN/2014/536410/EXPO_IDA%282014%29536410_EN.pdf. Accessed 1 Apr 2017.

Blanchfield, Mike. 2017. Human rights on the table in any Canada-China free trade deal: McCallum. *Globe and Mail*, March 29, 2017.

Burton, Charles. 2015. Canada's China policy under the Harper government. *Canadian Foreign Policy Journal* 21 (1): 45–63.

Conservative Party of Canada. 2015. Our conservative plan to protect the economy. Conservative Party of Canada. http://www.conservative.ca/media/plan/conservative-platform-en.pdf. Accessed 1 Apr 2017.

Council of the European Union. 2016. Joint interpretative instrument on the Comprehensive Economic and Trade Agreement (CETA) between Canada and the European Union and its member states. General Secretariat of the Council, October 27. http://data.consilium.europa.eu/doc/document/ST-13541-2016-INIT/en/pdf. Accessed 1 Apr 2017.

Dobson, Wendy, and Paul Evans. 2016. Living with global China: Agenda 2016. In *Moving forward: Issues in Canada-China relations*, ed. Asif B. Farooq and Scott McKnight, 2–10. Toronto: Asian Institute at the Munk School of Global Affairs.

European Commission. 2014a. CETA consolidated text. Council of the European Union General Secretariat Trade Policy Committee, August 5. www.tagesschau.de/wirtschaft/ceta-dokument-101.pdf. Accessed 15 July 2016.

———. 2014b. Trade for all: Towards a more responsible trade and investment policy. Luxembourg. Publications Office of the European Union, October, 2015. http://trade.ec.europa.eu/doclib/docs/2015/october/tradoc_153846.pdf. Accessed 16 July 2016.

———. 2015. Commission proposes new investment court system for TTIP and other EU trade and investment negotiations. European Commission, September 16. http://europa.eu/rapid/press-release_IP-15-5651_en.htm. Accessed 15 July 2017.

———. 2016. Investment provisions in the EU-Canada Free Trade Agreement (CETA). European Commission, February. http://trade.ec.europa.eu/doclib/docs/2013/november/tradoc_151918.pdf. Accessed 16 July 2017.

Finance Canada. 2015. Minister of Finance to launch the Canadian Renminbi clearing Centre & Trading Hub. Government of Canada, March 20. https://www.canada.ca/en/news/archive/2015/03/minister-finance-launch-canadian-renminbi-clearing-centre-trading-hub.html. Accessed 25 Mar 2015.

———. 2017. Building a strong middle class: Budget 2017. Finance Canada, March 22. http://www.budget.gc.ca/2017/docs/plan/budget-2017-en.pdf. Accessed 23 Mar 2017.

Freeland, Chrystia. 2012. *Plutocrats: The rise of the new global super-rich and the fall of everyone else*. New York: Penguin.

Global Affairs Canada. 2016a. Address by International Trade Minister Chrystia Freeland at the conference of Montreal. Global Affairs Canada, June 15. https://www.canada.ca/en/global-affairs/news/2016/06/address-by-international-trade-minister-chrystia-freeland-at-the-conference-of-montreal.html?=undefined&wbdisable=true. Accessed 20 June 2017.

———. 2016b. Address by International Trade Minister Chrystia Freeland at a Canadian Council for the Americas event on Canada and the Pacific Alliance. Global Affairs Canada, June 17. https://www.canada.ca/en/global-affairs/news/2016/06/address-by-international-trade-minister-chrystia-freeland-at-a-canadian-council-for-the-americas-event-on-canada-and-the-pacific-alliance-.html?=undefined&wbdisable=true. Accessed 19 June 2017.

———. 2016c. Address by Minister Freeland to the Toronto Region board of Trade on Canada's trade outlook. Global Affairs Canada, December 5. https://www.canada.ca/en/global-affairs/news/2016/12/address-minister-freeland-toronto-region-board-trade-canada-trade-outlook.html?=undefined&wbdisable=true. Accessed 19 June 2017.

———. 2016d. Economic impact of Canada's potential participation in the Trans-Pacific Partnership Agreement. Office of the Chief Economist, Global Affairs Canada, September 12. http://international.gc.ca/economist-economiste/analysis-analyse/tpp_ei-re_ptp.aspx?lang=eng. Accessed 5 Mar 2017.

———. 2016e. Open letter to Canadians on the Trans-Pacific Partnership from the Honourable Chrystia Freeland, Minister of International Trade. Global Affairs Canada, January 25. http://www.international.gc.ca/trade-agreements-accords-commerciaux/agr-acc/tpp-ptp/open_letter-lettre_ouverte.aspx?lang=eng. Accessed 5 Mar 2017.

———. 2017a. Address by Minister Champagne at the Canada-Australia Economic Leadership Forum. Global Affairs Canada, February 21. https://www.canada.ca/en/global-affairs/news/2017/02/address_by_ministerchampagneatthe-canada-australiaeconomicleaders.html. Accessed 15 Apr 2017.

———. 2017b. Address by Minister Champagne at the Canadian Chamber of Commerce – Mexico City. Global Affairs Canada, March 16. https://www.canada.ca/en/global-affairs/news/2017/03/address_by_ministerchampag-neatthecanadianchamberofcommerce.html. Accessed 25 Apr 2017.

———. 2017c. Address by Minister Freeland on Canada's foreign policy priorities. Global Affairs Canada, June 6. https://www.canada.ca/en/global-affairs/news/2017/06/address_by_ministerfreelandoncanadasforeignpolicypriori-ties.html. Accessed 6 July 2017.

———. 2017d. Trade and investment agreements. Global Affairs Canada. https://www.international.gc.ca/trade-commerce/trade-agreements-accords-commerciaux/agr-acc/index.aspx?lang=eng&menu_id=137. Accessed 1 Mar 2017.

Government of Canada. 2017a. Canada's feminist international assistance policy. Government of Canada. http://international.gc.ca/world-monde/issues_development-enjeux_developpement/priorities-priorites/policy-politique.aspx?lang=eng#5.3. Accessed 20 June 2017.

———. 2017b. Consultations on a potential free trade agreement with China. Canada Gazette Government notices. http://www.gazette.gc.ca/rp-pr/p1/2017/2017-03-04/html/notice-avis-eng.php#ne15. Accessed 25 Aug 2017.

Graham, David. 2017. Why is Trump risking a trade war with Canada? *The Atlantic*, April 26.

Gravelle, T.B. 2014. Partisanship, border proximity, and Canadian attitudes toward North American integration. *International Journal of Public Opinion Research* 26 (4): 453–474.

Lévesque, Céline. 2016. CETA's new system for the resolution of investment disputes: What a difference a few months make. Centre for International Governance Innovation, June 22. https://www.cigionline.org/publications/cetas-new-system-resolution-investment-disputes-what-difference-few-months-make. Accessed 1 May 2017.

Liberal Party of Canada. 2013. Statement by Liberal Party of Canada Leader Justin Trudeau on CETA. Liberal Party of Canada. https://www.liberal.ca/statement-liberal-party-canada-leader-justin-trudeau-ceta-2/. Accessed 5 Jan 2017.

———. 2015a. Real change: A new plan for a strong middle class. Liberal Party of Canada. https://www.liberal.ca/wp-content/uploads/2015/10/New-plan-for-a-strong-middle-class.pdf. Accessed 31 Oct 2015.

———. 2015b. Statement by Liberal Party of Canada Leader Justin Trudeau on the Trans-Pacific Partnership. Liberal Party of Canada, October 5. https://www.liberal.ca/statement-by-liberal-party-of-canada-leader-justin-trudeau-on-the-trans-pacific-partnership/. Accessed 5 Jan 2017.

Lilly, Meredith. 2016. Beijing plays by its own rules, so Canada shouldn't rush into a trade deal. *Globe and Mail*, August 26.

———. 2017. Managing relations under Trump will be about more than just NAFTA. *Policy Magazine*, January–February, 2017. http://www.policymagazine.ca/pdf/23/PolicyMagazineJanuary-February-2017-Lilly.pdf. Accessed 1 Mar 2017.

Massot, Pascale. 2016. The political economy of Canadian public opinion on China. In *Moving forward: Issues in Canada-China relations*, ed. Asif B. Farooq and Scott McKnight, 24–35. Toronto: Asian Institute at the Munk School of Global Affairs.

McCormick, James M. 2017. Pivoting toward Asia: Comparing the Canadian and American policy shifts. *Journal American Review of Canadian Studies* 46 (4): 474–495.

Paltiel, Jeremy. 2016. Resolute ambivalence: Canada's strategy toward China and the Asia-Pacific. *Canadian Foreign Policy Journal* 22 (1): 40–53.

Panetta, Alex. 2017. China: As Canada talks trade deal, Trump's Washington eyes it warily. *Canadian Press*, March 28.

Prime Minister of Canada. 2016a. 2016 North American Leaders' Summit statement. Prime Minister's Office, June 29. http://pm.gc.ca/eng/news/2016/06/29/economic-prosperity-trade-and-competitiveness. Accessed 30 June 2016.

———. 2016b. Joint statement by the Prime Minister of Canada and the President of the United States on softwood lumber. Prime Minister's Office, June 29. http://pm.gc.ca/eng/news/2016/06/29/joint-statement-prime-minister-canada-and-president-united-states-softwood-lumber. Accessed 15 July 2016.

———. 2016c. Prime Minister announces increased collaboration with China. Prime Minister's Office, September 23. http://pm.gc.ca/eng/news/2016/09/23/prime-minister-announces-increased-collaboration-china. Accessed 20 Nov 2016.

———. 2017a. Address by Prime Minister Justin Trudeau to the European Parliament. Prime Minister's Office, February 16. http://pm.gc.ca/eng/news/2017/02/16/address-prime-minister-justin-trudeau-european-parliament. Accessed 20 Feb 2017.

———. 2017b. Joint statement from President Donald J. Trump and Prime Minister Justin Trudeau. Prime Minister's Office, February 13. http://pm.gc.ca/eng/news/2017/02/13/joint-statement-president-donald-j-trump-and-prime-minister-justin-trudeau. Accessed 1 Mar 2017.

———. 2017c. Minister of Foreign Affairs mandate letter. Prime Minister's Office, January 2017. http://pm.gc.ca/eng/minister-foreign-affairs-mandate-letter. Accessed 15 Jan 2017.

———. 2017d. Minister of International Trade mandate letter. Prime Minister's Office, January 2017. http://pm.gc.ca/eng/minister-international-trade-mandate-letter. Accessed 15 Mar 2017.

Reinisch, August, and Lukas Stifter. 2016. CETA's new take on ISDS: Toward an international investment court. Centre for International Governance Innovation, June 22. https://www.cigionline.org/publications/cetas-new-take-isds-toward-international-investment-court. Accessed 1 May 2017.

Schlesinger, Jacob M., and Peter Nicholas. 2017. Trump drops NAFTA pullout threat. *Wall Street Journal*, April 27.

Schneiderman, David. 2016. Why CETA is unlikely to restore legitimacy to ISDS. Centre for International Governance Innovation, May 27. https://www.cigionline.org/publications/why-ceta-unlikely-restore-legitimacy-isds. Accessed 1 May 2017.

Simoes, Alexander C., and Cesar A. Hidalgo. 2017. The economic complexity observatory: An analytical tool for understanding the dynamics of economic development. Workshops at the Twenty-Fifth AAAI Conference on Artificial Intelligence. Observatory of Economic Complexity. http://atlas.media.mit.edu/en/profile/country/can/. Accessed 1 May 2017.

United States Trade Representative. 2017. Trump administration announces intent to renegotiate the North American Free Trade Agreement. Executive Office of the President, May 18. https://ustr.gov/about-us/policy-offices/press-office/press-releases/2017/may/ustr-trump-administration-announces. Accessed 25 May 2017.

VanDuzer, J.A. 2016. Investor-state dispute settlement in CETA: Is it the gold standard? C.D. Howe Institute. https://www.cdhowe.org/sites/default/files/attachments/research_papers/mixed/Commentary%20459.pdf. Accessed 1 June 2017.

Von Der Burchard, Hans. 2016. Cecilia Malmström finds her trade groove. *Politico*, March 7. http://www.politico.eu/article/eu-malmstroem-trade-court/. Accessed 1 June 2017.

White House Office of the Press Secretary. 2017. Presidential Memorandum Regarding Construction of the Keystone XL Pipeline. White House Office of the Press Secretary, January 24, 2017. https://www.whitehouse.gov/the-press-office/2017/01/24/presidential-memorandum-regarding-construction-keystone-xl-pipeline. Accessed 25 Mar 2017.

CHAPTER 8

Justin Trudeau's China Challenges

Philip Calvert

Justin Trudeau's Liberal government wants to reinvigorate and deepen the Canada-China relationship. This message was delivered early in the government's mandate, and was clearly demonstrated during the reciprocal back-to-back state visits undertaken by Trudeau and Chinese Premier Li Keqiang in September 2016. The message was also reciprocal: during his visit, Premier Li went so far as to express the hope that Sino-Canadian ties were entering a "golden decade" of renewed bilateral relations.[1]

CHALLENGING RELATIONSHIP IN A SHIFTING GLOBAL CONTEXT

As the son of the man who established diplomatic relations with China, Trudeau brings a certain cachet, as well as a new level of enthusiasm and energy, to a relationship that is consistently difficult to manage. The Canada-China relationship is most complex, difficult, and fraught with political tensions. Significant normative differences between the two countries, particularly with respect to human rights and the conduct of

P. Calvert (✉)
China Institute, University of Alberta, Edmonton, AB, Canada

© The Author(s) 2018
N. Hillmer, P. Lagassé (eds.), *Justin Trudeau and Canadian Foreign Policy*, Canada and International Affairs,
https://doi.org/10.1007/978-3-319-73860-4_8

international trade, lead to irritants, tension, miscommunication, and differing expectations, both between governments and among peoples.[2] China's own international actions often are the source of alarm as well, particularly in such regions as the South China Sea, where conflicting views over sovereignty are a source of conflict and increasing tension, or Hong Kong, where China appears to be disavowing its commitments to preserving Hong Kong's autonomy under the 1984 Joint Declaration. China's own discourse in the international media, while becoming increasingly sophisticated, can be blunt, confrontational, and lacking in nuance.

Canadian attitudes toward China are also shifting and often ambivalent. Surveys indicate that Canadians' views of China remain cautious and skeptical, even as many recognize the growing importance of China in the world.[3] The most recent survey by the Asia Pacific Foundation has found that, for the first time, a narrow majority (55 per cent) of Canadians support free trade with China. The same survey indicated that a large majority of 78 per cent believe that increasing economic ties will provide more business opportunities, but 64 per cent believe that these stronger ties would make Canada more vulnerable to pressure from the Chinese government, and 71 per cent believe that they would make Canada more vulnerable to economic volatility in China.[4]

Finding a balanced, constructive, and effective approach to China, and one that Canadians find acceptable, presents challenges to policy-makers and politicians, but is critical to Canada's interests. China is far too important, both bilaterally and as a global player, to not be treated as a key relationship. The economy has grown from a gross domestic product (GDP) of roughly $60 billion in the late 1950s and early 1960s, when the Canadian Wheat Board established long-term supply contracts, aided by Canadian export credits, to US$11 trillion in 2015.[5] With bilateral merchandise trade reaching $84 billion (or $203 million a day) in 2016, China is Canada's second-largest trading partner, and accounts for 12 per cent of our imports, and 4 per cent of our exports.[6] According to Canadian statistics, total Chinese investment in Canada was $21.3 billion in 2016.[7] Bilateral services trade was approximately $4 billion in 2015, making China our fifth-largest services trading partner.[8] Total Canadian investment in China, according to official Canadian statistics, was $6.8 billion, but this is likely an underestimate, depending on how investments are structured.[9] Canadian companies have established partnerships in China, producing goods and services that are essential to their profitability.

Sino-Canadian ties are also affected by flows of people. Roughly 120,000 Chinese students attend Canadian universities, and each year about 500,000 Chinese tourists visit Canada, affecting the bottom lines of universities and our hospitality industry.[10] China's environmental practices have a global impact on the production of greenhouse gases: mercury and other products from the burning of coal in China can be found in our trees and ice.

China is at a new phase in its global engagement: more assertive and more driven by nationalism and global ambitions. China is working to expand its influence through Central Asia and Southeast Asia via its "One Belt, One Road" initiative, an ambitious undertaking aimed at increasing connectivity through an extensive series of infrastructure projects in both regions. China's long-standing influence in Africa continues to grow, as it does in Latin America. China's power, both soft and hard, is extending outward regionally; its self-defined "core interests" have also spread to the South China Sea. China's multinationals, both state- and private-owned, have a global reach. Its manufacturers are at either the centre of global value chains or dominating global industries, such as in solar panels or steel. China's economic growth rates affect global commodity and other prices, as well as the export performance of its trading partners.

The global environment continues to shift dramatically since Trudeau and Li sipped beer on the dock at Harrington Lake, the prime minister's retreat. The Trump administration continues to espouse, as a default policy position, an uncertain international agenda that remains protectionist and driven by nativism. The United States has withdrawn from the Paris Accord, a blow to international action aimed at addressing climate change. In the face of this, as well as the Brexit vote, China's president, Xi Jinping, increasingly portrays China as the leading promoter of open global markets, and a champion in the fight against climate change and environmental degradation—moving, albeit somewhat reluctantly, into the global leadership vacuum left by the retreating United States. This shift should be treated with a healthy skepticism, given the continued levels of protectionism, lack of transparency, and weak adherence to the rule of law within the Chinese system.

Managing relations with China within this shifting global context while advancing other key relationships, and pushing an ambitious global agenda, is a significant challenge. It requires a comprehensive, balanced, and strategic China policy that advances Canada's commercial, security, and global interests while addressing issues of concern, in particular human rights and, increasingly, cyber and domestic security threats. While the Trudeau government has invested new energy and created new architecture in Canada's ties with China, it has yet to meet the challenge of finding that critical balance.

A New Approach?

The Trudeau government moved early to distinguish itself in its approach to China from that taken by the Conservative government under Stephen Harper. Both the Canadian and Chinese governments have sought to hearken back to days under earlier, particularly Liberal, governments, when Canadian ties with China were seen by many to have been better than those with other Western countries. This approach reflects the narrative reinforced by both the Canadian and Chinese governments that relations with China flourish under the Liberals, and that not much happened under the not-so-golden decade of bilateral relations under the Conservatives from 2006 to 2015.

This is a seductive but simplistic comparison. It is true that Justin Trudeau brings a famous name to the relationship and that there are obvious differences in styles of engagement between him and Stephen Harper. However, this assertion understates the engagement of the Conservatives—uneven as it was—and overstates the strategic vision and engagement of the Chrétien and Martin Liberals that preceded them. Indeed, over the last 25 years or more, each new Canadian government has attempted to draw a line between its approach to China and the approach of its predecessor. In the end, each government has reached a certain point of equilibrium; despite periods of diminished contact, commercial, political, and people-to-people ties have generally grown consistently through the years. The Trudeau government may differ in its approach to China, but it must address the same fundamental issues with which other governments have struggled: advancing Canada's interests, addressing issues of concern (especially human rights and governance), and coming to terms with China's swiftly changing reality.

Early Years of Diplomatic Relations

The People's Republic of China of today is a far different country than it was when Canada first reached out to it, and when we established diplomatic relations in 1970.[11] When the Wheat Board began selling to China, the country was in the midst of a debilitating famine, an economic crisis, and internal political conflict brought on by the disastrous policies of Mao Zedong's Great Leap Forward. The economy was largely insular and state-controlled. Contacts with Canada were limited to the odd visitor and trade hovered between $100 million and $200 million per year.[12]

The establishment of diplomatic relations sought to put Canada on an advantageous footing with China as compared with many Western countries. This led to a doubling of bilateral trade by the time of a 1973 trade mission, led by Foreign Minister Mitchell Sharp, which saw the signing of a trade agreement as well. However, while the lure of China with its market of 818 million people was a strong draw for some, the reality was that with a GDP of $96 billion, the Chinese economy was relatively small as well as state-driven, and the country itself was in the throes of continued internal political conflict.

Canada's interest in China as a commercial market burgeoned, ties broadened, and bilateral activity flourished—indeed skyrocketed—in the wake of economic reforms introduced by the paramount leader, Deng Xiaoping, in 1979.[13] Canadian companies became increasingly active, as well as some provinces, especially Alberta and Quebec. In 1982, the Canadian International Development Agency (CIDA) programme was established to assist in China's economic and social transformation, including the development of China's hydro sector, which was of great interest to Canadian engineering companies and equipment manufacturers. In June 1986, International Trade Minister James Kelleher agreed to help China in its quest to rejoin the General Agreement on Tariffs and Trade (GATT), which later became the World Trade Organization (WTO). At the time, China's trade regime remained essentially under state control, but rejoining GATT was seen by reformers as a way to drive structural change.[14]

These were heady, and at the same time somewhat naïve, times. Chinese society and economy were in swift transition and it was hard for both to keep up. For the government of Canada to shift its attention and resources to a market and country of growing interest and excitement for Canadians required a significant shift in priorities and culture that was beyond its grasp at the time. A sense of optimism about China and the future of Canada-China relations was evident during the visit of Prime Minister Brian Mulroney in 1986. From 1978 to 1988, Canadian exports grew by 18 per cent per year and the scope of products, while still mainly wheat and resources, began to become more diverse. Between 1980 and 1988, bilateral trade grew from $1 billion to $3.6 billion, and China became Canada's sixth-largest trading partner.[15] Canada opened a Consulate in Shanghai in 1986.

Despite extensive human rights problems in China, this issue was not at the forefront of Canada's agenda, or on the minds of Canadians, who were more aware of the plight of Soviet dissidents. Partly, this was because less information was available in China, and foreign journalists at the time operated on the assumption that any contact with dissidents in China would lead to a hasty expulsion. Many also believed that the loosening of political restraints would follow the opening up of the economy and looked to other means to support improved governance in the country. Chinese Premier (and later Communist Party General Secretary) Zhao Ziyang, who visited Canada in early 1984 and spoke in Parliament—the first leader of a Communist government to do so, and something we would not see now[16]—was pushing for new, more ambitious, and controversial economic reforms, including removing the Communist Party from state-owned enterprises. Under Communist Party General Secretary Hu Yaobang, it seemed that political reform was coming: there was even cautious debate about forms of government in state media. The minister of culture was a writer, his vice-minister an actor and translator of Shakespeare into Chinese. This optimism, mixed with naïveté, was at its height when Mulroney visited China in 1986.

The Tiananmen Watershed and the Chrétien-Martin Years

The Tiananmen massacre in June 1989 brought this to an end. By July 1989, Zhao Ziyang was under house arrest and the Tiananmen massacre had dramatically shifted popular perspectives on China, with human rights now taking the forefront. Tiananmen, as Charles Burton, a China specialist from Brock University, puts it, "brought home to Canadians the powerful realities of the Chinese Communist security apparatus."[17] The Mulroney government reduced Embassy staff, the size of the recently expanded trade section, and CIDA programmes, and ministerial visits halted until 1991. For the rest of the Mulroney government, little was advanced with China. The Chinese economy stagnated and reforms slowed as more conservative elements of the leadership came to power in the wake of Tiananmen.

Canada's approach shifted dramatically with the Liberal government of Jean Chrétien (1993–2003). The Chrétien government initiated a significant push on the trade file, seeing great opportunity in China's renewed economic growth and in the revival of its reform process, pushed with renewed vigour by Deng Xiaoping in a famous visit to Southern China. Chrétien led the first Team Canada mission to China, bringing provincial and territorial leaders (with the exception of Quebec's premier, Jacques Parizeau), federal ministers, and about 400 business representatives on a visit to Beijing and Shanghai in 1994—the first of three visits and two Team Canada visits during the Chrétien years. The trade agenda was broader and deeper, with agreements on the building of Canada deuterium uranium reactors, insurance services, and a host of business contract signings overseen by the prime minister. Chrétien established good personal ties with Chinese leaders, like Premiers Li Peng and Zhu Rongji (who famously called Canada China's "best friend in all the world" in 1998[18]) and President Jiang Zemin. Canada's development assistance programmes continued to grow, particularly in the environment, agriculture, and the judiciary.

Chrétien rarely pronounced publicly on human rights, preferring to keep such conversations to private meetings with his Chinese counterparts. During the first years of the Chrétien government, Canada continued to co-sponsor a United Nations resolution on the Chinese human rights situation. China's opposition to this resolution became increasingly vocal and vociferous, threatening commercial retaliation against countries participating in the resolution. In the end, following a visit to China and a meeting with Li Peng by Foreign Minister Lloyd Axworthy, Canada's participation in this resolution was dropped in favour of a bilateral human rights dialogue. China, through pressure and threats about the impact on trade relations, convinced other like-minded countries to adopt this approach as well.

Paul Martin's relatively short term as prime minister (2003–2006) saw, essentially, a continuation of the approach of his predecessor: heavily emphasizing business, a slightly stronger emphasis on human rights, and intent on promoting his idea of a Group of Twenty (G20) leaders meeting. His only visit to China as prime minister in January 2005 was complicated by the death of Zhao Ziyang. It not only changed his schedule, but forced Martin to address the issue of visiting Zhao's house to pay respects (he did not, much to the relief of China's Foreign Ministry), and placed

Tiananmen, human rights, and political reform high on the radar screen of the media, the public, and the Conservative Opposition in Canada.

Bilateral business ties continued to flourish, and there was a steady stream of business representatives and politicians in both directions. At the same time, the country remained a difficult place to do business: many regulations and other non-tariff measures, along with a system of commercial law that lacked objectivity and transparency, remained obstacles to foreign companies doing business in China. Bilaterally, negotiations for a Foreign Investment Protection Agreement, started in 1994, languished. China frequently complained about the presence in Canada of a Chinese citizen, Lai Changxing, who had fled in 1999 to avoid charges of corruption. Despite a vague promise to Paul Martin during his visit to China, the country still refused to grant Canada Approved Destination Status (ADS), which would allow Chinese package tours into Canada, thus providing the Canadian tourism industry with a much-needed source of additional revenue.

Conservative Engagement: From Coolness to Prickly Enthusiasm

The most significant break in continuity in Canada-China political relations came with the Conservative government of Stephen Harper, which sought to demonstrate a clear and decisive change from policies of the previous Liberal government, to project a "principled" foreign policy with greater emphasis on human rights, and to put greater emphasis on North America as opposed to Asia. In its approach to China, the combination of a high level of partisanship, little experience with China, and an innate mistrust of the bureaucracy led to a significantly different handling of China that endured for a few years. Early interactions between President Hu Jintao and Harper were reported to be terse and confrontational, particularly over the case of Huseyincan Celil, a Canadian of minority Uighur origin, who had been imprisoned in China on charges of separatism and terrorism and to whom access by Canadian consular officials was denied by China.

In this environment, senior-level engagement slowed down. There were a few visits by moderate ministers like Chuck Strahl (Agriculture), Jim Flaherty (Finance), and David Emerson (International Trade), with both Flaherty and Emerson delivering the message that Canada welcomed

Chinese investment. It took over a year before Foreign Minister Peter Mackay engaged with his recently promoted counterpart, Yang Jiechi, in April 2007.[19] Canadian media made much of the fact that Harper did not attend the opening ceremonies of the Beijing Olympics in 2008 (instead sending Emerson, who had been appointed foreign minister), but this did not appear to concern Chinese officials.

There was, however, a shift in the Conservative government's approach in 2009. There were a number of reasons for this: Stephen Harper's shifting perception of his role in the promotion of Canadian companies internationally; pressure from the business community and parts of the Chinese community, which the Conservatives had been courting; and the fact that he was out of step with his experienced Group of Eight (G8) counterparts in not having visited China. The promotion of Canada as a robust "energy superpower" was attractive to the Prime Minister's Office (PMO) and interested the Chinese government, as did the stability of Canada's banking system in the wake of the 2008 financial crisis.[20] The April 2009 visit of International Trade Minister Stockwell Day, a powerful member of cabinet and a strong supporter of Taiwan and the Dalai Lama, can also be seen as a watershed, as Day came away from the visit a strong supporter of building the China trade relationship. Day's visit was followed by that of Lawrence Cannon as foreign minister, and discussions were launched on a visit by Harper for later in the year. Chinese Foreign Minister Yang repeated the invitation when he met Harper during his June 2009 visit to Canada. This helped set the stage for Harper's first visit to China in 2009, and a return visit by President Hu to Canada in 2010, followed by visits by Harper in 2012 and 2014.

Eventually, as its position on China moderated and as China's interest in Canada's energy sources peaked, the Harper government enjoyed a number of successes in China, and was successful in strengthening institutional ties and settling long-standing irritants. Foreign Investment Promotion and Protection Agreement negotiations were concluded, Canada was granted ADS, and the two countries arrived at acceptable terms for returning Lai Changxing to China. Ministers cultivated ties with their counterparts regularly and enthusiastically, particularly Trade Minister Ed Fast and Foreign Minister John Baird. The government also managed to moderate its hosting of the Dalai Lama, reducing the profile of his meetings with senior Canadians, including the prime minister. A joint "complementarity study," which examined the complementarities in Chinese and Canadian economies and identified opportunities for growth in bilateral trade, was released in 2012.[21] Many saw this as a precursor to discussions regarding a free trade agreement (FTA), but, while there was public discussion about such an initiative, it did not move ahead, particularly after Canada entered negotiations on the Trans-Pacific Partnership (TPP). Chinese companies made several key investments, especially into the energy sector. The Canadian government's footprint expanded in China, through low-cost trade offices run by the Canadian Commercial Corporation and staffed by Chinese employees reporting to nearby diplomatic offices.

Despite these accomplishments and this shift, the Conservatives never settled on China, seemingly pulled one way by the trade agenda and then swinging like a pendulum to the other side in reaction to security and human rights concerns. Entrenched antipathy to the bilateral human rights dialogue, bolstered by a critical report produced by Charles Burton, led to Canada suspending the dialogue. This put an end to one institutionalized channel, however imperfect, for regular and ongoing engagement on this issue.[22] The Canadian government also sent mixed messages on investment, particularly by state-owned enterprises, which it excluded from higher thresholds in the review process.[23] After a very positive visit in 2014, which established an annual foreign ministers dialogue and contained significant initiatives to enhance bilateral ties, no Conservative cabinet minister visited China to follow up, leaving the Chinese side perplexed.

The Conservative approach to China has been criticized as "intermittent, conflicted and narrowly economic."[24] There is some truth to this assessment, although it understates the eventual breadth of the Conservative approach. While the PMO seemed to wax hot and cold, there was sustained growth in trade and investment, in education ties, and, eventually, in flows of Chinese tourists to Canada. What was lost was the opportunity to establish a long-term partnership, based on solid and sustainable working relations between leaders, at a time of significant change in China's domestic policies and in its view of its place in the world.[25]

A China Strategy?

The Conservative government's transactional approach to China and lack of an overarching strategy for Canada was not unique. Canada has rarely, if ever, had such an approach. As former Ambassador to China Fred Bild once commented, Canada's relationship with China has been usually conducted from "simultaneous and sometimes contradictory motives, and managed with the best of intentions by harried diplomatic staff."[26]

Through the years, there have been attempts to bring more coherence and strategic focus to an increasingly complex relationship, particularly as the number of provinces, non-governmental organizations (NGOs), and federal government departments with direct interests in China have grown. External affairs started such an exercise in 1987; however, it foundered after bilateral relations were reduced in the wake of Tiananmen.[27] As relations boomed again in the 1990s and early 2000s, more attempts were made to produce a whole of government, cabinet-endorsed, strategy along the lines of the 1987 attempt. None were successful.

Justin Trudeau has clearly signalled that he understands the importance of a constructive relationship with China's leadership, but it is not clear that his approach is any more strategic. The Trudeau and Li visits produced initiatives designed to push the relationship forward, but mostly they were an extension of previous prime-ministerial-level undertakings. In keeping with the tradition of joint statements around visits, some commitments were hortatory, like doubling trade volume by 2025 (essentially meaningless as the level of bilateral trade is essentially out of the hands of both leaders). Others aimed at strengthening the bilateral engagement architecture through new, high-level mechanism agreements. These included committing to an annual prime-minister-level dialogue, an annual Economic and Financial Strategic Dialogue at the vice-premier level, and dialogues on National Security/Rule of Law and Innovation. There was a host of memoranda addressing different issues aimed at increasing cooperation between Canadian and Chinese ministries. Canada announced its intention to join the China-led Asian Infrastructure Investment Bank (AIIB), and the two countries agreed to start discussions on a FTA. During separate talks, Canada's national security adviser agreed to discussions on a possible extradition agreement, a long-standing Chinese demand. The Trudeau visit also led to the release of Canadian Kevin Garratt, who had been held in China on accusations of spying.[28]

This was not the first prime-ministerial-level visit to produce a long list of results. Each government, for its own reasons, needs to show concrete actions arising out of high-level visits, and previous visits by Harper had produced lists of initiatives, although not a public commitment to an annual prime ministers' dialogue or undertaking discussions on a free trade or extradition agreements. It is not clear, though, that these last two undertakings were borne of a significant strategic discussion. The agreement on

FTA discussions was in response to a long-standing Chinese request, as well as growing demands from parts of the Canadian private sector, and it sent an ambitious message that was as much political as commercial. But it may not address many systemic barriers in China (such as full renminbi convertibility) that make doing business difficult for foreign countries and that are often outside standard FTAs.[29] Similarly, the commitment to begin discussions about an extradition agreement may have been instrumental in the release of Kevin Garratt and thus another good tactical move. Negotiation of such an agreement, while a good idea in principle, will face a number of hurdles that may in the end mean the talks go nowhere.[30]

Trudeau's Challenges

The Trudeau government's overall challenge is to develop and implement a strategic, balanced, and comprehensive approach to China. It means creating an environment that supports Canada's bilateral interests and global agenda, and in which there is room for frank and difficult discussions on sensitive issues, including human rights, cyber security, and the protection of Canada's interests. Achieving this goal means addressing a number of key, related challenges.

Understanding China's World View

The first challenge is understanding where Canada fits into China's world view. Chinese foreign policy-makers approach international issues with the overwhelming purpose of advancing China's interests. Foreign policy is driven by the need for stability: to maintain growth and to keep the Communist Party in power. In addition to domestic stability, economic growth requires regional stability, access to resources that can support and propel economic growth, and a workable relationship with the United States. Whereas Canada's support of the international rules-based system is based on principles and adherence to the rule of law, China sees the multilateral system and its legal framework more as tools and mechanisms than the conceptual basis of international engagement.[31] Faced with increasing middle-class activism against environmental degradation and the health impacts of heavy industry, China increasingly folds environmental protection into its stability considerations.

China's sense of history also informs its perspective on the world. It sees itself as a victim of the great Western powers of the nineteenth and early twentieth centuries and thus remains inherently suspicious of the West and what it sees as an unspoken agenda and coordinated effort to contain its growth. At the same time, China also sees itself as a leading world civilization, an empire that was once the centre of a far-reaching tribute system, and led the world in economic production, technology, and exploration—a position to which China sees itself as now returning.[32] In addition, the military in China is very powerful and has a strong influence on foreign policy positions, particularly with respect to sovereignty and territorial issues, including China's position with respect to its maritime claims in Asia. The political and foreign policy leadership therefore cannot afford to appear weak on these issues, especially as Chinese nationalist sentiments continue to rise. Finally, China is becoming increasingly adept at the use of soft power in international diplomacy. It has greatly expanded its use of cultural engagement, cultural diplomacy, and education to advance its interests and enhance its international image.[33]

Canada's place in China's world view is generally less prominent than many politicians would like to admit and lies, as Jeremy Paltiel has put it, "outside the inner circle of those states of immediate and permanent concern."[34] Although there is awareness of some major Canadian companies, like Bombardier, China tends to view Canada as a colder version of Australia (with which Canada is often compared): a source of natural resources that can help supply China's industrial demands; a good destination for tourists, students, and family; and an attractive investment target, stability, and access to the US market through the North American Free Trade Agreement (NAFTA) being particular assets. Canada's capacity to define the parameters of the relationship, much less single-handedly change China's governance or behaviour, is thus limited. Keeping Canada on China's international agenda requires sustained effort and a strong investment in branding.

A Pan-Canadian Approach

A second challenge Trudeau faces is developing a coherent, pan-Canadian approach to China. Many Canadian players have interests in China, including federal departments, provincial governments, the private sector, and NGOs. In some areas, such as investment and education, provinces are in competition with each other; in others, such as energy, policy differences are increasing. Uniting federal and provincial governments in a common purpose and advancing a coherent agenda for Canada is clearly in Canada's interest, but it has yet to be achieved in a sustainable way. Accomplishing this requires permanent coordinating mechanisms and ongoing communication between key players. Most of all, it requires that key players come together on a pan-Canadian strategy which identifies priorities in bilateral ties and sets out a roadmap for achieving them.

Developing the Economic Partnership

Developing an effective and fair economic partnership between Canada and China remains a priority for Trudeau, but also an ongoing challenge. Economic and commercial engagement will continue to be the driving forces of Canada-China relations. The overall indicators are positive: bilateral trade and investment are growing, and preliminary discussions on an FTA have started, but formal negotiations have not yet been launched, despite expectations that this would take place during Trudeau's December 2017 visit to China. However, ensuring that Canadian companies are fairly treated and continue to benefit from the Chinese market remains a challenge. The impact of an FTA will be limited unless it can go beyond traditional parameters and address systemic obstacles, particularly regulatory ones, which work against Canadian companies. An FTA would also need to address issues on which Canada and China differ widely, especially the inclusion of labour and environmental chapters.

The China FTA is likely to become a core element of Canada's China policy under Trudeau. However, Canada will need to accept that an FTA, should formal negotiations start, is likely to take two or more years to finalize and is unlikely to be concluded within the current government's mandate. Pressure on Canadian negotiators to reach a politically driven deadline will only undermine their negotiating leverage and make for a deal that does not fully meet Canada's interests.

Investment policy remains a particular economic policy challenge. The government must continue to send a consistent message supporting Chinese investment in Canada while, at the same time, squarely facing legitimate issues related to security, particularly in sensitive sectors, such as real estate, health care, and high technology—issues on which there has been significant public discussion. For example, by not subjecting transactions such as Hytera's purchase of the Canadian satellite company Norsat to a comprehensive security review, the Canadian government has appeared either naïve or blinded by Trudeau's own fascination with China. And US concerns about such investments need to be taken seriously and brought into the policy mix.

Questions on how to address human rights concerns will continue to be raised in the context of public discourse regarding the FTA, as there has already been public disagreement on whether and how they would be addressed in this context.

HUMAN RIGHTS

Developing a constructive and meaningful engagement on human rights remains a challenge for Canada. As the death of dissident Liu Xiaobo reminds us, however, these tough issues must be addressed. Canadians remain concerned about them, because of growing restrictions on political and minority rights and the jailing of human rights defenders. Determining when and how publicly to criticize China on specific cases is difficult: speaking out too little implies a lack of concern, and doing it too often diminishes the value of each statement. Canada and China lack a specific forum dedicated to addressing bilateral human rights issues, and neither Canada nor China wants to return to the old human rights dialogue, suspended in 2006. Finding a different approach, acceptable to both sides, will be a very difficult undertaking given China's resistance and Canada's need for short-term, concrete results. It would require, among other things, identification of some common ground from which to start. A focused, project-based approach might be one way forward, but requires the establishment of mutual trust and commitment.

CHINA AS A GLOBAL PLAYER

Finally, Canada faces the challenge of coming to terms with China as a global player, one who often plays by different rules. China continues to extend its influence in Africa, South and Southeast Asia, and Central Asia through development assistance and investment in infrastructure and now through the AIIB, China's answer to the Asian Development Bank. Its influence through economic associations and trade agreements, and through regional organizations like the East Asia Summit (of which Canada is not a member), continues to strengthen. With apparent diminishment of the global leadership role of the United States—as evidenced by its withdrawal from the Paris Accord and its isolation at the G20—China's President Xi is positioning China as a global leader in fighting protectionism and promoting the climate change agenda. These issues are important to Canada, but China's genuine and sustained commitment to them has yet to be demonstrated clearly in its domestic policies. On the other hand, China's increasingly aggressive encroachment on disputed territories in the South China Sea, and its equally aggressive undermining of Hong Kong's independence, both negatively affect Canada's interests. They also indicate China's growing disregard for international obligations and the rules-based system when it conflicts with China's global and domestic agenda. Under these circumstances, identifying areas of global cooperation for Canada and China requires careful consideration and a clear strategic purpose.

Conclusion

Managing China relations has been a challenge for many successive Canadian governments and will be a challenge for the Trudeau government as well. While sustained commercial, political, and other ties have expanded over the years, there is much more potential benefit that can be derived from a more strategic and comprehensive approach to Canada-China ties. To do so requires Canada to come to terms with China's current reality and to make policy decisions based on a realistic understanding of China today and its global role. Canada's former ambassador to China, David Mulroney, identifies Canada's biggest challenge as "seeing China as it is, and not through the prism of our wildest fears or our fondest hopes."[35] Canada must also keep in mind that diplomacy is a two-way street and that China's own interests and perspectives must be considered and addressed if the relationship is to flourish. Of all the lessons in relations management, this is often the hardest for Canada to learn.

Notes

1. This comment reflects the tendency to hyperbole, both positive and negative that often continues to characterize public statements from the government of China (Valiante 2016). See, also, Wentian (2016).
2. See Potter (2016, 47–55).
3. See, for example, Massot (2016, 24–35).
4. Asia Pacific Foundation of Canada (2017a).
5. World Bank (2017), Miner (2015, 12–13).
6. Asia Pacific Foundation of Canada (2017b).
7. Ibid., 2017c. See Jin and Ostaszewski (2016).
8. Lambert-Racine (2016).

9. Global Affairs Canada (2015).
10. Statistics Canada (2015); ICEF Monitor (2016).
11. Canada's contemplation of establishing diplomatic ties shortly after the Communist victory in 1949 had been derailed by the outbreak of the Korean War (Bild 2011, 17).
12. World Bank (2017), Holden (2004, 3–4).
13. See Evans (2014), Chap. 1, for an excellent summary of bilateral relations to 2013.
14. Personal observation, June 1986.
15. Holden (2004, 6).
16. Charles Burton makes this point well (Burton 2011).
17. Burton (2011, 38).
18. Paltiel (2011, 123).
19. Yang was promoted to foreign minister just a few days before the start of MacKay's visit, so he was the first foreign minister to meet Yang in his new capacity.
20. Nossal and Sarson (2013, 10–11).
21. Global Affairs Canada (2013).
22. Burton (2006), Evans (2014, 65).
23. See Mulroney (2015), especially 174–176 (kindle edition).
24. Dobson and Evans (2016, 3).
25. See Evans (2011, 2014), Nossal and Sarson (2013).
26. Bild (2011, 13).
27. Frolic (2011).
28. Prime Minister of Canada (2016a, b), Calvert (2016a, b).
29. Gruetzner and Calvert (2017a, b).
30. Calvert (2016b).
31. Shambaugh (2013, 23–26).
32. Paltiel (2011, 117).
33. See Shambaugh (2013), Chap. 6, for a good discussion of this approach.
34. Paltiel (2011, 118).
35. Mulroney (2015, 289).

References

Asia Pacific Foundation of Canada. 2017a. 2017 National opinion poll: Canadian views on engagement with China. Asia Pacific Foundation of Canada, May 3. https://www.asiapacific.ca/surveys/national-opinion-polls/2017-national-opinion-poll-canadian-views-engagement-china. Accessed 15 July 2017.

———. 2017b. Canada's merchandise trade with China. Asia Pacific Foundation of Canada. https://www.asiapacific.ca/statistics/trade/bilateral-trade-asia-product/canadas-merchandise-trade-china. Accessed 15 July 2017.

———. 2017c. Canadian inward foreign direct investment from Asia. Asia Pacific Foundation of Canada. https://www.asiapacific.ca/statistics/investment/inward-foreign-direct-investment/canadian-inward-foreign-direct-investment. Accessed 21 July 2017.

Bild, Fred. 2011. Canada's staying power: A diplomat's view. In *The China challenge: Sino-Canadian relations in the 21st century*, ed. Huhua Cao and Vivienne Poy, 12–31. Ottawa: University of Ottawa Press.

Burton, Charles. 2006. Assessment of the Canada-China bilateral human rights dialogue. Department of Foreign Affairs and International Trade, April 19. http://spartan.ac.brocku.ca/~cburton/Assessment%20of%20the%20Canada-China%20Bilateral%20Human%20Rights%20Dialogue%2019APR06.pdf. Accessed 5 Sept 2017.

———. 2011. The Canadian policy context of Canada's China policy since 1970. In *The China challenge: Sino-Canadian relations in the 21st century*, ed. Huhua Cao and Vivienne Poy, 32–46. Ottawa: University of Ottawa Press.

Calvert, Philip. 2016a. Canada's move to join the AIIB is smart politics and economics. *Nikkei Asian Review*, September 15. https://asia.nikkei.com/magazine/20160915-SOCIAL-REVOLUTION/Viewpoints/Philip-Calvert-Canada-s-move-to-join-the-AIIB-is-smart-politics-and-economics. Accessed 5 Sept 2017.

———. 2016b. Canada China extradition talks point to give and take diplomacy. *Nikkei Asian Review*, September 29. https://asia.nikkei.com/Viewpoints-archive/Viewpoints/Philip-Calvert-China-Canada-extradition-talks-point-to-give-and-take-diplomacy. Accessed 20 July 2017.

Dobson, Wendy, and Paul Evans. 2016. The political economy of Canadian public opinion on China. In *Moving forward: Issues in Canada-China relations*, ed. Asif B. Farooq and Scott McKnight, 24–35. Toronto: University of Toronto, Munk Institute of Global Affairs and China Open Research Network.

Evans, Paul. 2011. Engagement with conservative characteristics: Policy and public attitudes, 2006–2011. In *Issues in Canada-China relations*, ed. Pitman B. Potter and Thomas Adams, 19–30. Canadian International Council.

———. 2014. *Engaging China: Myth, aspiration and strategy in Canadian policy from Trudeau to Harper*. Toronto: University of Toronto Press.

Frolic, Michael B. 2011. Canada and China: The China strategy of 1987. In *The China challenge: Sino-Canadian relations in the 21st century*, ed. Huhua Cao and Vivienne Poy, 54–64. Ottawa: University of Ottawa Press.

Global Affairs Canada. 2013. Canada-China economic complementarities study. Global Affairs Canada, September 5. http://www.international.gc.ca/trade-agreements-accords-commerciaux/agr-acc/china-chine/study-comp-etude. aspx?lang=eng. Accessed 21 July 2017.

———. 2015. Canadian direct investment abroad (stocks). Global Affairs Canada, April. http://www.international.gc.ca/economist-economiste/assets/pdfs/Data/investments-investissements/FDI_by_Country/CDIA_stocks_by_Country-ENG.pdf. Accessed 16 July 2017.

Gruetzner, John, and Philip Calvert. 2017a. Canada-China free trade part 1: Business before politics. Centre for International Political Studies, March 10. http://www.cepi-cips.ca/2017/03/10/canada-china-free-trade-part-1-business-before-politics/. Accessed 20 July 2017.

———. 2017b. Canada-China free trade part 2: Forging an agreement. Centre for International Political Studies, March 10. http://www.cips-cepi.ca/2017/03/10/canada-china-free-trade-part-2-forging-an-agreement/. Accessed 10 Mar 2017.

Holden, Michael. 2004. *Canada's Trade Policy and Economic Relationship with China*. [Canada]: Parliamentary Information and Research Service, April 4.

ICEF Monitor. 2016. Canada's international student enrolment up 8%. *ICEF Monitor*, November 17. http://monitor.icef.com/2016/11/canadas-international-student-enrolment-up-8/. Accessed 10 July 2017.

Jin, Iris, and Valentine Ostaszewski. 2016. Differing methodologies causing stark discrepancies in Chinese and Canadian FDI statistics. Asia Pacific Foundation of Canada, June 21. http://www.asiapacific.ca/blog/differing-methodologies-causing-stark-discrepancies-chinese. Accessed 15 July 2017.

Lambert-Racine, Michaël. 2016. Canadian trade and investment activity: Canada-China. Library of Parliament Research Publications, September 19. https://lop.parl.ca/Content/LOP/ResearchPublications/2016-68-e.html. Accessed 15 July 2017.

Massot, Pascale. 2016. The political economy of Canadian public opinion on China. In *Moving forward: Issues in Canada-China relations*, ed. Asif B. Farooq and Scott McKnight, 24–35. Toronto: University of Toronto, Munk Institute of Global Affairs and China Open Research Network.

Miner, William M. 2015. The Rise and fall of the Canadian Wheat Board. Canadian Agricultural Economics Society. https://caes.usask.ca/meetings/the-rise-and-fall-of-the-canadian-wheat-board.pdf. Accessed 15 July 2017.

Mulroney, David. 2015. *Middle power, middle kingdom: What Canadians need to know about China in the 21st century*. Toronto: Allen Lane.

Nossal, Kim Richard, and Leah Sarson. 2013. About face: Explaining changes in Canada's China policy, 2006–2012. Paper presentation at the annual meeting of the Canadian Political Science Association, Victoria, BC, June 6.

Paltiel, Jeremy. 2011. Canada in China's grand strategy. In *Issues in Canada-China relations*, ed. Pitman B. Potter and Thomas Adams, 117–136. Canadian International Council.

Potter, Pitman B. 2016. Legal challenges in Canada-China relations. In *Moving forward: Issues in Canada-China relations*, ed. Asif B. Farooq and Scott McKnight, 47–55. Toronto: University of Toronto, Munk Institute of Global Affairs and China Open Research Network.

Prime Minister of Canada. 2016a. Joint press release between Canada and the People's Republic of China. Prime Minister's Office, September 1. http://pm.gc.ca/eng/news/2016/09/01/joint-press-release-between-canada-and-peoples-republic-china. Accessed 20 July 2017.

———. 2016b. Joint statement between Canada and the People's Republic of China. Prime Minister's Office, September 23. http://pm.gc.ca/eng/news/2016/09/23/joint-statement-between-canada-and-peoples-republic-china. Accessed 20 July 2017.

Shambaugh, David. 2013. *China goes global*. New York: Oxford University Press.

Statistics Canada. 2015. Travellers to Canada by country of origin, top 15 countries of origin. Statistics Canada, November 1, 2016. http://www.statcan.gc.ca/tables-tableaux/sum-som/l01/cst01/arts38a-eng.htm. Accessed 16 July 2017.

Valiante, Giuseppe. 2016. Chinese premier calls for 'new golden decade' with Canada. *Toronto Star*, September 23. https://www.thestar.com/news/canada/2016/09/23/chinese-premier-calls-for-new-golden-decade-with-canada.html. Accessed 15 July 2017.

Wentian, Wang. 2016. A new golden decade for Canada-China relations. *Globe and Mail*, October 9. https://www.theglobeandmail.com/opinion/a-new-golden-decade-for-canada-china-relations/article32300566/. Accessed 15 July 2017.

World Bank. China. The World Bank Group. http://data.worldbank.org/country/china. Accessed 15 July 2017.

CHAPTER 9

A Promise Too Far? The Justin Trudeau Government and Indigenous Rights

Sheryl Lightfoot

Canada is widely recognized as a global leader in human rights. One of the authors and drivers of the very first human rights document, the 1948 *Universal Declaration on Human Rights*, came from Canada. Canada has ratified all the major international human rights treaties, including the International Covenant on Civil and Political Rights; the International Covenant on Economic, Social and Cultural Rights; the International Covenant on the Elimination of Racial Discrimination; the Convention on the Rights of the Child; the Convention on the Elimination of All Forms of Discrimination Against Women; the Convention against Torture and Other Cruel, Inhuman or Degrading Treatment or Punishment; and the Convention on the Rights of Persons with Disabilities.[1] Canada has also signed and ratified numerous other international human rights instruments, making it one of the world leaders in human rights treaty ratification.[2] It has served on the United Nations (UN) Human Rights Council. When the international community looks for examples of states that

S. Lightfoot (✉)
University of British Columbia, Vancouver, BC, Canada

© The Author(s) 2018
N. Hillmer, P. Lagassé (eds.), *Justin Trudeau and Canadian Foreign Policy*, Canada and International Affairs,
https://doi.org/10.1007/978-3-319-73860-4_9

respect and support human rights, Canada is often referenced first. Because it lacks the influence of a superpower in foreign policy, Canada's global reputation and international leadership capability rely, to a great extent, on its human rights record and reputation.

Yet, when Indigenous peoples' rights are included in its human rights record, Canada's reputation loses some of its luster. Not only has Canada failed to ratify the most advanced Indigenous rights convention, the International Labour Organization (ILO) No. 169, it was also one of only four countries in the world to vote *against* the *United Nations Declaration on the Rights of Indigenous Peoples* in 2007. Canada not only voted against the Draft Declaration in the Human Rights Council in late 2006, but it was reported to have been the *most active country lobbying against* the UNDRIP in its final stage of negotiations in 2006 and 2007.[3] The UNDRIP is, in fact, the only international human rights instrument that Canada has ever failed to support. Canada is cited regularly and consistently in the Universal Periodic Review (UPR) and by the Committee on the Elimination of Racial Discrimination (or CERD, the independent body that monitors implementation of the Convention on the Elimination of All Forms of Racial Discrimination) as failing to live up to international standards where Indigenous peoples rights are concerned. Canada's Indigenous rights exception—to its otherwise good human rights reputation—compromises its global leadership and credibility.

Sensitive to Canada's shameful underperformance in Indigenous rights, the Justin Trudeau government, elected in 2015, set out to make a change. Trudeau promised that Canada would commit itself to a new, nation-to-nation relationship with Indigenous peoples, and he promised that his government would immediately adopt and implement the UNDRIP. This chapter will examine what implementation of the UNDRIP means for Canada and whether Canada's position on Indigenous rights has actually changed under the Trudeau government. I will argue that there is a notable gap between Trudeau's vision and rhetoric, on the one hand, and the policy realities on the ground. This troubling gap creates unnecessary risk to Canada's human rights reputation and leadership in the international community. While implementing Indigenous rights in Canada presents serious challenges, I will conclude by offering some recommendations for implementation strategies.

The Significance of the *United Nations Declaration on the Rights of Indigenous Peoples*[4]

The *United Nations Declaration on the Rights of Indigenous Peoples*, which passed the United Nations General Assembly on September 13, 2007, represents the global consensus on the minimum standard ("the floor") for Indigenous peoples' rights that all states are obligated to recognize, protect, and uphold. The UNDRIP emphasizes the nationhood and self-determination of Indigenous peoples: their right to exist, to maintain and strengthen their cultures, and to protect and enhance their own traditions and institutions. As a human rights declaration, it prohibits state discrimination against Indigenous peoples while also recognizing their collective right to remain distinct from their surrounding societies, to pursue their own visions of development, and to promote their full and effective participation in decision-making processes on issues that impact them.

As a human rights declaration, and not an international treaty or convention, the UNDRIP joins other important human rights declarations, such as the 1948 *Universal Declaration of Human Rights*, in articulating a global standard that states are morally and politically obligated to respect as well as promote. The text of the UNDRIP was negotiated and drafted by states and Indigenous groups over the course of several decades, but the final text was decided on by states alone. As with all General Assembly resolutions, only states can vote on the floor of the General Assembly, and state commitments to it, votes against it, or later endorsements of it, were entirely voluntary. As stated by the United Nations Permanent Forum on Indigenous Issues (UNPFII), all human rights declarations are "not generally legally binding; however, they represent the dynamic development of international legal norms and reflect the commitment of states to move in certain directions, abiding by certain principles."[5] According to a UN press release, the UNDRIP represents "a major step forward towards the promotion and protection of human rights and fundamental freedoms for all ... [through] ... the General Assembly's important role in setting international standards."[6] Furthermore, as former United Nations special rapporteur on the rights of Indigenous peoples, James Anaya, has stated, it is not the technical legal significance of the document that should be the focus but rather its normative legitimacy: "Whatever its legal significance, the Declaration has a significant normative weight grounded in its high degree of legitimacy. This legitimacy is a function not only of the fact that it has been formally endorsed by an overwhelming majority of United Nations member States, but also the fact that it is the product of years of advocacy and struggle by indigenous peoples themselves."[7]

Since normative change in international human rights can be expected eventually to alter human rights practices by states,[8] it is important to understand what implementation of the UNDRIP actually means. As Victoria Tauli-Corpuz, former chairperson of the UNPFII and current UN special rapporteur on the rights of Indigenous peoples, described it, "the Declaration will become the major foundation and reference [for UN agencies, but will also serve] as the main framework to guide States."[9] Tauli-Corpuz also noted that the UNDRIP is intended to serve as a "key instrument and tool for raising awareness on and monitoring progress of indigenous peoples' situations and the protection, respect and fulfilment of indigenous peoples rights."[10]

As a standard-setting tool, the 46 articles of the UNDRIP are intended to guide state action toward relationships with Indigenous peoples; they are based on justice and serve as a framework for mutual recognition and respect. Due to the comprehensiveness of the articles, many states have expressed confusion and/or misgivings about how they are expected to implement the UNDRIP in practice. James Anaya offered the following concrete suggestions for initial steps toward implementation:

> First, State officials as well as indigenous leaders should receive training on the Declaration and on the related international instruments, and on practical measures to implement the Declaration. ...
>
> Additionally, States should engage in comprehensive reviews of their existing legislation and administrative programmes to identify where they may be incompatible with the Declaration. This would include a review of all laws and programmes touching upon indigenous peoples' rights and interests, including those related to natural resource development, land, education, administration of justice and other areas. On the basis of such a review, the necessary legal and programmatic reforms should be developed and implemented in consultation with indigenous peoples.
>
> States should be committed to devoting significant human and financial resources to the measures required to implement the Declaration. These resources will typically be required for the demarcation or return of indigenous lands, the development of culturally appropriate educational programmes, support for indigenous self-governance institutions and the many other measures contemplated by the Declaration.

The United Nations system and the international community should develop and implement programmes to provide technical and financial assistance to States and indigenous peoples to move forward with these and related steps to implement the Declaration, as a matter of utmost priority.[11]

Clearly, these expectations are high for any state, but for the colonial settler states like Canada, which were originally settled on the basis of dispossession of Indigenous peoples' lands and which have profited for years from Indigenous peoples' lands and resources, these expectations will translate into major changes in practice. In fact, the UNDRIP calls on states to begin a process of resetting the entire framework of their relationship with Indigenous peoples, away from a colonial model and toward an entirely new relationship grounded in mutual respect and the principles of self-determination.[12]

Canada's Record on Indigenous Rights

In *Global Indigenous Politics: A Subtle Revolution*, I analyzed Indigenous rights and various state responses to Indigenous rights through December 2014. My study found that, while there was near global rhetorical consensus in original votes for, and later endorsements of, the *UN Declaration on the Rights of Indigenous Peoples*, states, in their actual behavior, are much more recalcitrant in their acceptance of the full body of Indigenous rights. I found that there are some strange and unexpected patterns of state behavior vis-à-vis Indigenous rights, especially among English-speaking settler states like Canada.

First, I observed a pattern that I call "selective endorsement." After originally voting against the UNDRIP in 2007, the four countries of the "Anglosphere" (Canada, United States, Australia, and New Zealand) each later shifted their official positions on the UNDRIP to "support" or "endorsement" during 2009 and 2010. Australia was the first, in April 2009, when Indigenous Affairs Minister Jenny Macklin announced the change in Parliament House.[13] A year later, on 19 April, New Zealand's Minister of Māori Affairs, Pita Sharples, surprised the world at the opening ceremony of the UNPFII, saying that his country would now support the Declaration.[14] Canada took a less public approach on 12 November 2010, when Indian and Northern Affairs Canada announced the country's formal endorsement online.[15] Finally, the United States changed its position on 16 December 2010, after extended review and tribal consultations.[16]

Each of these four countries also included important qualifiers and exclusions about how UNDRIP is to be interpreted in domestic law. Far from a full endorsement of Indigenous rights, the four countries engaged in more nuanced behavior. By selectively endorsing Indigenous rights, these four countries attempted to express their rhetorical support for Indigenous rights while also strategically, collectively, and unilaterally writing down the global consensus on Indigenous rights and constraining them so that these countries' current laws, policies, and practices automatically align with their own interpretation of the expectations of the global human rights consensus.

Second, Anglosphere states demonstrate "over-compliance." While compliance with international human rights is normally considered as a compliant or non-compliant calculation, my analysis shows five possible outcomes in Indigenous rights compliance by states, compliance, non-compliance, under-compliance, partial compliance, and a new concept, which I term "over-compliance." In order to analyze compliance, I constructed a data set of 58 countries with significant Indigenous populations. I compared such variables as percentage of Indigenous population, region, political system (parliamentary, presidential, semi-presidential, or one-party), legal system (common law, civil law, common/Islamic, or civil/Islamic), and political structure (federal or unitary). I then examined each country's position on the major human rights treaties and its position on Indigenous rights instruments: ILO 107 and 169 as well as the UNDRIP. Any changes in position since the 2007 UNDRIP vote were also noted. Next, I scored each of these countries on their Indigenous rights commitment, as well as their constitutional, legal, and policy behavior to devise a level of compliance with Indigenous rights.

The results show that ten countries, 17 percent, are non-compliant; 30 countries, about 52 percent, are under-compliant; 12 countries, about 21 percent, are partially compliant; two countries, about 3 percent, are compliant; and four countries, 7 percent, are over-compliant. The geographic results of each category are mixed, but the over-compliant countries are clearly the four countries of the Anglosphere: the United States, Australia, New Zealand, and Canada.

An "over-compliant" state, such as Canada, is one that paradoxically takes constitutional, legal, and/or policy actions that recognize specific rights, or a category of rights, that go beyond that state's international human rights treaty obligations or its normative international commitments. The term "over-compliance" does not indicate or imply that such states are completely complying with, or even exceeding, international Indigenous rights standards—they are not—only that these states are performing above the level that would be expected based upon their low commitments in Indigenous rights. It is a nuanced behavior that appears, like selective endorsement, to keep these countries' expectations low enough that they can interpret their status quo as being in line with global Indigenous rights.

The Trudeau Government's History with Indigenous Rights and the UNDRIP[17]

On 2 June 2015, in the last stages of the Stephen Harper Conservative government, at a press conference in Ottawa, the three commissioners of Canada's Truth and Reconciliation Commission (TRC), Justice Murray Sinclair, Chief Wilton Littlechild, and Dr. Marie Wilson, announced the release of the TRC summary report: *Honouring the Truth, Reconciling for the Future*.[18] This announcement concluded six years of intense and highly emotional work on the part of the TRC, which was created by the Indian Residential Schools Settlement Agreement.[19] The TRC was authorized to settle class action legal claims brought forward by residential school survivors. It conducted an extensive study of the century-long, church-run, and government-funded Indian Residential Schools program in Canada, in order to reveal the truth about the program and its legacy impacts on Indigenous peoples. At the June 2015 press conference, Justice Sinclair, the TRC chief commissioner, said, "The residential school experience is clearly one of the darkest, most troubling chapters in our collective history. ... In the period from Confederation until the decision to close residential schools was taken in this country in 1969,[20] Canada clearly participated in a period of cultural genocide."[21]

The second part of the TRC's mandate was to make recommendations on healing. It focused on how Indigenous individuals and families can heal, but also considered how to reset and renew the broken relationship between Indigenous and non-Indigenous peoples in Canada. Over the course of six years, the TRC held seven national and numerous regional events across Canada, collected tens of thousands of documents, and gathered witness statements from more than 6,000 individuals who had survived their attendance at residential schools.

The summary report notes that healing the harm done to the relationship between Canada and Indigenous peoples, lasting over a century and a half, will be hard. Reconciliation, it states, "is about establishing and maintaining a mutually respectful relationship between Aboriginal and non-Aboriginal peoples in this country."[22] While discovering the truth of residential schools was important, it was only the initial step in what is to be a very long process. The process of reconciliation will need to involve actions—actions that will fundamentally change behavior at all levels of government and in all facets of society. Citing the 1996 *Report of the Royal Commission on Aboriginal Peoples*[23] as a lost opportunity for fundamental change, the TRC saw itself as a second chance to redesign the relationship between Canada and Indigenous peoples.

The TRC's *Summary Report* ends with *94 Calls to Action*,[24] which are specific recommendations that the TRC views as essential to form the blueprint for reconciliation into the future. The Calls to Action urge all levels of government—federal, provincial, territorial, and municipal—to make fundamental changes in policies and programs in order to repair the harm caused by residential schools and work toward renewed relationships and, eventually, reconciliation. The Calls to Action are divided into two categories: the first set, 1–42, address "Legacy" effects of Indian Residential Schools. These include calling for changes in child welfare, education, language and culture, health, and justice to deal with significant gaps between Indigenous and non-Indigenous peoples and other various issues that all stem, in one form or another, from policy practices, including the Indian Residential Schools program. The second set of Calls, 43–94, charts a specific pathway toward "Reconciliation." This section begins with, "We call upon federal, provincial, territorial, and municipal governments to fully adopt and implement the *United Nations Declaration on the Rights of Indigenous Peoples* as the framework for reconciliation."[25] The very next Call to Action, 44, calls for a national action plan and other concrete measures designed to implement the UNDRIP. In total, 12 individual Calls to Action referenced the UNDRIP. Essentially, the TRC recommended that Canada's pathway to reconciliation should be grounded in the goals and principles of the UNDRIP. Upon its release, Prime Minister Harper icily received the TRC Summary Report. Justice Sinclair reported that, while the prime minister seemed "open to listening to some of our concerns and inquired about some of our recommendations," the government remained steadfast in its resistance to adoption of the UNDRIP.[26]

The UNDRIP became an issue during the 2015 federal election, which began in mid-summer, on the heels of the June TRC announcement of 94 *Calls to Action*. Within weeks of the TRC announcement, Liberal Party leader Trudeau addressed the Assembly of First Nations 36th Annual General Assembly in Montreal. He noted that the TRC and the Calls to Action serve as "an especially important conversation as we prepare to commemorate the 150th anniversary of Confederation. We need to recognize that ours was a nation forged without the meaningful participation of Aboriginal Peoples. ... This commemoration stands as a reminder that much work remains. One hundred and fifty years on, we've yet to complete the unfinished business of Confederation."[27] Trudeau continued, stating that there is an "urgent need for a renewed relationship between the federal government and Indigenous Peoples in Canada – one built on trust, recognition and respect for rights, and a commitment that the status quo must end." Railing against a paternalistic approach to Indigenous peoples and charging the Harper government with a series of failed Aboriginal policies, Trudeau promised an honorable and renewed nation-to-nation relationship, based on "recognition, rights, respect, co-operation and partnership…[and] rooted in the principles of the United Nations Declaration on the Rights of Indigenous Peoples." Later in the address, Trudeau specifically mentioned that the Liberal Party's response to the TRC's 94 recommendations would start with implementation of the UNDRIP. The full Liberal Party platform, released shortly thereafter, used the same language.[28]

Fueled by anger over Harper government policies, including voter suppression legislation and the parliamentary actions that sparked the Idle No More movement in 2012, Indigenous peoples surged to the ballot box during the 2015 federal election, helping Justin Trudeau's Liberal Party win the election. Some Indigenous communities saw voter turnout spike more than 200 percent over the previous election.[29] Even Indigenous individuals who had previously been opposed, in principle, to participating in Canadian federal or provincial elections were so outraged by Harper policies that the mantra "anyone but Harper" brought many of them to the polls for the very first time.[30] Many Indigenous communities reported very long lines, and some polling stations even ran out of ballots.[31]

Many Indigenous leaders greeted the electoral victory of Justin Trudeau and the Liberal Party with hope, optimism, and high expectation; others remained cautious, especially given past Liberal Party positions on

Indigenous issues, which leaned heavily toward assimilative policies. Initial moves seemed positive. Prime Minister Trudeau crafted a Cabinet that included two Indigenous members, Jody Wilson-Raybould as Justice Minister and Hunter Tootoo as Minister of Fisheries and the Canadian Coast Guard. The appointment of Carolyn Bennett, as Minister of Indigenous and Northern Affairs, was also seen by many Indigenous leaders as a positive sign.[32]

The mandate letter from the new prime minister to Bennett, which was made public in November 2015, further fueled high expectations on Canada's new approach to the UNDRIP. The prime minister directed that the relationship between Aboriginal peoples and Canada must be renewed on a "nation-to-nation" basis because "no relationship is more important to me and to Canada than the one with Indigenous peoples." In particular, the prime minister wrote:

> I expect you to work with your colleagues and through established legislative, regulatory, and Cabinet processes to deliver on your top priorities: To support the work of reconciliation, and continue the necessary process of truth telling and healing, work with provinces and territories, and with First Nations, the Métis Nation, and Inuit, to implement recommendations of the Truth and Reconciliation Commission, starting with the implementation of the *United Nations Declaration on the Rights of Indigenous Peoples*.[33]

One month later, in December 2015, Prime Minister Trudeau addressed the Assembly of First Nations Special Chiefs Assembly and announced his five-point plan to reset Canada's relationship with Indigenous peoples: "it is time for a renewed, nation-to-nation relationship with First Nations peoples, one that understands that the constitutionally guaranteed rights of First Nations in Canada are not an inconvenience but rather a sacred obligation."[34] Alongside promises to repeal Harper legislation, to launch a national inquiry on missing and murdered Indigenous women and girls, and to address education funding issues, Trudeau promised fully to implement the 94 recommendations of the Truth and Reconciliation Commission, including adoption and implementation of the UNDRIP.

In May 2016, Wilson-Raybould and Bennett went to New York to address the UNPFII. Wilson-Raybould addressed the opening session with a special statement on Canada's new position on the UNDRIP, the *Indian Act*, reconciliation, and the principle of free, prior, and informed consent (FPIC). In this statement, she indicated the need for Canada to reform the ways it conducts business with Indigenous peoples, and the central role that the UNDRIP should play in that re-ordering and renewal. She said:

> We need to find long-term solutions to decades old problems as we seek to deconstruct our colonial legacy. Important to this work will be implementing the Calls to Action set out in the recent report of the Truth and Reconciliation Commission which considered the legacy of the Indian Residential schools.
> One of the significant challenges to this work is that although strengthening the nation-to-nation relationship is the goal, practically speaking the administration of Indigenous affairs in Canada is not organized around Indigenous Nations. For the most part, it is organized around an imposed system of governance. With respect to Indians this is through "bands," which are creatures of federal statute under the Indian Act. The Indian Act being the antithesis of self-government as an expression of self-determination.
> Simply put, we need to move beyond the system of imposed governance.
> ... Tied to the fundamental work of Nation rebuilding and implementing the UNDRIP, one of the biggest legal questions we need to unpack is how to implement the concept of "free, prior and informed consent."
> The Declaration recognizes that Indigenous peoples have both individual and collective rights. Participation in real decision-making is at the heart of the Declaration's concept of free, prior and informed consent – that Indigenous peoples must be able to participate in making decisions that affect their lives.

The next day, Minister Bennett addressed the first day of the UNPFII. She stated—unequivocally—that her purpose in speaking at the UNPFII was to address Canada's position on the UNDRIP. She announced that Canada would hereafter be a "full supporter of the Declaration, without qualification."[35] Following loud applause and a standing ovation, she continued, "We intend nothing less than to adopt and implement the Declaration."[36] She then added some important qualifying terms, "in accordance with the Canadian Constitution,"[37] the first indication from the new government that their agenda for change in their relationship with Indigenous peoples was actually limited by existing governance structures.

Bennett continued with an explanation of the new government's position. She said, "By adopting and implementing the Declaration, we are breathing life into section 35 [of the Constitution] and recognizing it as a full box of rights for Indigenous peoples." Next, she said that the new Canadian government believes that its existing constitutional obligations already fulfilled the principles of the UNDRIP, including the important but controversial principle of FPIC. Further, she noted, in an important pivotal shift in the new government's rhetoric, "We see modern treaties and self-government agreements as the ultimate expression of free, prior and informed consent among partners."[38] In other words, Bennett's statement, in stark contrast to Wilson-Raybould's statement the day before, indicated that the new government is actually quite satisfied that Canada's existing constitutional, legal, and policy positions are already in line with the principles of the UNDRIP and no fundamental structural change is needed.

Only six weeks later, Justice Minister Wilson-Raybould came to the Assembly of First Nations, at their Annual General Assembly in Niagara Falls, to discuss the hard work that lay ahead for Canada and First Nations to rebuild and transform their relationship into one that better reflects the inherent self-determination of Indigenous peoples.[39] She intended to set out a course of action, of "transformative change" that would turn all of the "good words" and "good will" into "meaningful progress." As she did several weeks earlier at the United Nations, Wilson-Raybould took aim at the *Indian Act*, as a legacy of colonial administration, and one of the major elements of current governance that is "fundamentally inconsistent with the United Nations Declaration"[40] and requires change. Referring to whole-scale adoption of the UNDRIP into Canadian law as "unworkable" and a "simplistic approach," she, rather, urged a cautious, thoughtful, controlled, and deliberate "process of transition" to finding alternatives to the *Indian Act*. She said, "the way the UNDRIP will get implemented in Canada will be through a mixture of legislation, policy, and action initiated and taken by Indigenous Nations themselves." However, she also noted that "ultimately, the UNDRIP will be articulated through the constitutional framework of section 35." In other words, while certain policy changes can be expected to proceed slowly, no fundamental constitutional change is planned, anticipated, or, seemingly, desirable.

In February 2017, the prime minister announced the creation of a Working Group of Ministers, headed by Wilson-Raybould, that would be charged with conducting a full review of laws and policies related to

Indigenous peoples. According to the prime minister's press release, this group

> will examine relevant federal laws, policies, and operational practices to help ensure the Crown is meeting its constitutional obligations with respect to Aboriginal and treaty rights; adhering to international human rights standards, including the United Nations Declaration on the Rights of Indigenous Peoples; and supporting the implementation of the Truth and Reconciliation Commission's Calls to Action.[41]

The Working Group made its first public announcement in July 2017, when it released ten guiding principles.[42]

Meanwhile, the Trudeau government has taken other steps that cause many to doubt its real commitment to change. It approved a liquefied natural gas project in British Columbia, and continues to push through the Kinder Morgan pipeline and the Site C dam, in spite of vocal opposition and legal challenges by many First Nations. It launched the Missing and Murdered Indigenous Women inquiry, but has faced intense criticism over its form, scope, and speed of operations. The Canadian Human Rights Tribunal issued two non-compliance orders against the federal government that was found to be discriminating against First Nations children, and rather than comply, the federal government choose to fight the orders in court. An October 2016 article in *Maclean's* magazine noted, "It's getting pretty hard to figure out what differentiates this government from the one Stephen Harper ran before it." By January 2017, a Privy Council Office report card gave the Trudeau government harsh marks for not living up to its lofty promises for Indigenous peoples.[43] It has still failed to produce a promised national action plan for the implementation of the UNDRIP.

In August 2017, the Committee on the Elimination of Racial Discrimination issued its periodic review on Canada's record along with its recommendations for action. The report applauded Canada's new position on the UNDRIP but also expressed significant concern over the lack of a national action plan and full implementation.[44] Only a month later, in September 2017, Prime Minister Trudeau addressed the UN General Assembly and spent a significant portion of his speech on Indigenous issues, acknowledging Canada's history of colonialism, pledging to rely on the norms, principles, and standards in the UNDRIP as the path forward to reconciliation in Canada, and noting that "the world expects Canada to strictly adhere to international standards including the United Nations Declaration on the Rights of Indigenous Peoples."[45] Both the CERD report and Trudeau's speech continue to highlight the central importance of implementation of Indigenous rights to Canada's global leadership position.

AT A CROSSROADS

Canada and the Trudeau government stand at a crossroads. On the one hand, the Liberal Party and Prime Minister Trudeau wish to respond to the recommendations of the TRC, and set out on a new course, with a renewed relationship with Indigenous peoples based on the UNDRIP. On the other hand, the Trudeau government recognizes just how wide sweeping such change would ultimately be and the political and practical challenges involved.

There are multiple challenges. First, there is tremendous diversity among Indigenous peoples that live within the borders of what we call Canada. Their needs, concerns, and views of self-determination vary tremendously. Some Indigenous peoples have historical treaty relations that pre-date Confederation, others are engaged in the numbered treaties and other land claim agreements of the nineteenth and twentieth centuries, and still others remain outside of treaty: existing in a state of pure colonial imposition and control, but with their full Aboriginal rights still intact. Some Indigenous peoples desire a Western-style democracy, while others prefer to maintain traditional forms of governance. Implementing the UNDRIP means responding to, and negotiating with, each group to ensure that their self-determination is achieved.

Second, there is the complexity of competing priorities in the economic realm. Some Indigenous peoples wish to engage in capitalism, either natural resource and/or commercial development to improve the socioeconomic conditions of their nations, while others feel that their very existence as Indigenous peoples depends upon resisting such projects in their territories. Not only are there vast differences in economic priorities between Indigenous peoples and industry but also differences in perspective among Indigenous nations, so that there are many conflicts and in multiple directions. Yet, implementing the UNDRIP requires government and industry to negotiate with each Indigenous people to obtain their FPIC to projects that impact them, before approving or launching such projects. It means that Indigenous peoples may give their consent, or they may withhold it.

In short, implementing the UNDRIP is difficult, expensive, and complex on many levels. It is a process that will involve significant and sustained political will and commitment over a long period of time by all layers of government. The Trudeau government is engaged in a difficult dance. It has promised to adopt and implement the UNDRIP, yet it is cognizant of the scope of structural changes to do so, and so it remains hesitant—even resistant—to making real change, a policy position that is quite consistent with the Harper government. While rhetoric on Indigenous rights has changed remarkably from the Harper government, the Trudeau government remains engaged in both selective endorsement and "over-compliance" behavior. Critics of the Trudeau government have noticed the "troubling gap between Trudeau's lofty talk and his government's actions."[46] Citing the government's "incoherent half-embrace of the United Nations Declaration on the Rights of Indigenous Peoples," a *Toronto Star* editorial noted a dearth of practical difference between the Trudeau and Harper governments, in terms of actual policy and programs, particularly on issues related to natural resource development projects.[47]

Recommendations for Implementing the UN Declaration

Implementing the UNDRIP is a difficult and expensive long-term project, and yet Canada has an opportune moment to become a global leader in Indigenous rights *and* human rights if it quickly takes actions that align with its rhetorical commitments on Indigenous rights. I conclude with some initial steps that Canada can take to work co-operatively with Indigenous peoples toward implementation and to fulfill its international obligations:

1. Announce a comprehensive national action plan. In the Outcome Document of the World Conference on Indigenous Peoples, held in 2014, all nation states committed to working co-operatively with Indigenous peoples to co-create a national action plan for the implementation of the UNDRIP.[48] As of mid-2017, no state has done so. Canada could be the first and could lead the world in this direction.

2. Domesticate the UNDRIP through legislation. In 2016, Member of Parliament Romeo Saganash introduced a private members bill[49] to establish a legislative framework for the implementation of the UNDRIP. Such frameworks ensure that future governments are not able to reverse any legislative, constitutional, or administrative measures taken. Passage of this legislation would be a significant practical and symbolic step toward implementation.
3. Engage in a constructive dialogue with Indigenous peoples about how to move from the Canadian standard of "consultation" on development projects to the international standard of FPIC. Consent is a key definitional feature of a people's right to self-determination, a people that is not able to give or withhold its consent is not truly self-determining. Therefore, to ensure that Indigenous peoples enjoy the right of self-determination equal to all other peoples, new legal structures and administrative systems must be co-designed by states and Indigenous peoples so that this international standard will be met in Canada.
4. Establish a domestic monitoring body for the implementation of the UNDRIP. The monitoring body should have representation from government and Indigenous peoples and should provide an annual progress report on implementation, along with suggestions for improvement. This monitoring body can also consult with the United Nations for technical advice on constitutional reforms and specific legislation as well as policy recommendations.

Notes

1. United Nations (2015).
2. University of Minnesota Human Rights Library (2008).
3. Continuing Legal Education Society of British Columbia (2008).
4. This section is drawn from Sheryl Lightfoot (2016). *Global Indigenous Politics: A Subtle Revolution*. Oxfordshire, Routledge. Reprinted by permission.
5. United Nations Permanent Forum on Indigenous Issues (2007).
6. United Nations General Assembly (2007).
7. Anaya (2010).
8. Risse et al. (1999).
9. Tauli-Corpuz (2007).
10. Ibid.
11. Anaya (2010).

12. Lightfoot (2010).
13. Macklin (2009).
14. Sharples (2010).
15. Indigenous and Northern Affairs Canada (2010).
16. Obama (2010).
17. Portions of this section were previously published in Sheryl Lightfoot (2017). Reprinted by permission.
18. Truth and Reconciliation Commission (2015).
19. Indian Residential Schools Settlement Agreement (2006).
20. Even though the decision to begin closing the schools was made in 1969, the last school did not close until 1996.
21. The Canadian Press (2016).
22. Truth and Reconciliation Commission (2015, 6).
23. Royal Commission on Aboriginal Peoples (1996).
24. Truth and Reconciliation Commission (2015, 319–337).
25. Ibid., 325.
26. Fedio (2015).
27. Trudeau (2015b).
28. Liberal Party (2016).
29. Puxley (2015).
30. Ayers (2015).
31. Baum (2015).
32. Wilson (2015).
33. Trudeau (2015a).
34. Mas (2015).
35. Bennett (2016).
36. Ibid.
37. Ibid.
38. Ibid.
39. Wilson-Raybould (2016).
40. Ibid.
41. Office of the Prime Minister (2017).
42. APTN (2017).
43. *National Post* (2017).
44. Committee on the Elimination of Racial Discrimination (2017).
45. Trudeau (2017).
46. *Toronto Star* (2016).
47. Ibid.
48. United Nations General Assembly (2014).
49. Bill C-262, an Act to ensure that the laws of Canada are in harmony with the United Nations Declaration on the Rights of Indigenous Peoples, introduced 21 April 2016.

References

Akin, David. 2017. In a report card on Trudeau government's first year, indigenous affairs work gets an 'incomplete.' *National Post*, January 23. http://nationalpost.com/news/politics/trudeau-aides-give-liberal-government-failing-grade-on-meeting-indigenous-affairs-objectives/wcm/615244f8-ed98-4801-a49a-a6e66283448e. Accessed 12 Apr 2017.

Anaya, James A. 2010. Statement by James Anaya, Special Rapporteur on the Rights of Indigenous Peoples on the obligations of states to implement the Declaration on the Rights of Indigenous Peoples. Speech, United Nations, New York, October 18.

APTN. 2017. Canada releases 10 'principles' on government's relationship with Indigenous peoples. *APTN National News*, July 14. http://aptnnews.ca/2017/07/14/78213/. Accessed 31 July 2017.

Ayers, Tom. 2015. N.S. First Nations group suggests voting for anyone but Harper. *Herald News*, June 22. http://thechronicleherald.ca/novascotia/1300839-n.s.-first-nations-group-suggests-voting-for-anyone-but-harper. Accessed 25 Nov 2016.

Baum, Kathryn Blaze. 2015. On-Reserve voters endure lines and ballot issues for historic election. *Globe and Mail*, October 20. http://www.theglobeandmail.com/news/politics/some-first-nations-polling-stations-run-out-of-ballots-amid-high-turnout/article26899907/. Accessed 25 Nov 2016.

Bennett, Carolyn. 2016. Announcement of Canada's support for the United Nations Declaration on the Rights of Indigenous Peoples. Speech, United Nations Permanent Forum on Indigenous Issues, New York, May 10.

Canadian Press. 2016. Commission offers 94 ways to redress 'cultural genocide.' *Maclean's*, June 2. http://www.macleans.ca/news/canada/trc-offers-94-ways-to-redress-cultural-genocide/. Accessed 1 Nov 2016.

Committee on the Elimination of Racial Discrimination. 2017. Concluding observations on the combined twenty-first to twenty-third periodic reports of Canada. CERD/C/CAN/CO/21–23.

Continuing Legal Education Society of British Columbia. 2008. *Aboriginal Law Conference 2008, Paper 2.1: United Nations Declaration on the Rights of Indigenous Peoples*. Vancouver: Continuing Legal Education Society of British Columbia.

Fedio, Chloe. 2015. Truth and Reconciliation report brings calls for actions, not words. *CBC News*, June 2. http://www.cbc.ca/news/politics/truth-and-reconciliation-report-brings-calls-for-action-not-words-1.3096863. Accessed 1 Nov 2016.

Indian Residential Schools Settlement Agreement. 2006. Indian residential schools settlement agreement. Official court website, May 8. http://www.residentialschoolsettlement.ca/IRS%20Settlement%20Agreement-%20ENGLISH.pdf. Accessed 1 Nov 2016.

Indigenous and Norther Affairs Canada. 2010. ARCHIVED – Canada's statement of support of the United Nations Declaration on the Rights of Indigenous Peoples. Government of Canada, November 12. http://www.ainc-inac.gc.ca/ai/mr/nr/s-d2010/23429-eng.asp. Accessed 10 Jan 2011.

Liberal Party of Canada. 2016. Truth and Reconciliation. Liberal Party of Canada. https://www.liberal.ca/realchange/truth-and-reconciliation-2/. Accessed 24 Nov 2016.

Lightfoot, Sheryl. 2010. Emerging international indigenous rights norms and 'over-compliance' in New Zealand and Canada. *Political Science Sage* 62 (1): 84–104.

———. 2016. *Global indigenous politics: A subtle revolution*. Oxfordshire: Routledge.

———. 2017. Adopting and implementing the United Nations Declaration on the Rights of Indigenous Peoples: Canada's existential crisis. In *Surviving Canada: Indigenous peoples celebrate 150 years of betrayal*, ed. Kiera L. Ladner and Myra Tait, 440–459. Winnipeg: ARP.

Macklin, Jenny. 2009. Statement on the United Nations Declaration on the Rights of Indigenous Peoples. Australian Government, April 3. http://parlinfo.aph.gov.au/parlInfo/download/media/pressrel/418T6/upload_binary/418t60.pdf;fileType=application%2Fpdf#search=%22media/pressrel/418T6%22. Accessed 4 Apr 2009.

Mas, Susana. 2015. Trudeau lays out plan for new relationship with Indigenous peoples. *CBC News*, December 8. http://www.cbc.ca/news/politics/justin-trudeau-afn-indigenous-aboriginal-people-1.3354747. Accessed 25 Nov 2016.

Obama, Barack. 2010. *Remarks by the president at the White House Tribal Nations conference*. Washington, DC: The White House, December 16.

Prime Minister's Office. 2017. Prime Minister announces working group of ministers on the review of laws and policies related to Indigenous peoples. Prime Minister's Office, February 22. http://pm.gc.ca/eng/news/2017/02/22/prime-minister-announces-working-group-ministers-review-laws-and-policies-related. Accessed 27 Feb 2017.

Puxley, Chinta. 2015. Anger at Stephen Harper, disenfranchisement fueled turnout of Aboriginal voters. *Canadian Press*, October 25. http://www.nationalobserver.com/2015/10/25/news/anger-stephen-harper-disenfranchisement-fuelled-turnout-aboriginal-voters. Accessed 24 Nov 2016.

Risse, Thomas, Stephen C. Ropp, and Kathryn Sikkink, eds. 1999. *The power of human rights: International norms and domestic change*. Cambridge: Cambridge University Press.

Royal Commission on Aboriginal Affairs. 1996. Report of the Royal Commission on Aboriginal peoples. Library and Archives Canada. http://www.collectionscanada.gc.ca/webarchives/20071115053257/http://www.ainc-inac.gc.ca/ch/rcap/sg/sgmm_e.html. Accessed 1 Nov 2016.

Sharples, Pita. 2010. UNPFII opening ceremony New Zealand statement. Speech, United Nations Permanent Forum on Indigenous Issues, New York, April 19.

Tauli-Corpuz, Victoria. 2007. Message of Victoria Tauli-Corpuz, Chairperson of the UN Permanent Forum on Indigenous Issues, on the occasion of the adoption by the General Assembly of the Declaration on the Rights of Indigenous Peoples. Speech, United Nations, New York, September 13.

Toronto Star. 2016. For Indigenous reconciliation, words are not enough: Editorial. *Toronto Star*, November 25. https://www.thestar.com/opinion/editorials/2016/11/25/for-indigenous-reconciliation-words-are-not-enough-editorial.html. Accessed 27 Nov 2016.

Trudeau, Justin. 2015a. Minister of Indigenous and Northern Affairs mandate letter. Office of the Prime Minister, November 13. http://pm.gc.ca/eng/minister-indigenous-and-northern-affairs-mandate-letter. Accessed 25 Nov 2016.

———. 2015b. Real change: Restoring fairness to Canada's relationship with Aboriginal peoples: Justin Trudeau's remarks at the Assembly of First Nations General Assembly. Liberal Party of Canada, July 7. https://www.liberal.ca/justin-trudeau-at-assembly-of-first-nations-36th-annual-general-assembly/. Accessed 24 Nov 2016.

———. 2017. Address to the United Nations General Assembly. Speech, United Nations, New York, September 21.

Truth and Reconciliation Commission of Canada. 2015. Honouring the Truth, reconciling for the future: Summary of the final report of the Truth and Reconciliation Commission of Canada. TRC. http://nctr.ca/assets/reports/Final%20Reports/Executive_Summary_English_Web.pdf. Accessed 1 Nov 2016.

United Nations. 2015. United Nations treaty collection. United Nations. https://treaties.un.org/Pages/Treaties.aspx?id=4&subid=A&lang=en. Accessed 15 July 2015.

United Nations General Assembly. 2007. General Assembly adopts Declaration on the Rights of Indigenous Peoples. United Nations, September 13. https://www.un.org/press/en/2007/ga10612.doc.htm. Accessed 21 Aug 2017.

———. 2014. United Nations General Assembly resolution A/RES/69/2, outcome document of the high-level plenary meeting of the General Assembly known as the World Conference on Indigenous Peoples, 22 September 2014. United Nations General Assembly, September 25. http://www.un.org/en/ga/search/view_doc.asp?symbol=A/RES/69/2. Accessed 25 Sept 2016.

United Nations Permanent Forum on Indigenous Issues. 2007. Frequently asked questions – Declaration on the Rights of Indigenous Peoples. United Nations Permanent Forum on Indigenous Issues, August. http://www.un.org/esa/socdev/unpfii/documents/FAQsindigenousdeclaration.pdf. Accessed 25 Sept 2009.

University of Minnesota Human Rights Library. 2008. Ratification of International Human Rights Treaties. University of Minnesota Human Rights Library. http://www1.umn.edu/humanrts/research/ratification-index.html. Accessed July 2015.

Wilson, Tiar. 2015. Hopeful Indigenous reaction to Justin Trudeau's Cabinet picks. *CBC News*, November 4. http://www.cbc.ca/news/indigenous/aboriginal-leaders-react-cabinet-choices-1.3303972. Accessed 25 Nov 2016.

Wilson-Raybould, Jody. 2016. Address to Assembly of First Nations. Speech, Niagara Falls, July 12.

CHAPTER 10

Canada's Feminist Foreign Policy Promises: An Ambitious Agenda for Gender Equality, Human Rights, Peace, and Security

Rebecca Tiessen and Emma Swan

Several important signals emerging from the Liberal government under Prime Minister Justin Trudeau have raised the profile of Canada's commitments to gender equality and to feminist foreign policy. While the rhetoric of feminist foreign policy is gaining traction in Canada, calls for integrating a feminist approach to foreign policy and international relations (IR) are hardly new. There is an important body of feminist scholarship documenting the value and significance of understanding feminist goals in foreign policy and redressing gender inequalities in world interactions.[1] Additionally, there is a long history of women's rights movements promoting government policies that address gender inequality and women's concerns, particularly around issues related to peace and security. Yet, the buzz generated around the notion of a "feminist foreign policy" since the election of Trudeau, in 2015, facilitated a renewed set of conversations and debates in the Canadian context. The questions emerging from these

R. Tiessen (✉) • E. Swan
University of Ottawa, Ottawa, ON, Canada

contemporary commitments to feminist foreign policy and gender equality include the following: How is this rhetoric different from previous governments' approaches to promoting gender equality in foreign policy commitments? Do the commitments (resources, programs, funding, staffing, policy creation) match the discourse?

The recent enthusiasm coming out of Canada's capital around an explicit effort to feminize foreign policy and commit to human rights and gender equality represents a welcome shift—one that presents an opportunity to move toward a foreign policy dedicated to addressing gender equality and human rights in, and beyond, Canada's peace and security work. In order to understand some of the opportunities and challenges of implementing a feminist foreign policy, particularly in areas related to peace and security, this chapter explores the current international policy context, specifically related to United Nations Security Council Resolution (UNSCR) 1325 on Women, Peace and Security and subsequent resolutions (UNSCR 1325+). Feminist literature and scholarship analyzing UNSCR 1325+ offer insights into some of the challenges, shortcomings, and silences within the resolution and policy framework itself. Civil society organizations (CSOs) have also highlighted the challenges of rhetorical promises without substantive practical commitments. The chapter concludes with a summary of the current "feminist friendly" environment, ongoing considerations, and the possibilities for a renewed commitment to gender equality in Canada's National Action Plan (NAP) on Women, Peace and Security.

Feminist Foreign Policy in the Spotlight

In 2016, Trudeau made headlines for his remarks on feminism. These remarks correspond to other international events putting feminist action into the spotlight. For example, when Sweden committed to a feminist foreign policy, attention turned to Margot Wallström, the first minister who publicly declared her government would pursue a feminist foreign policy. Such important international commitments underscore the strides made in establishing foreign policy and security goals that put gender equality at the center of all strategies. Appointing women to half of the positions in the Canadian federal cabinet and naming women to some of the key ministerial positions were the first strategic moves by Trudeau. When pushed on why half the cabinet comprised women, Trudeau stated, "because it's 2015." His remark signaled that it is *about time* gender equality was considered a core value of the Canadian government. Subsequent remarks reaffirmed that Trudeau is "proud to be a feminist," a statement made at a UN conference organized by UN Women in March 2016.[2] He went on to note: "It shouldn't be something that creates a reaction. It's simply saying that I believe in the equality of men and women and that we still have an awful lot of work to do to get there."

Trudeau's remarks call for a normalization of gender equality and a feminist approach as an important first step to destigmatize, normalize, and humanize what it means to be a feminist; establish gender equality as integral to human rights and an equality perspective; and signal to the world how something so fundamental and basic as equality often remains sidelined, ignored, or even ridiculed, thus reemphasizing the ongoing struggle for gender equality. These commitments were further bolstered by the House of Commons Standing Committee on Foreign Affairs and International Development's report, *An Opportunity for Global Leadership: Canada and the Women, Peace and Security Agenda*, released in October of 2016, which recommended Canada make women, peace, and security a foreign policy priority.

Similar optimism for a focus on human rights has emerged under Trudeau's Liberal government. This can be seen, inter alia, in the stated commitments on Lesbian, Gay, Bisexual, Trans, and Queer (LGBTQ) rights, as highlighted by Trudeau's statement on the International Day against homophobia, transphobia, and biphobia:

> In Canada and around the world, we must continue to fight against homophobia, transphobia, and biphobia, and to defend gender expression, gender identity and sexual orientation rights. We deplore the recent, reprehensible reports of violations of the human rights of gay and bisexual men in Chechnya. We call for the protection of all people in Chechnya whose sexual orientation makes them a target for persecution. Human rights have no borders.[3]

In addition to LGBTQ rights, gender equality has also been an important focus of the government's human rights rhetoric as demonstrated in the statement by Trudeau for International Development Week, in which he called for a refocusing of efforts to "help the world's poorest and most vulnerable people, including by promoting human rights, women's empowerment and gender equality, and respect for diversity and inclusion."[4]

Gender equality is therefore established as a central tenet to the human rights approach offered by Trudeau and the Liberal government. These promises have culminated, at the time of writing this chapter, in the launching of an official feminist foreign policy in the release of the Canada's Defence Policy (6 June 2017) and the Feminist International Assistance Policy (9 June 2017). The Defence Policy makes explicit reference to a feminist approach to international policy noting that "Canada is committed to working with the UN to end conflict-affected sexual violence and the use of child soldiers. This includes advancing the implementation of the United Nations Security Council Resolution 1325 on Women, Peace and Security, and ensuring UN peacekeepers are held accountable for meeting the highest standards of conduct."[5] Other examples of a feminist or gender equality approach to defence highlight opportunities for recruitment, improved integration of female military personnel, and enhanced training opportunities. This includes the integration of the Gender-Based Analysis-Plus (GBA+) training in all activities (from program design to equipment procurement) of the Canadian Armed Forces and the Department of National Defence.

The emphasis on a feminist foreign policy is even more apparent in the Feminist International Assistance Policy.[6] According to this policy document, Canada's international assistance will be feminist in orientation with commitments to ensuring no less than 95 percent of Canadian bilateral aid advances gender equality and promotes the empowerment of women and girls by 2021–2022, up from the 2017 figures of merely 2 percent bilateral assistance allocated to projects with primary objectives to ensure gender equality and women's empowerment. In launching the Feminist International Assistance Policy, Minister Bibeau remarked that this policy "is the most ambitious and progressive in the history of Canada's diplomacy. It will make Canada a global leader in promoting gender equality and the empowerment of women and girls."[7]

Future commitments to the promotion of gender equality (as one of Canada's core priorities) include the prime minister's promise that gender equality will be a major focus of the 2018 Group of Seven (G7) Summit hosted by Canada.[8] The long-awaited release of the second Canadian National Action Plan on Women, Peace and Security (launched in 2017) is another possible commitment to feminist foreign policy that is aligns with the goals and aspirations of recent policy documents and government commitments.

Early Evaluations of the Feminist Foreign Policy Rhetoric

Civil society organizations were quick to praise Trudeau's open discussion of a feminist approach, noting the significance of this rhetoric and the potential impacts of such remarks for practice. In the months to follow, however, this praise quickly shifted toward critically evaluating tangible commitments beyond his feminist friendly rhetoric. The rhetoric and discourse coming out of the new government around a feminist foreign policy and commitments to gender equality were quickly matched by calls for action.

Similar evaluations were provided by government critics such as New Democratic Party critic Hélène Laverdière, who offered a succinct summary and critique of the current Canadian context in March 2017. She argued that a feminist foreign policy is going to require more than rhetoric from the Trudeau Liberals. She went on to note that,

> A truly feminist government would also fund the Women, Peace and Security Agenda. Over the last decade, the issue of women, peace and security was largely neglected by the Canadian government, despite Canada's leading role in achieving United Nations Security Council Resolution 1325. Reports on Canada's National Action Plan were frequently late, and the Agenda was underfunded. The scarcity of funds has been one of the key challenges of implementing the WPS agenda at both the national and global level.[9]

In a blog post for the McLeod Group, Beth Woroniuk reported on the early indications of movement beyond the Liberal rhetoric of "feminist" as "mixed."[10] For example, CSOs were concerned with "business as usual" in the form of selling military vehicles to Saudi Arabia, given the country's poor track record on women's rights and human rights. Choices such as these have raised questions about the extent to which gender equality and women's rights are truly integrated into a Canadian feminist foreign policy approach. Other important gestures made by Trudeau pointed to re-engaging meaningfully in UN commitments to peace operations; renewing the Canadian National Action Plan on Women, Peace and Security; and committing in 2017 to redirect existing development funding to sexual and reproductive health for women around the world.[11] Yet these gestures, while positive first steps or "jumping off points" as Woroniuk argues, are insufficient for "shifting how we understand security and bringing women peacebuilders and gender perspectives to the centre of conflict prevention and response."[12] Similarly, in a more recent assessment, Sarah Rieger argues that the feminist approach by the Canadian government under the Trudeau Liberals is "more talk than action."[13]

As a result of critiques such as these, Oxfam Canada came out with a "Feminist Scorecard" to document the actions taken by the Liberal government. The first set of results were released in March 2017, in the lead up to International Women's Day, and called for the government to turn feminist words into action. The scorecard measures Canada's progress on affecting the lives of women in Canada and around the world with attention to eight categories: representation, taxation, climate and natural resources, violence against women, care work, global development, jobs, and response to conflict and crises. Noting Trudeau's commitment to gender parity in cabinet, the report highlighted progress in the area of representation. Other important commitments noted in Oxfam's 2017 gender scorecard included Canadian-focused priorities, such as the launching of the national inquiry on violence against Indigenous women and girls, a concern that was not "on the radar" of the Harper Conservatives,[14] and international priorities, such as increased funding for sexual and reproductive health care.

Concerns coming out of civil society, party critics, and the public around translating feminist rhetoric into policy and action have not gone unnoticed by the government. Some of the opportunities for improved gender equality programming were documented in the Global Affairs Canada (GAC) initial report of the International Assistance Review (IAR), also known as *What We Heard*. In this report, as the Canadian Council for International Cooperation (CCIC) notes, GAC highlighted the importance of a gendered approach to policy coherence for sustainable development in the Sustainable Development Goals, noting the importance of Canada's IAR being "guided by a feminist and human rights-based approach that intends to be transformative."[15] Furthermore, the report noted that aid effectiveness was to be measured in terms of the realization of human rights, gender equality, women's empowerment, and gender transformative change.[16]

A commitment to addressing gender equality is highlighted throughout the GAC discussion paper, *What We Heard*, with the terms "gender" and "gender equality" repeatedly mentioned.[17] This is an important shift from the previous federal government, whereby references to gender equality were removed from key policy statements and replaced with "equality between women and men."[18] The discussion paper explicitly puts advancing gender equality "at the heart of Canada's international assistance," noting that a "feminist lens will be applied throughout all of Canada's international assistance activities" ranging from, among other priorities, activities in health and rights of women and children to peace and security. These commitments, at least rhetorically, reflect the large and growing body of scholarship documenting the importance of adopting a feminist lens for addressing gender inequality that affects men, women, boys, girls, and trans communities around the world. The discussion paper and subsequent commitments also reflect the nature of the evaluation process, including CSOs that are eagerly watching this self-described feminist prime minister and the government he leads, while also scrutinizing his commitments to gender equality.

The release of the government's Feminist International Assistance Policy is a significant step forward in the ambitious agenda for a Canadian feminist foreign policy. Commitments to increased funding for women's organizations (though no overall additional funding for international assistance) mean that CSOs are being heard. A real test of the commitment to gender equality and a feminist foreign policy will be in the evaluations of how well policy translates into practice, and to what extent a feminist foreign policy influences other foreign policy strategies including, but not limited to, the development of the Canadian National Action Plan on Women, Peace and Security.

Feminist scholars and practitioners have long argued for a feminist approach to foreign policy, arguing that gender equality must be more than targeting women for development assistance. We turn now to a discussion of the international commitments and feminist scholarship, and how these contributions have advanced our understanding of gender equality writ large, and specifically within the foreign policy priority area of peace and security.

INTERNATIONAL POLICIES ON WOMEN, PEACE, AND SECURITY AND SCHOLARLY INSIGHTS

Reflecting back to 1979, the current international policy priorities for gender, peace, and security were built on the framework set out in The Convention on the Elimination of all Forms of Discrimination Against Women (CEDAW). Sixteen years later, but profoundly influenced by and benefitting from the commitments laid out in CEDAW, the Beijing Declaration and Platform for Action further developed an international agenda for women's empowerment and gender equality.[19] A major commitment in the twenty-first century, UNSCR 1325 on Women, Peace and Security, was adopted in 2000. UNSCR 1325 built on previous UN initiatives, yet was the first of its kind to focus exclusively on the impact of war on women and women's contributions to conflict resolution and sustainable peace.[20]

Feminist analyses of conflict and insecurity have been critical to the adoption of important international policy commitments and these policy priorities have subsequently played a leading role in promoting feminist goals in peace and security initiatives. Important achievements are noteworthy in UNSCR 1325+. However, this guiding framework has been criticized for being weak on gender equality discourse and recommendations,[21] focusing instead on essentialist characterizations of women's roles in peace and conflict, and instrumentalist strategies targeting women without addressing underlying gender inequalities and human rights considerations. In addition to weaknesses inherent in the UNSCR 1325+ guiding framework, similar limitations are noted in many of the national level policy documents and National Action Plans on Women, Peace and Security that have been developed by more than 60 countries.[22]

Notwithstanding the tremendous importance and potentially transformative agenda embodied in UNSCR 1325+, the general consensus among feminist scholars and practitioners is that the significance of UNSCR 1325+ has not been matched by the inclusion of appropriate gender considerations in the design of policies related to peace and security globally.[23] Feminist scholars argue that there is a profound discrepancy between the sentiments of UNSCR 1325+ and the policy and practice of the Security Council and member countries.[24] This is due largely to the fact that many member countries—Canada included—make bold public statements in support of gender equality (particularly in fragile and conflict-affected states), the broader UNSCR 1325+ agenda, and policy commitments in the form of NAPs, all the while failing to incorporate a feminist epistemology, or feminist lens, into their larger foreign policy agenda. As a result, notwithstanding the rhetorical nod to sentiments encapsulated in UNSCR 1325+, such as protection and participation of women, it is widely argued that policies and practice fail to respond to the holistic calls of UNSCR 1325+, in particular around issues related to prevention of conflict, and fall short of invoking the desired improvements because their foreign policy remains locked into narrow, rigid, and often essentialist understandings of gender and gender equality.

This "failed foreign policy" extends to areas typically understood as outside of the reach of gender, such as arms deals (as seen in the Saudi Arabian example given in the Pedersen chapter below) and action on climate change, among other areas of limited consideration. Furthermore, the limitations of Resolution 1325+ and many of the National Action Plans, including the targeting of women as "objects" of security reform and peace processes, and the overall limited attention to gender equality, highlight additional gaps and weaknesses in the international and national commitments to addressing gender inequality in peace/conflict and (in)security.[25]

Together, CEDAW, Beijing Platform for Action, and UNSCR 1325+, along with other commitments, frameworks, and resolutions,[26] have contributed to a normative agenda that drives international donors' commitments on gender equality. Nonetheless, neither the language of UNSCR 1325+ nor the policies emerging from subsequent NAPs holistically reflect the impressive gains and strategies employed in previous initiatives. Not only does UNSCR 1325+ fail to reflect gains made by initiatives such as CEDAW, this resolution and subsequent NAPs do not reflect lessons learned and best practices gathered from the wider feminist scholarship, particularly in feminist international relations scholarship and feminist foreign policy literature.

Feminist International Relations Scholarship

In regard to the arguments put forth in this paper, a key insight drawn from feminist IR scholarship is the ways in which conventional IR and political science theories, politics, the state, and international institutions are gendered and imbued with patriarchal underpinnings and assumptions.

Emerging in the late 1980s, feminist IR literature has been integral to uncovering why international polices and commitments such as UNSCR 1325+ have either not translated into foreign policy priorities or, if they have translated rhetorically into policies, why they have not resulted in meaningful change in the lives of women and girls. This literature offers analysis and insights that illuminate the underlying androcentric epistemology of the state, its institutions, and subsequent policies. Feminist scholars argue that institutions of the state are deeply gendered and reflect an unchallenged male-centricity. This literature thus encourages us to interrogate the normative foundations of theories, policies, and practice. Given the androcentric "default" of the state and international relations, feminist IR literature suggests that taking an approach that siloes efforts to achieve gender equality into certain areas—and fails to integrate it into others—is destined to perpetuate the status quo rather than challenge it. Given the pervasive favoring and unrecognized privileging of masculinist norms in much of the normative international and state relations, without a holistic feminist foreign policy that sees gender in all aspects of policy intervention, government policy commitments, and NAPs on UNSCR 1325+ risk becoming stuck at "add women (as victims/peace-builders) and stir," thereby instrumentalizing women as either "useless or useful to" peace and security initiatives.[27]

FEMINIST CONTRIBUTIONS TO CANADIAN FOREIGN POLICY SCHOLARSHIP

Feminist insights into Canadian foreign policy have also been central to how we make sense of, and analyze, Canada's past and present commitments to gender equality. The 2003 collection by Turenne-Sjolander, Smith, and Stienstra provided one of the earliest and most comprehensive analyses of the need for a critical analysis of Canadian foreign policy through a feminist lens, highlighting the "multiple sites of foreign policy" in classrooms, government departments, refugee recipient communities, and much more.[28] Documenting the foreign policy approaches in the period between 1992 and 2012, the collection by Smith and Turenne-Sjolander offers additional insights into feminist and critical foreign policy scholarship.[29] Tiessen and Baranyi build on this essential Canadian foreign policy scholarship by tracking gender equality programming under the Harper Conservative governments, noting a range of missed opportunities and ambiguous actions in the promotion of gender equality in "othered" communities within Canada and abroad.[30,31] As documented in the chapters in the Tiessen and Baranyi collection, there are several examples of inroads to addressing gender equality when committed personnel are actively engaged in ensuring such outcomes.[32]

Among the missed opportunities, however, are examples of targeting women with development programming rather than addressing the causes of gender inequality and addressing human rights and strategic priorities.

In other cases, Canadian foreign policy priorities have been silent on the role of women and on gender relations (as in the case of mining projects) or have created parallel projects and hypocritical stances focusing on empowering the girl child[33] while maintaining business as usual in other projects that undermine women's and girls' rights. Here, too, the "multiple sites of foreign policy" are examined to include the failure to employ an intersectional approach that will facilitate improved programming for people with disabilities[34] or the treatment of Indigenous women as targeted outsiders who were not on the government's "radar," despite sweeping commitments to addressing global maternal mortality and health.[35] Other scholars examining Canadian foreign policy and practice in Afghanistan have further documented a range of gender issues, including the instrumentalization of women's rights and girls' access to education as rationales for military intervention.[36]

Feminist analyses of Canadian foreign policy have thus documented many significant lessons learned over the past 25 years or more. The summary provided above is a mere glimpse into this scholarship guiding our critical analysis of contemporary practices in Canadian foreign policy. An evaluation of the stated commitments, policy announcements, and public pledges of a *feminist* prime minister, Justin Trudeau, marks a significant shift from the Harper government rhetoric (a shift from the "erasure of gender equality"[37]). This welcomed shift has put gender equality at the center of all foreign policy priorities and places Canada in a position to be a global leader in gender equality.

Drawing from the feminist foreign policy literature and the feminist scholarship specific to international relations and gender, peace, and security, several important themes emerge from the literature and shed light on the current limitations of policy and practice. These include weak approaches to gender mainstreaming, essentialism, and a failure to take masculinities into consideration. Based on these critical analyses of policy and practice, several recommendations can be drawn from the feminist scholarship and are central to ensuring a feminist foreign policy for Canada. The early signals from the Trudeau government point to increased efforts to engage in multilateral efforts to protect human rights through deeper engagement with the UN among other avenues, as well as focusing on human rights and the broad range of gender equality issues through improved aid programming. These rhetorical commitments thus demonstrate a shift away from the Harper government's limited commitments[38] and a move toward much deeper strategies and sustained practices for tackling a broad range of human rights issues and gender inequalities in particular. In effect, Canada is positioning itself as a global voice and leader on gender equality. This commitment was reaffirmed in Minister Bibeau's comments during the launch of the Feminist International Assistance Policy in June 2017, perhaps with even greater ambition and dedication than in the past, and most certainly with a heightened focus on women's rights and gender equality. Such an ambitious plan will be watched closely and with great scrutiny as CSOs and scholars continue to document the extent to which rhetoric is transformed into practice, and promises result in improved human rights and gender equality.

CONCLUSION

In order to build on the work of feminists over the last five decades and to contribute to the ever-evolving international policy priorities for global women, peace, and security commitments, policy and practice must be based on *a feminist epistemological foundation* that adequately addresses the broad, latent, and pervasive nature of gender inequality from the grassroots through to state institutions and the UN. This feminist epistemological foundation must serve as the basis of a feminist foreign policy. A gender-informed foreign policy strategy must also be sophisticated about the diverse needs and roles of women, as well as about patterns of masculinity. It needs to be embedded in a practicable strategy to sustain structural change in power dynamics and gender relations.[39]

A feminist foreign policy, furthermore, recognizes that gender equality arises from a commitment to understanding diverse forms of oppression experienced by a range of actors because of their gender. Thus, transgender individuals face specific challenges and require programs and opportunities for empowerment and meaningful participation. Addressing gender equality begins by recognizing that certain gender norms and expectations (ones that reproduce gender inequality) are harmful to many, including women and men. Programs geared to engaging men and boys, for example, can be an important complement to other gender programming to ensure that problematic and conflict-oriented masculinist practices are identified and efforts are in place to address deficiencies.

Feminist academic scholarship has been instrumental in pointing to these more nuanced understandings of gender equality. Civil society organizations are also actively engaged in setting the agenda for improving Canada's foreign policy commitments to women, peace, and security. One of the core strategies identified by civil society organizations in ensuring success in peace and security programming is to increase funding for locally based, or "grassroots," women's organizations. These women's organizations can be instrumental in employing culturally effective and comprehensive strategies to engage community members in gender equality practices. Civil society organizations, such as those actively engaged in the Women, Peace and Security Network Canada (WPSN-C), are important partners in the design and delivery of Canadian foreign policy priorities because many of these organizations are able to respond to the local context in a timely manner and liaise with locally based knowledge experts who understand the causes and consequences of gender inequality.[40] The knowledge, experience, and understanding of gender issues held by members of civil society, particularly those comprising the feminist expertise in the WPSN in Canada, are essential for building an active engagement across sectors in the design, monitoring, and evaluation of the second Canadian National Action Plan on UNSCR 1325. This document must serve as a core foreign policy priority for Canada in all that we do abroad in our efforts to promote peace and security.[41]

With the announcement of Canada's first Feminist International Assistance Policy, combined with a number of promises to put gender equality at the center of Canada's future leadership opportunities (including the 2018 G7 meetings), there are indeed many positive first steps made toward full integration of a feminist approach to Canada's foreign policy, and an apparent departure from the previous government that actively erased gender equality from official policies and commitments. However, we must not lose sight of the importance of integrating this same approach beyond our international assistance policy, toward, for example, policy areas such as defence, trade, and climate change. Ongoing evaluation of how these commitments are translating into practice will be the focus of scholar and civil society analyses in the years to come as outcomes are measured in line with the goals and commitments made by the federal government. The early stages of the Trudeau government, however, point to significant feminist aspirations and to crucial foreign policy promises designed to make gender equality a core feature of Canada's international work.

Notes

1. See Smith and Cornut (2016), Tiessen and Carrier (2015), and Turenne-Sjolander (2005).
2. For full interview, see Trudeau and Mlambo-Ngcuka (2016).
3. For full statement, see Trudeau (2017b).
4. For full statement, see Trudeau (2017a).
5. National Defence (2017, 55).
6. To read the full Feminist International Assistance Policy, see Government of Canada (2017).
7. Zilio (2017).
8. To read the full article, see Canadian Press (2017).
9. Laverdière (2017).
10. Woroniuk (2016).
11. See Global Affairs Canada (2017), official news release on redirecting existing development funding to sexual and reproductive health here.
12. Woroniuk (2016).
13. Rieger (2017).
14. For a deeper discussion, see Smith (2017).
15. Canadian Council for International Cooperation (2017, 2).
16. Ibid., 3.
17. For full report, see Global Affairs Canada (2016).
18. Tiessen and Carrier (2015).
19. Organization for Economic Co-operation and Development (2013).
20. Parpart (2014), Willett (2010), Valasek and Nelson (2006).
21. Parpart (2017).
22. An indication of the inconsistent application of UNSCR 1325+ is evident in UN member countries' NAPs, which vary greatly in quality between countries. Some NAPs are 14 page "highly generalist" documents, while others are more comprehensive documents consisting of 80+ pages of text. They also vary greatly in regard to the level of engagement and integration of civil society; proposed financing mechanisms; and plans on monitoring, reporting, and feedback processes (Fritz et al. 2011, 5–6). Many NAPs, such as Canada's, have been criticized for consisting of "loose promised and vague reporting." (Tiessen and Tuckey 2014, 14).
23. Villellas et al. (2016), Puechguirbal (2010), Valasek and Nelson (2006).
24. Cohn (2004, 2), Willett (2010). Cohn et al. (2004, 135), draw attention to a similar frustration with the human security agenda. They argue that a rhetorical commitment to "human security" in the UN will not translate into changed priorities and practices without a member state network devoted to raising the issue again and again, and infusing it throughout the institution of the UN. There is a clear parallel to UNSCR 1325.

25. Parpart (2017).
26. Such as the 2005 Paris Declaration on Aid Effectiveness, the Millennium Development Goals, and the Sustainable Development Goals.
27. Cohn et al. (2004).
28. Turenne-Sjolander et al. (2003).
29. Smith and Turenne-Sjolander (2012).
30. Tiessen and Baranyi (2017).
31. For a discussion on indigenous communities, see Chap. 11 Smith (2017).
32. Tiessen and Baranyi (2017).
33. Butler (2017).
34. Stienstra (2017).
35. Smith (2017).
36. Swiss (2012), Tuckey (2017).
37. Tiessen and Carrier (2015).
38. Petrasek and Tiessen (2016).
39. Connell (2001), Wright (2014).
40. Warden (2016).
41. For an in-depth reflection of the House of Commons Standing Committee on Foreign Affairs and International Development (the Committee) report, An opportunity for global leadership: Canada and the women, peace and security agenda by WPSN-C, see WPSNCANADA (2016).

REFERENCES

Butler, Paula. 2017. Gold and girls: Why Canada weds gender equality with mining capitalism in Burkina Faso. In *Obligations and omissions Canada's ambiguous actions on gender equality*, ed. Rebcca Tiessen and Stephen Baranyi, 141–164. Montreal/Kingston: McGill-Queen's University Press.

Canadian Council for International Cooperation (CCIC). 2017. Analysis of Global Affairs Canada's *What We Heard* summary of Canada's International Assistance Review. Canadian Council for International Co-Operation 2017. http://www.ccic.ca/_files/en/what_we_do/February2017_What_We_Heard_EN_.pdf. Accessed 15 Sept 2017.

Canadian Press. 2017. Gender equality to top agenda at G7 summit in Quebec: Trudeau. *Globe and Mail*, June 8. https://beta.theglobeandmail.com/news/politics/gender-equality-to-top-agenda-at-g7-summit-in-quebec-trudeau/article35250874/?ref=http://www.theglobeandmail.com&. Accessed 15 Sept 2017.

Cohn, Carole. 2004. Feminist peacemaking: In resolution 1325, the United Nations requires the inclusion of women in all peace planning and negotiation. *The Women's Review of Books* 21 (5): 8–9.

Cohn, Carole, Helen Kinsella, and Sheri Gibbings. 2004. Women, peace and security resolution 1325. *International Feminist Journal of Politics* 6 (1): 130–140.
Connell, Bob. 2001. Masculinities, violence, and peacemaking. *Peace News*, Issue 2443, June–August. http://www.peacenews.info/issues/2443/connell.html. Accessed 10 May 2017.
Fritz, Jan Marie, Sharon Doering, and Belgin Gumru. 2011. Women, peace, security and the national action plans. *Journal of Applied Social Science* 5 (1): 1–23.
Global Affairs Canada. 2016. International assistance review: Discussion paper. Government of Canada. http://international.gc.ca/world-monde/assets/pdfs/iar-consultations-eai-eng.pdf. Accessed 15 Sept 2017.
———. 2017. Minister Bibeau champions sexual and reproductive health and rights: News release. Government of Canada, March 2. https://www.canada.ca/en/global-affairs/news/2017/03/minister_bibeau_championssexualandreproductivehealthandrights.html. Accessed 15 Sept 2017.
Government of Canada. 2017. Canada's feminist international assistance policy. Government of Canada, August 22. http://international.gc.ca/world-monde/issues_development-enjeux_developpement/priorities-priorites/policy-politique.aspx?lang=eng. Accessed 15 Sept 2017.
House of Commons Standing Committee. 2016. *An opportunity for global leadership: Canada and the women, peace and security agenda*. Report of the Standing Committee on Foreign Affairs and International Development. 42nd Parliament, 1st Session.
Laverdière, Hélène. 2017. Federal budget 2017: Feminist foreign policy needs more than rhetoric. *Huffington Post*, March 21. http://www.huffingtonpost.ca/helene-laverdiere/federal-budget-2017-women_b_15470868.html. Accessed 10 May 2017.
National Defence. 2017. Strong, secure, engaged: Canada's defence policy. National Defence. http://dgpaapp.forces.gc.ca/en/canada-defence-policy/docs/canada-defence-policy-report.pdf. Accessed 20 June 2017.
Organisation for Economic Co-operation and Development (OECD). 2013. *Gender and statebuilding in fragile and conflict-affected states, conflict and fragility*. Paris: OECD Publishing.
Parpart, Jane. 2014. Exploring the transformative potential of gender mainstreaming in international development institutions. *Journal of International Development* 26 (3): 382–395.
———. 2017. Rethinking women, peace and security: Incorporating masculinities, gender relations and conflict. Paper presented at the International Studies Association (ISA), Baltimore, USA, February 24.
Petrasek, David, and Rebecca Tiessen. 2016. The shaping of a conservative human rights policy in the Harper era. In *The Harper era in Canadian foreign policy: Parliament, politics, and Canada's global posture*, ed. Adam Chapnick and Christopher J. Kukucha, 181–195. Vancouver: University of British Colombia Press.

Puechguirbal, Nadine. 2010. Discourses on gender, patriarchy and resolution 1325: A textual analysis of UN documents. *International Peacekeeping* 17 (2): 172–187.
Reiger, Sarah. 2017. Canada's feminist government is more talk than action: Report. *Huffington Post Canada*, March 7. http://www.huffingtonpost.ca/2017/03/06/canada-feminism_n_15195382.html. Accessed 3 June 2017.
Smith, Heather. 2017. Not high on our radar? The Harper government missing and murdered aboriginal women in Canada. In *Obligations and omissions Canada's ambiguous actions on gender equality*, ed. Rebecca Tiessen and Stephen Baranyi, 261–282. Montreal: McGill-Queen's University Press.
Smith, Heather, and Jérémie Cornut. 2016. The status of women in Canadian foreign policy analysis. *Journal of Women, Politics & Policy* 37 (2): 217–233.
Smith, Heather, and Claire Turenne-Sjolander. 2012. *Canada in the world: Internationalism in Canadian foreign policy*. Toronto: Oxford University Press.
Stienstra, Deborah. 2017. Lost without wayfinders? Disability, gender and Canadian foreign and development policy. In *Obligations and omissions Canada's ambiguous actions on gender equality*, ed. Rebecca Tiessen and Stephen Baranyi, 115–140. Montreal/Kingston: McGill-Queen's University Press.
Swiss, Liam. 2012. Gender, security and instrumentalism: Canada's foreign aid in support of national interest? In *Struggling for effectiveness: CIDA and Canadian foreign aid*, ed. Stephen Brown, 135–158. Montreal: McGill-Queen's University Press.
Tiessen, Rebecca, and Stephen Baranyi, eds. 2017. *Obligations and omissions Canada's ambiguous actions on gender equality*. Montreal/Kingston: McGill-Queen's University Press.
Tiessen, Rebecca, and Krystel Carrier. 2015. The erasure of 'gender' in Canadian foreign policy under the Harper conservatives: The significance of the discursive shift from 'gender equality' to 'equality between women and men. *Canadian Foreign Policy Journal* 21 (2): 95–111.
Tiessen, Rebecca, and Sarah Tuckey. 2014. Loose promises and vague reporting: Analyzing Canada's national action plan and reports on women, peace and security. In *Worth the wait? Reflections on Canada's national action plan & reports on women, peace & security*, ed. Beth Woroniuk and Amber Minnings, 14–18. https://wpsncanada.files.wordpress.com/2012/05/worth-the-wait-report.pdf. Accessed 12 June 2017.
Trudeau, Justin. 2017a. Statement by the Prime Minister of Canada on International Development Week. Prime Minister's Office, February 5. http://pm.gc.ca/eng/news/2017/02/05/statement-prime-minister-canada-international-development-week. Accessed 15 Sept 2017.
———. 2017b. Statement by the Prime Minister of Canada on the International Day against Homophobia, Transphobia and Biphobia. Prime Minister's Office,

May 17. http://pm.gc.ca/eng/news/2017/05/17/statement-prime-minister-canada-international-day-against-homophobia-transphobia-and. Accessed 15 Sept 2017.

Trudeau, Justin, and Phumzile Mlambo-Ngcuka. 2016. Headline politics: March 16, 2016 – Just Trudeau at UN Women. Cpac video, 0:49:31, March 16. http://www.cpac.ca/en/programs/headline-politics/episodes/90006936/. Accessed 15 Sept 2017.

Tuckey, Sarah. 2017. Discourse and whole-of-government: The instrumentalization of gender in the Kandahar provincial reconstruction team. Paper presented at the *Canadian Association for the Study of International Development (CASID)*, Conference, Ryerson University, Toronto, Canada.

Turenne-Sjolander, Claire. 2005. Canadian foreign policy: Does gender matter? *Canadian Foreign Policy Journal* 12 (1): 19–31.

Turenne-Sjolander, Claire, Heather Smith, and Deborah Stienstra. 2003. *Feminist perspectives on Canadian foreign policy*. Toronto: Oxford University Press.

Valasek, Kristin, and Kaitlin Nelson. 2006. Securing equality, engendering peace: A guide to policy and planning on women, peace and security (UN SCR 1325): A practical guide to promoting women's participation in peace and security initiatives. *United Nations International Research and Training Institute for the Advancement of Women*. http://www.responsibilitytoprotect.org/files/1325guide-finalen.pdf. Accessed 25 July 25 2017.

Villelas, María, Pamela Urrutia, Ana Villelas, and Vicenç Fisas. 2016. Gender in EU Conflict Prevention and Peacebuilding Policy and Practice. *WOSCAP*, March 31. http://www.woscap.eu/documents/131298403/131553554/Scoping+Study+-+Gender.pdf/ebda2ef3-ac44-4555-b721-ec159246bf4d. Accessed 21 July 2017.

Warden, Rachel. 2016. Canadian government must support women's rights organizations in these troubled times. *Hill Times*, November 30. http://www.hilltimes.com/2016/11/30/canadian-government-must-support-womens-rights-organizations-troubled-times/89145?ct=t(RSS_EMAIL_CAMPAIGN)&goal=0_8edecd9364-0287e19f78-90953389&mc_cid=0287e19f78&mc_eid=61391a85f9. Accessed 15 May 2017.

Waroniuk, Beth. 2016. A feminist foreign policy? What about women, peace and security? *McLeod Group Blog*, June 27. http://www.mcleodgroup.ca/2016/06/26/a-feminist-foreign-policy-what-about-women-peace-and-security/. Accessed 5 June 2017.

Willett, Susan. 2010. Introduction: Security council resolution 1325: Assessing the impact on Women, Peace and Security. *International Peacekeeping* 17 (2): 142–158.

WPSNCANADA. 2016. Response of the Women, Peace and Security Network-Canada (WPSN-C) to the report of the Standing Committee on Foreign Affairs and International Development: An opportunity for global leadership: Canada and the Women, Peace and Security Agenda. *WPSN-Canada*, December 16. https://wpsn-canada.org/2016/12/16/response-of-the-women-peace-and-security-network-canada-wpsn-c-to-the-report-of-the-standing-committee-on-foreign-affairs-and-international-development-an-opportunity-for-global-leadership-canada/. Accessed 15 Sept 2017.

Wright, Hannah. 2014. Masculinities, conflict and peacebuilding: Perspectives on men through a gender lens. *Saferworld*. UK Department for International Development.

Zillio, Michelle. 2017. Ottawa unveils new feminist foreign-aid policy. *Globe and Mail*, June 9. https://www.theglobeandmail.com/news/politics/ottawa-unveils-new-feminism-focused-foreign-aid-policy/article35260311/. Accessed 10 June 2017.

CHAPTER 11

"We Will Honour Our Good Name": The Trudeau Government, Arms Exports, and Human Rights

Jennifer Pedersen

Justin Trudeau's government was elected in 2015 after a campaign promising "sunny ways," re-engagement with the international community, and a return to open and accountable government. Despite Trudeau's feel-good proclamations that "Canada is back," his new government was quickly hindered by the challenge of navigating Canadian arms exports to Saudi Arabia amid accusations of human rights abuses and questions about his government's lack of transparency.

This chapter examines the political debate surrounding Canadian arms exports to Saudi Arabia over the first two years of the Trudeau government.[1] I focus on how critics, particularly the New Democratic Party of Canada (NDP), challenged the Liberal government's narrative in the House of Commons and unsuccessfully tried to improve parliamentary oversight of Canadian arms exports. I discuss troubling reports of misuse of Canadian arms against civilians in Saudi Arabia and in Yemen, and the Canadian government's inadequate reactions to those reports. I also

J. Pedersen (✉)
Independent Scholar, Ottawa, ON, Canada

examine problems with the government's legislation to accede to the Arms Trade Treaty,[2] which regulates the international trade in conventional arms. I argue that there is a gap between the Liberal government's rhetoric on human rights and transparency on the one hand and its actions with regard to arms exports to Saudi Arabia on the other. The overall picture reveals a confused, inconsistent, and disappointing Liberal policy on arms exports, amounting to a failure of foreign policy under Trudeau.

Canada's Arms Exports and the Saudi Deal in Context

In 2014, Stephen Harper's Conservative government announced the largest arms contract in Canadian history. The deal for light-armoured vehicles (LAVs), which was brokered by the Canadian Commercial Corporation on behalf of London-based General Dynamics Land Systems of Canada (GDLS) and the Kingdom of Saudi Arabia, was worth $15 billion over 15 years and would create an estimated 3000 jobs in Southwestern Ontario. The LAV deal with Saudi Arabia followed a long history of exports from Canada to the Kingdom and the region. What made this particular deal so significant was the scale, as well as the government's public celebration of the contract as a "win" for Canada, particularly for manufacturing in Southwestern Ontario.[3]

Canada's defence industry contributes an estimated $6.7 billion (in 2014 figures) to Canada's gross domestic product and accounts for over 60000 jobs across the country. In 2016, Canadian military exports to countries other than the United States[4] amounted to nearly $718 million, the majority of the sales going to North Atlantic Treaty Organization (NATO) partners and Australia, with Saudi Arabia accounting for $142 million in Canadian arms exports that year.[5] Canada's arms sales are consistent with global trends. The world's biggest arms exporters[6] have increased exports to the Middle East and Asia over the past decade as exports to Europe, the Americas, and Africa have decreased. Canada is now the second-largest arms exporter to the Middle East, exporting to Saudi Arabia, Bahrain, United Arab Emirates, Algeria, and other countries in the region.[7]

Though Saudi Arabia has been repeatedly criticized by human rights groups and the United Nations (UN) for violating the human rights of its citizens, this has not hindered its status as the second-largest arms importer in the world.⁸ In Canada, critics of the GDLS-Saudi deal have argued that Saudi Arabia's human rights record should make the country ineligible to buy Canadian arms and that the deal violates Canadian arms export rules. Under export rules in effect when the deal was negotiated in 2014, a human rights assessment should have been conducted to determine that there is "no reasonable risk" that Canadian goods would be used against civilians. This is an important point on which much of the 2015–2017 arms exports debate hangs; "reasonable risk" of human rights abuses, not *evidence of* abuses, is the standard under which export permits should be assessed. Further, Canada is, according to its export policy, supposed to "closely control" exports to countries "whose governments have a persistent record of serious violations of the human rights of their citizens."⁹ However, Canada's Department of Foreign Affairs (now Global Affairs Canada—GAC) did not produce a human rights assessment for Saudi Arabia in 2013 or 2014, when the Saudi LAV deal was signed by the Conservatives.¹⁰ For the Harper government, the economic benefits of the LAV deal clearly outweighed Canada's human rights concerns about Saudi Arabia.

Election 2015: What Was Said and Why It Matters

Prior to the 2015 election, key Liberals were highly critical of the Saudi LAV deal. Gerald Butts and Roland Paris, advisors to Trudeau, had criticized the deal in the months before the Liberals formed government. Paris, Trudeau's foreign policy advisor, told the CBC that with this deal, "we've allowed an arms sale to trump human rights."¹¹ A senior policy advisor to Foreign Affairs Minister Stéphane Dion, Jocelyn Coulon, had also criticized the deal before joining Dion's staff in 2016, writing in *La Presse* that: "For a long time now, Saudi Arabia has bought the silence of Westerners with its juicy civilian and military contracts."¹² But opposition to the deal wasn't limited to advisors; in fact, a few days after the 2015 election was called, Trudeau himself said Canada must "stop arms sales to regimes that flout democracy such as Saudi Arabia."¹³ Yet two months later, only days before the election and during an appearance on the television show *Tout le monde en parle*, Trudeau promised that the Liberals would not cancel the LAV contract, and downplayed the military importance of the vehicles, likening them to "jeeps." When challenged on this point a few days later, Trudeau replied, "we will … behave in a way that is transparent and open going forward, to ensure that Canadians have confidence that their government is abiding by the rules, principles and values that people expect of their government."[14]

Trudeau's about-face on arms sales to Saudi Arabia may have come down to electoral politics. The challenges of navigating the Saudi contract were evident when the three main federal parties began campaigning in London, Ontario, the home of the General Dynamics plant where the LAVs were manufactured. The plant was in the electoral riding of London-Fanshawe, held by New Democratic Party incumbent Irene Mathyssen—a riding that the Liberals hoped to take. For the NDP, the deal put the party in a difficult position. On the one hand, as Canada's only labour party, good jobs for workers are a priority. On the other hand, the party's history of support for human rights meant a deal with Saudi Arabia was not just unpalatable to many members, but unacceptable. NDP Leader Thomas Mulcair attempted to balance those concerns when he promised in London that the NDP would not cancel the contract. At the same time, he also expressed concerns about the deal: "I think Mr. Harper is in fact breaking the rules that we set up here in Canada a long time ago. Look, you have to look at the record of human rights of people before giving a contract."[15] In an election debate, Mulcair said the NDP would investigate the Saudi deal if elected. Mulcair's comments put him in a difficult position with the Unifor (a general trade union) local in London, whose members worked at the GDLS plant.[16] The Liberals used Mulcair's hesitation to attack Mathyssen. A letter sent out to voters in the riding by the Liberal candidate accused the NDP of being "wishy-washy" on the deal, and claimed that "If (the NDP) get their way, this will cost us and our children thousands of high quality jobs."[17] Mathyssen, who had met repeatedly with union members and General Dynamics officials, reassured voters "that this is a signed contract and that we are going to be honouring the contract."[18] On election day, while many New Democrat Members of Parliament (MP) across Ontario lost their seats to the Liberal surge, Mathyssen held London-Fanshawe with nearly 38 per cent of the popular vote, beating her Liberal rival by 3400 votes. Of the three other ridings in London, two were won by Liberals and one was held by the Conservatives.

January 2016: The Turning Point

For the next few months, the Saudi deal and arms exports went largely undiscussed as the Trudeau government began its mandate. But in January 2016, the Saudi Arabian government executed 47 people, including a popular dissident Shia cleric, in the largest mass execution in decades.

The Liberals faced renewed calls to cancel the Saudi deal. However, a spokesperson for Foreign Minister Dion promised that Canada would move forward with the contract, arguing that "a private company is delivering the goods according to a signed contract with the government of Saudi Arabia."[19] The use of the term "private company" was misleading, as it downplayed the role the state played in brokering the deal between General Dynamics Land Systems and Saudi Arabia. Over the following weeks, Liberal rhetoric on the deal fluctuated widely. Dion at first insisted "what is done is done,"[20] arguing his government had inherited the contract from the Conservatives and could not go back on it. Yet this argument ignored the responsibility Dion himself had to approve or reject export permits for the LAVs—export permits that, at that point, had not been signed, though this was not yet public information. Only days later, GAC stated, "should we become aware of reports that would be relevant to Canada's export control regime, the government can consider whether existing permits should be suspended or cancelled."[21] What was odd about this statement was that it was made at the same time as near-daily reports of human rights abuses in Saudi Arabia and the increasingly deadly Saudi bombing campaign in Yemen.[22]

Dion also suggested that Canada could face penalties if the Saudi contract was cancelled. GAC was asked repeatedly what those penalties might be, but no answers were given due to commercial confidentiality. (Some have since suggested the penalties for contract cancellation could be in the billions.)[23] The government repeatedly pivoted back to its electoral promise that it would sign and implement the ATT while also suggesting the Saudi deal would not be subject to the ATT. Further arguments from the government suggested that they were working closely with the Saudis to improve their human rights situation. Yet the government provided no evidence that the Saudis paid notice to Canada's concerns.[24]

The NDP Position: Transparency Please

The events of January 2016 would seem to have provided an immediate opportunity for the progressive opposition, the NDP, to pursue the Liberals on the Saudi deal. But the electoral promise made by the NDP in London complicated matters. Despite the urging of disarmament advocates, the NDP was not willing to risk its support in London by calling for suspension of the Saudi deal. After difficult internal conversations,[25] a decision was made to focus on the lack of public information on Canadian arms exports and the need for increased governmental transparency and accountability—both areas in which the Liberals had promised to do better than the Conservatives. Rather than make an immediate call for a cancellation of the LAV deal, the NDP instead asked to see GAC's human rights assessment on Saudi Arabia, a prerequisite for signing export permits, and proposed a new way to increase transparency on arms exports, through a new parliamentary committee.

NDP foreign affairs critic Hélène Laverdière (for whom I work) tabled a motion to create a new parliamentary sub-committee of the House of Commons Standing Committee on Foreign Affairs and International Development. Laverdière explained that she wanted to see a "national dialogue on Canadian arms exports, human rights and our international obligations." The new committee would enable parliamentarians to hear from witnesses from government, business, and human rights sectors, and identify loopholes in existing legislation and practices.[26]

Laverdière's proposal was based on the United Kingdom (UK) Parliamentary Committees on Arms Exports Controls, which had studied the use of UK-manufactured arms in Yemen.[27] Laverdière's motion sat at the Foreign Affairs Committee for several weeks, as the NDP continued to grapple with internal division over the issue. But a turning point for the NDP position came at its policy convention in Edmonton in early April 2016, thanks to a speech by Stephen Lewis, in which the former leader of the Ontario NDP and former Canadian ambassador to the UN tore into the Liberals: "What in heaven's name possesses the Liberal government to consummate the sale of light-armoured vehicles to Saudi Arabia," he asked. To shouts of "Shame!" Lewis continued: "It reveals so much about this government – so much that cries out for an aggressive political response. The arms sale shows astonishing contempt for human rights ... We're talking about a regime whose hands are drenched in blood .... What do you mean, you can't break the contract? What you mean is that you *won't* break the contract!" Lewis then attacked Trudeau's claim to be a feminist, asking "What kind of feminism is it that sells weapons to a government steeped in misogyny?"[28] He also acknowledged "the elephant in the room," the question of jobs, noting "a serious progressive government" would create jobs "in another manufacturing environment, or another sector, or using infrastructure funds in Southwestern Ontario, whatever it takes."[29]

Lewis's speech was a subtle reprimand to NDP leadership that they had not been doing enough to speak out against arms exports to Saudi Arabia. As CBC commentator Neil Macdonald wrote of Lewis' "masterful" speech, "Lewis actually understated the government's lack of transparency ... Not that the NDP or Conservatives are pushing (Minister Dion) on the issue, which was the subtext of Lewis's message."[30] After months of overly cautious NDP policy, Lewis's bold message gave the party the green light to increase pressure on the Liberal government and criticize their handling of the deal. Serendipitously, the NDP convention ended the day before news broke that Dion had quietly approved $11 billion worth of export permits for the Saudi LAV deal—over 70 per cent of the transaction.[31]

THE SAUDI ARMS DEAL IN PARLIAMENT, 2016–2017

In Question Period in the House of Commons, the day after the news of the approved export permits broke, Mulcair and Laverdière accused the Liberals of misleading Canadians about the "done deal." Trudeau replied that the NDP had also promised to honour the LAV contract, noting "the fact is that there are jobs in London relying on this ... we will honour our good name." Mulcair retorted, "our good name includes standing to defend human rights around the world .... The situation in Saudi Arabia has only become worse, and the Prime Minister knows it."[32]

The NDP's line of questioning focused on two claims. First, the government had "lied to Canadians" by insisting that the Saudi contract was a "done deal." According to Canadian export rules, arms only ship when the export permits are signed, following human rights assessments. The decision to follow through with the contract, then, was Stéphane Dion's. The second line of attack focused on the question of human rights. Under pressure, Dion released a heavily redacted human rights assessment prepared by GAC before the export permits were approved. But the NDP argued that this assessment was weak. Nowhere in the assessment, or in any of the Liberal talking points, was any serious understanding of the concept of "reasonable risk" that Canadian-made arms could be used to commit human rights violations.³³

Dion claimed that the export permit approval was a simple administrative step and then promised in the House, "Should I become aware of credible information of violations related to this equipment, I will suspend or revoke the permits." (It was later revealed that Dion had not been briefed by human rights officials at GAC before signing the export permits.)³⁴ Speaking to reporters, he also suggested that, if Canada was not selling arms to Saudi Arabia, other countries would: "if we drop the contract, we will simply hand the contract to a non-Canadian, potentially more ambivalent provider."³⁵

At the Foreign Affairs Committee, Laverdière put her motion to create a sub-committee for increased parliamentary oversight of arms exports to a vote. The Liberals quickly blocked the motion and accused the NDP of playing politics with the issue. Bob Nault, the Liberal chair of the Committee, said, "Our committee is too high profile and too important to play politics with issues, and we weren't, quite frankly, very impressed that people were trying to seize on one issue when we think it's a lot larger and more complex than that."³⁶

During May and June of 2016, debate in the House was fuelled by a series of front-page reports in the *Globe and Mail* about human rights violations by Saudi Arabia, including the use of LAVs against Saudi civilians.³⁷ During 2016, the NDP raised concerns about Canadian arms exports 32 times in Question Period. Yet, during this time, the most common answer by the Liberals to questions on arms sales was that the NDP had made an electoral promise to honour the Saudi contract, along with the oft-repeated assertion that "Canada has some of the strongest export controls in the world." Direct questions about allegations of human rights abuses and misuse of Canadian arms went unanswered.

During the summer of 2016, while the House was not sitting, troubling allegations emerged that Streit Group, a Canadian company operating out of the United Arab Emirates, had sold arms to Libya, Sudan, and South Sudan in contravention of UN sanctions. The Streit case demonstrated a major loophole in Canadian arms export controls: Canadian companies operating overseas are not required to apply for export permits for weapons manufactured outside of Canada. The Liberals responded to the Streit Group allegations by saying they had referred the case to the Royal Canadian Mounted Police (RCMP). (In the year since these allegations surfaced, the RCMP has repeatedly refused to confirm whether there is, or has been, an investigation into Streit Group, let alone fines or prosecution, and the Liberal government still refuses to provide updates to parliamentarians on this case.)[38]

Canadian media also reported that military gear stamped "Made in Canada" was used in an attack against civilians in Saudi Arabia's Eastern Province—important evidence that Canadian weapons were, in fact, being used by Saudi Arabia in human rights violations. The response from the Canadian government was another in a long list of excuses: notably, this particular equipment was not subject to arms export controls, as it was militarized post-export.[39] The government was insisting on a very limited and technical understanding of "evidence" of human rights abuses— which, again, went against the standard of "reasonable risk." During this same time period, the *Globe and Mail* also revealed that the government had watered down its arms exports controls.[40]

When Parliament resumed in the fall of 2016, the NDP used their first Opposition Day[41] to attempt, once again, to create a parliamentary committee to examine arms exports.[42] During the full day of debate on the NDP motion, Liberal MPs repeatedly questioned the opposition's intentions and referred to the NDP promise made a year before not to cancel the Saudi contract. Several of the Liberal speakers attacked the NDP MP for London-Fanshawe, Irene Mathyssen, who was not speaking in the debate. One Liberal MP accused the NDP of trying to "break the promise they made to the constituents of London-Fanshawe." Another said, "the New Democrats have consistently attacked the Canadian defence industry. The only time they broke from their attacks was during the last election, in an effort to hold onto a seat in London." A third reminded the House that "we are talking about a lot of good, solid union jobs."[43] The Liberal talking points insisted that the NDP proposal for parliamentary oversight was a threat to the defence industry. Pamela Goldsmith-Jones, parliamentary secretary to the minister of foreign affairs, asked, "Is the defence industry really something we wish to cut back on? ... we are disappointed by the (NDP's) disregard for tens of thousands of Canadians' livelihoods."[44] On 5 October 2016, the Liberal government voted down the NDP motion. Following the defeat, Laverdière told the press, "It goes against everything—the Liberal government rhetoric—that promises more transparency, more open government."[45]

Yemen, the Forgotten Conflict

An under-examined consequence of exporting Canadian arms to Saudi Arabia is the likely use of that weaponry in Yemen. Largely ignored by Canadian media, the conflict in Yemen has raged since March 2015, when a Saudi-led coalition embarked on a bombing campaign against Houthi rebels. The bombing campaign has caused massive damage to infrastructure, in particular hospitals and sewage facilities, and restricted access to humanitarian aid. As a result, Yemen now faces one of the world's worst humanitarian crises, with over half a million people infected with cholera as of August 2017.[46]

In February 2016, the CBC revealed that Canadian-made guns originally sold to the Saudis had found their way into the hands of the Houthis in Yemen. (Canada has sold over $28 million in guns and rifles to Saudi Arabia in the past ten years.) The government launched an investigation, with one spokesperson saying, "we committed ourselves in the election campaign to greater transparency on these kinds of transactions—we intend do that."[47] Since those reports, however, the government has refused to release any findings of this investigation. Nor have they since answered questions about whether other Canadian weaponry sold to the Saudis have been used in Yemen.

Laverdière raised the conflict in Yemen 17 times in the House of Commons in 2016 and 2017, repeatedly seeking assurances from the government that no Canadian-made weapons were used by the Saudi coalition in Yemen.[48] Foreign Minister Dion promised, "we are monitoring the situation very closely to ensure that arms sold by Canadian companies are used with respect for human rights and in the interests of Canada and its allies."[49] But the Liberal government separately admitted, in an April 2016 document stamped "Secret" and tabled in Federal Court, that the Saudi-led campaign in Yemen was "consistent with Canada's defence interests in the Middle East."[50] In December, *VICE* reported that the government conceded in a document filed in court that it was unable to collect information on the use of Canadian weapons in Yemen. Further, the government said Saudi Arabia was a "key military ally who backs efforts of the international community to fight the Islamic State in Iraq and Syria and the instability in Yemen. The acquisition of these next-generation vehicles will help in those efforts."[51]

This astonishing admission once again exposed Liberal doublespeak regarding Saudi Arabia and human rights. The same government that had stated that it would suspend the LAV contract upon evidence of human rights abuses was also arguing in court that Saudi efforts in Yemen, and the use of Canadian weapons in that conflict, were "compatible with Canadian defence interests." This was despite enormous amounts of evidence indicating human rights violations in Yemen by the Saudi coalition, and a worsening humanitarian crisis.[52]

Evidence and Investigations in the Summer of 2017

In the summer of 2017, fresh allegations emerged that Saudi Arabia was using Canadian weaponry against Saudi civilians. The *Globe and Mail* reported that Terradyne armoured vehicles, known as Gurkhas, had been deployed against Shia minorities in Saudi Arabia's Eastern Province.[53] Only days later, the CBC reported new images showing the use of Canadian-made LAVs by General Dynamics in the same conflict.[54] The new minister of foreign affairs, Chrystia Freeland, expressed her "deep concern" and announced that she had ordered an investigation into the allegations. A spokesperson for GAC added that Minister Freeland would "take action" if it was confirmed that Canadian-made military equipment had been used to violate human rights. Yet the spokesperson provided no details on what "action" would be taken.[55]

These allegations prompted opposition parties and civil society to renew calls on Canada to suspend export permits to Saudi Arabia.[56] The NDP questioned the minister's newfound "deep concern." Said Laverdière, "I am wondering where the Trudeau government was over one year ago when people raised concerns over armoured vehicles sales to Saudi Arabia."[57] Laverdière sent a public letter to Freeland recalling former Minister Dion's April 2016 promise to reverse his decision on export permits should new evidence come to light. The letter argued that "based on [Dion's] clear commitment, the Liberal government has an indisputable responsibility, beyond conducting a thorough review that fully respects our domestic and international commitments, to immediately reverse the decision to permit the exportation of these military goods." Laverdière's letter also included a request that the government prepare "contingency plans to ensure that Canadian workers are not adversely affected" by the suspension of export permits.[58]

Other political opponents of the Liberals also criticized the inaction of the government. Conservative foreign affairs critic Peter Kent asked Canada to terminate contracts should there be "tangible evidence" that

Canadian weapons were used to commit human rights violations, and Green Party leader Elizabeth May argued Canada should "suspend any sales while we investigate."[59] The former Liberal cabinet minister, Irwin Cotler, an internationally respected human rights lawyer, also weighed in: "we shouldn't be selling any more arms to Saudi Arabia."[60] Daniel Turp, a former Bloc Québécois MP who had taken the Canadian government to court over the General Dynamics deal, threatened to renew his legal challenge to the government.[61]

Newspapers across Canada called on the government to cancel the LAV contract. The *Globe and Mail*, which had published many exclusive reports on the scandal since 2015, published a scathing editorial arguing Trudeau's government had "handled [the deal] poorly from the minute it came to power in 2015 ... in order to be respected—and to support human rights and the desire for a more peaceful world—there has to be a line in the sand that Canada will not cross. Let this be that line."[62] The *Toronto Star* published an editorial titled "Don't supply terror tools to tyrants," saying Trudeau's government "had better not rag the puck on this. If the reports are true, the government needs to stop further shipments, kill the deal and tell Canadians in no uncertain terms it has done so and will not support new deals that carry the same risk. ... We may not be able to stop tyrannical foreign governments from slaughtering their own people, but we don't have to supply the bullets."[63] The *Halifax Chronicle Herald* described Canada's position as "morally bankrupt," arguing that Minister Freeland "doesn't seem worried enough to take effective action."[64]

Facing such extensive criticism, on August 7, Freeland held a teleconference with the press where she insisted Canada had "expressed our concerns ... to the Kingdom of Saudi Arabia." But while Freeland said Canada expected end users of Canadian equipment to "abide by the terms of our export permits," she then refused to confirm that there were export permits for the Terradyne vehicles, "citing commercial confidentiality."[65] It was unclear why Minister Freeland would use commercial confidentiality as an excuse not to answer questions about export permit approvals for the Terradyne vehicles—especially considering that permits must have been granted for the vehicles to have ended up in Saudi Arabia.

For two weeks Freeland defended her government by insisting that it was investigating the allegations. However, on August 17, the Saudis made a stunning revelation, telling the *Globe and Mail* that Canadian-made weaponry was, in fact, being used by the Saudi government in the Eastern Province. The Saudi Embassy in Canada argued it was using its military equipment to fight terrorism, though their claims conflicted with reports from human rights groups that Saudi Arabia was targeting civilians.[66] Perhaps the Saudi government did not understand that, by confirming the use of Canadian weaponry in the Eastern Province, they had effectively thrown the Liberals and their "investigation" under the bus. For over a year, Trudeau's government had insisted that evidence of Canadian-made weaponry in human rights abuses would warrant cancellation of export permits. That this evidence would come from the Saudis themselves, in a letter to a leading national newspaper, was certainly surprising. Only days later, CBC journalist Neil Macdonald revealed that he had been given "strong indications that Terradyne's export permits have been suspended pending the investigation's outcome." But, even if true, "the government will not even confirm the cancellation"—so Canadians may never know what action the government has, or has not, taken in response to the evidence. Macdonald also confirmed a "bitter split at Global Affairs between diplomats who help sell arms and diplomats who are appalled that we're selling the Saudis anything."[67]

At the time of writing, it is unclear how the Trudeau government has responded to the new evidence beyond vague promises of "action." Will the government confirm it will cancel export permits for the Terradyne vehicles, or, as the CBC suggested, have they already cancelled them? Will the government release details or results of the investigation, or will this, like all the other investigations in the last two years, remain secret, with the government insisting no *conclusive* proof was found that Canadian weapons were used to violate the human rights of Saudi citizens?[68]

"A Troubling International Precedent": The Liberals and the Arms Trade Treaty

Throughout the political controversy over arms exports to Saudi Arabia, the Liberals insisted that their promise to accede to the Arms Trade Treaty (ATT) was evidence that they took arms control and human rights seriously. In April 2017, Minister Freeland finally tabled Bill C-47 in the House of Commons[69]; it contains amendments to the *Export and Import Permits Act* that would make Canada eligible to join the ATT. While the minister said the new legislation will "raise the bar with a stronger and more rigorous system for our country," the bill, as tabled, includes at least two glaring omissions. First, C-47 does not address Canadian military exports to the United States. The government of Canada does not currently collect data on most military exports to the United States, though at least half of Canadian exports are destined for that country.[70] (Given that the ATT does not permit exceptions, the exclusion of the United States would violate Canada's obligations under the treaty.) A second major concern with Bill C-47 is the omission of new assessment criteria for authorization of export permits. While the bill creates a legal requirement that the minister of foreign affairs considers assessment criteria before authorizing a new export permit, the new criteria are not included in the legislation. Instead, the criteria will be determined by the government following the enactment of the bill—which means parliamentarians and members of the Canadian public will have no opportunity to examine the criteria to ensure that they uphold both the letter and the spirit of the ATT.

In choosing not to include these two major points in its legislation, the Liberal government seems to have dismissed advice provided by civil society experts. Project Ploughshares, Amnesty International, Oxfam Canada, and Oxfam Quebec had, in the year prior to the tabling of C-47, met with government officials on multiple occasions and provided a 30-page briefing note to the government with recommendations on improving Canada's military export controls in order to accede to the Treaty.[71] These civil society organizations (CSOs) have worked on disarmament issues at the global level for decades and have participated in ATT negotiations at the United Nations. But when C-47 was tabled in April 2017, it became clear that much of their advice was not taken by the Liberal government. Said Cesar Jaramillo of Project Ploughshares, "Rather than heed [our] recommendations, GAC left in place precisely the type of scenario that not only runs contrary to the spirit and objective of the Treaty, but also could set a troubling international precedent."[72]

If passed without amendment, Bill C-47 will not strengthen export controls to the standard required by the ATT, and it is unlikely that this legislation would ensure that future arms deals with human rights-abusing countries would be prohibited. In other words, with this legislation another Saudi deal could be possible.[73]

Beyond 2017

Despite two years of political debate on whether to continue selling arms to Saudi Arabia, the Liberals have yet to take a clear position. For the past two years, they have permitted arms sales to Saudi Arabia to continue while making weak and often implausible claims about respect for human rights. On multiple occasions, they have refused to answer important questions about the Saudi-LAV deal and about Canadian arms exports in general. They have also twice refused to permit greater parliamentary debate on, and oversight of, Canadian arms exports. They have hidden behind secretive "investigations" into allegations of sanctions-busting by Streit Group, and allegations that Canadian weaponry has been used to commit human rights violations in Saudi Arabia and Yemen. They have tabled weak legislation in Parliament that clearly runs counter to the spirit and the letter of the ATT, while at the same time claiming that it will strengthen arms export regulations. As this happens, the Trudeau government has continued to promote the Canadian arms industry abroad, through the Department of Global Affairs and the Canadian Commercial Corporation.[74]

The leading civil society expert on Canada's arms exports policy, Project Ploughshares' Jaramillo has raised five excellent questions that should be considered beyond 2017. First, does Canada have the capacity to monitor misuse of arms exports, and how realistic or effective is that capacity? All prior indications have been that the government relies mainly on the assurances of state recipients of arms and that there is little to no monitoring of use of arms by the end user. Second, what other instances of misuse of Canadian arms have occurred? Has the government previously asked these questions of Saudi Arabia or other states, and if so, what answers have they received? So far, the government has refused to answer questions on reported misuse and refused to provide results of their investigations. Third, to what extent is an eventual transition of power in Saudi Arabia relevant to these discussions and what potential impact could new leadership have on conflict in the region? Fourth, what action will the government take following the findings of the investigation? And finally, does the Liberal government's insistence on requiring evidence of misuse—and not reasonable risk of misuse—create a new precedent, "whereby future arms deals would be judged on a basis that is blatantly incongruous with domestic export regulations and the spirit and obligations of the international Arms Trade Treaty?"[75] Jaramillo's five questions should drive much of the debate moving forward—but in the absence of a forum for discussion in Parliament, it is hard to say if these questions will find answers.

There is also the larger and more troubling issue of Canadian arms exports in general. In their 2017 article in *Canadian Foreign Policy Journal*, Ellen Gutterman and Andrea Lane question whether Canada should have an arms industry at all and argue for a "public evaluation of Canada's participation in the global arms industry" and a "wholesale, informed reevaluation of priorities."[76] Along similar lines, Jaramillo suggests this debate should make us consider "fundamental questions about Canada's role in the world ... and its very character as a nation."[77] But a public conversation about Canada's overall approach to arms exports does not seem likely to occur under the Liberal government—despite the efforts of the NDP to foster parliamentary discussion on arms exports, despite the concerns of many Canadians that Canada should not be exporting to human rights abusers like Saudi Arabia, and despite the many criticisms of Canada's arms exports regime from disarmament advocates.

In the absence of this conversation, and given the important role the Canadian arms industry plays in the Canadian economy, how will the Trudeau Liberals walk the line between human rights and arms exports moving forward? Will the Liberals make significant policy changes over the coming months, perhaps in the form of a stronger bill to accede to the ATT? Will they suspend existing export permits to Saudi Arabia, or even prevent all future sales to the country? Or will they continue to express their concern for human rights on the one hand, and sign export permits to countries like Saudi Arabia on the other hand?

It is not only the Liberal Party that should reflect on these questions. In the near future, the Conservatives may continue to play both sides of the argument while in opposition, taking advantage of a weak Liberal response—though in government, the Conservatives were as lacking in transparency as the Liberals. And to what extent will the progressive opposition NDP balance its commitment to human rights with their support for (and from) Canadian labour, parts of which depend on jobs provided by the arms industry? The new NDP leader, Jagmeet Singh, may have an impact on the direction the party takes on this issue.

Also worth further examination is how Trudeau's disheartening approach to arms exports fits within the larger frame of Canadian foreign policy under his government. The government's lack of transparency on the arms exports file comes at the same time as an announced 70 per cent increase in Canada's defence budget over the next ten years—coinciding with a declining international assistance envelope—as well as the Canadian government's withdrawal from international disarmament efforts, including its scandalous absence at UN negotiations for a nuclear weapons ban treaty.

Whether Canada changes its policy on arms exports to potential human rights violators will likely depend on how much Canadians actually speak out on this issue and put pressure on their elected representatives. There is certainly public interest in policy change: in September 2017, a Nanos poll revealed that a majority of Canadians oppose arms exports to Saudi Arabia.[78] But interest doesn't equate to action, and without greater public pressure, there is little incentive for the Liberals to change their position. Perhaps the Liberals have calculated that they can weather this scandal without serious consequences, since foreign affairs rarely affect election outcomes in Canada and most Canadians will not be thinking about this issue at the ballot box. What is clear is that, in the continuing absence of honest, principled, and moral leadership by the Trudeau government, little will change.

Notes

1. I work for the New Democratic Party Foreign Affairs Critic, Hélène Laverdière. This chapter is partially based on my work on this file while a parliamentary staffer, but is not endorsed by the NDP or by the House of Commons. I have made every effort to respect confidences, and any errors and omissions are mine alone.
2. See United Nations (2013).
3. For analysis of the deal, see Chase (2016a), Marwah (2017), and Jaramillo (2015a).
4. Canada does not collect data on military exports to the United States, although these amount to half or more of Canadian military exports. This is due to the Defence Production Sharing Agreement, in place since the 1950s. Most military goods exported to the United States do not require export permits. For more information, see Global Affairs Canada (2017b) and Powers (2016).
5. For more details, see Canadian Association of Defence and Security Industries (2017) and Marcoux and Brewster (2017).
6. The five biggest arms exporters are the United States, Russia, China, France, and Germany, which account for nearly three quarters of the world's arms exports (Stockholm International Peace Research Institute 2017).
7. For a more detailed discussions of Canada's record as a global arms dealer, see Shiab (2017), Khan (2017), and Chase (2016e).
8. India was the largest arms importer in the world between 2012 and 2016 (Stockholm International Peace Research Institute 2017).
9. See Jaramillo (2015b).

10. See Jaramillo (2015a).
11. See Petrou (2016).
12. As quoted (Chase 2016b).
13. As quoted *London Free Press* (2015, B2).
14. See Chase and Leblanc (2016).
15. See Gloria Galloway (2015).
16. Galloway (2015).
17. Dubinski (2015).
18. Ibid.
19. Chase (2016a).
20. Jaramillo (2016a).
21. Quoted in Jaramillo (2016b).
22. Jaramillo (2016b).
23. See Gibson (2017).
24. Jaramillo (2016c, d).
25. I was privy to some, but not all, of these conversations.
26. This was articulated in an article by Hélène Laverdière published by the *Sun* newspaper chain (Laverdière 2016a).
27. The UK Parliamentary Committees on Arms Export Controls draw members from several other committees, including Trade, Business, Defence, and Foreign Affairs and International Development. Their studies have been widely reported in the British press, and have contributed to public discussions on the role of the UK arms industry in Middle Eastern conflicts, including the devastating conflict in Yemen. See United Kingdom Parliament (2017).
28. The question of feminism and Canadian arms deals is discussed by Srdjan Vucetic in his working paper (Vucetic 2017).
29. Stephen Lewis' full speech can be viewed at Lewis (2016).
30. See Neil Macdonald's analysis of Lewis' speech (Macdonald 2016a).
31. Chase (2016c).
32. House Publications (2016a).
33. Global Affairs Canada (2015).
34. Paul Webster reported this exclusively in the National Observer (Webster 2017).
35. See Thompson (2016).
36. Chase (2016d).
37. Most of these reports were by Steven Chase, whose articles can be found at https://www.theglobeandmail.com/authors/steven-chase
38. The NDP has raised this question in the House of Commons, in Committee, and as a question on the Order Paper. Answers from the government provide no details or confirmations of an RCMP investigation into Streit Group's actions.
39. Jaramillo (2016e).

40. See Chase (2016f), and Rettino-Parazelli (2016).
41. An Opposition Day is a day in which the House of Commons debates a motion tabled by an opposition party.
42. The motion read in part: "That: (a) the House recognize that (i) Canadian arms exports have nearly doubled over the past decade, and that Canada is now the second-largest exporter of arms to the Middle East, (ii) Canadians expect a high standard from their government when it comes to protecting human rights abroad, (iii) Canadians are concerned by arms sales to countries with a record of human rights abuses, including Saudi Arabia, Libya, and Sudan, (iv) there is a need for Canadians, through Parliament, to oversee current and future arms sales." See New Democratic Party of Canada (2016). See, also, for the full debate House Publications (2016b).
43. For these quotes and the full debate, see House Publications (2016b).
44. Quoted in Chase (2016g).
45. Chase (2016g).
46. See Almosawa et al. (2017).
47. CBC News (2016).
48. See, for example, House Publications (2016c, d). See also Laverdière (2016b).
49. House Publications (2016c).
50. Macdonald (2016b).
51. See Justin Ling's exclusive published in Vice: Ling (2016).
52. The Canadian government pledged $34 million for the humanitarian crisis in Yemen in March 2017 (Global Affairs Canada 2017a).
53. Shia dissidents had circulated videos and photos on the Internet of Saudi Arabian security operations in the area of al-Awamiya, in the al-Qatif region (Chase and Fife 2017).
54. CBC TV *The National* (2017).
55. Gibson (2017).
56. Amnesty International Canada secretary-general Alex Neve called on Canada to "put an immediate end to the Canadian/Saudi LAV deal" (Chase and Fife 2017).
57. Chase (2017d).
58. Letter from Helene Laverdière to the Hon. Chrystia Freeland, July 31, 2017.
59. Chase (2017a).
60. Ibid., (2017b).
61. See Goujard (2017), CBC *As it Happens* (2017), and Chase (2017c).
62. *Globe and Mail* (2017).
63. *Kitchener-Waterloo Record* (2017).
64. *Halifax Chronicle-Herald* (2017).
65. Chase (2017d).
66. Ibid., (2017e). See also Cornellier (2017).

67. Macdonald (2017).
68. CBC journalist Neil Macdonald asked Global Affairs multiple times over two years for results of investigations into images of Canadian LAVs used in Yemen, as well as other investigations. He was told on several occasions that there was no conclusive proof that weapons were used against civilians (Macdonald 2017).
69. Minister of Foreign Affairs (2017).
70. Canadians may falsely assume that military exports to the United States are used solely by the US military. This is not the case, as Canadian components are often incorporated into US made weapons systems and exported elsewhere. For more information on this, see Jaramillo (2017b).
71. For the full briefing, see Project Ploughshares et al. (2017).
72. Jaramillo (2017b).
73. At the time of writing, it was expected that C-47 would be debated in Parliament in the fall of 2017.
74. Two interesting commentaries on the Canadian government's promotion of arms sales abroad are by researcher Anthony Fenton and by CBC opinion columnist Neil Macdonald. See a March 2016 Canadaland podcast with Anthony Fenton (Sexton 2016; Neil Macdonald 2017).
75. Jaramillo (2017c).
76. See Gutterman and Lane (2017, 88).
77. Jaramillo (2017a).
78. Chase (2017f).

References

Almosawa, Shuaib, Ben Hubbard, and Troy Griggs. 2017. 'It's a slow death': The world's worst humanitarian crisis. *New York Times*, August 23. https://www.nytimes.com/interactive/2017/08/23/world/middleeast/yemen-cholera-humanitarian-crisis.html. Accessed 15 Sept 2017.

Canadian Association of Defence and Security Industries (CADSI). 2017. The defence sector and innovation-led growth: submission to the standing committee on finance. *CADSI*. https://www.defenceandsecurity.ca/UserFiles/File/Presentations/Finance%20Submission/CADSI_%20Finance_PreBudgetsubmission2017.pdf. Accessed 15 Sept 2017.

CBC *As it Happens*. 2017. Former Bloc MP Daniel Turp says videos of Canadian armoured vehicles being used in civilian areas of Saudi Arabia are all the evidence the government should need to block further sales. CBC *As it Happens*, radio broadcast, August 8.

CBC News. 2016. Investigation underway after Canadian rifles end up in Yemen rebel hands. *CBC News*, February 23. http://www.cbc.ca/news/canada/manitoba/winnipeg-made-sniper-rifles-fall-into-yemen-rebel-hands-1.3459551. Accessed 15 Sept 2017.

CBC TV *The National*. 2017. New video purports to show Canadian-made LAVs being used in Saudi crackdown. CBC TV *The National*, television broadcast, August 8.

Chase, Steven. 2016a. Ottawa going ahead with Saudi arms deal despite condemning executions. *Globe and Mail*, January 4. https://www.theglobeandmail.com/news/politics/ottawa-going-ahead-with-saudi-arms-deal-despite-condemning-executions/article28013908/. Accessed 15 Sept 2017.

———. 2016b. Dion adviser Jocelyn Coulon critical of Saudi arms deals. *Globe and Mail*, March 27. http://www.theglobeandmail.com/news/politics/dion-adviser-jocelyn-coulon-critical-of-saudi-arms-deals/article29400881/. Accessed 15 Sept 2017.

———. 2016c. Dion quietly approved arms sale to Saudi Arabia in April: documents. *Globe and Mail*, April 12. http://www.theglobeandmail.com/news/politics/liberals-quietly-approved-arms-sale-to-saudis-in-april-documents/article29612233/. Accessed 15 Sept 2017.

———. 2016d. Liberals block NDP motion to create arms exports oversight body. *Globe and Mail*, April 20. http://www.theglobeandmail.com/news/politics/liberals-blasted-for-blocking-move-to-create-arms-exports-oversight-body/article29697820/. Accessed 15 Sept 2017.

———. 2016e. Canada now second-biggest arms exporter to the Middle East. *Globe and Mail*, June 14. https://www.theglobeandmail.com/news/politics/canada-now-the-second-biggest-arms-exporter-to-middle-east-data-show/article30459788/. Accessed 15 Sept 2017.

———. 2016f. Ottawa rewrites mandate for screening arms exports. *Globe and Mail*, July 31. https://www.theglobeandmail.com/news/politics/ottawa-rewrites-mandate-for-screening-arms-exports/article31216740/. Accessed 15 Sept 2017.

———. 2016g. Liberals reject NDP motion to increase scrutiny of arms exports. *Globe and Mail*, October 4. https://www.theglobeandmail.com/news/politics/liberals-reject-ndp-motion-to-increase-scrutiny-of-arms-exports/article32252484/. Accessed 15 Sept 2017.

———. 2017a. Critics urge Ottawa to suspend arms exports to Saudi Arabia. *Globe and Mail*, July 31. https://www.theglobeandmail.com/news/politics/critics-urge-ottawa-to-suspend-arms-exports-to-saudi-arabia/article35851117/. Accessed 15 Sept 2017.

———. 2017b. Human-rights lawyer calls for end to Canadian arms sales to Saudi Arabia. *Globe and Mail*, August 1. https://www.theglobeandmail.com/news/politics/human-rights-lawyer-calls-for-end-to-canadian-arms-sales-to-saudi-arabia/article35861007/. Accessed 15 Sept 2017.

———. 2017c. Saudi video revives push to ban exports. *Globe and Mail*, August 5. https://www.theglobeandmail.com/news/politics/montreal-professor-renews-legal-effort-to-block-canadian-combat-vehicle-exports-to-saudi-arabia/article35887899/. Accessed 15 Sept 2017.

———. 2017d. Ottawa conveys concerns to Saudis, allies over alleged vehicle use. *Globe and Mail*, August 8. https://www.theglobeandmail.com/news/politics/trudeau-government-registers-concern-with-saudi-arabia-over-apparent-armoured-vehicle-use/article35896121/. Accessed 15 Sept 2017.

———. 2017e. Saudi Arabia defends use of Canadian-made armoured vehicles against civilians. *Globe and Mail*, August 17. https://www.theglobeandmail.com/news/politics/saudi-arabia-defends-use-of-canadian-made-armoured-vehicles-against-civilians/article36007932/. Accessed 15 Sept 2017.

———. 2017f. Most Canadians oppose arms deals with Saudi Arabia, poll finds. *Globe and Mail*, September 14. https://beta.theglobeandmail.com/news/politics/most-canadians-oppose-arms-deals-with-saudi-arabia-poll-finds/article36256402/. Accessed 15 Sept 2017.

Chase, Steven, and Robert Fife. 2017. Review ordered of Saudis' use of Gurkhas. *Globe and Mail*, July 29.

Chase, Steven, and Daniel Leblanc. 2016. Duceppe takes aim at Trudeau over Saudi arms sales. *Globe and Mail*, October 13, 2015. https://www.theglobeandmail.com/news/politics/gilles-duceppe-accuses-justin-trudeau-of-lying-about-saudi-arms-sales/article26779801/. Accessed 15 Sept 2017.

Cornellier, Manon. 2017. Un aveu incontournable. *Le Devoir*, August 19. http://www.ledevoir.com/politique/canada/506066/vente-d-armes-a-l-arabie-saoudite-un-aveu-incontournable. Accessed 15 Sept 2017.

Dubinski, Kate. 2015. The NDP's Irene Mathyssen fires back at Liberal Khalil Ramal's claim the NDP will sink the lucrative military contact. *London Free Press*, October 17. http://www.lfpress.com/2015/10/16/the-ndps-irene-mathyssen-fires-back-at-liberal-khalil-ramals-claim-the-ndp-will-sink-the-lucrative-military-contact. Accessed 15 Sept 2017.

Galloway, Gloria. 2015. Mulcair's concerns over Saudi arms deal put him in tricky spot with union. *Globe and Mail*, September 30. http://www.theglobeandmail.com/news/politics/saudi-arms-deal-puts-mulcair-in-tricky-spot-with-ontario-union/article26606571/. Accessed 15 Sept 2017.

Gibson, Victoria. 2017. Ottawa to probe alleged breach of Saudi deal. *Toronto Star*, July 29.

Global Affairs Canada. 2015. Human rights report: Saudi Arabia. Global Affairs Canada. http://s3.documentcloud.org/documents/2804181/Global-Affairs-Canada-Human-Rights-Report-Saudi.pdf. Accessed 15 Sept 2017.

———. 2017a. Canada provides funding to respond to food crises in Nigeria, Somalia, South Sudan, and Yemen. Global Affairs Canada, March 17. https://www.canada.ca/en/global-affairs/news/2017/03/canada_provides_fundingtorespondtofoodcrisesinnigeriasomaliasout.html. Accessed 15 Sept 2017.

———. 2017b. Exports of military goods 2016. Global Affairs Canada. www.exportcontrols.gc.ca. Accessed 15 Sept 2017.

Globe and Mail. 2017. On Saudi arms sale, Ottawa must be prepared to say no. Editorial. *Globe and Mail,* August 1. https://beta.theglobeandmail.com/opinion/editorials/globe-editorial-on-saudi-arms-sale-ottawa-must-be-prepared-to-say-no/article35858862/. Accessed 15 Sept 2017.

Goujard, Clothilde. 2017. Outraged lawyer gives Chrystia Freeland three weeks to stop Saudi arms deal. *National Observer,* August 10. http://www.nationalobserver.com/2017/08/10/news/outraged-lawyer-gives-chrystia-freeland-three-weeks-stop-saudi-arms-deal. Accessed 15 Sept 2017.

Gutterman, Ellen, and Andrea Lane. 2017. Beyond LAVs: Corruption, commercialization and the Canadian defence industry. *Canadian Foreign Policy Journal* 23 (1): 77–92.

Halifax Chronicle Herald. 2017. Editorial: A round of tut-tuts. *Halifax Chronicle Herald,* August 7. http://thechronicleherald.ca/editorials/1492597-editorial-a-round-of-tut-tuts. Accessed 15 Sept 2017.

House Publications. 2016a. 42nd Parliament, 1st Sessions edited hansard – number 039. *House of Commons,* April 14. http://www.ourcommons.ca/DocumentViewer/en/42-1/house/sitting-39/hansard. Accessed 15 Sept 2017.

———. 2016b. 42nd Parliament, 1st Sessions edited hansard – number 084. *House of Commons,* September 29. https://www.ourcommons.ca/DocumentViewer/en/42-1/house/sitting-84/hansard. Accessed 15 Sept 2017.

———. 2016c. 42nd Parliament, 1st Sessions edited hansard – number 092. *House of Commons,* October 18. https://www.ourcommons.ca/DocumentViewer/en/42-1/house/sitting-92/hansard. Accessed 15 Sept 2017.

———. 2016d. 42nd Parliament, 1st Sessions edited hansard – number 128. *House of Commons,* December 14. http://www.ourcommons.ca/DocumentViewer/en/42-1/house/sitting-128/hansard. Accessed 15 Sept 2017.

Jaramillo, Cesar. 2015a. Saudi Arabia doesn't measure up to Canada's rights recommendations. *Huffington Post,* October 8. http://www.huffingtonpost.ca/cesar-jaramillo/human-rights saudi-arabia_b_8259422.html. Accessed 15 Sept 2017.

———. 2015b. We must not downplay Canada's arms deal with Saudi Arabia. *Huffington Post,* October 28. http://www.huffingtonpost.ca/cesar-jaramillo/canada-saudi-arabia-military-vehicles_b_8399476.html. Accessed 15 Sept 2017.

———. 2016a. Saudi arms deal will shape Canada's character (for better or worse). *Huffington Post,* January 14. http://www.huffingtonpost.ca/cesar-jaramillo/canada-saudi-arms-deal_b_8973038.html. Accessed 15 Sept 2017.

———. 2016b. Trudeau's handling of the Saudi arms deal will define his legacy. *Huffington Post,* January 28. http://www.huffingtonpost.ca/cesar-jaramillo/justin-trudeau-saudi-arms-deal_b_9102670.html. Accessed 15 Sept 2017.

———. 2016c. Here's an entirely legitimate exit strategy on the Saudi arms deal. *Huffington Post*, March 7. http://www.huffingtonpost.ca/cesar-jaramillo/canada-saudi-arms-deal_b_9375302.html. Accessed 15 Sept 2017.

———. 2016d. The big, fat Saudi-arms deal spin. *Huffington Post*, April 18. http://www.huffingtonpost.ca/cesar-jaramillo/saudi-arms-deal_b_9721988.html. Accessed 15 Sept 2017.

———. 2016e. Ottawa cannot continue to deny dangers of Saudi arms deal. *Huffington Post*, July 14. http://www.huffingtonpost.ca/cesar-jaramillo/saudi-arms-deal-canada_b_10973218.html. Accessed 15 Sept 2017.

———. 2017a. Despite ruling, many questions on Saudi arms deals linger. *Globe and Mail*, January 25. https://www.theglobeandmail.com/opinion/despite-ruling-many-questions-on-saudi-arms-deal-linger/article33742260/. Accessed 15 Sept 2017.

———. 2017b. Canada's ATT legislation: A loophole you could drive a tank through. *Ploughshares Monitor*, 38 (2): 3–4. http://ploughshares.ca/pl_publications/the-ploughshares-monitor-summer-2017/. Accessed 15 Sept 2017.

———. 2017c. Five urgent questions in light of an investigation into Saudi use of Canadian arms. *OpenCanada*, August 15. https://www.opencanada.org/features/five-urgent-questions-light-investigation-saudi-use-canadian-arms/. Accessed 15 Sept 2017.

Khan, Adnan. 2017. Canada's abysmal record as an arms dealer. *Macleans*, August 4. http://www.macleans.ca/news/world/canadas-abysmal-record-as-an-arms-dealer/. Accessed 15 Sept 2017.

Kitchener Waterloo-Record. 2017. Don't supply terror tools to tyrants. *Kitchener-Waterloo Record*, August 3.

Laverdière, Helene. 2016a. Why Canada needs a committee on arms exports. *Toronto Sun*, March 13. http://www.torontosun.com/2016/03/13/why-canada-needs-a-committee-on-arms-exports. Accessed 15 Sept 2017.

———. 2016b. When it comes to arms exports, Canada isn't 'back'. *Huffington Post*, October 4. http://www.huffingtonpost.ca/helene-laverdiere/canada-arms-exports_b_12322030.html. Accessed 15 Sept 2017.

———. 2017. Letter to Hon. Chrystia Freeland, July 31.

Lewis, Stephen. 2016. 2016 NDP convention – Stephen Lewis. *Cpac video*, 0:37:52, April 9. https://www.youtube.com/watch?v=CJ2_-nYvU9I. Accessed 15 Sept 2017.

Ling, Justin. 2016. Canada admits the weapons it sells to Saudi Arabia could be used in Yemen civil war. *VICE News*, December 20. https://news.vice.com/story/canada-admits-the-weapons-it-sells-to-saudi-arabia-could-be-used-in-yemen-civil-war. Accessed 15 Sept 2017.

London Free Press. 2015. Daily Briefing. *London Free Press*, August 10.

Macdonald, Neil. 2016a. In masterful oration, Stephen Lewis reminds NDP convention what left-wing means. *CBC News*, April 10. http://www.cbc.ca/news/politics/stephen-lewis-speech-at-ndp-convention-1.3529470. Accessed 15 Sept 2017.

———. 2016b. On Saudi arms deal, the new boss in Ottawa is just like the old boss. *CBC News*, April 14. http://www.cbc.ca/news/politics/canada-saudi-arabia-arms-lav-contract-liberals-conservatives-neil-macdonald-1.3534795. Accessed 15 Sept 2017.

———. 2017. Canada's review of arms sales to Saudi Arabia runs into a bit of a snag. *CBC News*, August 24. http://www.cbc.ca/news/opinion/canada-arms-sales-1.4259338. Accessed 15 Sept 2017.

Marcoux, Jacques, and Murray Brewster. 2017. Saudi Arabia top non-U.S. destination for Canadian arms exports: federal report. *CBC News*, June 22. http://www.cbc.ca/news/politics/saudi-arabia-top-non-u-s-destination-for-canadian-arms-exports-federal-report-1.4172182. Accessed 15 Sept 2017.

Marwah, Sonal. 2017. Arms and forced displacement: The case of the Canada-Saudi Arabia arms deal. *Ploughshares Monitor*, 38 (2): 5–11. http://ploughshares.ca/pl_publications/the-ploughshares-monitor-summer-2017/. Accessed 15 Sept 2017.

Minister of Foreign Affairs. 2017. Bill C-47: *An Act to amend the Export and Import Permits Act and the Criminal Code (amendments permitting the accession to the Arms Trade Treaty and other amendments)*. April 13.

New Democratic Party of Canada. 2016. NDP proposes oversight on arms sales. New Democratic Party of Canada, September 28. https://www.ndp.ca/news/ndp-proposes-oversight-arms-sales. Accessed 15 Sept 2017.

Petrou, Michael. 2016. Why is Canada making arms deals with the Saudis? *Macleans*, January 14. http://www.macleans.ca/politics/worldpolitics/why-is-canada-making-arms-deals-with-the-saudis/. Accessed 15 Sept 2017.

Powers, Lucas. 2016. Canadian arms trade much larger than data suggests, expert says. *CBC News*, February 23. http://www.cbc.ca/news/business/canada-arms-technology-trade-1.3458608. Accessed 15 Sept 2017.

Project Ploughshares, Oxfam Canada, Amnesty International Canada, and Oxfam Quebec. 2017. *Briefing: Canada's Accession to the Arms Trade Treaty*. April.

Rettino-Parazelli, Karl. 2016. Les libéraux adoptent le ton conservateur. *Le Devoir*, August 2. http://www.ledevoir.com/politique/canada/476842/exportation-de-materiel-militaire-les-liberaux-marchent-dans-les-pas-des-conservateurs. Accessed 15 Sept 2017.

Sexton, Kevin. 2016. Canada's arms deals: beyond Saudi Arabia. *Canadaland*, March 21. http://www.canadalandshow.com/podcast/canadas-arms-deals-beyond-saudi-arabia/. Accessed 15 Sept 2017.

Shiab, Naël. 2017. Marchandises militaries: la grande hypocrisie canadienne. *L'Actualité*, February 5. https://lactualite.com/societe/2017/02/05/marchandises-militaires-la-grande-hypocrisie-canadienne/. Accessed 15 Sept 2017.

Stockholm International Peace Research Institute. 2017. *Trends in international arms transfers, 2016*. February.

Thompson, Elizabeth. 2016. Canada will cancel Saudi arms sale if it's used to violate human rights. *iPolitics*, April 13. http://ipolitics.ca/2016/04/13/scrap-the-saudi-arms-deal-says-clement/. Accessed 15 Sept 2017.

United Kingdom Parliament. 2017. United Kingdom Parliament Committees on Arms Export Controls Website. United Kingdom Parliament. https://www.parliament.uk/business/committees/committees-a-z/other-committees/committee-on-arms-export-controls/. Accessed 15 Sept 2017.

United Nations. 2013. Arms Trade Treaty. United Nations. https://www.un.org/disarmament/convarms/att/. Accessed 15 Sept 2017.

Vucetic, Srdjan. 2017. The nation of feminist arms dealers? Canada and military exports. Working paper.

Webster, Paul. 2017. Dion not properly briefed on human rights before Saudi arms deal. *National Observer*, January 31. http://www.nationalobserver.com/2017/01/31/news/exclusive-dion-not-properly-briefed-human-rights-saudi-arms-deal. Accessed 15 Sept 2017.

CHAPTER 12

The Trudeau Government, Refugee Policy, and Echoes of the Past

Julie F. Gilmour

Press accounts in the *The New York Times, The Guardian, Al-Jazeera,* and other mainstream outlets over the last two years have made special mention of Canada's efforts to welcome refugees from Syria in contrast to closed-door policies in the United States that their editorial boards and journalists found alarming or misguided. This was particularly true for *The New York Times*, in the wake of the 27 January 2017 Trump administration executive order banning the entry of individuals from Iraq, Syria, Sudan, Iran, Somalia, Libya, and Yemen.[1] The refugee issue has thus reinforced, in the phrasing of the Canadian Broadcasting Corporation, the "perception of Canadians as 'friendly and welcoming.'"[2]

Prime Minister Justin Trudeau himself became a central part of the narrative when he made the Syrian refugees a pivotal part of the Liberal platform in the 2015 federal election and personally welcomed refugees arriving in Canada as a result of his policies. The refugee policy promise was central to the Liberal victory in 2015 and has been widely judged a success, since the goal of bringing 25,000 Syrians to Canada was reached quickly. This chapter aims to describe the extensive government response

J. F. Gilmour (✉)
Trinity College, University of Toronto, Toronto, ON, Canada

required to fulfill this promise, to put it in a historical context, and to emphasize the important role of private citizens and civil service initiatives in previous and current refugee resettlement programs. We will come to see that, as in the refugee crises of 1947 and 1979, Canada's large refugee resettlement programs are successful when the civil service is encouraged to partner actively with the public to find creative ways to direct both federal and private resources.

According to Liberal Party materials circulated during the 2015 election, a Liberal-led government would focus on a number of changes designed to ensure an "immigration system that is grounded in compassion and economic opportunity for all."[3] This included the party's promise to directly sponsor 25,000 Syrian refugees; support private sponsorship programs to encourage the movement of additional families; spend $200 million to increase capacity in refugee processing, sponsorship, and settlement; and contribute $100 million to the United Nations High Commissioner for Refugees (UNHCR).[4] It is therefore not surprising that, soon after taking office, the Trudeau government returned to its refugee pledge. The original promise of the movement of 25,000 Syrian refugees to Canada by the end of 2015 was revised to a commitment to meet that target by February 2016 and then to add another 10,000 by 2017.[5] The government was signaling that refugees generally, and Syrian refugees, in particular, were a priority.

Refugee Programs in the Harper and Trudeau Governments

The previous Stephen Harper government's 2015 budget plan included no references to refugees or to Canada's refugee system. All relevant spending by Immigration and Citizenship Canada in 2015 was left out of the government's Economic Action Plan, which mentioned immigration briefly in sections entitled "Supporting Canadian Workers," "Reforming the Temporary Foreign Worker Program," and "Protecting the Integrity of our Borders."[6] This is not to say that there was no "Refugee Protection Program." On the contrary, the Harper government underlined, in another document, its stated target of resettling 8–12 percent of the world's refugees in 2014 and its intention to spend $35,205,049 to protect "refugees in need of resettlement" and to continue "to strengthen the integrity of Canada's refugee protection system by collaborating with domestic and international partners to ensure that those who need protection can receive it in a timely fashion and to deter abuse."[7] Included in this group of "those who need protection" by the Harper government were largely Christian Syrians, who were given priority over members of the much larger Muslim population of Syria.[8]

The Harper government projected a reduction in planned spending on refugees in 2015–16 and 2016–17,[9] while maintaining the per year target for government-assisted refugees (GARs) at 6,900–7,200 admissions and 4,500–6,500 admissions of privately sponsored refugees (PSRs).[10] GARs are brought to Canada in a program underwritten by the federal government that assures them basic financial support for a year, as well as settlement assistance. PSRs come in the Privately Sponsored Refugee Program (PSRP), which is supported financially by individuals and groups who undertake to provide the financial and settlement assistance for a year within a program managed by the federal government. Medical care is available in both of these programs under Canada's single-payer provincial health care systems.

In contrast, in a portion of its 2016 Budget Plan, the Liberal government announced the allocation of the enormous sum of $678 million over six years to respond broadly to the Syrian refugee crisis, as well as the promised $100 million immediately for the UNHCR.[11] This document also framed the new government's immigration priorities in the context of a Liberal interpretation of the lessons of Canada's immigration history and strongly reflected former Prime Minister Pierre Trudeau's approach to multiculturalism, which emphasized the contributions of Canada's ethnic communities in a nation-building project whose sum was greater than its parts. "Canada's history," the Justin Trudeau Liberals asserted, "has been shaped by immigration. Immigrants bring unique cultures and perspectives, and make distinctive contributions to Canadian society and the economy. Our immigration system works best when it strikes a balance between Canada's economic needs and Canadians' core values of compassion and opportunity for all."[12] The budget plan items intended to build on this commitment addressed family reunification through permanent resident admissions, reducing processing times,[13] and the expansion of ongoing Syrian refugee policy by allocating $245 million for that purpose over five years, starting in 2016–17 and taking in the additional 10,000 refugees.[14]

One might think that the commitment to expanding GAR applications would entail an increase in spending estimates under existing programs within the renamed Immigration, Refugees and Citizenship Canada (IRCC) departmental budget. But it seems, instead, that spending was increased in human resource expenditures (Full-time Equivalents, FTEs) across departments rather than by increasing the budget of IRCC itself. In addition to the IRCC, a "Team of Federal Departments and Agencies" was involved in the Syrian program: The Canada Border Services Agency (CBSA); the Department of National Defence/Canadian Armed Forces; Global Affairs Canada (GAC); the Public Health Agency of Canada (PHAC); Public Services and Procurement Canada (PSPC); and the Royal Canadian Mounted Police (RCMP).[15] Planned spending in Refugee Protection in 2016–17 was $28,013,358, down from $30,059,852 in 2015, but the number of FTEs delegated to refugee matters across departments was 300, up from earlier estimates of 194.[16] Regular program spending is not, therefore, an adequate measure by itself of the government's commitment to refugee resettlement. Evidence of the scope of activity across departments suggests that the shift of resources to refugee resettlement was a "whole-of-government effort" rather than constituting a permanent increase in the IRCC budget.[17]

One measure of the government's success in fulfilling its campaign commitment to the refugee program is the number of refugees assisted. Since November 2015, when the government officially announced its initiative, 40,081 Syrians have, reportedly, resettled. But the groups that make up this number are significant because of the relatively high spending on government-assisted refugees compared to private sponsorship: 21,876 refugees have arrived as GARs, an additional 3,931 have been "blended" (a combination of private and government sponsorship), and 14,274 have come as PSRs, a program for which, since 2015, the Liberal and Conservative governments both budgeted only about $4,000,000 per year.[18] Thus, PSRs accounted for a large number of the admissions from Syria between November 2015 and the end of January 2017. We conclude that the Privately Sponsored Refugee Program is an inexpensive and relatively efficient method for successfully admitting individuals in crisis abroad and is an engine for the expansion in the numbers of refugees.

Private Refugee Initiatives: Past and Present

The relative importance of the private refugee initiative places the Trudeau government's refugee policy firmly in the tradition of Canadian refugee assistance in two ways. First, it is one of many movements over time supporting the migration and resettlement of refugees in Canada underwritten by a group of energetic private individuals. Second, solutions for managing the crisis and the unusually large numbers being processed by the federal government were found in ad hoc creative choices made in collaboration between government, the civil service, and segments of the Canadian public that mobilized to give support.

While there have been moments when immigration to Canada was viewed negatively, there have been others when there was demonstrable enthusiasm for refugee sponsorship. In 1947 and in 1979, when the government could assure Canadians that their jobs were safe and when there was an international refugee crisis requiring a solution, private citizens, churches, and special interest groups were willing to act. When there were European Displaced Persons (DPs) in 1947, private citizens simultaneously demonstrated a humanitarian impulse to help those who were unable to return home after the Second World War, and a practical instinct when they put pressure on the Liberal government under William Lyon Mackenzie King to take action. Informal channels between the Department of Labour and industry managers to solve pressing wartime labor shortages by using prisoner of war (POW) labor were transformed into a conversation regarding the needs of refugees for work and the needs of industry for workers.

In February 1947, members of the National Selective Service Woods Labour and Camp Conditions Advisory Committee, a body established during the Second World War to advise on labor conditions in the pulp and paper industry, turned its attention to the labor crisis arising from the repatriation of German prisoners of war. A number of businesses had received letters from former POWs (who would not be allowed to come until after 1950) and DPs waiting in camps in Europe. These men desired work in the Ontario forests in order to escape refugee centers and emerging Cold War conflicts in Europe. There was a consensus among industry representatives that "these people would make suitable and desirable immigrants," and that the Ontario firms should send knowledgeable representatives to Europe to help choose "suitable" workers. They forwarded a resolution to the Department of Labour to make their position official: the "only solution to the problem is in immigrating (sic) able bodied persons from the Continent of Europe."[19]

This practical interest, combined with the federal government's desire to take action to solve the international crisis, led directly to the selection of DPs in Europe to come to Canada on one-year contracts. On 20 May

1947, C.D. Howe, the acting minister of the Department of Mines and Resources, submitted a draft resolution to Cabinet citing the need to address "a very distressing situation," allow for the selection of "the most desirable" refugees, and "attain a wide degree of recognition abroad and bring very favourable publicity to Canada."[20] By the end of 1953, more than 160,000 individuals were admitted to Canada and given status as permanent residents.[21] This solution was an extension of the wartime problem-solving of the federal government and the managers of priority industries, such as pulp and paper and mining.

By the 1970s, the Privately Sponsored Refugee Program administrative option had been added to the government's immigration repertoire. In lieu of industry providing work for groups of applicants, the PSRP relied on the philanthropy of individuals, churches, and ethnic organizations to cover the expenses of an individual refugee, identified abroad as being in need, for a one-year term. The possibilities inherent in this program became obvious in July 1979, as the crisis in Indochina worsened and Canadian individuals responded to it.[22] The government was led at the time by Progressive Conservative Prime Minister Joe Clark, who announced a plan to admit 50,000 refugees from the region. Significantly, his government also made a public commitment to match the number of government-assisted refugee admissions with any commitments made by the public in the form of privately sponsored refugees.

At the close of 1980, just over a year after these promises were made, approximately 32,000 of the 60,000 refugees admitted to Canada had been supported by citizens, church groups, and private organizations, and not by family or government sponsorship.[23] It was acknowledged at the time by Lloyd Axworthy, the minister of employment and immigration, that the outpouring of support from the Canadian public was one of the fundamental keys to the success of the undertaking, as "7,000 sponsoring groups and organizations donated their time, energy and funds."[24]

It would be a mistake to assume that the whole process moved smoothly. Despite the great enthusiasm that many Canadians felt for the PSRP, it was clear that a review of the process was in order. Howard Adelman, a philosopher at York University, wrote an assessment of the PSRP in 1991 and elaborated on it in the journal, *Refuge*. "What was originally viewed as a very incidental part of the system of refugee intake," the PSRP "quickly became the most imaginative innovation in refugee resettlement with the massive intake of Indochinese refugees beginning in 1979 and 1980."[25]

Despite his conclusion that the PSRP was a successful Canadian innovation, Adelman was in no way blind to the complications of this unusual process. The fluid crisis state created by the pressure abroad and the sheer numbers of desperate refugees required the federal government to respond to changing circumstances.[26] Their "informal procedures" echoed some of the informal improvisation of the 1940s during the DP program and were a sign of creative problem solving in the midst of a high-pressure administrative dilemma.[27] Michael J. Molloy and his colleagues, in their studies of the Indochina refugee crisis, have recently outlined the inadequacy of Canada's processing capacity and yet the way in which those working within it introduced "modifications and innovations" to "handle the dramatic deluge of refugees" who needed a safe harbor.[28] It is also clear from their piece that flexibility and low level decision-making were encouraged, as they had been in the 1940s. And while maintaining proper legal procedures, the government was also "highly receptive to operational flexibility in the delivery of the refugee operation."[29] When unanticipated challenges arose, those on the spot needed to find answers and were encouraged to do so.

Today's refugee enthusiasm echoes this early private sponsorship wave. Private citizens from across the country (including former Vietnamese refugees who arrived in the 1979–80 wave[30]) have not only organized, raised money, and applied to sponsor Syrian refugees, but followed up with government agencies after long waits, pressured the government to do more, and have given the global media a case study in engaged citizenship.[31] In the months before the 2015 election, Canadians waited impatiently for the refugees they had sponsored to arrive.[32] Increasing frustration over perceived bottlenecks and interference from the Prime Minister's Office (PMO), because of the Harper government's preference for Christian families, further linked Syrian lives to the election outcome in the minds of Canadians.[33] There was a growing discussion about Canada's complicity in the deaths of Syrian refugees as a result of the publication of a tragic photo of the drowned body of young Alan Kurdi after his family chose to escape by boat in the Mediterranean. When it was reported that the boy's aunt lived in British Columbia, the links between Canadian choices and Syrian lives became a powerful campaign issue. In addition, more and more Canadians submitted applications under the PSRP.[34] News reports said that there were more eager sponsors than available Syrian refugees in December 2015.[35] Eventually, the resources diverted into refugee processing increased the number of Syrians ready for resettlement, and Syrian refugees found new homes across the country.[36]

CHALLENGES AND CONCLUSIONS

This government's focus on Syrian refugees has not solved some of the primary and most challenging dilemmas of refugee resettlement, such as the problem of extended processing times. Even before the emergence of an official "American First" foreign policy in the Donald Trump White House, Prime Minister Trudeau made it plain that Canada's role was to "#WelcomeRefugees."[37] New challenges have arisen from that blanket statement, particularly in the context of growing fears among asylum seekers in Trump's America that they may be detained at any time, and especially at border crossings. This has led to increasing numbers of refugees choosing to enter Canada illegally, in remote areas, and be arrested and detained for a brief period in Canada, rather than face a hostile fate in the United States.[38] The growing number of such crossings in remote locations has put pressure on local and provincial governments, and raised questions about maintaining the effective security of Canada's borders.[39] In the meantime, across the country, creative solutions to housing and staffing pressures have been found. The installation of a temporary trailer at a remote border point in Manitoba and the creation of a shelter in the Olympic stadium in Montreal are examples of attempts to balance pressure on the system with the goal of maintaining security without jettisoning compassion.[40]

However, pressures on Canada will rise as uncertainty around immigration and refugees grows in the United States. The number of unplanned refugee arrivals at the Canadian border may increase in the coming years if Canada's reputation as a welcoming state persists, and the United States remains an unpredictable place to be. For example, in the summer of 2017, we have seen the level of uncertainty around the legal status of those brought illegally to the United States as children, the "Dreamers," who had benefitted from a certain amount of stability, until recently, under the Deferred Action for Childhood Arrivals (DACA) program. President Trump was elected on the promise that DACA would be eliminated and immigration from Mexico tightened. Canada, easily accessible from the United States and having recently removed visa requirements for Mexican citizens, may find itself a very desirable destination.

The federal government must give thought to how it wishes to respond to requests (both legal and illegal) for permission to settle in Canada. It may also have to revisit the question of the conditions under which Canada will remain a participant in the "Safe Third Country Agreement," in effect since 2004 and requiring "refugee claimants...to request refugee protection in the first safe country they arrive in, unless they qualify for an exception to the Agreement."[41] Solutions to these challenges will require a political climate in which refugees continue to be welcome and in which further commitments to Immigration, Refugee and Citizenship Canada over an extended period remain fiscally viable.

The refugee file has been a success. The Liberal election promise to bring 25,000 Syrian refugees has been fulfilled and more.[42] The funds for capacity building, family reunification, and the UNHCR have been allocated and either spent, or are available to be spent, and an Interim Federal Health Program is in effect to support refugees.[43] On the "not yet" side, we can see that the government has not yet established an "expert panel" to "make recommendations on designated countries of origin," or to provide a forum for a "right to appeal." But planning documents indicate that it is on the government agenda.[44]

The Trudeau government bound itself closely to the Syrian refugee crisis. The refugee issue had saliency during the election and had a clearly defined goal that was closely scrutinized both at home and abroad. It would have been a blow to the new government had it failed to make rapid progress toward its goal of resettling 25,000 Syrian refugees. And so the program became a priority across a number of powerful departments. Emergency funding was promised and delivered, human resources were channeled toward the processing and moving of applicants, and highly public signals were sent to both domestic and international audiences in the press and on social media that refugees were welcome in Canada. Innovative solutions required when unusual numbers were involved were found in the mutual cooperation of multiple levels of government and an engaged public. While some Canadians worried about the dangers of refugee resettlement within the country's borders, the Trudeau government was able to assure Canadians that the program would both maintain the security of citizens and aid thousands of individuals at risk in Syria and the surrounding areas. It was able to provide a structure for those Canadians who sought a humanitarian answer to support the resettlement of thousands of new Canadians.

The more than 40,000 Syrian refugees who have come to Canada under the Trudeau government do not match the large numbers that came from Europe as DPs after 1947 or later from Indochina. The Syrian program, however, is less than two years old. And, the government now knows, other groups will be knocking at Canada's door as well.

Notes

1. Department of Homeland Security (2017).
2. O'Neil (2015).
3. Liberal Party of Canada (2015, 1).
4. Ibid., 2.
5. Government of Canada (2015a, 2016, 199).
6. Ibid. (2015b, 160, 167, 329).
7. Citizenship and Immigration Canada (2015, 40).
8. Friesen et al. (2015).
9. Citizenship and Immigration Canada (2015, 40).
10. Ibid., 41–42.
11. Government of Canada (2016, 196).
12. Ibid., 199.
13. Ibid., 200.
14. Ibid., 199.
15. Immigration, Refugees and Citizenship Canada (2016a).
16. Compare Citizenship and Immigration Canada (2016, 21), and Immigration, Refugees and Citizenship Canada (2017a, 42).
17. Immigration, Refugees and Citizenship Canada (2017a, 44).
18. Ibid. (2016a).
19. Library and Archives Canada (1947b, 7).
20. Ibid. (1947a).
21. Gilmour (2009a).
22. For the most recent work on the movement to Canada from Indochina, see Molloy et al. (2017).
23. Employment and Immigration Canada (1982b, 27).
24. Employment and Immigration Canada (1982a, 5).
25. Adelman (1992, 2).
26. Ibid., 8.
27. For more on the movement of Displaced Persons to Canada, see Gilmour (2009b).
28. Molloy et al. (2017, 10).
29. Ibid. (2017, 123).
30. Black (2015).

31. *The New York Times* has been particularly interested in sharing Canadian refugee resettlement stories (Kantor and Einhorn 2017).
32. Howlett (2015).
33. Friesen (2015).
34. White and Hui (2015).
35. Goodyear (2015).
36. Immigration, Refugees and Citizenship Canada (2017b)
37. Zerbisias (2015).
38. Hauser (2017).
39. Hoye (2017).
40. Ibid. Levin (2017).
41. Immigration, Refugees and Citizenship Canada (2016b).
42. Ibid. (2016a).
43. Ibid. (2017c).
44. Ibid. (2017a, 44).

References

Adelman, Howard. 1992. Discussion paper: Private sponsorship of refugees program, employment and immigration Canada. *Refuge* 12 (3): 2–10.

Black, Debra. 2015. Vietnamese refugees prepare to sponsor Syrian families. *Toronto Star*, December 16. https://www.thestar.com/news/immigration/2015/12/16/vietnamese-refugees-prepare-to-sponsor-syrian-families.html. Accessed 8 Sept 2017.

Citizenship and Immigration Canada. 2015. Report on plans and priorities 2014–15. Government of Canada. http://www.cic.gc.ca/english/resources/publications/rpp/2014-2015/. Accessed 11 Apr 2017.

———. 2016. Report on plans and priorities 2015–16. Government of Canada. http://www.cic.gc.ca/english/resources/publications/rpp/2015-2016/. Accessed 11 Apr 2017.

Employment and Immigration Canada. 1982a. Indochinese refugees: The Canadian response, 1979 and 1980. Narrative. Employment and Immigration Canada. http://cihs-shic.ca/wp-content/uploads/2015/03/Indochinese-Refugees-Cdn-Response-report-ENG.pdf. Accessed 15 July 2017.

———. 1982b. Indochinese refugees: The Canadian response, 1979 and 1980. Statistics. Employment and Immigration Canada. http://cihs-shic.ca/wp-content/uploads/2015/03/Indochinese-Refugees-Cdn-Response-statistics-ENG.pdf. Accessed 14 Apr 2017.

Friesen, Joe. 2015. Prime Minister's Office ordered halt to refugee processing. *Globe and Mail*, October 8. http://www.theglobeandmail.com/news/

national/prime-ministers-office-ordered-halt-to-refugee-processing/article26713562/. Accessed 16 Apr 2017.

Friesen, Joe, Ian Bailey, and Gloria Galloway. 2015. Harper defends how refugees are processed. *Globe and Mail*, October 9. https://beta.theglobeandmail.com/news/politics/government-prioritized-some-refugees-because-they-are-being-targeted-by-isis-harper-says/article26746945/?ref=http://www.theglobeandmail.com&. Accessed 18 Sept 2017.

Gilmour, Julie F. 2009a. 'And who is my neighbour?' Refugees, public opinion, and policy in Canada since 1900. In *Canada among nations 2008*, ed. Robert Bothwell and Jean Daudelin, 159–182. Montreal/Kingston: McGill-Queen's University Press.

———. 2009b. "The kind of people Canada wants": Canada and the displaced persons, 1943–1953. University of Toronto. https://tspace.library.utoronto.ca/bitstream/1807/29949/1/Gilmour_Julie_Frances_200906_PhD_thesis.pdf. Accessed 11 Apr 2017.

Goodyear, Sheena. 2015. Syrian refugees not always available for sponsorship, Canadians learn. *CBC News*, December 25. http://www.cbc.ca/news/canada/refugee-sponsors-non-syrians-1.3376790. Accessed 18 Sept 2017.

Government of Canada. 2015a. Canada offers leadership on the Syrian refugee crisis. Government of Canada. http://news.gc.ca/web/article-en.do?nid=1021919. Accessed 11 Apr 2017.

———. 2015b. Strong leadership: A balanced budget, low-tax plan for jobs, growth and security. Government of Canada. http://www.budget.gc.ca/2015/docs/download-telecharger/index-eng.htm. Accessed 11 Apr 2017.

———. 2016. Growing the middle class. Government of Canada. http://www.budget.gc.ca/2016/docs/plan/budget2016-en.pdf. Accessed 11 Apr 2017.

Government of the United States. 2017. Department of Homeland Security. Fact sheet: Protecting the nation from foreign terrorist entry to the United States. Government of the United States. https://www.dhs.gov/news/2017/01/29/protecting-nation-foreign-terrorist-entry-united-states. Accessed 15 Sept 2017.

Hauser, Christine. 2017. Fleeing U.S. for asylum, and handcuffed in Canada. *New York Times*, February 24. https://www.nytimes.com/2017/02/24/world/americas/canada-border-crossing-arrests.html. Accessed 16 Apr 2017.

Howlett, Karen. 2015. Toronto man still waiting on application to sponsor Syrian family. *Globe and Mail*, September 3. http://www.theglobeandmail.com/news/national/toronto-man-still-waiting-on-application-to-sponsor-syrian-family/article26223103/. Accessed 16 Apr 2017.

Hoye, Bryce. 2017. Border services sets up emergency trailer to make space for refuge seekers. *CBC News*, February 27. http://www.cbc.ca/news/canada/manitoba/emerson-refugees-manitoba-1.4000668. Accessed 16 Apr 2017.

Immigration, Refugees and Citizenship Canada. 2016a. #WelcomeRefugees: The road ahead. Government of Canada. http://www.cic.gc.ca/english/refugees/welcome/overview.asp. Accessed 17 Apr 2017.

———. 2016b. Canada-U.S. Safe Third Country Agreement. Government of Canada. http://www.cic.gc.ca/english/department/laws-policy/menu-safethird.asp. Accessed 18 Sept 2017.

———. 2017a. Report on plans and priorities 2016–17. Government of Canada. http://www.cic.gc.ca/english/resources/publications/rpp/2016-2017/. Accessed 17 Apr 2017.

———. 2017b. Map of destination communities and service providers. Government of Canada. http://www.cic.gc.ca/english/refugees/welcome/map.asp. Accessed 16 Apr 2017.

———. 2017c. Interim federal health program: Summary of coverage. Government of Canada. http://www.cic.gc.ca/english/refugees/outside/summary-ifhp.asp. Accessed 16 Apr 2017.

Kantor, Jodi, and Catrin Einhorn. 2017. Canadians adopted refugee families for a year. Then came 'month 13.' *New York Times*, March 25. https://www.nytimes.com/2017/03/25/world/canada/syrian-refugees.html?_r=0. Accessed 14 Apr 2017.

Levin, Dan. 2017. Facing wave of refugees, Montreal opens up stadium for housing. *New York Times*, August 3. https://www.nytimes.com/2017/08/03/world/americas/montreal-refugees-stadium-housing.html. Accessed 18 Sept 2017.

Liberal Party of Canada. 2015. Real change: A new plan for Canadian immigration and economic opportunity. Liberal Party of Canada. https://www.liberal.ca/wp-content/uploads/2015/09/A-new-plan-for-Canadian-immigration-and-economic-opportunity.pdf. Accessed 11 Apr 2017.

Library and Archives Canada. 1947a. Department of Labour. Cabinet Committee on Immigration. RG27, v. 895, 8-9-63-1, pt. 1, 10 May. Minister of Mines and Resources, "To his excellency the Governor General in Council- Proposal that Canada admit 5,000 selected displaced persons without waiting for an International Agreement on this subject."

———. 1947b. Department of Labour. Woods Labour Advisory Council. RG27, v. 1521, T6, pt. 2, 14 February. Minutes of the fifth meeting of the WLAC, Port Arthur, Ontario, 7.

Molloy, Michael J., Peter Duschinsky, Kurt F. Jensen, and Robert Shalka. 2017. *Running on empty: Canada and the Indochinese refugees, 1975–1980*. Montreal/Kingston: McGill-Queen's University Press.

O'Neil, Laureen. 2015. Canada's reputation takes top spot in international survey. *CBC News*, July 16. http://www.cbc.ca/news/trending/canada-has-the-worlds-best-reputation-global-survey-shows-1.3155500. Accessed 31 Aug 2017.

White, Patrick and Ann Hui. 2015. Toronto Mayor John Tory joins group sponsoring Syrian refugee family. *Globe and Mail*, September 4. http://www.theglobeandmail.com/news/toronto/toronto-mayor-john-tory-to-sponsor-family-of-syrian-refugees-in-canada/article26225377/. Accessed 16 Apr 2017.

Zerbisias, Antonia. 2015. Note to world leaders: This is how to welcome refugees. *Al-Jazeera*, December 14. http://www.aljazeera.com/indepth/opinion/2015/12/note-world-leaders-refugees-trudeau-canada-syria-151214051232043.html. Accessed 16 Apr 2017.

CHAPTER 13

Justin Trudeau's Quest for a United Nations Security Council Seat

Andrea Charron

"It's time. It is time for Canada to step up once again." This declaration on 16 March 2016 in New York City was Justin Trudeau's way of beginning Canada's campaign to win a seat on the United Nations Security Council (UNSC) for the two-year term running from 1 January 2021 to 31 December 2022. The competition will be stiff. Canada's main competitors will be Norway and Ireland, countries which, while both elected fewer times to the UNSC than Canada's six previous terms, enjoy popular and widespread support for bids of their own.

The most powerful organ in the world, the UNSC can make instant and mandatory international law when it so chooses. A seat on the UNSC is highly coveted by some states: Japan, Brazil, and Argentina have been elected no less than eleven, ten, and nine times, respectively. There are, however, at least 66—of the current 193—UN member states[1] that have never held a seat. A variety of reasons explain this, including the drain on personnel and financial resources to keep pace with the demanding UNSC agenda, as well as the frustration with the Council and its frequent deadlocks on crucial issues.

A. Charron (✉)
University of Manitoba, Winnipeg, MB, Canada

© The Author(s) 2018
N. Hillmer, P. Lagassé (eds.), *Justin Trudeau and Canadian Foreign Policy*, Canada and International Affairs,
https://doi.org/10.1007/978-3-319-73860-4_13

Why would the Trudeau government choose to run? His Liberals may not even be in power by the time of the election in 2020 for a 2021–2022 seat. A campaign for the UNSC requires considerable political and economic investment. There is no guarantee that a seat will be won, and embarrassment if an election is lost. Furthermore, there is a great deal of discord among UNSC members, not unusual given the political nature of the Council, but a condition not helped by the election of an anti-UN American president, Donald Trump. The Trudeau government has decided to campaign vigorously nonetheless,[2] and this chapter will examine its motivations, the powers and importance of the UNSC, Canada's history on the Council, and the costs, benefits, and challenges of mounting a Canadian run for a Council seat.

The UNSC: A Primer[3]

The UNSC is one of six organs of the United Nations (UN) and is special because of its role and powers. State members "confer on the Security Council primary responsibility for the maintenance of international peace and security, and agree that in carrying out its duties under this responsibility the Security Council acts on their behalf,"[4] which means that the UNSC can make binding decisions on behalf of the UN, such as employing the use of force or application of sanctions. State members must assist to those ends. Furthermore, the UNSC is a body that can make instantaneous international law—no treaty need be signed, and no other authority may interpret and/or challenge the legality of a decision made by the UNSC. The UNSC is exceptional in that it combines the powers of the judiciary, legislature, and executive in a single body.

The UNSC is made up of 15 states: the Permanent Five (P5) (the United States, Russia, China, France, and the United Kingdom) and ten elected state members representing regions in the world for (usually) two-year terms.[5] Every year, however, five of the ten elected members are replaced, so that there are always new faces around the UNSC's famous horseshoe-shaped table. Two seats are reserved for the Western European and Others Group (WEOG): Canada belongs to this regional grouping and will run for one of these two seats.[6] Decisions of the UNSC, usually written in the form of resolutions, are taken by vote. Each of the 15 members has one vote (which is usually cast by the ambassador to the UN of the state raising his or her hand), but each member of the P5 has the power to veto any proposals of a substantial nature by casting, or suggesting they will cast, a "no" vote. Absent a veto, a vote is held and only nine affirmative votes are needed to adopt a resolution. Given that there are ten non-permanent members, their votes do matter: the non-permanent members can outvote the P5, assuming that none of the five casts a veto.

Each month, one of the members of the UNSC acts as the Council's president, chairs meetings, and helps to set the agenda. The rotation of presidents is set by alphabetical order based on the English spelling of the state's name. Because there are only 12 months of the year and 15 members on the UNSC, a state is likely to be president only once in its two-year term. The work schedule of UNSC representatives is punishing. They deal with the world's most egregious conflicts, must be available for emergency meetings at a moment's notice, and sit on an average of 15 other UNSC committees (often dedicated to sanctions), for which they must be briefed, prepped, and prepared to represent their government's wishes during often acrimonious debates that can last for hours. From the first day in January, the beginning of their UNSC term, until the last day of December, in the second year, ambassadors and their staff are in a marathon sprint.

The UNSC has evolved over its more than 70 years of existence. The number of non-permanent members was increased from six to ten in 1965 to reflect better the growing number of new states created after post-1945 decolonization. The Council has established a number of committees to review its working methods and standardize the language used in resolutions so that they are more easily interpreted; after all, no decision of the UNSC is given effect until member states act on the instructions outlined in the resolutions. Despite these attempts to improve UNSC working methods, many states have called for the UNSC to be reformed to reflect the power dynamics of the world in 2018 as opposed to the world of 1946 when the UNSC adopted its first resolution establishing a Military Staff Committee that was never of much use.[7] Suggestions have included expanding the number of non-permanent members and adding some new permanent members, such as Brazil, South Africa, Germany, or Japan. Reform is unlikely, however, as any changes to the Council makeup or working processes must have the acquiescence of current UNSC members, including the veto-wielding P5.

Liberal Manifest Destiny?

The Liberals and their governments are tempted to think that they have a special hold on an internationalist foreign policy, a manifest destiny to make a (righteous) mark on the world. That would make running for and winning a seat on the UNSC a mandatory part of Liberal foreign policy doctrine. Instead, the record shows that, when Liberal governments have made UNSC bids, they have done so sometimes reluctantly and after a sober analysis of the advantages and disadvantages of Council membership. Indeed, the Liberals do not have a monopoly on interest in the UNSC. Both Liberal and Conservative governments over the years have vied for a seat and won elections to the Council—the Liberals four times and the Conservatives twice.

Canada's first attempt for a seat on the UNSC failed in January 1946 with Canada withdrawing its candidacy. Australia, which was elected, was seen as the better defender and voice of "small" and "middle" states and was the first choice of the United States and the United Kingdom. As observed by historian Adam Chapnick, Canada chose prudence over popularity in its approach to the UN in its early days.[8] Several of Canada's top officials had little enthusiasm for a seat on the UNSC, as Cold War politics froze the Council's work. Diplomat John Holmes nevertheless remarked that, while Council membership would add "a crushing load" to the Department of External Affairs, "it would make a great difference to the morale of our officers abroad who spend a good deal of their time reporting international politics which impinge only very indirectly on Canadian policy."[9] A bid for a 1948–1949 seat was successful and was keenly supported by the United Kingdom and the United States.

Canada was elected again for a non-permanent UNSC seat for two-year terms in 1958–1959, 1967–1968, 1977–1978, 1989–1990, and 1999–2000—once a decade, in other words often enough that it made it seem that service on the Council was a Canadian diplomatic duty, perhaps even a right. In 2010, the run of successful UNSC bids was ended. The Stephen Harper Conservative government, having inherited the campaign from the Liberal Chrétien government, failed to secure a seat, withdrawing its candidacy after the second round of voting. The Trudeau Liberals now seek to restore Canada's record. Prime Minister Trudeau, however, advertises his interest in a UNSC seat in terms that would be surprising to his predecessors, particularly in his ambition to "advance current reform efforts."[10] The Liberal prime ministers who served before Justin Trudeau, including his father, might well find the idea that Canada could remake the UNSC, especially given today's fractious Council, unrealistic and perhaps even vainglorious.

In the National Interest?

Much of the literature on Canada's role in the UN tends to focus on what Canada contributes rather than how Canada benefits from a seat on the UNSC.[11] Given the amount of money and resources required to campaign and then hold a seat, it is curious more is not written about what Canada intends to gain from a seat on the UNSC. It is as if Canada approaches the UNSC like a job interview—it is more interested in outlining what it will bring to the UNSC, and not the other way around.

Sovereign states have three common and fundamental national interests. While the order of importance of these interests will vary from state to state and from time to time, they are enduring and enshrined in international law. They are the defence of the state from armed aggression, the health of the national economy and society as a whole, and maintenance of world order.[12] These three national interests are found in various chapters within the UN Charter. The first and third interests are directly tied to the mandate of the UNSC; the second interest is achieved via many UN agencies, and other organs of the UN, including the General Assembly and the Economic and Social Council (ECOSOC).

David Bosco, the author of *Five to Rule Them All*, a study of P5 dynamics and the true purpose of the UNSC, speaks of two Council functions: governance and concert. The governance function consists of maintaining peace and security among member states; the concert function prevents war between members of the P5. Bosco argues that the real purpose of the UNSC is not to keep peace among member states, but to prevent war from breaking out between or among members of the P5.[13] The governance function of the UNSC takes a back seat to the concert function, which ensures that P5 interests are protected, limiting the likelihood of conflict among the P5. The governance function, defending UN member states against aggression, only becomes possible with the acquiescence of the P5. Indeed, any decision or action taken by the UNSC requires the P5's approval. Any suggestion of dissent by any member of the P5 will immediately end the drafting of a resolution.

It has been in the Canadian national interest to give support to its allies, the United States, the United Kingdom, and to some extent, France, and through them to preserve a world order that places the United States in a dominant position. A review of every vote by Canada while on the UNSC reveals that, of the 318 votes it has cast, all but 11 were "yes" or "for" resolutions drafted nearly always by Western-aligned states and especially the United States. Of the 11 times that Canada did not vote "yes" or "for" a given resolution, only five of the votes were not in the same direction as the United States. All 11 resolutions were either vetoed by one of the great powers or did not strike at specifically American interests. Thus, 98 percent of the time (313 of 318 votes) Canada has voted specifically with the United States. Furthermore, as the United States or Western-aligned states are the most frequent drafters of resolutions,[14] Canada and its allies are "for" the action (or non-action) prescribed the vast majority of the time.

Canada's real mark on the UNSC has been in niche areas that pertain more to the governance function of the UNSC and fall into two categories: first, to take initiatives that speak to the Canadian value of respect for human rights; and second, to address "machinery of government" issues. Canada has championed a number of thematically-based resolutions while on the UNSC. One of many was tied to the protection of individuals and was adopted in Canada's 1989–1990 term. Finland and Canada drafted a resolution[15] condemning abduction and hostage-taking unequivocally.[16] The Canadian government also supported Resolution 1325—Women, Peace and Security—adopted on 31 October 2000. And Canada is well known for its support of the human security agenda on the UNSC, which led to discussions about the protection of civilians and ultimately the Responsibility to Protect doctrine (R2P).[17] R2P promoted an ambitious agenda focused on protecting vulnerable peoples from the abuses of states and their governments. It called for states around the world to prioritize the protection of civilians, with force if necessary, especially in the case of massive abuses and loss of life, either by neglect or by design, as had been the case in the Rwandan genocide in 1994.

What is less well known, or perhaps not fully appreciated, is how important Canada is as a fixer of Council working processes and machinery of government issues. For example, it was Canada that called for a new funding formula for one of the longest UN peacekeeping missions—the UN Peacekeeping Force in Cyprus (UNFICYP). Greater UNSC transparency was at the heart of Canada's 1998 campaign for a Council seat,[18] which sought to encourage more open debate and greater participation from third-party actors,[19] better standardization of language in resolutions, and clearer, more fulsome, updates by member states on the actions taken to give effect to UNSC actions. Pressure from Canada, and other like-minded states, resulted in an agenda on transparency and the allowing of non-members to participate actively in discussions. Between 1999 and 2000, Canadian Permanent Representative to the UN Robert Fowler revolutionized how UNSC sanctions committees monitored and verified sanctions effectiveness. Canada also circulated an informal paper with regard to the secretary-general's selection process.[20] The 2016 acclamation of António Guterres (Portugal) as the ninth UN Secretary-General reflected several of these recommendations.[21] Canada's reputation for competent and hardworking diplomats means that Canada is often asked to chair subsidiary committees and collaborate on penning draft resolutions both in the UNSC and the other UN organs.

Based on the initial rhetoric and enthusiasm of the current Trudeau government for a UNSC seat, a concern is that the Prime Minister has designs on the concert function of the P5—interfering with the powers of the P5 and their (admittedly increasingly rare) comity[22]—rather than concentrating on the governance function of the UNSC. That would be a mistake. Based on current geopolitical realities and a US President who seems to hold little but disdain for the UN, nothing but a pragmatic approach, similar to that practised by previous prime ministers, is advisable. While the concert function remains the prerogative of the P5, Canada has limited effect on the promotion of its national interests except as they are tied to the Western members of the P5. Where Canada can make a difference is by improving the bureaucratic processes of the UNSC which, while rarely newsworthy, have made the UN more efficient and more aware of the need to protect innocent civilians.

The Campaign's Challenges

Canada's failure, under the Harper government, to secure the required votes for a non-permanent seat on the UNSC in the 2010 bid has been attributed to Canada's late entry into the campaign and policies that were likely to have alienated large voting blocs.[23] Canada's support in the Middle East, Africa, Southeast Asia, and small island nations' voting blocs was adversely affected by a strongly pro-Israel policy, reduction in aid to underdeveloped African nations, and perceived indifference to Southeast Asia and the issue of climate change.[24]

While few thought Canada could beat Germany in the 2010 balloting, it was taken for granted that Portugal, a much smaller state and contributor to the UN, could be easily defeated. Canada's campaign did appear from the outside as an afterthought, but one likely, nevertheless, to result in success. Yet Canada had learned in its 1946 bid for a seat, its only unsuccessful attempt before 2010, that there were certain WEOG states against which Canada could not or should not compete. Australia is most definitely one. The failed 2010 bid suggests that states which had overseas possessions in the past (such as Portugal, but one could add Italy, Spain, Netherlands, Belgium—all within the WEOG) seem to be able to attract votes from their former colonies. In the case of bloc-voting African states, representing 54 of the 129 votes required for election (or 2/3 of the votes), such influence is difficult to beat, especially if Canada is presumed to be indifferent to or to have withdrawn support from Africa as a whole, a charge often leveled at the Harper government.

Paying attention to Africa, Asia, and South America at the UN, as Trudeau is doing, should bring voting dividends. States also need to feel that Canada cares about their particular needs and concerns. The perception that development assistance is absent is particularly injurious to Canada's chances of winning a seat on the UNSC. Norway and Ireland do not have foreign state colonial ties, but they do have very strong support in Africa and Asia as stalwart development supporters. Given the fiscal realities faced by the Trudeau government, it is hardly in a position to promise significant increases in development assistance funding; it is better, from a voting perspective, to spread limited funds far and wide. But Trudeau's development policy concentrates, as did Harper's, on a few very poor states, many in Africa.

The main advantage Canada has against its competition is its membership in La Francophonie, the Association of Southeast Asian Nations (ASEAN)—as a dialogue partner—and the Asia-Pacific Economic Cooperation (APEC) forum, which lends Canada privileged access to many African and Asian states.[25] The blind voting process, however, means that all bets will be off in terms of guaranteeing support when the UNSC elections take place in June 2020. Unless Canada maintains sustained (read costly) attention to and support of its campaign with the horse trading that comes with such efforts, there is absolutely no guarantee that Canada will win. Given the migration crisis in Europe, many are calling for more Europeans on the UNSC. And, if Trudeau continues to suggest that the UNSC needs to be structurally reformed, endangering the concert function of the P5, this could be counter to a long-held Canadian interest, which is maintaining the Western-led world order. A UNSC dominated by

Russia or China is unlikely to support, meaningfully, the many human rights-themed resolutions Canada has championed. Nor has either country been particularly interested in improving the working processes of the UNSC, thus compromising Canada's two niche Council roles.

In addition, Trudeau faces realities that Harper encountered in 2010: competing priorities that draw attention away from Canada's campaign[26] and a public service that has perhaps lost some of its UN expertise. In 2010, Harper was preoccupied with the war in Afghanistan, the economy, wooing the United States, and making a "mark" in the world. Substitute Iraq/Syria/Latvia, where the Canadian Armed Forces are currently deployed, for Afghanistan, and the rest remains true today. The focus of Prime Minister Trudeau and Global Affairs Canada (GAC), rightly so, is on maintaining the North American Free Trade Agreement and other trade deals with the United States in the face of Trump protectionism. As for the public service, UNSC experience has atrophied since its last term ending in 2000. Canada's campaign will be poorer without key, engaged, and experienced public servants with a keen sense of Canada's role at the UN and of the UNSC's history.

Why the UNSC for Canada?

For Global Affairs Canada, the UNSC is undoubtedly one of the most exciting, complex, and multifaceted foreign policy files. After nearly ten years of feeling marginalized by a Harper government that kept files close to its chest and showed open contempt for the United Nations, one can appreciate why GAC is looking for a new challenge.

The public is also onside. According to a national survey conducted by Nanos for CTV News in October 2016, a majority of Canadians support (42 percent) or somewhat support (32 percent) making the UNSC a priority, while 8 percent "somewhat oppose this" and 9 percent "oppose this." 4 percent are unsure.[27] Canadians, when polled, continue to support the aims of the UN and want to feel Canada has a role there. And while Canada consistently makes significant contributions to ECOSOC, the General Assembly, the International Court of Justice, and the UN Secretariat, these activities do not garner the attention of the media and public the way that the seat on the UNSC inevitably does.[28]

A seat on the UNSC has also been a way to demonstrate tangible support to allies. Since the West, and especially the United States, United Kingdom, and France, remain the dominant drafters, or pens, of resolutions and Canada is often asked to assist in resolution drafting, opportunities are presented to meet and liaise with allies on issues of concern, especially to the United States. Since Canada is on board with Western-based resolutions 98 percent of the time, allegiance to the United States and its international aims is easily demonstrated.

Even if the number of Canadian troops in support of UN missions has dropped in favour of assistance to NATO and United States-led coalition missions, Canada will find it helpful to be at the UNSC to understand the competing agendas and priorities of parties to conflicts thus providing Canada with the inside "scoop", especially as it relates to changes to peace operations. As well, the UNSC approves all International Court of Justice judges, all new state members of the UN, and secretary-generals. In addition, the UNSC may establish ad hoc criminal courts and tribunals and it can recommend cases to the prosecutor of the International Criminal Court for investigation. The UNSC also takes up issue areas of concern, such as climate change and regulation of armanents and weapons of mass destruction, takes military action, and decides on all measures short of force.

In the beginning and early years of the United Nations, Canada had an earnest belief that the organization and the UNSC were crucial to the prevention of a major international conflict. Canada understood its role would be modest when great power politics dominated the agenda during the Cold War. And great power politics have returned once again. If Trudeau's Canada (if it is still Trudeau's Canada in 2020) holds to the pragmatic and realistic Canadian foreign policy tradition and the role Canada can play in the world, the UNSC can be a productive place for Canada to be in the 2020s. Sitting on the UNSC, Canada can, as it is has done in the past, keep agendas on point or offer to fund solutions to improve the effectiveness of the UN and UNSC, such as the creation of the sanctions database that Canada helped to underwrite in 2000. The niche areas of support to human rights advancements/protection of civilians and better UNSC working methods are further areas to which Canada has contributed in the past.

If all states abandon the UN and the UNSC, the world may witness the marginalization of an organization that has fed, vaccinated, educated, supported, and protected millions. To hold a seat on the UNSC is very expensive in time, personnel, and resources—the UNSC functions nearly 24 hours a day, 365 days a year. Many states simply cannot afford such an enterprise, but Canada can.

Notes

1. For a list of member states never elected to the UNSC, see United Nations Security Council, (n.d.-a). I am grateful to a number of excellent students from the Norman Paterson School of International Affairs for their ideas, including Geneviève Fauteux, Uriel Marantz, Alysha Pannu, and Erika Schneidereit. I particularly thank Alayna Jay from the Royal Military College of Canada for her outstanding research in calculating every Canadian vote in the UNSC's history.
2. Note, however, that Minister Freeland's foreign policy priorities speech on 6 June 2017 did not make reference to the UN Security Council, although mention was made of peacekeeping, the 2030 Sustainability Goals, and other UN programs (Freeland 2017).
3. The UN has a very good Frequently Asked Questions on the UNSC found at http://www.un.org/en/sc/about/faq.shtml.
4. United Nations Charter (1945). Article 24 (1).
5. There have been cases of states only serving for 1 year. For example, Italy and then the Netherlands are sharing a two-year term (2017–2018). It is also something for Canada to consider—perhaps splitting a two-year term with Ireland.
6. For a full list of all of the regional group arrangements for the UNSC, see http://www.un.org/depts/DGACM/RegionalGroups.shtml.
7. The Military Staff Committee was to be made up of the five chiefs of defence of the P5 to advise on military matters. Cold War dynamics and the lack of a UN military meant that the MCC, while it continued to meet, was of limited value.
8. Chapnick (2005, 138). See, also, Mackenzie (2009, 454).
9. The original quote was from a letter from Holmes to Riddell, July 24, 1947 (Hilliker and Barry 1995).
10. Panetta (2016).
11. Riddell-Dixon (2006/2007); von Riekoff (2002).
12. I argue that national interests are not the same as values. Vital national interests speak to the continued survival of a state; values describe the aspirational conduct of a state within its borders and in its relations with other states.
13. Bosco (2009, 4).
14. Security Council Report (2016).
15. S/20757, which became S/RES/638 (1989).
16. The impetus for the resolution was the hanging of US Marine Lt Col William Higgins by pro-Iranian Shiite Muslim extremists in retaliation for the Israeli abduction of a Hezbollah spiritual leader. Lt Col Williams served on the UN Lebanon mission (UNOGIL) (United Press International 1989).

17. United Nations Office on Genocide Prevention and the Responsibility to Protect, (n.d.).
18. Malone (2009, 8).
19. Malone (1997, 403).
20. Security Council Report (2015).
21. United Nations News Centre (2016).
22. Bosco (2014).
23. Ibbitson and Slater (2010).
24. Blanchfield (2015).
25. Norway is only a Sectoral Dialogue Partner of ASEAN.
26. Hampson and Paris (2010).
27. CTV News (2016).
28. The sixth organ of the UN, the Trusteeship Council, discharged its final trust territory Palau in 1994. The Trusteeship Council, therefore, is now dormant.

References

Blanchfield, Mike. 2015. Why Canada should try again for UN Security Council seat according to France. *Toronto Star*, January 28. https://www.thestar.com/news/canada/2015/01/28/why-canada-should-try-again-for-un-security-council-seat-again-according-to-france.html. Accessed 30 Oct 2016.

Bosco, David. 2009. *Five to rule them all: The UN security council and the making of the modern world*. Oxford: Oxford University Press.

———. 2014. Assessing the UN security council: A concert perspective. *Global Governance* 20 (4): 545–561.

Chapnick, Adam. 2005. *The middle power project: Canada and the founding of the United Nations*. Vancouver: University of British Columbia Press.

CTV News. 2016. Views on Canada's role in peacekeeping missions. Nanos Research, October. http://www.nanosresearch.com/sites/default/files/POLNAT-S15-T703.pdf. Accessed 6 Oct 2017.

Department of General Assembly and Conference Affairs. (n.d.). United Nations Regional Groups of Member States. United Nations, May 9, 2014. http://www.un.org/depts/DGACM/RegionalGroups.shtml. Accessed 6 Oct 2017.

Freeland, Chrystia. 2017. Address by Minister Freeland on Canada's foreign policy priorities. Global Affairs Canada, June 6. https://www.canada.ca/en/global-affairs/news/2017/06/address_by_ministerfreelandoncanadasforeignpolicypriorities.html. Accessed 6 Oct 2017.

Hampson, Fen Osler, and Roland Paris. 2010. Introduction: Leadership challenges in an era of uncertainty. *Centre for International Policy Studies*, 1–12. http://www.cips-cepi.ca/wp-content/uploads/2015/01/Priorities_Report.pdf. Accessed 5 Oct 2017.

Hilliker, John, and Donald Barry. 1995. *Canada's department of external affairs II: Coming of age 1946–1948*. Montreal/Kingston: McGill-Queen's University Press.

Ibbitson, John, and Joanna Slater. 2010. Security Council rejection a deep embarrassment for Harper. *Globe and Mail*, October 10. http://www.theglobeandmail.com/news/politics/security-council-rejection-a-deep-embarrassment-for-harper/article1370239/. Accessed 31 Oct 2016.

Mackenzie, Hector. 2009. Knight errant, cold warrior or cautious ally? Canada on the United Nations security council, 1948–1949. *Journal of Transatlantic Studies* 7 (4): 453–475.

Malone, David. 1997. Canada and the UNSC in the post-cold war era: 1987–1997. *Security Dialogue* 28 (4): 393–408.

———. 2009. Eyes on the prize: The quest for nonpermanent seats on the UN security council. *Global Governance* 6 (1): 3–23.

Panetta, Alexandre. 2016. Trudeau announces bid for seat on UN Security Council: 'It is time for Canada to step up once again.' *National Post*, March 16. http://news.nationalpost.com/news/canada/canadian-politics/trudeau-announces-bid-for-seat-on-u-n-security-council-it-is-time-for-canada-to-step-up-once-again. Accessed 6 Oct 2017.

Riddell-Dixon, Elizabeth. 2006/2007. Canada at the United Nations: 1945–1980. *International Journal* 62 (1): 145–160.

Security Council Report. 2015. Appointing the UN Secretary-General. Security Council Report, October 16. http://www.securitycouncilreport.org/atf/cf/%7B65BFCF9B-6D27-4E9C-8CD3-CF6E4FF96FF9%7D/research_report_2_secretary_general_appointment2015.pdf. Accessed 5 Nov 2016.

———. 2016. In hindsight: The Security Council penholders. Security Council Report, April. http://www.securitycouncilreport.org/monthly-forecast/2016-10/in_hindsight_the_security_council_penholders.php. Accessed 6 Oct 2017.

United Nations, Charter of the United Nations, 24 October 1945, 1 UNTS XVI, available at: http://www.un.org/en/charter-united-nations/

United Nations General Assembly. 1950. Uniting for Peace Resolution A/RES/377V. United Nations, November 3. http://www.un.org/en/sc/repertoire/otherdocs/GAres377A(v).pdf. Accessed 6 Oct 2017.

United Nations News Centre. 2016. António Guterres appointed next UN Secretary-General by acclamation. United Nations, October 13. http://www.un.org/apps/news/story.asp?NewsID=55285#.WBkkDoWcFYc. Accessed 25 Oct 2016.

United Nations Office on Genocide Prevention and the Responsibility to Protect. n.d.. Responsibility to Protect. United Nations. http://www.un.org/en/genocideprevention/about-responsibility-to-protect.html. Accessed 7 Oct 2017.

United Nations Security Council. 1989. Draft resolution on acts of hostage-taking and abduction (28 July 1989) S/20757. Dag Hammarskjöld Library. http://repository.un.org/handle/11176/58536. Accessed 7 Oct 2017.

———. n.d.-a. Countries never elected members of the Security Council. United Nations Security Council. http://www.un.org/en/sc/members/notelected.asp. Accessed 6 Oct 2017.

———. n.d.-b. Frequently asked questions. United Nations Security Council. http://www.un.org/en/sc/about/faq.shtml. Accessed 6 Oct 2017.

———. n.d.-c. Functions and Powers. United Nations Security Council. http://www.un.org/en/sc/about/functions.shtml. Accessed 6 Oct 2017.

United Press International. 1989. Col. Higgins was hanged, Shiites say; Bush outraged: Another hostage threatened. *Los Angeles Times*, July 31. http://articles.latimes.com/1989-07-31/news/mn-492_1_hezbollah. Accessed 5 Oct 2017.

von Riekoff, Harald. 2002. Canada and the United Nations security council, 1999–2000 – A reassessment. *Canadian Foreign Policy* 10 (1): 111–130.

CHAPTER 14

Manning Up: Justin Trudeau and the Politics of the Canadian Defence Community

Andrea Lane

In setting out to assess the Trudeau government's defence performance, two things become immediately clear. First, the expectations surrounding the Trudeau Liberals in the area of national defence were different, but no less dramatic, than those awaiting them in other portfolios, in spite of—or perhaps because of—the general lack of prominence of defence and security issues in the traditional Liberal election platform. While the Liberal Party of Canada (LPC) might not usually be thought of as one whose core support is drawn from either "hawks" or "doves," the 2015 election saw the Liberals attempting to woo disgruntled voters from the Conservative and New Democratic Party (NDP) respectively. With the contentious issue of Canada's participation in the mission against the Islamic State in Iraq and Syria (ISIS) in the news, defence policy was animating voters the Liberals could ill afford to ignore. This placed Trudeau's team in a difficult position: hew too far to one side or the other, and those swing votes disappear.

Second, there is a relatively small amount of "bandwidth" available for discussion of Canadian defence policy, both in the sense of the small audience for such discussions and in the narrow range of opinions advanced by

A. Lane (✉)
Dalhousie University, Halifax, NS, Canada

© The Author(s) 2018
N. Hillmer, P. Lagassé (eds.), *Justin Trudeau and Canadian Foreign Policy*, Canada and International Affairs,
https://doi.org/10.1007/978-3-319-73860-4_14

261

defence commentators in Canada. Defence and military issues are not top of mind for most Canadians, and, as I will explain in this chapter, the few who specialize in defence commentary are likely to have different opinions than the average voter. Few voices speaking on defence and security, and even fewer listening—this skews the conversation in such manner, I argue, that an objective evaluation of Justin Trudeau's defence policy is difficult to come by.

This chapter offers a feminist analysis of both the nature of the Canadian defence community and its expertise in general, and the manner in which that community discusses the defence policy of Liberal governments in particular. A feminist lens recognizes sex and gender as important, constitutive "inputs" in the creation and discussion of Canadian defence policy, and is particularly useful to the analysis of a policy domain in which the main actors—ministers, military officers, and defence industry executives—are overwhelmingly male. In lieu of embarking on a broad assessment of Trudeau's defence policies directly, I will explore the way in which all such assessments, with their assumptions of neutrality and objectivity, should be viewed with suspicion due to both the "unrepresentative author" bias inherent to much Canadian defence commentary and the gendered manner in which Liberal, francophone, politicians are discussed in Canada. Then, I will briefly discuss two defence policy case studies—the fighter replacement programme and the UN peacekeeping mission—as high-profile examples of the politics of defence in Canada. Finally, I conclude with a discussion of the government's 2017 defence policy statement, with a focus on the way in which sex and gender are at play not only in the policy itself, but in its critical reception and political impact.

In all of this chapter's themes, defence decisions as *politics* and defence decisions as *governance* will be deliberately intermingled. This I chose to do explicitly, in order to highlight the way in which Canadian defence commentary has a tendency to be portrayed as ostensibly neutral and governance-focussed, while remaining wildly partisan. In particular, I seek to refute the common refrain that Canadian governments—especially Liberal governments—are far too wont to sacrifice defence and military issues on the altar of domestic politics. In doing so, I reject the division between the "high politics" of foreign and defence policy, and the "low politics" of social welfare and domestic governing, a normative division that works to suppress discussion and dissent of national security issues, and one that feminist theorists[1] have identified as rooted in a sexed and gendered public/private divide. Instead, I accept—nay, *embrace*—national defence as a continuation of domestic politics by other means, and argue that to wilfully exclude party politics from defence policy is to omit an important real-world variable, leading to an incomplete analysis.

Assessing Defence Policy Fairly?

A feminist methodology encourages us to pay attention to knowledge claims—to both the *what* is being touted as fact and to the *who* is being described as an expert. The provision of "expert opinion" on defence policy matters is, at first glance, straightforward: experts are those who have acquired specialist knowledge by dint of experience, study, or both, such that they know more about an issue area than most Canadians, politicians, and civil servants included. In this reading, the provision and utilization of expert knowledge is *instrumental*, or designed to improve policy performance by the filling of knowledge gaps within government, the military, and the civil service. Defence policy in Canada is widely viewed as a technocratic realm, one in which objective expert testimony and analysis ought to be the foundation for government decision-making, as opposed to a democratic realm, in which public opinion or popular support are the determinative criteria for policy success.[2] In Canada, the defence policy "expert knowledge" community and the government exist in a symbiotic and mutually legitimizing relationship. Within the mainstream defence community, to provide solicited advice to government is the hallmark of defence expertise. In turn, governments are quick to advertise when they have academic or industry support for a defence decision, while opposition parties seize upon expert dissatisfaction with wolfish glee.

While it may be a truth universally acknowledged that Canadians care little for defence policy, defence stakeholders themselves seem split as to whether Canadians don't pay enough attention to defence issues,[3] or that defence platforms are *too* salient and thus too easily "politicized."[4] Those who do care, the academics, practitioners, and politicians who comment regularly on defence issues, are nearly universally of the opinion that the public *ought* to care more—not only care, however, but support the spending of more money on defence. While the material demand for defence expenditure in Canada has been calculated according to economic principles,[5] the demand for defence expenditure according to defence stakeholders seems at times infinite.[6] Even the recognition that Canada does not suffer from any existential or territorial threats[7] doesn't seem to dissuade endless commentary suggesting Canada "needs" a conventional, well-equipped, combat-capable military, "combat capable" here being a sort of incantation to ward off those who suggest specialization or "niche" capabilities.[8]

The persistent discrepancy between Canadian public opinion and defence community commentary can be partially explained by who is writing about defence issues in Canada: thinly veiled industry stakeholders, serving and retired military officers, partisan opinion journalists, and academics whose investment in time and resources gaining knowledge of (and access to) the military make them sympathetic to its cause. In short, the defence policy conversation in Canada is a small one, whose members are self-selected and thus, one suspects, subject to distortion by sample bias. As defence scholars Lagassé and Robinson have noted, "an exaggerated perception of threat and of the utility of force currently prevails within the Canadian defence community,"[9] commentators included. Indeed, such is the mainstream consensus that one recent analysis described the two "camps" in the Canadian defence policy debate as "pro- Western collective defence" and "pro- multilateral collective security," with neither side advocating for a reduction in defence spending, and both sides accepting the need for a substantial expeditionary Canadian Armed Forces (CAF), even as they recognized that "it is only in the international context that the country has any real defence problem necessitating modern armed forces of any composition."[10] Indeed, even while analysts recognize that "the main and overriding motive for the maintenance of the Canadian military establishment since the Second World War has had little to do with national security as such,"[11] it is rare to find one recommending that spending on the military be reduced.

The consensus of defence expert opinion in Canada is often treated as a virtue, as evidence that such expert opinion can be trusted. However, this ostensible consensus ought to give rise to serious questions as whether there is selection bias at play. This consensus serves to delegitimize dissenting opinion, by casting it as outside the circle of Canadian defence expertise, and thus suspect as to its technical knowledge and policy suitability. Given the somewhat narrow range of opinions expressed by most non- and quasi-academic defence commentators, it seems reasonable to conclude that partisan politics are involved in the formation of said opinions. Researchers Gravelle et al. found that large-C Conservatives were substantially more likely to agree with the statement that "sometimes war is the only solution to international problems" than people who supported other parties—57 versus 28 percent.[12] Forty-three per cent of Conservatives disagreed that Canada should use its military "only when the country's security is directly threatened," versus 25 per cent of supporters of other parties.[13] Moreover, those relatively few citizens who pay attention to defence and security issues have been found to support spending more on defence and using force more readily than those who do not.[14]

Another factor likely contributing to this near-unanimity is sex: as is evident from the bibliography of any article on Canadian defence policy, military issues are the almost-exclusive purview of male commentators. Feminist international relations scholarship has shown that an absence of women's voices in the security and defence community means that male opinions, concerns, and research questions are apt to be viewed as objective and universal, even as they are biased or unrepresentative.[15] It is unlikely that the gender imbalance in the Canadian defence community is without substantive effect; indeed, there is ample social science evidence to the contrary. For example, men are much more likely to support higher defence spending and increased combat involvement than women,[16] and women's support for military action is more sensitive to humanitarian or peacekeeping objectives.[17] Women are more likely to prioritize social welfare spending over defence, and less likely to vote with military issues as their primary motivation.[18] In general, women are more sceptical as to the "cost" of war, especially when it comes to the loss of human life.[19] Thus, if Canadian defence commentary—and the expert advice given to government—is created in the main by men, it is almost certainly slanted towards the expansion of the defence budget and the continued use of the CAF in combat missions overseas, even as these positions are not supported by all Canadians.

Assessing Trudeau Fairly?

The self-selection effects of the Canadian defence community become readily apparent when discussing the Liberal Party of Canada. To many in the defence community, "Liberal" is synonymous with neglect, indifference, disrespect, and—*peccatum peccatorum*—peacekeeping. Above all, Liberal governments are accused of responding to the Canadian public's demand, or not, for defence expenditure, and for prioritizing social welfare spending over military equipment.[20] Beyond this general scepticism of the Liberal Party's commitment to investing tax dollars in the military,[21] Justin Trudeau comes under unique scrutiny in their respect as the son of former Liberal Prime Minister Pierre Trudeau, himself having been described by critics as "the man who irreparably damaged the Canadian Forces."[22] Much as Pierre Trudeau's attempt at creating a National Energy Policy marked his name forever as traitorous to Alberta and made his son (and his party) virtually unelectable in the Prairies, his father's surname means that Justin Trudeau will be viewed with implicit suspicion by the many defence stakeholders whose starting position is that Canada needs to give *more*—more money, more respect, more influence over policy—to the military.

Trudeau's offhand comment while in opposition about "whipping out our CF-18s and showing off how big they are" saw him excoriated in the press,[23] and cemented his position in the minds of many within the military as, at best, an ignorant lightweight, and, at worst, an effeminate, antimilitary, buffoon. The question of whether Trudeau's quip might have had some substantive insight into both the token nature of the Canadian contribution to the anti-ISIS air campaign and to the highly gendered manner in which defence decisions are made and effected was lost in the general rush to condemn his comments as silly and disrespectful of the CAF. It seemed inevitable that parallels be drawn with former Liberal Prime Minister Jean Chrétien's oft-disparaged description of Canadian peacekeepers as "Boy Scouts," and his assumed dislike of the military.[24] Moreover, it seems difficult to not conclude that there is something pointedly different in the way in which Justin Trudeau, Jean Chrétien, and Pierre Trudeau are spoken of with regard to defence, when compared to Stephen Harper or Paul Martin.

Since becoming prime minister, Justin Trudeau has been accused of both ideological pacifism[25] *and* of not being a true pacifist[26] but instead having being lured by the calculations of base electoral politics into playing a pacifist on the Cable Public Affairs Channel (CPAC).[27] Jean Chrétien had been castigated as a pacifist whose ostensibly "gauzy" reasoning included such unthinkable thoughts as considering whether Western arrogance and military interventionism might have contributed to the 11 September 2001 attacks,[28] whose reluctance to brag about the CAF's military prowess was alleged evidence of his antimilitarist feelings,[29] and whose Human Security agenda has been denigrated as "quasi-pacifism" and "foreign policy for wimps."[30] Pierre Trudeau, whose decision not to enlist in the military in the Second World War seems inexplicably prominent in even more contemporaneous analyses of his defence policy,[31] is also remembered as someone whose primary focus was on the nurturing of fragile, nascent Canadian unity and nationalism,[32] and whose White Paper, "Defence in the 70s," stressed the subordination of defence spending and policy to the promotion of social justice, economic growth, and civilian quality of life.[33] Whatever the specific allegation, these Liberal prime ministers are frequently portrayed in mainstream analyses as effete, anti-military, security dilettantes, whose focus on domestic politics, Canadian (read: anti-American) nationalism, and social welfare marks their defence policies as harmful to the CAF, even as numbers show that "pinko" Pierre Trudeau and other Liberal prime ministers outspent their Conservative rivals on defence—a popular, if flawed, metric for evaluating the hawkishness of governments.[34]

In all of these characterizations—and this chapter could easily have been a "Mad Libs" of derogatory comments assembled from countless sources—there is an unmistakable undercurrent of gendered, anti-francophone, sentiment. *Gendered* because of the persistent, if sometimes subconscious, association of traits such as "belligerence, fierce independence, [the promotion of] self-interested actions over community interests" with masculinity, and the concomitant designation as feminine traits like "pacificity, passivity, cooperative problem-solving and mediation."[35] Women, and by extension "effeminate" men, are seen as less competent and trustworthy leaders on issues of foreign policy and national security.[36] Left-of-centre political parties in general suffer[37] from an association with femininity, in part because of the "caring" or "egalitarian" social welfare issues they are more likely to feature in their electoral platforms.[38] In Canada, the manner in which francophone Quebecer Prime Ministers are discussed (and derogated) exceeds this gendered partisanship and is amplified by the long-standing stereotyping of French–Canadians—and the French more generally—as effeminate, or at the least "feminine" in comparison to their anglophone counterparts.[39] The coding of francophone Quebecers as pacifist—and by extension feminine—is part of the way in which the "otherness" of Quebec is constructed,[40] and contributes to concern as to the "undue influence" Quebec wields in Canadian international affairs.[41] As analysts Roussel and Boucher have noted, the supposed Québécois pacifism myth can also be used against commentators from the rest of Canada whose positions might align with Québécois liberal internationalism, branding them doves by association.[42]

This gendered stereotyping was in full view during the 2015 federal election campaign. Opposition parties played up Trudeau's schoolteacher past (teaching is a feminized profession), and his interest in drama (the theatre is historically associated with homosexuality and thus effeminacy), and mocked both his physical appearance (nice hair, though!) and his embracing of the modern selfie phenomenon, something which is often disparagingly associated with the "vapidity" of teenage girls. Tellingly, questions as to whether Trudeau represented the triumph of "style over substance" began to be asked almost immediately after the election, with polling firm Ipsos going so far as to put the question to Canadians in the fall of 2016. Pierre Trudeau also faced this criticism from the English-language press as prime minister,[43] and, while the question seems innocuous enough on the surface, it rests on gendered assumptions of a divide between the deemed serious, masculine world of proper policy-making and the deemed vain, feminine frivolity of image-conscious performance politics. In spite of the expressed importance of tone and style in political discourse to Canadian public, and polls showing Trudeau's style in particular appeals to voters,[44] the question continues to be asked as if style ought to play no part in Canadian politics. One can hardly imagine Canadians being asked if Stephen Harper's "substance over style" politics were illegitimate in the same way, even as Harper's cold, controlling, and mechanical demeanour is alleged to have lost the Conservative Party the 2015 election.[45] At its root, the attention to and criticism of Trudeau's appearance is part of a larger questioning of his overall masculinity, and thus his fitness for office.[46]

AND YET, YOU CANCEL ONE HELICOPTER, AND...

The association of both the Liberal Party of Canada and francophone Quebecers with the soft, interior, and pacifist *feminine* helps to explain why the "politicization" label sticks to Liberals like Chrétien more perniciously, too. The Chrétien decision to honour his campaign promise and cancel the EH-101 helicopter purchase is commonly held up as the height of partisan procurement interference, a nonsensical, "rash decision rooted in partisan politics and symbolism,"[47] "politically expedient,"[48] and "overtly political."[49] And yet the Harper decision to acquire C-17 Globemaster heavy lift aircraft through a sole sourced military off the shelf procurement, in spite of its not being an identified capability requirement, is rarely correctly identified as having been driven by "political expediency, not need,"[50] and is instead celebrated as a procurement success—a quick, off-the-shelf purchase for a CAF at war by a supportive government. If, as Lagassé and Robinson allege, the Globemaster purchase was undertaken wholly or in part simply because the Liberal Defence Policy Statement had not included it, that is comparably egregious Conservative politicking.

Such is the persistence of the Liberals-as-politicizers label that commentators have criticized Trudeau for being too sensitive to "political" pressure from the United States, as if there were not compelling geostrategic reasons for responding to American signals. Defence analyst Andrew Richter notes with scorn that Trudeau committed Canada to leading the multinational North Atlantic Treaty Organization (NATO) battalion in Latvia "*just one day*"[51] after President Obama's request for "more Canada"; and yet, Trudeau's failure to meet the 2 per cent gross domestic product defence spending target has *also* been criticized as irresponsible, as it ignores President Trump's rather undiplomatic requests. At once too political, and also not political enough—it seems Trudeau, like other Liberal prime ministers, just cannot win.

MIXING POLITICS AND POLICY

The inescapable realities of geography, as the US' closest neighbour, and history, having an enduring cultural and emotional linkage to NATO and Western Europe, mean that the changes in Canadian defence policy made by successive governments tend for the most part to be distinctions without a difference. While accepting this, there are nevertheless two areas of specific policy to focus on that are most salient to analysis of the "politics" and "Liberal -ness" of Trudeau's defence policy thus far. The first is Canada's engagement with the United Nations (UN), which is explicitly linked to the Trudeau government through campaign promises and party platform statements. The second is Trudeau's handling of the long-standing and controversial CF-18 fighter replacement file, where the gap between the "expert consensus" and the Liberal government looks like an unbridgeable gulf.

It is difficult to think of a topic within Canadian defence policy that animates stakeholders, analysts, and laypeople to the same degree as peacekeeping. The persistent gap between what defence commentators say Canadians *ought* to think about peacekeeping—that it is a fantastical, anachronistic chimera, completely out of touch with the realities of modern combat missions[52]—and the support for peacekeeping that Canadians themselves continue to assert in public opinion polls, reaffirms the disconnect between ordinary civilians and the defence policy community. One common criticism of the LPC is their promotion of peacekeeping, especially UN peacekeeping, as a Canadian value, and as a good in its own right. That the LPC in general, and the Trudeau government in particular, value peacekeeping is not in doubt: a promise to "renew Canada's commitment to United Nations peacekeeping operations" was part of Trudeau's first Throne Speech in 2015.[53] This commitment is not only an assumed expression of the personal beliefs of Trudeau and his advisers but also an extension of the anti-Harper positioning that propelled the LPC to a majority in 2015. In the LPC platform materials, the language used is both explicit—"under Stephen Harper, Canada has dramatically scaled back its involvement in peace operations"—and implicit, with references to "renewing" and "recommitting" that paint Trudeau as restoring Canada to its natural place in the world.[54] While being the anti-Harper party has thus far returned domestic electoral dividends, the election of Donald Trump in 2016 has made the corollary Liberal position—being the "anti-USA" party—an alluring, low-hanging, but potentially poisonous fruit.

The international media attention which greeted Justin Trudeau when elected, however easy for critics to scorn as frivolous and embarrassing, has made Canada's actions on the world stage more noteworthy.[55] With Trump in the White House, Canada has become a liberal international rock star, and this in turn could be an unprecedented source of practical global strength, as it arguably was in negotiating the Canada–European Union trade deal. Canada's Goldilocks comparative advantage—occupying the sweet spot between Europe and America—is at the foundation of what passes for Canada's "Grand Strategy,"[56] and Trudeau's commitment to UN peacekeeping serves to further this. But that advantage, while powerful, is also potentially risky; anger the volatile and erratic President Trump, and Canada's economy and national security could suffer. It is as yet unclear what material expressions Trump's rhetoric on the UN will find; a proposed reduction in the US share of the UN peacekeeping budget, from 28 per cent to a historical ceiling of 25 per cent, is in itself not a meaningful disengagement.[57] Some have suggested that the anti-terrorism mandate of some UN peacekeeping operations, such as the Mali mission rumoured to be the most likely destination for Canadian troops, is likely to find favour with the Trump administration.[58] Whatever the eventual outcome, the Trudeau government's decision to delay an announcement on troop deployments until a clearer signal from Trump can be established seems like a sensible middle option, even if, as has been alleged, waiting has denied Canada the opportunity to command the UN mission in Mali.

However laudable pausing to consider the ramifications of the Trump election might be, there is a political risk for the Liberals if the delay continues much longer. The November 2017 UN Peacekeeping summit in Vancouver looms as a pressing deadline; were it to commence without Canada having made a troop commitment somewhere, it would leave open the Trudeau government to domestic and international ridicule. Continued indecision on the African peacekeeping mission originally announced in October of 2016—especially since troop numbers and funding have already been committed—is politically dangerous for the Liberals, as it calls into question the government's moral rationale for the mission. Leaving aside the debate as to whether Mali, or other African conflicts or indeed any international conflicts at all, do in fact threaten Canadian national interests, a UN peacekeeping mission is optional for Canada. The legitimacy of that option rests with the Liberal Party's commitment to the mission as an extension of the Canadian public's belief in the value of peacekeeping *qua* peacekeeping. For the mission to be successful, for the spending of blood and treasure to be palatable to Canadians (and casualties seem inevitable), the Trudeau government must be able to defend it on Liberal and liberal grounds. Continuing to delay the sending of troops signals a moral wobbliness, which could compromise the mission before it starts, hamstringing its resources, muddying its goal, and vitiating its public support.

Crazy Like a Fox? The CF-18 Replacement

Although it is unclear what effect, if any, it had on the outcome of the 2015 election, there was a notable campaign promise on defence procurement in the Liberal platform. If elected, the Trudeau Liberals would not buy the F-35 Joint Strike Fighter, and instead "launch an open and transparent competition to replace the CF-18 fighter aircraft," a competition presumably tailored to the party's stated focus on "the defence of North America, not first-strike capability."[59] Given the extent to which the CF-18 replacement programme has already been the subject of both extensive media commentary and substantive academic research,[60] it was tempting to omit the Trudeau government's actions on this file from my analysis altogether. Admittedly, some of this reticence is rooted in cowardice: the Liberals' 2016 decision to purchase "interim" fighter aircraft has been universally condemned by the defence community, academic and practitioner alike. While there are a few diligent American researchers who continue to question the F-35 both as an aircraft and as a cost-effective procurement,[61] in Canada, the voices arguing for a different fighter jet for

Canada[62] have dwindled away as the narrative of "fifth-generation," "interoperability," and "industrial benefits" has ascended, unassailable. To suggest that there was some method to the Liberals' madness is, in effect, to mark oneself as on the lunatic fringe. And yet, if one considers the decisions made by the Trudeau Liberals thus far from a partisan politics perspective, the assessment seems less clear-cut than most defence commentary suggests.

The most common criticism of the Trudeau government's handling of the CF-18 replacement is that they are "playing politics" by opposing the purchase of the F-35—a plane whose merits are to most commentators as settled as climate science—and delaying the launch of a competitive bid process for the replacement, instead wasting time and money on an unnecessary "interim" purchase of lesser F/A-18E/F Super Hornets.[63] Put this way, the comparisons with the Chrétien decision to cancel the EH-101 deal seem unavoidable. But those comparisons neglect what is arguably the most important lesson from that previous cancellation: how little negative political cost it had for the Liberals, even as the cancellation costs mounted and the ageing Sea King helicopters continued to be flown.

Successive governments have gambled successfully on no CAF members being killed or injured due to flying unsafe helicopters. While the age of the Sea Kings made for a palatable and readily understood news story, there is little evidence to connect the narrative of "Sea Kings are old and unsafe" to "the Canadian public is angered by Chrétien's decisions to cancel the replacement." There is even less evidence to suggest that the public has retained any interest in the helicopter file. The helicopter chosen to replace the Sea King, the Sikorsky CH-148 Cyclone, has taken an extraordinarily long time to procure, with one estimate putting the time needed to reach fully operational status at 21 years since the contract was signed. The Cyclone procurement has been plagued by problems, some due to the folly of purchasing a helicopter that did not exist (the Cyclones are a Canada-only military variant of a civilian helicopter) and some due to governments' reluctance to enforce penalties against Sikorsky for delays and technical inadequacies.[64] When compared to the media (and academic) coverage of the cancellation of the original contract, current interest in the Cyclones seems minimal at best, suggesting once again that making procurement decisions for partisan political reasons is a not unreasonable strategy, with little, if any, long-term negative effects.

The Harper Conservatives' pro-military branding and multi-term reign were insufficient to insulate them from criticism over the F-35 purchase, especially throughout the platform's problem-plagued infancy.[65] So poor is the F-35's image in "laymen's" eyes that the Liberal Party has been calling for the F-35 contract to be cancelled since 2011. Accordingly, the Trudeau government's delay in moving forward on the permanent CF-18 replacement, and the uncertainty as to whether the F-35 will be included in any eventual open bidding process, ought not to be surprising to anyone. There is quite clearly political hay to be made with the fighter replacement, and the election results of 2015 arguably provided evidence that the Liberals were smart to do so.

Building on the public's discontent with the F-35, the announcement of the government's "consideration" of an interim fleet of Super Hornets—to fill a capability gap most analysts argue persuasively was at least partially manufactured to suit the government's desires—is a breathtakingly canny political move. If one assumes the "interim" decision was originally designed to force the CF-18 replacement issue and ensure that the Super Hornet became the only feasible choice for the permanent replacement, then the Liberal decision-making makes both short- and long-term sense and leaves the Trudeau government ample room to manoeuvre should circumstances, either domestic or international, change. As Richter notes, "by purchasing a small number of aircraft as an 'interim measure' to fill a supposed 'gap,' the government could avoid a legal challenge [by Lockheed Martin] while at the same time being able to say they had not broken a campaign promise"[66]—a deft coup indeed. Moreover, both the announcement of the interim Super Hornet option and subsequent government comments on the project have been carefully worded to stress that the acquisition of the interim fleet is "contingent on getting the Super Hornets at the right price, on the required schedule, and with the required economic spinoff."[67] This, in effect, leaves the Liberals in the enviable position of being able to wait and see whether the US Navy's stated desire to purchase more Super Hornet airframes, and President Trump's direct intervention in January 2017 to investigate the F-35 versus F-18 price differential, has an effect on the pricing, American and allied usage, and long-term availability of the plane—three significant obstacles to the adoption of the Super Hornet as the permanent CF-18 replacement.

If, on the other hand, the Trudeau government wishes to reconsider the decision to acquire the interim fighters, they have in their contingency list a built-in "get out of jail free" card, which could allow them to re-commit to the F-35, but with the attempt to acquire Super Hornets serving to mitigate against political fallout from violating a campaign promise.

The 2017 trade spat with Boeing over alleged illegal Canadian government support of Bombardier has only strengthened the government's position: now it could renege on the interim Super Hornet purchase while fulfilling campaigning promises and being able to appear tough on nationalist trade policy, a win-win. So long as the CAF is able to acquire the new fighter aircraft it needs—*needs*, not wants—when it needs them, and given the domestic cost/benefit analysis that would seem to encourage "playing politics" with procurement, perhaps we ought to be thinking of politics as a feature, not a bug, of Canadian defence policy?

Manning Up? The 2017 Defence Policy Statement

In June 2017, the Trudeau government launched its long-awaited defence policy statement, which followed extensive consultation with the "defence stakeholder" community. Titled "Strong, Secure, Engaged," the policy has been lauded for its substantial investment in the military, particularly in procurement, and for its focus on service members' well-being. The content of the policy seems to have taken many commentators—this author included—by surprise: more jets, more ships, more money than expected from a Liberal government, particularly a Liberal government under constant opposition attack for its deficit spending. Paying attention to the gendered nuance of both the policy statement and its reception, however, sheds some light on the Trudeau government's possible motivations for crafting it as they did, and on the relatively positive reception the policy has received thus far.

While there has been muted criticism of the defence policy statement from both the NDP ("too hot!") and the Conservative Party ("too cold!), "Strong, Secure, Engaged" has shown itself to be carefully constructed porridge, able to satisfy the palate of even those Liberal voters who aligned themselves with the party for the first time in 2015. Taken alone, the policy's massive increase in spending might well have put paid to the "Decade of Darkness." Beyond the money, however, the Trudeau government has gone even further to position itself as serious, security-minded, and supportive of its military. For example, there is a new aggressive role for the CAF in the cyber domain, marking for the first time that Canada will be attacking, not merely defending, in this arena. Other acquisitions also allude to a robust, active, and offensive vision for the CAF: ground-based air defence systems, and "medium altitude remotely piloted systems"—that is, drones, and CP-140 Auroras, recently revamped from

Maritime Patrol to Multimission Aircraft and the centrepieces of the Canadian contribution to the anti-IS fight, to be replaced with "next generation aircraft."[68] In order to ensure that Canadian "sovereignty is well-defended,"[69] the "combat ready" CAF will increase in authorised strength by 3500 personnel, with an expanded Reserves and enlarged Special Operations Forces Command. Photos illustrating the "Global Context" chapter, which speaks to complex, emerging threats, emphasize a decidedly military response to the world's next crises. An embarrassment of treacly words of praise for CAF members, "the brave women and men who wear the uniform,"[70] abounds throughout the policy. In sum, this would seem to not be the defence policy of Trudeau the pacifist, nor of Trudeau the antimilitarist.

Buffering all this talk of equipment, technology, action, innovation, aggression, and strength, however, is a distinctly softer, more caring focus on service members and their families. Combined with the policy's stated goal of having 25 per cent of the CAF be women by 2027,[71] the focus on family support services and policies like tax relief for members on named deployments mean that women and children are also the intended beneficiaries of the policy's largesse. The images illustrating the policy, too, belie the hawkish, more masculinist message of the acquisition, context, and technology pieces: a majority feature women and people of colour, including Indigenous peoples. Moreover, for every image of a camouflage-painted, ghillie-suited, soldier brandishing a rifle, there are four or five more of CAF members hugging children, providing medical care, helping in a humanitarian crisis, or partaking in a powwow. A quick rundown of the photos in which demographic indicators could be easily ascertained shows there are 37 photos featuring women or people of colour versus 17 featuring white men. Given the white, male face of the CAF, such disproportionality can only be assumed to be both intentional and aspirational.

If commentators noticed the preponderance of female faces and "feminine" foci of the policy statement, their criticism has been for the most part mild. Indeed, with the advent of numerous private veterans' charities and their patronage by prominent Conservative Party and NDP supporters, critics are likely loath to condemn the policy's investment in service-member support. Since, as conservative columnist John Ivison put it, "the policy unveiled by Defence Minister Harjit Sajjan is a defence plan you might expect from a Conservative government,"[72] the wind seems to have left many critics' sails. The most common critical position—even from analysts whose pre-policy statement position might be summarized as anti-Liberal (or, more charitably, pro-military)—seems to be grudging admission that the size and shape of the promised investment in defence is good, coupled with suspicion that the Liberals will not follow through and emphasis on the fact that many of the policy's promises will require future governments to implement and fund them.[73] "Putting up" the defence budget has seemingly "shut up" critics on both sides of the aisle, even as both Conservative and New Democrats were once united in condemning the Trudeau government for underfunding the military.

Conclusion

As the Trudeau government seeks to define its place on the world stage in 2017 and beyond, two related challenges await it. First, as the Trump presidency alienates allied leaders (and citizens) around the globe, will Canada be able to maintain its traditional position midway between the United States and Western Europe? And second, will the new defence policy, with its concomitant funding increases, be both sufficiently hawkish to lastingly neuter opposition criticism, and sufficiently Liberal to sustain base support? That is, can Trudeau's modern, feminist visage[74] appear sufficiently "masculine" to appease domestic and international hawks, while remaining caring, sympathetic, and thus "feminine" enough to assuage voters wary of increased military engagement abroad? For both challenges, the advice of the mainstream Canadian defence policy community—mine included—ought to be taken with a grain of salt. The North American defence partnership has produced a CAF that is closely integrated with its US partners, even as their respective civilian governments have drifted apart. Serving and retired military advice on potential United States-led military operations is therefore less likely to be sensitive enough to the "politics" of such a mission, whether domestic or international. Care should also be taken to distinguish between those voices calling for sensible caution in the selection of an African UN peacekeeping mission for Canada and those for whom the idea of Canadian troops dying in blue helmets is ideological anathema. In spite of the oft-reiterated criticism of morality and partisanship in defence policy-making from many within the Canadian defence community, Trudeau and his team ought to seek for themselves the balance between what Canada ought to do as *Canada*—replace the ageing CF-18 fleet, work with our allies in international military endeavours—and what the government is free to do as

Liberal, including choosing the details of those commitments so that they are on-brand. Thus far, the Trudeau government has been walking a canny path between maintaining the crucial United States–Canada relationship, while signalling their support for liberal internationalism to non-American allies. Canny, too, is the Liberal defence policy's blending of masculine and feminine, tough and tender, killing and caring. Whether it can continue to do so in face of geopolitical circumstance remains to be seen, but in 2017, "playing politics" and being unabashedly Trudeauvian seems to have bought Canada international traction, wrong-footing naysayers.

Notes

1. Crosby (2003, 93).
2. Boswell (2008).
3. Shadwick (2011, 64), Richter (2016).
4. Gravelle et al. (2010, 113).
5. Solomon (2005).
6. Leuprecht and Sokolsky spend an entire article outlining the Walmart strategy behind Canadian defence spending, and then at the end—after explaining how it works so well—inexplicably state that Canada should spend more, in order to achieve Target status, pay more, and get some more "flair" (Leuprecht and Sokolsky 2015, 557).
7. I was consulted as an "expert" for the report (Collins and Speer 2017, 12).
8. "Combat capability" meaning expeditionary warfare, versus residual tasks such as sovereignty protection. The phrase has its roots in the Trudeau government's 1974 Defence Structure Review (Keeble 1997, 555). Somewhat ironically, this "combat capability" was put forward in opposition to what was viewed the heavy, specialized equipment required by Canadian NATO-supporting troops in Europe.
9. Lagassé and Robinson (2008, 55).
10. Sokolsky and Jockel (2016).
11. This is an astonishing admission, but is glossed over with barely a mention (James Eayrs, in Leuprecht and Sokolsky, "Walmart," 545).
12. Gravelle et al. (2010, 116).
13. Ibid., 117.
14. Fitzsimmons et al. (2014, 507).
15. Tickner (2006).
16. For an overview of the cross-country literature on this phenomenon, see Fitzsimmons et al. (2014).
17. Eichenber (2003, 128).

18. Eichenberg and Stoll (2011).
19. Note that Boucher (2010), did not find sex to be statistically significant when assessing the impact of casualties on Canadian public support for the war in Afghanistan.
20. Bland (2016), Shadwick (2004).
21. Simpson (2016).
22. Lagassé and Robinson (2008, 23).
23. Nossal et al. (2015, 315).
24. Shadwick (2004).
25. Tandt (2015), Nossal (2016b).
26. Bercuson (2015).
27. Saideman (2014).
28. Kay (2012).
29. Nossal (2016b).
30. Crosby (2003, 103).
31. Granatstein and Bothwell (1991, 67).
32. Keeble (1997, 559).
33. Lagassé and Robinson (2008, 25).
34. Pugliese (2007).
35. Neck et al. (1995, 168), in Smith (2003, 28).
36. Lawless (2004).
37. I use the word *suffer* deliberately, because the feminine in patriarchal societies like Canada is devalued.
38. Winter (2010, 591). This gender association goes beyond the linking of specific policy issues such as abortion, healthcare, or defence spending to certain parties, but rather that gendered traits like "statesmanlike" or "compassionate" were viewed as reasons to either support or reject each party; that is to say, Republican supporters viewed their party's masculinity as favourable, and the Democratic Party's femininity as undesirable, and vice versa.
39. The origins of this stereotype are complex, transcending the "two solitudes" narrative to include perceptions of national character, the existence of a Protestant (versus Catholic) ethos, and colonial assumptions of gender. For non-feminist analyses of this differentiation, see Haglund and Massie (2016), and Vucetic (2011).
40. For a non-feminist analysis, see Boucher and Roussell (2008).
41. Haglund and Massie (2016), Massie et al. (2010).
42. Boucher and Roussel (2008).
43. English (2009, 20).
44. Anderson and Coletto (2014).
45. Kennedy (2015).
46. Sabin and Kirkup (2016).

47. Lagassé and Robinson (2008, 33).
48. Shadwick (2004).
49. Nossal (2016, 66).
50. Lagassé and Robinson (2008, 46).
51. Italics in original (Richter 2016, 6).
52. For a particularly florid and personal version of this argument, see Maloney (2016, 200).
53. Hltaky (2016, 4).
54. Liberal Party of Canada (2015a).
55. Akin (2017).
56. Kennedy, in Leuprecht and Sokolsky, "Walmart," 2.
57. Foroohar (2017).
58. McCormick and Lynch (2017).
59. Liberal Party of Canada (2015b).
60. See, for example, the special issue of *Canadian Foreign Policy Journal* dedicated to the F-35 question: *Canadian Foreign Policy* 17:3 (2011) "Canada and the F-35: What's at stake?"
61. Grazier (2017).
62. Bezglasnyy and Ross (2011).
63. Schaub and Shimooka (2017).
64. Gutterman and Lane (2017), Cudmore (2014).
65. Vucetic (2011).
66. Richter (2016, 6).
67. Sajjan, quoted in Canadian Press staff, "Liberals take next step on Super Hornet fighter jet deal." (Canadian Press 2017).
68. National Defence (2017, 39).
69. Ibid., 14.
70. Ibid., 11.
71. Ibid., 23.
72. Ivison (2017).
73. In addition to Ivison (2017), see: Hlatky and Nossal (2017); Nossal is notably suspicious of Trudeau's pacifist tendencies, and has written extensively of the dangers of "politicizing" defence matters; (Richter 2017); any commentary by Dr. David Perry, senior analyst with the Canadian Global Affairs Institute. Criticism on the left has also focused on the potential funding pitfalls, as well as the vagueness on peacekeeping (Rideau Institute 2017).
74. Sabin (2016).

References

Akin, David. 2017. Trudeau's celebrity can actually help us. *Toronto Sun*, March 7.
Anderson, Bruce, and David Coletto. 2014. Harper, Mulcair, Trudeau – Overall impressions. *Abacus Data*, August 29. http://abacusdata.ca/harper-mulcair-trudeau-impressions/. Accessed 21 Aug 2017.
Bercuson, David. 2015. Canada deserves better answers about the ISIS mission. *Globe and Mail*, December 18.
Bezglasnyy, Anton, and Douglas Alan Ross. 2011. Strategically superfluous, unacceptably overpriced: The case against Canada's F-35A lightning II acquisition. *Canadian Foreign Policy Journal* 17 (3): 239–250.
Bland, Douglas. 2016. Trudeau cannot continue the neglect of the Canadian military. *Ottawa Citizen*, November 18, 2016.
Boswell, Christina. 2008. The political functions of expert knowledge: Knowledge and legitimation in European Union immigration policy. *Journal of European Public Policy* 15 (4): 471–488.
Boucher, Jean-Christophe. 2010. Evaluating the 'Trenton effect': Canadian public opinion and military casualties in Afghanistan (2006–2010). *American Review of Canadian Studies* 40 (2): 237–258.
Boucher, Jean-Christophe, and Stéphane Roussel. 2008. From Afghanistan to 'Quebecistan': Quebec as the Pharmakon in Canadian foreign and defence policy. In *Canada among Nations 2007: What room for manoeuvre?* ed. Jean Daudelin and Daniel Schwanen, 128–158. Montreal/Kingston: McGill-Queen's University Press.
Canadian Foreign Policy Journal. 2011. Canada and the F-35: What's at stake. *Canadian Foreign Policy Journal* 17 (3): 193–284.
Canadian Press. 2017. Liberals take next step on Super Hornet fighter jet deal. *Global News*, March 14. http://globalnews.ca/news/3308918/liberals-super-hornet-fighter-jets/. Accessed 21 Aug 2017.
Collins, Jeffrey, and Sean Speer. 2017. First principles and the National Interest: Recommendations for a new Canadian defence policy. Macdonald Laurier Institute, March 2017. http://macdonaldlaurier.ca/files/pdf/MLI_NationalInterestDefenceF_Web.pdf. Accessed 15 Sept 2017.
Crosby, Ann Denholm. 2003. Myths of Canada's human security pursuits: Tales of tool boxes, toy chests, and tickle trunks. In *Feminist perspectives on Canadian foreign policy*, ed. Claire Turenne Sjolander, Heather A. Smith, and Deborah Stienstra, 90–107. Don Mills: Oxford University Press.
Cudmore, James. 2014. Sea King replacements: $7.6B Cyclone maritime helicopters lack key safety requirement. *CBC News*, June 23. http://www.cbc.ca/news/politics/sea-king-replacements-7-6b-cyclone-maritime-helicopters-lack-key-safety-requirement-1.2684036. Accessed 15 Sept 2017.

Eichenberg, Richard. 2003. Gender differences in public attitudes towards the use of force by the United States, 1990–2003. *International Security* 28 (1): 110–141.

Eichenberg, Rchard, and Richard Stoll. 2011. Gender difference or parallel publics? The dynamics of defense spending opinions in the United States, 1965–2007. *Journal of Conflict Resolution* 56 (2): 331–348.

English, John. 2009. *Just watch me: The life of Pierre Elliot Trudeau: 1968–2000*. Toronto: Knopf.

Fitzsimmons, Scott, Alan Craigie, and Marc Andre Bodet. 2014. Canadian public opinion about the military: Assessing the influences on attitudes towards defence spending and participation in overseas combat missions. *Canadian Journal of Political Science* 47 (3): 503–518.

Foroohar, Kambiz. 2017. UN peacekeepers face new peril in Trump's push to cut budget. *Bloomberg*, March 22. https://www.bloomberg.com/news/articles/2017-03-22/un-s-peacekeepers-face new-peril-in-trump-s-push-to-cut-budget. Accessed 15 Sept 2017.

Granatstein, J.L., and Robert Bothwell. 1991. *Pirouette: Pierre Trudeau and Canadian foreign policy*. Toronto: University of Toronto Press.

Gravelle, Thomas, Thomas Scotto, Jason Reifler, and Howard Clarke. 2010. Foreign policy belief and support for Stephen Harper and the conservative party. *Canadian Foreign Policy* 20 (2): 111–130.

Grazier, Dan. 2017. F-35 continues to stumble. Project on Government oversight, March 20. http://www.pogo.org/straus/issues/weapons/2017/f35-continues-to-stumble.html. Accessed 21 Aug 2017.

Gutterman, Ellen, and Andrea Lane. 2017. Beyond LAVs: Corruption, commercialization and the Canadian defence industry. *Canadian Foreign Policy* 23 (1): 77–92.

Haglund, David, and Justin Massie. 2016. Southern (over) exposure? Quebec and the evolution of Canada's grand strategy, 2002–2012. *American Review of Canadian Studies* 46 (2): 1–21.

Ivison, John. 2017. Liberal defence plan puts national interest ahead of its own partisan concerns, for now. *National Post*, June 7.

Kay, Jonathan. 2012. How the tragedy of 9/11 made Canada a better, more sensible country. *National Post*, September 11.

Keeble, Edna. 1997. Rethinking the 1971 white paper and Trudeau's impact on Canadian defense policy. *American Review of Canadian Studies* 27 (4): 550–562.

Kennedy, Mark. 2015. Stephen Harper: The political outsider who sought a revolution. *Ottawa Citizen*, October 20.

Lagassé, Philippe, and Paul Robinson. 2008. *Reviving realism in the Canadian defence debate*. Kingston: Queen's Centre for International Relations.

Lawless, Jennifer. 2004. Women, war, and winning elections: Gender stereotyping in the post-9/11 era. *Political Research Quarterly* 57 (3): 479–490.

Leuprecht, Christian, and Joel Sokolsky. 2015. Defence Walmart style. *Armed Forces and Society* 41 (3): 541–562.

Liberal Party of Canada. 2015a. Promoting international peace and security. Liberal Party of Canada. https://www.liberal.ca/realchange/promoting-international-peace-and-security/. Accessed 21 Aug 2017.

———. 2015b. F-35. Liberal Party of Canada. https://www.liberal.ca/realchange/f-35/. Accessed 21 Aug 2017.

Maloney, Sean. 2016. Towards a new national security policy for Canada. *Defense and Security Analysis* 32 (2): 199–206.

Massie, Justin, Jean-Christophe Boucher, and Stéphane Roussel. 2010. Hijacking a policy? Assessing Quebec's "undue" influence on Canada's Afghan policy. *American Review of Canadian Studies* 40 (2): 259–275.

McCormick, Ty, and Colum Lynch. 2017. To save peacekeeping from Trump's budget axe, will the UN embrace fighting terrorism? *Foreign Policy*, March 29.

National Defence. 2017. Strong, secure, engaged: Canada's defence policy. *National Defence*. http://dgpaapp.forces.gc.ca/en/canada-defence-policy/docs/canada-defence-policy-report.pdf. Accessed 21 Aug 2017.

Nossal, Kim Richard. 2016. *Charlie foxtrot: Fixing defence procurement in Canada*. Toronto: Dundurn.

———. 2016b. Canada is back, part 2: Trudeau and the use of force. CDA Institute, January 28. http://cdainstitute.ca/canada-is-back-part-2-trudeau-and-the-use-of-force/. Accessed 21 Aug 2017.

Nossal, Kim Richard, Stéphane Roussel, and Stéphane Paquin. 2015. *The politics of Canadian foreign policy*. Montreal/Kingston: McGill-Queen's University Press.

Pugliese, Daivd. 2007. Trudeau was Canada's top defence spender: Study. *National Post*, December 3.

Richter, Andrew. 2016. The Liberal government of Justin Trudeau and defence policy. CDA Institute, November. http://cdainstitute.ca/wp-content/uploads/2016/07/Richter_Analysis_November_2016.pdf. Accessed 15 Sept 2017.

———. 2017. A muscular new Canada? Not so fast. Macdonald-Laurier Institute, July 31. http://www.macdonaldlaurier.ca/a-muscular-new-canada-not-so-fast-andrew-richter-for-inside-policy/. Accessed 21 Aug 2017.

Rideau Institute. 2017. New Canadian defence policy neither credible nor affordable. Rideau Institute, June 12. http://www.rideauinstitute.ca/2017/06/12/new-canadian-defence-policy-neither-credible-nor-affordable/. Accessed 23 Aug 2017.

Sabin, Jerald. 2016. Are you man enough? Masculinity in the 105 election. *Policy Options*, May 26. http://policyoptions.irpp.org/2016/05/26/man-enough-masculinity-2015-federal-election/. Accessed 21 Aug 2017.

Sabin, Jerald, and Kyle Kirkup. 2016. Competing masculinities and political campaigns. Paper presented at the *2016 Annual meeting of the Canadian Political Science Association*, Ryerson University, Toronto, Canada.

Saideman, Steven. 2014. On Harper's strategy and Trudeau's quandary. *Open Canada*, October 6. https://www.opencanada.org/features/on-harpers-strategy-and-trudeaus-quandary/. Accessed 21 Aug 2017.

Schaub, Jr., Gary, and Richard Shimooka. 2017. Super Hornets, eh? Canadian airpower falls short on North American defense. *War on the Rocks*, February 17. https://warontherocks.com/2017/02/super-hornets-eh-canadian-airpower-falls-short-on-north-american-defense/. Accessed 21 Aug 2017.

Shadwick, Martin. 2004. The Chretien legacy. *Canadian Military Journal* 4 (4): 68–72.

———. 2011. Defence and the 2011 election. *Canadian Military Journal* 11 (4): 62–67.

Simpson, Jeffrey. 2016. Why Sajjan will be wrestling with military spending. *Globe and Mail*, January 16.

Smith, Heather. 2003. Disrupting internationalism and finding the others. In *Feminist perspectives on Canadian foreign policy*, ed. Claire Turenne Sjolander, Heather Smith, and Deborah Stienstra, 24–39. Oxford: Oxford University Press.

Sokolsky, Joel, and Joseph Jockel. 2016. A defence policy review? Not really necessary. CDA Institute, April, 2017. http://cdainstitute.ca/wp-content/uploads/Analysis/Sokolsky_Jockel_Analysis_April_2016.pdf. Accessed 27 Aug 2017.

Solomon, Binyam. 2005. The demand for Canadian defence expenditures. *Defence and Peace Economics* 16 (3): 171–189.

Tandt, Michael den. 2015. Isis war needs military might, not pacifism. *London (Ontario) Free Press*, November 17.

Tickner, J. Ann. 2006. Feminism meets international relations: Some methodological issues. In *Feminist methodologies for international relations*, ed. Brooke A. Ackerly, Maria Stern, and Jacqui True, 19–41. Cambridge: Cambridge University Press.

Hlatky, Stéphanie von. 2016. Trudeau's Promises: From coalition operations to peacekeeping and beyond. CDA Institute, June. http://cdainstitute.ca/wp-content/uploads/Analysis/images_Analysis_Hlatky_Analysis_June_2016.pdf. Accessed 15 Sept 2017.

Hlatky, Stéphanie von., and Kim Richard Nossal. 2017. Canada's new defence policy: The short version. CDA Institute, July. http://cdainstitute.ca/wp-content/uploads/2017/07/CDA-Institute-Analysis-vonHlatkyNossal-July-2017FINAL.pdf. Accessed 15 Sept 2017.

Vucetic, Srdjan. 2011. *The Anglosphere: A genealogy of a racialized identity in international relations.* Stanford: Stanford University Press.

Winter, Nicholas. 2010. Masculine republicans and feminine democrats: Gender and Americans' explicit and implicit images of the political parties. *Political Behavior* 32 (4): 587–618.

CHAPTER 15

Trudeau the Reluctant Warrior? Canada and International Military Operations

Jeffrey Rice and Stéfanie von Hlatky

Canada has been a member of the Global Coalition to Counter the Islamic State of Iraq and Syria (ISIS) since it began in 2014. Prime Minister Stephen Harper decided to commit Canada to a role in both Iraq and Syria at that time, one of few allies to offer contributions on both fronts. When Prime Minister Justin Trudeau took office on 4 November 2015, one of the first foreign policy decisions he made was to halt Canada's combat role as part of Operation IMPACT, the Canadian Armed Forces' (CAF) counter-ISIS campaign. This decision provoked public debate about what constitutes combat versus non-combat operations, owing to the role Canadian special operations forces (SOF) played in assisting and advising local forces, but the reaction was largely predictable since it had been a core message during Trudeau's electoral campaign.[1]

In defending the decision to end airstrikes against ISIS, Trudeau's minister of national defence, Harjit S. Sajjan, sought to assure the House of Commons, and the Canadian public, that the Liberal government was committed to continuing the fight against global terrorism. Acknowledging that the operational mandate would transition away from combat and

---

J. Rice (✉) • S. von Hlatky
Queen's University, Kingston, ON, Canada

© The Author(s) 2018
N. Hillmer, P. Lagassé (eds.), *Justin Trudeau and Canadian Foreign Policy*, Canada and International Affairs,
https://doi.org/10.1007/978-3-319-73860-4_15

would be replaced with a greater emphasis on training, he noted that: "When planning a fight, we have to look at the entire picture, not each individual piece of the puzzle. We have to look at what we are bringing to the table, what our allies are also bringing to the table, and how the enemy is evolving. If we focus too closely on a singular, short-term option, we lose sight of what is needed to win the fight in the long run."[2]

In making this statement, Sajjan raised a number of important questions. Among its allies and among other nations, what does Canada bring to the table in terms of international military operations? Are its contributions sufficient to satisfy its international obligations and alliance commitments? And do these types of contributions signify either a qualitative or quantitative change in the way Canada participates in international military operations? This final question may be of special interest, given that Trudeau's electoral success arguably hinged on the idea of "breaking with the past." Since Canada is committed to over 18 international military operations—three of which can be regarded as major military operations (defined as a commitment involving 200 or more CAF personnel)—these three questions guide the discussion of this chapter to help better understand Canada's role in international military operations.

We offer the following arguments. First, Trudeau's approach to international military operations shares many similarities to that of his predecessor because he has not withdrawn Canada from any of the operations Harper had signed the CAF up for. However, whereas the Harper government was more likely to deploy overt military assets to combat roles, albeit with less enthusiasm over time, Trudeau appears to be a "reluctant warrior," more interested in strengthening the role of SOF and developing capacity with local security forces in theatres of operations and surrounding countries. Between 2011 and 2015, the Harper government tended toward more symbolic and politically motivated military action. To be sure, Harper did rely on SOF for training and advising, but his government engaged the Royal Canadian Air Force (RCAF) to perform airstrikes in Iraq. In contrast, Trudeau's emphasis instead appears to be on the creation and professionalization of local forces, offering tactical and strategic support where possible but steering clear of kinetic operations.

Second, although Canada falls short of two per cent of gross domestic product (GDP) on defence spending—a number it formally committed itself to during the Wales Summit of the North Atlantic Treaty Organization (NATO) in 2014—Canada does contribute a significant amount to international military operations, by placing its focus on training, supporting allies, and SOF contributions.³ Reinforcing that message, namely, that Canada is a reliable contributor, would prove even more important with the election of President Donald Trump. In contributing actively to these three areas, it is not altogether clear whether Canada, or its allies, would benefit substantially from reaching that two per cent benchmark by the agreed deadline of 2024. In fact, the government's 2017 defence policy statement makes clear that, at best, Canada would reach 1.4 per cent within the next ten years.⁴ Third, given the relative size and capability of the CAF and of the Canadian defence budget as a whole, Canada is better suited at developing niche capabilities for military operations and should be emphasizing SOF and training of indigenous security capabilities. This military skillset has been well developed over the course of the CAF's involvement in Afghanistan and that relative success can be replicated in places like Iraq and in neighbouring countries, such as Jordan and Lebanon.

This chapter, in making the above arguments, develops in the following way. It provides an overview of historical trends in international military operations undertaken by the CAF. It then proceeds to outline Canada's role in military operations through an analysis of the three major military operations: Operation IMPACT, which involves the deployment of SOF personnel with the mandate of training Kurdish forces in North-Eastern Iraq in their campaign to retake Mosul; Operation REASSURANCE, the deployment of conventional forces to Eastern Europe; and Operation UNIFIER, the special training mission to assist Ukraine in combating Russian aggression. In each of these cases, we must recognize an important, but also humbling, element of Canada's contributions: they are of limited scope, given its position as a middle power and its limited defence spending. Although Canada does play an important role in international military operations, its overall impact is predicated in large part on the contribution of its other middle- and great-power allies. Canada's presence can only be felt when it is among other nations.

What It Brings and What It Has Brought

If the attacks on 11 September 2001 ushered in a security era of uncertainty, the threats that have emerged since are now fairly clear: terrorism, hybrid warfare (see below), and asymmetrical warfare from non-state or sub-state actors that are either supported by a state or are themselves, as in the case of ISIS (also known as Daesh), pursuing statehood. These kinds of threats have, for the most part, replaced the threat posed by conventional forces of advanced industrialized nations. Even with the resurgence of traditional foes, such as Russia, following its annexation of Crimea in 2014, conflict has taken on a different form, referred to as hybrid warfare.[5] The utility of procuring and developing conventional forces is not as clear-cut as it once was. The Cold War, itself replete with uncertainties, did carry with it a degree of certainty with respect to what capabilities one should develop. Nuclear parity, as well as maintaining an edge with respect to military power—peace through strength, in other words—was a cornerstone of US foreign policy during this time.[6] Yet, NATO experiences in Afghanistan demonstrated that, even when in possession of an overwhelming asymmetry in military capabilities, victory is not always guaranteed. Nor have NATO's superior capabilities deterred Russia from provoking unrest on its Eastern flank.

This uncertainty is troubling for the United States and its allies and has been made worse by the emergence of a mild transatlantic rift with the participation of President Donald Trump in international summitry. But some allies have more options than others. Given that the United States spends over 400 times more than Canada on defence, it can afford to develop the broad spectrum of capabilities necessary to address most security threats—Canada cannot. Even without the United States (Fig. 15.1), Canada is not part of NATO's top tier.

With its defence budget slightly above one per cent of its GDP, thanks to recent increases promised in the 2017 defence policy review, Canada should be very specific and clear about how the capabilities proposed in the review will contribute to current and future military operations. Ultimately, debates about procurement, force development, and participation all relate to the role and position that it occupies in the world and in international military operations. That role has been defined broadly, from emergency assistance and peacekeeping to rotational forces in Europe. In the 2015 edition of *Canada Among Nations*, Hampson and Saideman noted that Canadian peacekeeping contributions have been in steady decline, but the number of missions has remained roughly the same throughout this time. Of course, the nature of the missions has changed. Peacekeeping has been de-emphasized in favour of training, combat, and support.[7] What this means is that, as the nature of the missions change, the operational demands placed upon the CAF will continue to increase and become more complex. Nonetheless, there is a trade-off between breadth and depth, with Canada opting for the former. In the uncertain environment of the post-Cold War era, successive Canadian prime ministers have

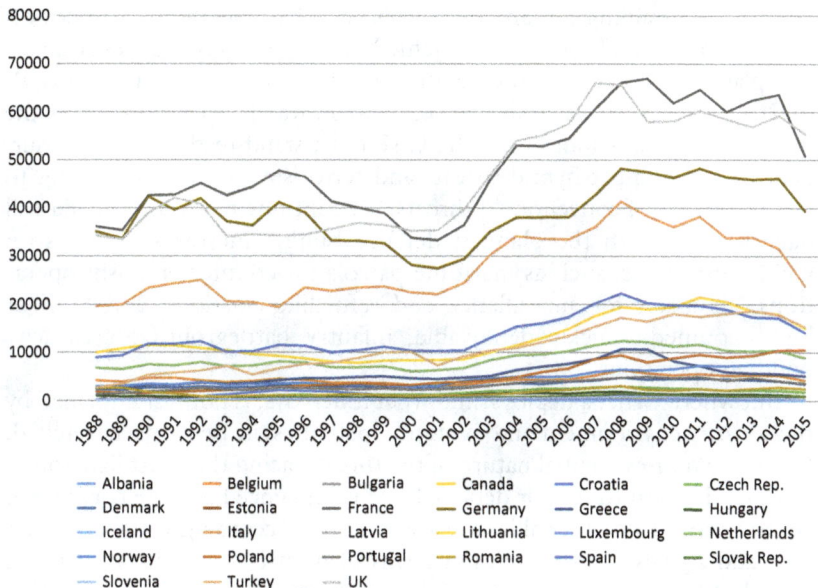

Fig. 15.1 Mil Exp (without United States)

deprioritized defence budgets, but continued to insist that the CAF remain a multi-role, combat capable force, able to deploy in support of US-led operations and United Nations peacekeeping missions. Trudeau is no exception in this respect, as most of the money and capabilities he has promised are slated for far down the road.[8]

Today's conflicts, from Ukraine to Northern Iraq, may seem more complex, but this also presents an opportunity for Canada to meaningfully contribute to military operations in unique and unconventional ways. The fluidity demanded of a modern military was made clear to Canadians during the war in Afghanistan. From 2001 until 2011, the CAF mandate in Afghanistan vacillated between combat and reconstruction before shifting to a training role. Although armed forces personnel played an integral role in helping to rebuild Afghanistan through the Provincial Reconstruction Teams (PRTs), CAF casualties in Afghanistan also ranked third highest among all other participating member-states.

In 2011, the Harper government ended Canada's combat mission in Afghanistan and transitioned to a training mission. In spite of the new emphasis on training for land operations, combat operations were not off the table for the Harper government. Under the Conservatives, Canada also played an active role in Operation UNIFIED PROTECTOR (OUP) in 2011, the NATO-led air campaign in Libya. If operations from the recent past are any indication, the CAF must stand ready to battle insurgencies and combat hybrid threats and terrorism, while contributing to the deterrence of conventional threats. To continue to do so, Canada will have to stick with the planned defence budget increases or focus on niche capabilities, such as maritime patrols for counterterrorism operations, air assets for surveillance and refuelling missions, and SOF or highly trained, quickly deployable, infantry battlegroups for capacity building operations.[9]

But where Canada deploys, and what it deploys, is not just informed by the security environment and existing capabilities, however overstretched. Given the non-existential nature of the threats facing the Canadian homeland, its decision to use, or deploy, force is influenced in large part by the contributions that other allies are also making. Accordingly, Canada takes cues and signals from its allies in terms of what it contributes. Strategic considerations as well as other alliance commitments help determine Canada's contributions to international military operations. It is therefore useful to understand Canada's decisions on military operations through the prism of its alliance relationships.[10]

At the domestic level, a lack of public support for combat operations is something that has affected most Western states. Public support is crucial, as low public support often means a reduction in political will and interest in deploying boots on the ground, especially when there is risk of political fallout from casualties. For example, public support for the Canadian war in Afghanistan declined fairly significantly in the final years.[11] For Prime Minister Harper, the period between 2006 and 2011 was a constant struggle to reconcile Canada's commitment in Afghanistan with political tactics at home. Force exhaustion, coupled with a public unwilling to support prolonged combat operations, forced Canada to think critically about what aspects of international military operations to which it would contribute to. As such, an emphasis on training for the land forces, and working with regional and local forces in theatre to develop counterterrorism or deterrence capabilities, characterizes many of Canada's current contributions to operations. This stance permits the CAF to be a player in all major allied operations. And President Trump is keeping attendance.

The airstrikes of Operation IMPACT run counter to these trends, at least according to an Ipsos poll conducted in November 2015, showing that a majority of Canadians supported the airstrikes against Daesh.¹² But the utility of these airstrikes, beyond their symbolism, is less clear. Indeed, Canada has conducted less than two per cent of the coalition's 145,469 sorties to date.¹³ But, how significant were Canada's 1,378 CF-18 sorties in 2015 and 2016 in terms of broader coalition efforts?¹⁴

Training: Operation IMPACT

In October 2014, Canada, one among 66 other states participating in the coalition, entered the fight against ISIL with a series of airstrikes undertaken by CF-18s, targeting ISIL fighting positions and equipment depots. For two years, CF-18s took part in the coalition bombing campaign, the purpose and mandate of which was somewhat ambiguously defined as degrading and defeating ISIL. Following Trudeau's electoral victory in 2015, the mission underwent a fairly significant reorganization, and shortly after taking power, the Liberals ended the airstrikes on 15 February 2016, fulfilling one of their campaign promises. Although Trudeau has expanded the number of personnel on the ground in Iraq, from 69 to 200, the mission was initially criticized by Trudeau, mainly on the basis that it placed too much emphasis on combat operations. The official information offered by the CAF is that, during the course of the airstrike campaign (from 4 October 2014 to 15 February 2016), the RCAF bombed 267 Daesh positions, eliminating 102 vehicles and equipment, as well as destroying 30 Daesh improvised explosive devices (IEDs) factories.¹⁵ Although these accomplishments represent a fairly significant contribution, at least for Canada, it is impossible to discern what their overall effect has been on degrading and eliminating Daesh. The uncertain nature of the contribution was, in part, one of the reasons why Trudeau chose to withdraw the CF-18s in the first place. In addition, the Trudeau government is quick to emphasize the "non-combat nature" of its contributions.

In making the decision to withdraw the six CF-18s taking part in Operation IMPACT, Trudeau drew the ire of the Conservative Party of Canada (CPC). Rona Ambrose, the interim Leader of the CPC and of the official Opposition in the House of Commons, declared it to be a "shameful step backward." Other Conservative Members of Parliament (MPs) also rejected the decision on the basis that it was important for Canada to be seen to be contributing equally with coalition allies in the bombing campaign[16] and cited the fact that the majority of Canadians (68 per cent) supported the airstrikes. Although the decision was unpopular with the CPC, the termination of the bombing mission was defended by the chief of the defence staff, General Jonathan Vance, who stated that "there is sufficient air power available in the coalition to continue the air bombardments with the support of Canada's re-fueller and our targeting."[17] Whether these sentiments were echoed by allies is unclear, but US President Barack Obama did at the time accept and acknowledge the new mission as a meaningful contribution. Trump seems equally satisfied with Canada's role in operations.

Operation IMPACT now represents the single largest deployment of CAF personnel to theatre since the war in Afghanistan, with roughly 880 training and SOF personnel deployed to Iraq and supporting the operation all around the Middle East. Since then, the CAF actively engaged in training and advising Peshmerga forces in North-Eastern Iraq as they prepared for the campaign to liberate Mosul from ISIL. Even though one of Trudeau's criticisms of the Harper government was a lack of clarity concerning mandate and endpoint, the role of the CAF in Iraq has been no less opaque. Despite a pledge for greater transparency, there have been few mission briefings under Trudeau. Although the Canadian Special Operations Forces Command (CANSOFCOM) is mandated with a strictly defensive role, what are described as "defensive combat operations" during the fall of 2016 also increased fairly significantly. Further tactical and strategic support has been offered by the CAF, for example, with the establishment of a Role 2 Military Hospital in Erbil, Iraq, to provide medical support for coalition and international partners as well as the deployment of a Polaris refuelling tanker. In spite of this, CAF officials have been adamant that the focus on training has not changed.

DETERRENCE: OPERATION REASSURANCE

On 9 September 2016, Stéphane Dion, then Minister of Foreign Affairs, announced to the House of Commons "the deployment of troops to Latvia for a mission of deterrence against Russian aggression."[18] Earlier that summer, following the Warsaw Summit, NATO allies agreed to the deployment of soldiers to the Baltic states and Poland in order to "unambiguously demonstrate, as part of our overall posture, Allies' solidarity, determination and ability to act by triggering an immediate Allied response to any aggression."[19] Dubbed Enhanced Forward Presence (eFP), these efforts contributed, in part, to the Readiness Action Plan (RAP) that was agreed upon in 2014 during the Wales Summit, in direct response to the Russian annexation of Crimea. A multinational land force was deployed in support of Operation REASURANCE through the Framework Nations concept. Canada, in volunteering to serve as one of the Framework Nations, leads one of the four battlegroups, along with the United States, the United Kingdom, and Germany. The Canada-led battlegroup, consisting of a multinational force of roughly 1,000 soldiers, was deployed to Latvia in May 2017. Approximately 450 of the 1,000 soldiers are CAF personnel serving on a rotational basis. The deployment of conventional capabilities to Eastern Europe serves as an important reminder to Canada's allies that it remains committed to European security and the transatlantic relationship while also shouldering a significant part of the alliance burden as a Framework Nation.

This deployment as part of eFP would be insufficient to defend against a Russian invasion, but it may contribute to both deterrence and reassurance.[20] Amid uncertainty and conflicting rhetoric from President Trump, small degrees of reassurance and signals of stability appear to be quite welcome. The Latvian ambassador to Canada, Karlis Eihenbaums, has, on numerous occasions, praised the Canadian decision to deploy to Latvia and even went so far as to underline the value of Canadian leadership in the region while simultaneously defending the decision from criticism emerging from Moscow.[21] Given that President Trump has wavered on multiple occasions as to whether or not the United States would come to the aid of the Baltic states if they were the targets of Russian aggression, Canada, in this instance, has defined its position in contradistinction to that of the Americans. It should also be noted that the United States is, itself, leading a battlegroup in Poland and this deployment has proceeded as scheduled, starting in January of 2017. Despite Trump's ambivalent stance toward NATO, his statements have been increasingly supportive of the alliance. While it seems that Canada itself has fairly modest assets to offer with respect to deterrence, it is important to note that eFP is limited in scope, with fewer than 5,000 troops in the theatre. Canada has limited conventional forces to deploy, which is why it has to rely on the contributions of Albania, Italy, Poland, Slovenia, and Spain to complete its battlegroup.

Yet, the government of Canada and the CAF can bring valued leadership to the mission in Latvia, as shown by its ability to secure the role of a Framework Nation, alongside the United States, the United Kingdom, and Germany. On multiple occasions, Canada has been tasked with taking a commanding role in international military operations, as was the case with both the International Security Assistance Force (ISAF) in Afghanistan and OUP in Libya, as will be discussed below.

Training and (Weak) Deterrence: Operation UNIFIER

An extension to Operation UNIFIER, until March 2019, was announced by Foreign Affairs Minister Chrystia Freeland and Defence Minister Sajjan during a press conference in March 2017. The mission's official mandate is to provide support and assistance in the development of Ukrainian armed forces capabilities in order to ensure the integrity and continued sovereignty of Ukraine. Much as in the case of Operation REASSURANCE, Operation UNIFIER has been denounced by Russian officials, but the Ukrainian ambassador to Canada has described it as "a powerful signal of deterrence to Russia and a strong sign of Canadian leadership in dealing with global challenges."[22] Although deterrence is not found within the official CAF mandate, Ukrainian officials have been keen to label it as such. Words spoken by Department of National Defence officials lend credence to the idea of deterrence. Minister Sajjan, for instance, during a parliamentary session on the 20 March 2017, stated that "through Operation UNIFIER, we sent a clear signal of deterrence to Russia, and we also sent a strong message of solidarity and support to Ukraine."[23] Sajjan also reiterated this point and echoed the words of the Ukrainian ambassador in stating that Operation UNIFIER, in conjunction with Operation REASSURANCE, "is sending a very strong message of deterrence to Russia."[24] Nevertheless, mention of deterrence as a part of Operation UNIFIER is a recent development and CAF officials have been, historically, slightly more restrained in declaring Operation UNIFIER's objective as being one of deterrence.

Hence, although conventional fighting forces have not been deployed to Ukraine, Operation UNIFIER serves as an interesting example of what can be achieved through alternative and bilateral contributions, reassurance, and a modicum of deterrence. Given the focus that the mission places on training, it again highlights a growing niche area for the CAF to make active contributions in international security without having to commit soldiers to risky operations. In other words, it fulfils allied goals at low cost, a benefit that was recognized by both Harper and Trudeau.

Trudeau chose to stay the course after Harper decided to send roughly 200 military trainers in April 2015 to help support the Ukrainian armed forces in their efforts to defeat Russia-backed rebels in its Eastern regions. The difficulty with training missions, however, is that it is hard to assess the overall impact that the training mission is having in helping Ukrainian forces stabilize the region and resolve the situation in Eastern Ukraine. Given that any effects will be indirectly experienced, since CAF soldiers are only involved in advising and training and not direct combat, it is much more difficult to ascertain what the effects of the mission are beyond counting the number of Ukraine soldiers trained.

Canada's Worth as an Ally

The previous sections of this chapter have focused on what Canada contributes as part of coalition- and alliance-led military operations. The question that flows from this brief comparison of Canada's top missions is whether or not these efforts are meeting the expectations of the United States, key allies, and NATO. Unwilling to follow the trends of apparent isolationism that permeate the rhetoric of many in the Trump administration, Canada, in both rhetoric and practice, continues to make international engagement a leading priority. Indeed, Trudeau has insisted that "Canada is back." But how can that be evaluated? With the contributions noted above, Ottawa can certainly make the case that it is fulfilling its international obligations.

Yet, for scholars of burden-sharing, there is no easy answer to this question.[25] For example, NATO's rough burden-sharing measure is the two per cent pledge. Although Canada is failing to meet the two per cent of GDP in defence spending that it committed to at the Wales Summit, there is little reason to believe that this metric is actually an accurate assessment of Canada's overall contributions.[26] What is clear is that, even though the CAF does possess limited capabilities when compared with its larger European allies, its contributions tend to be well-received and even praised, especially by its Eastern European allies. As well, there is general agreement that Canada, when it does participate, demonstrates its worth as an ally and this in turn pays off in terms of Canada's visibility within NATO.

Taking a leadership role in an operation is an important qualitative indicator of burden-sharing. Canada has held a number of notable and public leadership positions in international military operations over the last decade and a half. Lieutenant-General Rick Hillier took command of ISAF in 2004 for seven months, Lieutenant-General Charles Bouchard commanded Operation UNIFIED PROTECTOR (OUP) in Libya, and Canada once more assumed a leadership position in international military operations by leading the deployment of a multinational battlegroup in Latvia as part of Operation REASURANCE. Scholars have emphasized exposure to risk as yet another example of how allies can prove their worth in the context of operations.[27] Risk can be assessed by measuring the number of casualties relative to the size of the deployment. This metric was a significant one for ISAF but was less salient for OUP or Operation REASSURANCE.

When assessing an ally's contributions, other scholars have focused on the political and military restrictions that governments place on their soldiers on the battlefield (known as caveats) and the rules of engagement that soldiers are required to follow. National variation in the amount of restrictions, in terms of how restrictive or permissive they are, or even different rules of engagement, may affect the ability of coalitions to coordinate effectively.[28] A US Congressional Research Service report notes that "certain coalition actors can often work at cross-purpose without intending to do so," thereby reinforcing the significance of leadership and coordination capacity.[29] The same report identifies the conflicting regional objectives that certain coalition partners may pursue, noting that they might "contradict US interests."[30] Given that the United States is more often than not the largest contributor to international military operations, working against US interests can have the effect of undermining mission cohesion.

The United States and NATO, for operations under their command, have developed the practice of doing tallies of military and non-military contributions offered by allies and partners. For example, Washington tracks contributions for its counter-ISIS operations, which is named Operation INHERENT RESOLVE in the United States. The United States assesses the military contributions across three categories: training and advising, airstrikes, and other contributions.[31] Canada's air refuelling and surveillance assets would fit under the last category. Of the 66 partners that offer contributions in support of Operation INHERENT RESOLVE, only 26 countries provide military assets (excluding the United States). And of those 26 countries, only eight provide assets across the three categories (training, strikes, and *others*). Canada belonged to that category until it withdrew its CF-18s from the fight in February 2016. In quantitative terms, countries stand out if they belong to the top tier of allies and partners who contribute military assets. Canada most often misses the mark, though not by much.

Canada does well when we look at qualitative assessments of burden-sharing: it is often able to secure command appointments, it has few political and military restrictions, and it has a high level of interoperability with coalition leaders. Canada does not fare as well when contributions are assessed using strictly quantitative indicators. This is enough to avoid being perceived as a free-rider, but it puts pressure on Ottawa to make sure the value of its military contributions is emphasized by using diplomatic and political channels to underscore the message. In addition, Canada continues to have some comparative advantages when compared with other allies, as is apparent in the realm of intelligence with the "Five Eyes" intelligence sharing agreement between Australia, Canada, New Zealand, the United Kingdom, and the United States.

Beyond these qualitative and quantitative indicators of burden-sharing, we can also look at more immediate signals from allies about whether or not contributions are meeting expectations. American Secretaries of Defense have openly criticized their fellow NATO allies for not investing enough in building their own defence capabilities. This type of pressure is also quite present during force generation conferences, the meetings that are intended to solicit troop contributions from allies. For example, during the 2016 meeting of the coalition to counter ISIS, US Secretary of Defense Ash Carter said, "And we need everybody, and that's all the Europeans—the Gulf States, which aren't doing [enough], Turkey, which is right there on the border. So, there are a lot that need to make more contributions."[32] By singling out allies and partners in this way, Washington is engaging in public shaming and putting pressure on the capitals to bring more to the fight.

Canada has so far escaped the type of harsh criticisms that European allies and Turkey have received, and has done so in spite of even spending $20 billion dollars annually on defence—though this is now improving under the new defence policy. In a context in which the US President has called NATO *obsolete*, Canada may once again feel some pressure to contribute more to alliance or coalition operations. Contributing more to training and relying heavily on its SOF pose a dilemma for Canada in that it is more difficult to ascertain the impact of these contributions. Even though these special forces are active in training the Kurdish forces (known as the Peshmerga) as they prepare to retake the remaining sectors of Mosul, it is not altogether clear what they are actually doing. Operations that rely on SOF make assessing the impact of missions all the more difficult, given that historically—and the Trudeau government is no better in this respect—SOF missions have been shrouded in secrecy. However, world-class SOF capabilities are high-value assets in short supply, so when they are in demand, Canada can offer contributions that will get noticed and inch into the top tier. SOF capabilities have been boosted in the 2017 defence policy, including a planned increase of 605 personnel.

Conclusion

As a "reluctant warrior," Trudeau has been less willing than Stephen Harper to commit to overt displays of military force, in both rhetoric and practice. In surveying the three major international military operations being undertaken by the CAF, there is a clear preference for capacity building over direct military action, except in cases where SOF are being deployed. Nevertheless, we have identified many enduring trends in the conduct of Canada's international military operations, and Trudeau has kept the CAF engaged in the main operations that he inherited from Harper.

Canada has demonstrated its reliability as an ally in terms of security contributions in spite of resource constraints, thanks in part to the emphasis that Canadian governments have placed on multilateral and bilateral capacity building, and the selective usage of SOF around the world. Canada has avoided the harsh criticism of its largest allies and partners for now, and the government has pre-empted greater scrutiny by announcing headline-grabbing defence budget increases in June 2017. Whether the money and capabilities will materialize is still quite uncertain. Ottawa will have to decide whether or not the contributions that it is making to international military operations are the types of contributions it will want to make in the future.

What is sure to be challenging beyond the defence policy's promised spending boost is how to navigate any new demands that President Trump might place on its military allies, especially in terms of counterterrorism operations. As the Global Coalition to defeat ISIS consolidates its gains, what will Canada's future role be in Iraq? The timeline of operations is not clear. While certain missions have end dates, these are often extended. Will simultaneous involvement in deterrence, counterterrorism, and peace support operations prove too much for the "reluctant warrior"? At least until the next election, Trudeau is likely to stick to a status quo strategy of high-visibility and low-risk missions.

NOTES

1. Pugliese (2015).
2. Sajjan (2015).
3. An important caveat is that the Trudeau government has discussed increasing its UN peacekeeping commitments with 600 troops and a budget of roughly $450 million. In principle and in rhetoric, this denotes a modest shift in stance when discussing UN peacekeeping operations, but neither troops nor money have yet to be committed to specific operations to date.
4. The 2017 defence policy statement forecasts that by 2024–25, total defence spending will reach 1.4 per cent of GDP (National Defence 2017).
5. Kofman and Rojansky (2013).
6. Nau (2013, 181).
7. Hampson and Saideman (2015, 3).
8. Hlatky (2016), Hlatky and Nossal (2017).
9. The 2017 defence policy statement plans for a 70 per cent increase of the defence budget in the next ten years (National Defence 2017).
10. Hlatky (2013).
11. Ettinger and Rice (2016). See, also, Boucher and Nossal (2015).
12. Russel (2015).
13. Department of National Defence (2017b). Canada has carried out a total of 2,835 sorties, which includes the 1378 sorties by the CF-18 Hornets (Department of National Defence 2017a). See also Department of National Defence (2016).
14. Department of National Defence (2016).
15. Department of Defence (2017a).
16. Connoly (2016).
17. Mas (2016).
18. Dion (2016). Prior to that, Canada was contributing to NATO's air policing mission in the Baltics.
19. North Atlantic Council (2016).
20. Shlapak and Johnson (2016).
21. Chase (2016).
22. Brewster (2017).
23. Sajjan (2017).
24. Brewster (2017).
25. Zyla (2015).

26. Alexander (2015, 7). See, also, Lanoszka (2015, 133–152).
27. Zyla (2015).
28. Auerswald and Saideman (2014).
29. McInnis (2016, 6).
30. McInnis (2016).
31. Ibid.
32. Mehta (2016).

References

Alexander, John. 2015. Canada's commitment to NATO: Are we pulling our weight? *Canadian Military Journal* 15 (4): 4–11.
Auerswald, David, and Stephen Saideman. 2014. *NATO in Afghanistan: Fighting together, fighting alone*. Princeton: Princeton University Press.
Boucher, Jean-Christophe, and Kim Richard Nossal. 2015. Lessons learned?: Public opinion and the Afghanistan mission. In *Elusive pursuits: Lessons from Canada's interventions abroad. Canada among nations 2015*, ed. Fen Osler Hampson and Stephen M. Saidemen, 59–79. Montreal/Kingston: McGill-Queen's University Press.
Brewster, Murray. 2017. Canada extending military mission in Ukraine to 2019. *CBC News*, March 6. http://www.cbc.ca/news/politics/canada-ukraine-military-mission-1.4011870. Accessed 10 Sept 2017.
Chase, Steven. 2016. Latvian envoy defends Canadian led NATO mission. *Globe and Mail*, December 22. http://www.theglobeandmail.com/news/politics/latvian-envoy-defends-canadian-led-nato-mission/article33409058/. Accessed 10 Sept 2017.
Connoly, Amanda. 2016. ISIS mission debated in the House, DND confirms end of airstrikes. *iPolitics*, February 17. http://ipolitics.ca/2016/02/17/battle-lines-drawn-as-isis-mission-debate-begins-in-commons/. Accessed 10 Sept 2017.
Department of National Defence. 2016. Operation IMPACT. Government of Canada, February 15. http://www.forces.gc.ca/en/operations-abroad-current/op-impact.page. Accessed 10 Sept 2017.
———. 2017a. Operation IMPACT – Airstrike History. Government of Canada, February 14. http://www.forces.gc.ca/en/operations-abroad-current/op-impact-airstrikes.page. Accessed 10 Sept 2017.
———. 2017b. Operation IMPACT. Government of Canada, April 11. https://www.defense.gov/News/Special-Reports/0814_Inherent-Resolve. Accessed 10 Sept 2017.
Dion, Stéphane. 2016. Statement in house of commons. Parliament of Canada, September 19. http://www.parl.gc.ca/HousePublications/Publication.aspx?DocId=8381558. Accessed 10 Sept 2017.

Ettinger, Aaron, and Jeffrey Rice. 2016. Hell is other people's schedules: Canada's limited term military commitments, 2001–2015. *International Journal* 71 (3): 371–392.
Hampson, Fen Olser, and Stephen Saideman, eds. 2015. *Canada among nations 2015: Elusive pursuits: Lessons from Canada's interventions abroad.* Montreal/Kingston: McGill-Queen's University Press.
Hlatky, Stéfanie von. 2013. *American allies in times of war: The great asymmetry.* Oxford: Oxford University Press.
———. 2016. Trudeau's promises: From coalition operations to peacekeeping and beyond. CDA Institute Analysis, June. https://www.cdainstitute.ca/images/Analysis/Hlatky_Analysis_June_2016.pdf. Accessed 10 Sept 2017.
Hlatky, Stéfanie von, and Kim Richard Nossal. 2017. Canada's new defence policy: The short version. CDA Institute Analysis, July 11. http://cdainstitute.ca/stefanie-von-hlatky-and-kim-richard-nossal-canadas-new-defence-policy-the-short-version-cda-institute-analysis/. Accessed 10 Sept 2017.
Kofman, Michael, and Matthew Rojansky. 2013. A closer look at Russia's hybrid war. Kennan Cable, No. 7, April. https://www.wilsoncenter.org/sites/default/files/7-KENNAN%20CABLE-ROJANSKY%20KOFMAN.pdf. Accessed 10 Sept 2017.
Lanoszka, Alexander. 2015. Do allies really free ride? *Survival* 57 (3): 133–152.
Mas, Susana. 2016. ISIS airstrikes by Canada to end Feb. 22, training forces to triple. *CBC News*, February 9. http://www.cbc.ca/news/politics/justin-trudeau-canada-isis-fight-announcement-1.3438279. Accessed 10 Sept 2017.
McInnis, Kathleen J. 2016. Coalition contributions to countering the Islamic State. Congressional Research Service, No. 6, August 24. https://fas.org/sgp/crs/natsec/R44135.pdf. Accessed 10 Sept 2017.
Mehta, Aaron. 2016. Carter again slams anti-ISIS partners on lack of assistance. *Defense News*, February 2. http://www.defensenews.com/story/war-in-syria/2016/02/02/carter-slams-isis-coaltion-isil-syria-iraq-fight/79698804/. Accessed 10 Sept 2017.
National Defence. 2017. Strong, secure, engaged: Canada's defence policy. National Defence. http://dgpaapp.forces.gc.ca/en/canada-defence-policy/docs/canada-defence-policy-report.pdf. Accessed 15 Sept 2017.
Nau, Henry R. 2013. *Conservative internationalism: Armed diplomacy under Jefferson, Polk, Truman, and Reagan.* Princeton: Princeton University Press.
North Atlantic Council. 2016. Warsaw Summit communique. North Atlantic Treaty Organization, July 9. http://www.nato.int/cps/en/natohq/official_texts_133169.htm?selectedLocale=en. Accessed 10 Sept 2017.
Pugliese, David. 2015. Canadian participation in Iraq combat would end under NDP government, says Mulcair. *Ottawa Citizen*, September 10. http://ottawacitizen.com/news/national/defence-watch/canadian-participation-in-iraq-combat-would-end-immediately-under-ndp-government-says-mulcair. Accessed 10 Sept 2017.

Russel, Andrew. 2015. Majority of Canadians support airstrikes against Islamic State: Ipsos poll. *Global News*, November 23. http://globalnews.ca/news/2353190/majority-of-canadians-support-airstrikes-against-islamic-state-ipsos-poll/. Accessed 10 Sept 2017.

Sajjan, Harjit S. 2015. House of Commons statement. The Parliament of Canada, December 10. http://www.parl.gc.ca/HousePublications/Publication.aspx?Language=E&Mode=1&Parl=42&Ses=1&DocId=8067275. Accessed 10 Sept 2017.

———. 2017. House of Commons statement. The Parliament of Canada, March 20. http://www.parl.gc.ca/HousePublications/Publication.aspx?Language=E&Mode=1&DocId=8832958. Accessed 10 Sept 2017.

Shlaplank, David A., and Michael W. Johnson. 2016. Reinforcing deterrence on NATO's eastern flank: war gaming defense of the Baltics. The Rand Corporation. https://www.rand.org/content/dam/rand/pubs/research_reports/RR1200/RR1253/RAND_RR1253.pdf. Accessed 10 Sept 2017.

Zyla, Benjamin. 2015. *Sharing the burden? NATO and its second-tier powers*. Toronto: University of Toronto Press.

Index[1]

NUMBERS AND SYMBOLS
11 September 2001, 62, 97, 266, 287

A
Afghanistan, 13, 61, 62, 67,
    197, 278n19, 287–290,
    292, 294
  and Harper, Stephen, 255, 289, 290
Arms export rules, 209
Arms Trade Treaty (ATT), 208, 211,
    219–222
Artificial intelligence (AI), 94
Asia-Pacific Economic Cooperation
    (APEC), 1, 21, 254
Association of Southeast Asian Nations
    (ASEAN), 136, 254
ATT, *see* Arms Trade Treaty
Australia, 96, 157, 169,
    170, 208, 250,
    254, 297

B
Beyond the Border (BTB), 85, 86
Bill C-47, 219, 220
Boeing, 12, 38, 44, 274
Bombardier, 12, 44, 157, 274

C
CAF, *see* Canadian Armed Forces
California's Air Quality Resources
    Board (CARB), 112
Canada-Korea Trade Agreement, 4
Canadian Armed Forces (CAF), 7, 13,
    38, 39, 190, 236, 255, 264–268,
    272, 274–276, 285–295, 298
  anti-ISIS campaign, 266
  defence policy, 7, 190, 264–267,
    274–276, 287, 288
  Ukrainian assistance, 294
Canadian Commercial Corporation
    (CCC), 67, 68, 154, 208, 221

---

[1] Note: Page numbers followed by 'n' refer to notes.

© The Author(s) 2018
N. Hillmer, P. Lagassé (eds.), *Justin Trudeau and Canadian Foreign Policy*, Canada and International Affairs,
https://doi.org/10.1007/978-3-319-73860-4

Canadian International Development
    Agency (CIDA), 149, 150
Capitalism, 3, 58–60, 178
Carbon dioxide (CO_2), 90, 110
Carbon pricing, 107, 109, 111,
    116, 118
  and Canada, 109, 111, 116, 118
  and Mexico, 109, 116, 118
  and the United States, 109, 116, 118
Carbon Pricing Leadership Coalition
    (CPLC), 106, 118
Carbon Pricing Panel (CPP), 107, 109
Carbon tax, 90, 111, 116
CEDAW, *see* Convention on the
    Elimination of all Forms of
    Discrimination Against Women
CETA, *see* Comprehensive Economic
    and Trade Agreement
CF-18, 6, 22, 23, 32, 33, 35, 39, 40,
    42, 44, 47, 70, 266, 269,
    271–274, 276, 291, 297, 299n13
China, 4–6, 10, 14n11, 20, 22, 24,
    27, 28, 32, 56, 62, 87, 104, 114,
    115, 118, 126, 133–136,
    145–161, 223n6, 248, 255
  Approved Destination Status (ADS),
    152, 153
  Asian Infrastructure Investment
    Bank (AIIB), 134, 155, 159
  Canadians and, 5, 104, 114, 115,
    118, 126, 134, 135, 146–150,
    152–160
  economic growth of, 115, 147,
    151, 156
  foreign policy of, 5, 134, 135, 152,
    156, 157
Chrétien, Jean, 27, 43–45, 113, 134,
    148, 150–152, 266, 268, 272
CIDA, *see* Canadian International
    Development Agency
Civil society organization (CSO), 188,
    191, 193, 198,–199, 220

Climate change, 2, 9, 10, 17, 20, 21,
    26, 34, 36, 56, 83, 90, 92, 93,
    99n2, 103, 105, 106, 108–116,
    118, 147, 159, 195, 199,
    253, 256
  and Trudeau, 2, 9, 17, 21, 26, 36,
    56, 103, 108, 110–112,
    147, 199
Cold War, 60, 72n18, 237, 250, 256,
    257n7, 288
Comprehensive Economic and Trade
    Agreement (CETA), 3, 4,
    126–131, 133, 136
Conservative Party of Canada (CPC),
    291, 292
Convention on the Elimination of all
    Forms of Discrimination Against
    Women (CEDAW), 165, 193–195
Conference of Parties, Twenty-First
    Session (COP21), 1, 106–108
  See also Paris Agreement; United
    Nations Framework
    Convention on Climate Change
    (UNFCCC)
Crimea, 38, 65, 66, 288, 293

D
Defence community, 7, 261–279
Defence policy, 6, 7, 12, 35, 46, 190,
    261–269, 274–277, 297, 298
Defence Policy, Canada (2017), 190,
    262, 274–276, 287, 288, 298,
    299n4, 299n9
Deferred Action for Childhood
    Arrivals (DACA), 240
Development assistance, 3, 9, 18, 21,
    34, 151, 159, 193, 254
Dion, Stéphane, 24, 46, 68, 69,
    105, 209, 211, 213, 214,
    216, 217, 292, 299n18
Displaced persons (DPs), 237, 239, 242

E

Eastern Europe, 17, 20, 35, 37–38, 47, 59, 65–71, 287, 293
Election, 2015 Canadian federal, 2, 6, 8, 19–24, 29n1, 32, 39, 44, 125, 126, 173, 209, 233, 234, 239, 261, 267, 268, 271
  and Indigenous peoples, 173
  and the niqab, 42
  and Syrian refugees, 8, 233, 234, 239
  and TPP, 125
  and Trudeau's positions, 19, 39, 126, 210, 261
Enhanced Forward Presence (eFP), 38, 293
Environmental Protection Agency (EPA), 108, 110, 111
Environment and Climate Change Canada (ECCC), 105, 112, 120n44
EU, see European Union
European Union (EU), 17, 24, 66, 73n66, 125–130, 136, 270
  and the EU Commission, 127

F

F-35 (Lockheed Martin), 6, 32, 35, 42–44, 47, 271–273, 279n60
Feminist foreign policy, see International relations theory
Feminist International Assistance Policy, 9, 56, 136, 190, 193, 198, 199
First Nations, see Indigenous peoples
Five Eyes, 297
Fourth industrial revolution, 85, 93–95, 97
FPIC, see Free, prior, informed consent

Freeland, Chrystia, 12, 18, 24–26, 46, 106, 126–132, 135, 136, 137n23, 217–219, 225n58, 257n2, 294
Free, prior, informed consent (FPIC), 174–176, 178, 180
Full-time equivalents (FTEs), 236

G

G20, see Group of Twenty
GAC, see Global Affairs Canada
GDP, see Gross domestic product
Gender-Based Analysis-Plus (GBA+), 190
Gender equality, viii, 9, 17, 26, 56, 135, 187–201
General Dynamics Land Systems (GDLS), 67, 208–211
GHG, see Greenhouse gas
Global Affairs Canada (GAC), 56, 68, 192, 200n11, 209, 211–214, 217, 220, 223n4, 225n52, 236, 255
Globalization, 61, 67, 100n26, 129, 137
Globe and Mail, 36, 48n18, 94, 214, 215, 217, 218
Government-assisted refugees (GARs), 235, 236, 238
Greenhouse gas (GHG), 10, 20, 23, 90, 96, 106, 108, 110, 111, 114, 116, 147
Gross domestic product (GDP), 12, 26, 146, 149, 208, 269, 286, 288, 295, 299n4
Group of Eight (G8), 38, 153
Group of Twenty (G20), 1, 21, 22, 87, 105, 151, 159
Gulf Cooperation Council (GCC), 68, 69

H

Harper, Stephen, 2–9, 22, 27, 31–37, 39, 41, 42, 47, 69, 104, 105, 107, 108, 112, 113, 125, 126, 134, 137n1, 148, 152, 153, 155, 171–174, 177, 179, 192, 196, 197, 208–210, 234–236, 239, 250, 253–255, 266, 268, 270, 272, 285, 286, 289, 290, 292, 295, 298
 and Afghanistan, 255, 289, 290, 292
 anti-ISIS policies of, 266
 and China, 5, 126, 134, 148, 152, 153
 environmental policies of, 104, 113
 and the Saudi–LAV deal, 221
 and Syrian refugees, 3, 8, 36, 41–42, 47, 239
 and the UNSC, 7, 8, 37, 250, 253–255
House of Commons, 2, 5, 9, 34, 49n52, 189, 201n41, 207, 212, 213, 216, 219, 223n1, 224n38, 225n41, 285, 291, 292
Hydrofluorocarbons (HFCs), 107–109

I

Illiberal regimes, 57
Immigration, Refugees and Citizenship Canada (IRCC), 236
IMPACT, Operation, 39, 285, 287, 291, 292
India, 56, 62, 87, 126, 133, 223n8
Indigenous peoples, 4, 26, 27, 87, 99n2, 166–169, 171–180, 275
Indigenous rights, 165–181
Industry 4.0, *see* Fourth industrial revolution
INHERENT RESOLVE, Operation, 296

International Assistance Review (IAR), 23, 192
International Defence Exhibition and Conference (IDEX), 68
International Labour Organization (ILO), 166, 170
International relations theory
 feminist, 187, 195–197, 265
 liberal, 37, 57
 Marxist, 58
 realist, 57
Investor-state dispute settlement (ISDS), 127–129, 137
Iraq, 3, 6, 22, 23, 35, 39, 40, 47, 62–64, 68, 69, 233, 255, 285–287, 289, 291, 292, 298
ISDS, *see* Investor-state dispute settlement
Islamic State (IS), *see* Islamic State of Iraq and Syria (ISIS)
Islamic State of Iraq and Syria (ISIS), 40, 261, 285, 287, 297, 298
Islamic State of Iraq and the Levant (ISIL), *see* Islamic State of Iraq and Syria (ISIS)

K

Keystone XL pipeline, 131
Kinder Morgan pipeline, 177
Kurdi, Alan, 41, 42, 239

L

Latvia, 24, 38, 70, 91, 255, 269, 289, 292–294, 296
LAVs, *see* Light-armoured vehicles
Lesbian, Gay, Bisexual, Trans, and Queer (LGBTQ), 189
Liberal government, *see* Trudeau, Justin

INDEX 307

Liberal internationalism, 1, 37, 267, 277
Liberal Party of Canada (LPC), 55,
  261, 265, 268–270
  See also Trudeau, Justin
Light-armoured vehicles (LAVs), 4,
  67, 208–214, 217, 218, 225n56,
  226n68
Low Carbon Fuel Standards (LCFS),
  112, 118

M
McKenna, Catherine, 9, 10, 105, 106,
  108, 114, 115
Malmström, Cecilia, 127–129
Martin, Paul, 45, 113, 134, 148,
  150–152, 266
Mega-regions, 95, 96
Methane, 23, 107–110, 116
Mexico, 10–12, 23, 85, 88, 104–106,
  109, 116–118, 131, 133,
  136, 240
Middle East, 19, 59, 63–71, 91, 208,
  216, 225n42,
  253, 292
Mosul, 287, 292, 298
Mulcair, Thomas, 21, 32, 36, 41, 42,
  210, 213
Mulroney, Brian, 27, 43, 46, 125,
  149, 150

N
NAFTA, see North American Free
  Trade Agreement
NATO, see North Atlantic Treaty
  Organization
NATO Flying Training in Canada
  (NFTC), 67
NDP, see New Democratic Party

New Democratic Party (NDP), 2, 5,
  21, 32–34, 36, 41, 42, 137n3,
  191, 207, 210, 212–215, 217,
  222, 223n1, 224n38, 225n42,
  261, 274, 275
  opposition to LAV–Saudi arms
    deal, 215
  support for LAV–Saudi arms
    deal, 213–215
New York Times, 8, 12, 56, 85,
  233, 243n31
Non-governmental organizations
  (NGOs), 89, 155, 157
North American Free Trade
  Agreement (NAFTA), 2, 11, 12,
  18, 25, 27, 45, 85, 86, 97, 111,
  131–133, 135, 136, 157, 255
  and Trump, 2, 11, 12, 25, 45, 85,
    86, 97, 111, 131–133,
    135, 255
North American Leaders Summit
  (NALS), 85, 109
North Atlantic Treaty Organization
  (NATO), 12, 17, 20, 24, 27, 35,
  37–38, 40, 45, 60, 62, 65, 67,
  70, 208, 256, 269, 277n8, 286,
  288, 290, 292, 293,
  295–297, 299n18
  and Afghanistan, 62, 287–289
  enlargement, 65
  Wales Summit, 286, 295
  Warsaw Summit, 292

O
Obama, Barack, 10, 11, 23, 56, 61,
  64, 71n6, 84, 90, 108–110, 127,
  131, 134, 181n16, 269, 292
Organization of the Petroleum
  Exporting Countries (OPEC), 91

P

Pan-Canadian Framework on Clean Growth and Climate Change, 111, 112, 117–118
Paris agreement, 9, 90, 92, 110
  See also Conference of Parties, Twenty-First Session (COP21); United Nations Framework Convention on Climate Change (UNFCCC)
Peacekeeping, 2, 7–8, 13, 27, 35–37, 46, 252, 257n2, 262, 265, 269–271, 276, 279n73, 288, 289, 299n3
Permanent Five (P5), *see* United Nations Security Council (UNSC)
Peshmerga, 39, 292, 298
Poland, 38, 70, 289, 292, 293
Populism, 10, 89, 92
Prisoner of war (POW), 237
Privately Sponsored Refugee Program (PSRP), 235, 236, 238, 239
Privately-sponsored refugees (PSRs), 235, 236, 238

R

REASSURANCE, Operation, 38, 287, 292–294, 296
Regulatory Cooperation Council (RCC), 85, 86
Russia, 10, 20, 22, 38, 65, 70, 223n6, 248, 255, 288, 294
  and Syria, 22, 255
  and Ukraine, 22, 38, 65, 66, 70, 287, 294, 295

S

Sajjan, Harjit S., 12, 37, 44, 46, 275, 279n67, 285, 286, 294, 299n2, 299n23

Saudi Arabia, 4, 24, 63, 64, 67–69, 191, 207–223, 225n42
  LAV-deal with Canada, 4, 208, 209, 221, 225n56
  and Yemen conflict, 216–217, 221
Second World War, 27, 34, 59–61, 107, 237, 264, 266
SOF, *see* Special operation forces
Softwood lumber, 23, 131, 132
South China Sea, 146, 147, 160
Special operation forces (SOF), 285–287, 290, 292, 297, 298
Streit Group, 214–215, 221, 224n38
Strong, Secure, Engaged, *see* Defence policy; Defence policy, Canada (2017)
Syria, 22, 35, 39, 63, 64, 67, 68, 72n53, 216, 233, 235, 236, 242, 285
Syrian refugees, 3, 8, 24, 35, 36, 41–42, 47, 56, 233–235, 239–242

T

Tiananmen massacre, 150
Toronto Star, 39, 179, 218
TPP, *see* Trans-Pacific Partnership
Transatlantic Trade and Investment Partnership (TTIP)
Trans-Pacific Partnership (TPP), 4, 125–127, 130–133, 136, 154
TRC, *see* Truth and Reconciliation Commission
Trudeau, Justin, vii, viii, 1–14, 17–29, 31–49, 55–74, 83, 85, 86, 91, 98, 103–120, 125–139, 145–161, 165–181, 187–192, 197, 199, 200n2–4, 207–226, 233–243, 247–258, 261–279, 285–300
  campaign against ISIS, 266, 285

and China, 4, 5, 10, 22, 27, 32, 56, 118, 126, 133–136, 145–161
electoral positions, 2, 43, 45, 131, 133, 173, 210, 266, 267, 270, 285, 286, 291
environmental policies, 10, 103–120
and feminism, 188, 213
and Harper continuity, 3, 152
and Harper contrast, 286
and Indigenous peoples, 4, 26, 27, 166, 171–179
and media praise, 8, 12, 13, 23, 40, 241, 270, 272
and Putin, 21, 22
and Syrian refugees, 3, 8, 36, 42, 47, 56, 233–235, 240–242
and Trump strategy, 17, 117, 132, 136
and the UNSC, 7, 8, 37, 190, 191, 247–258
Trudeau, Pierre, 27, 235, 265–268
Trump, Donald J., vii, 1–14, 17, 19, 21–26, 29, 32, 37, 44–47, 83–100, 103, 109–112, 114, 117, 119n34, 126, 127, 131–136, 147, 209, 233, 240, 248, 255, 269, 270, 273, 276, 287, 288, 290, 292, 293, 295, 298
DACA position, 240
electoral positions, 24, 45, 131, 133, 270
environmental policies, 10, 103, 117
impact on Canadian policy, 37, 132
NAFTA position, 2, 11, 12, 25, 85, 86, 131–133, 135
NATO position, 12, 17, 269, 286, 288, 293, 295
travel ban, 86
Truth and Reconciliation Commission (TRC), 171–175, 177, 178

U
Ukraine, 6, 22, 38, 65, 66, 70, 126, 137n1, 287, 289, 294, 295
UN, *see* United Nations
UNDRIP, *see* United Nations Declaration on the Rights of Indigenous Peoples
UNFCCC, *see* United Nations Framework Convention on Climate Change
UNIFIED PROTECTOR, Operation, 290, 296
UNIFIER, Operation, 38, 287, 294–295
United Nations (UN), 2, 4, 7–10, 13, 20, 21, 24, 26, 34, 35, 37, 55, 56, 60–64, 69, 83, 87, 104–106, 151, 165, 167–169, 176, 177, 179–180, 189–191, 194, 197, 198, 200n22, 200n24, 208, 212, 214, 220, 222, 247, 248, 250–256, 257n2, 257n7, 257n16, 258n28, 262, 269–271, 276, 289, 299n3
United Nations Declaration on the Rights of Indigenous Peoples (UNDRIP), 2, 4, 166–180, 181n49
Canadian implementation of the, 166, 168, 173, 174, 177, 179, 180
United Nations Framework Convention on Climate Change (UNFCCC), 106, 108–110
See also Conference of Parties, Twenty-First Session (COP21); Paris Agreement
United Nations High Commissioner for Refugees (UNHCR), 234, 235, 241

United Nations Security Council
  (UNSC), 7, 8, 188, 190, 191,
  194–196, 199, 200n22,
  200n24, 247–258
  Canadian support for, 8, 194, 247,
    251–256
  Permanent Five (P5), 248, 249,
    251, 253, 254
  Resolution 1325, 188, 190,
    191, 194, 195, 199,
    200n24, 252
  Resolution 1325+, 188,
    194–196, 200n22
  Western European and Others
    Group (WEOG), 248, 254
UNSC, *see* United Nations Security
  Council

V
Visible minorities, 88

W
Wallonia, 129
Welfare spending, 265
White identity, 88, 89
Women, Peace and Security Network
  Canada (WPSN-C), 199, 201n41
World Trade Organization (WTO), 149

Y
Yemen, 63, 67, 68, 207, 211, 212,
  216–217, 221, 224n27, 225n52,
  226n68, 233

GPSR Compliance
The European Union's (EU) General Product Safety Regulation (GPSR) is a set
of rules that requires consumer products to be safe and our obligations to
ensure this.

If you have any concerns about our products, you can contact us on

ProductSafety@springernature.com

In case Publisher is established outside the EU, the EU authorized
representative is:

Springer Nature Customer Service Center GmbH
Europaplatz 3
69115 Heidelberg, Germany

www.ingramcontent.com/pod-product-compliance
Lightning Source LLC
LaVergne TN
LVHW020327260326
834688LV00037B/907